Democracy or Bonapartism

Democracy or Bonapartism

Two Centuries of War on Democracy

Domenico Losurdo
Foreword by Luciano Canfora

Translated by David Broder

VERSO
London • New York

This English-language edition first published by Verso 2024

First published as *Democrazia o bonapartismo. Trionfo e decadenza del suffragio universale*

1 3 5 7 9 10 8 6 4 2

Verso
UK: 6 Meard Street, London W1F 0EG
US: 388 Atlantic Avenue, Brooklyn, NY 11217
versobooks.com

Verso is the imprint of New Left Books

ISBN-13: 978-1-78478-731-8
ISBN-13: 978-1-78478-732-5 (UK EBK)
ISBN-13: 978-1-78478-733-2 (US EBK)

British Library Cataloguing in Publication Data
A catalogue record for this book is available from the British Library

Library of Congress Cataloging-in-Publication Data

Names: Losurdo, Domenico, author. | Broder, David, translator. | Canfora, Luciano, writer of foreword.
Title: Democracy or Bonapartism : two centuries of war on democracy / Domenico Losurdo ; foreword by Luciano Canfora ; translated by David Broder.
Other titles: Democrazia o bonapartismo. English
Description: London ; New York : Verso, 2024. | First published as Democrazia o bonapartismo. Trionfo e decadenza del suff ragio universale, Torino, Italy : Bollati Boringhieri, 1993. | Includes bibliographical references and index.
Identifiers: LCCN 2023041748 (print) | LCCN 2023041749 (ebook) | ISBN 9781784787318 (hardback) | ISBN 9781784787332 (ebook)
Subjects: LCSH: Suffrage—History. | Representative government and representation—History. | Bonapartism—History.
Classification: LCC JF831 .L6713 2024 (print) | LCC JF831 (ebook) | DDC 325.3209—dc23/eng/20231229
LC record available at https://lccn.loc.gov/2023041748
LC ebook record available at https://lccn.loc.gov/2023041749

Typeset in Minion by Hewer Text UK Ltd, Edinburgh
Printed and bound by CPI Group (UK) Ltd, Croydon CR0 4YY

Contents

Foreword
Luciano Canfora

Here, I have chosen to speak of Domenico Losurdo as a militant.[1] Indeed, Losurdo was not only a teacher and scholar of the history of philosophy, but was also, in the full sense, a historian and a militant, throughout his life. A militant – that is, someone who does not hold himself back from the fray, who commits himself, who puts himself out in the open. This, not only in the way that occurs within political formations, in their life and their functioning, but also in his written work.

I believe that the most militant part of Losurdo's activity were the books he produced and disseminated with important publishers over a long period. In my opinion – and I hope I am not mistaken on this score – the start of his activity and his strong commitment coincided, we might say, with the world crisis, with the historical turning point of 1989–91, the beginning of the final decade of the twentieth century. Why? This was a trigger for his activity, but for self-evident reasons, we could say that this historical turning point was an opportunity for everyone, an opportunity to understand.

It was as if we were witnessing a new restoration. Restoration is a word used to indicate a certain period in the history of the nineteenth

1 Luciano Canfora was among the speakers at 'A Life for a World Without Wars: Domenico Losurdo', the panel that marked the official opening of the academic year for the Italian Institute for Philosophical Studies on 7 December 2018. This text is a lightly edited translation of Canfora's talk, which was given five months after Losurdo's death.

century, the end of the quarter-century cycle from 1789 to the end of Bonaparte. While, strictly speaking, the word refers to the restoration of the *ancien régime*, that is not what it was – nor could it have been, as we learn from a great Italian historian who died young, Adolfo Omodeo. He devoted a large part of his studies – which are still authoritative, and which we can even today benefit from reading – precisely to this era, showing that no restoration is truly a restoration. There is never a return *ad pristinum*, to just how things were before. In those dramatic years of clashes, of conflicts, of breakdown, Losurdo grasped that it was time to understand what had happened. So, he reckoned with a great defeat, with a great disillusionment, with the need to understand.

This is especially true of the period starting in 1993, a year in which he produced two texts, the first of which was *Democracy or Bonapartism*, which I will be pausing to reflect on in a little greater depth. Its subtitle in Italian, which is highly telling, is *The Triumph and Decadence of Universal Suffrage*. In 1993, alongside this book – which is very dear to me, and which I have long been studying – he also published *Marx and the Historical Balance-Sheet of the Twentieth Century*. In 1996 there was *Historical Revisionism: Problems and Myths*, and in 1998 *The Original Sin of the Twentieth Century* – obviously this title was meant ironically.[2] From 1997 to 1999 he co-edited, together with Ruggero Giacomini, *USSR: Balance-Sheet of an Experience*, and in 1999 he published his *Escape from History?* This is a very cutting book, taking on what he calls the self-phobia of the communist movement after the Soviet collapse. Then, in 2005 – I will look more closely at this one, too – there was *Liberalism: A Counter-history*, which gave rise to related works like *Language of Empire: Lexicon of the American Ideology*, in 2013 *The Class Struggle: A Political and Philosophical History*, and in 2014 *The Absent Left*. This is a brief panorama of his titles; obviously, I will not dwell on them all, but rather on the two I have noted already – the volume on the apparent alternatives of *Democracy or Bonapartism*, and *Liberalism: A Counter-history*. I do so because of my preference for these works, but also because I am convinced that they are central to Losurdo's production.

Losurdo was an acute scholar of history and thought, and it could not escape him that, while on the one hand the turning point in 1989–91

2 The former was published in English as *War and Revolution: Rethinking the Twentieth Century* (London: Verso, 2015), and it included the latter as an appendix.

brought to completion a perhaps foreseeable crisis of actually existing socialism – perhaps forcing a revision of categories but also of the philosophy of history, as the expectation of a fullness of time instead suddenly receded, causing an almost unbearable trauma for those who had dedicated their lives to that cause – it was in that precise situation, in those years and the ones that followed, that the mask of so-called Western democracy fell. This latter is an entity of which we speak ever less often, with less enthusiasm and with greater fatigue. This is the fundamental point – we can say, the trench that Losurdo defended. There are newspaper pundits – usually paid very handsomely – who sing the praises of the 'great democracies'. But these meaningless words are ever less heartfelt, and less convincing. Losurdo clear-sightedly grasped the concomitance of these two things – that is, the fact that the enemy had disappeared, or seemed to have disappeared, and thus the rhetoric and the self-representation of so-called Western democracy also fell away.

Losurdo therefore took as his cue for *Democracy or Bonapartism* the history of universal suffrage, which I think is the appropriate, concrete move for a scholar himself faced with a historical problem. While this subject has repeatedly been addressed by scholars showing greater or lesser originality – for instance, Giovanni Sartori, a very well-known political scientist and editor who enjoyed great success – Losurdo instead reframed the starting point. That is, he framed it in terms of the fact that the conflict that characterised the nineteenth century after the defeat of the revolution and the end of Bonaparte was a conflict *between* liberalism and democracy – that is, democracy as a product of the workers' movement, organising itself against a liberal vision that is restricted, elitist, based on property qualifications. This took the form of concocting various means to restrict suffrage, which Losurdo sets at the forefront of his analysis in *Democracy or Bonapartism*.

It had not been very well known that such a revered and widely vaunted thinker as John Stuart Mill was among the theorists most convinced of the need to, yes, perhaps resign oneself to the extension of suffrage, but also take the precaution of ensuring it would be a suffrage-by-degrees. Mill speaks of how the master works with his brain and his worker works with his muscles, in a famous line which Losurdo cites from the *Considerations on Representative Government* from 1861. Starting from this consideration, Mill suggests that the vote should thus be proportionate; he says that the plural vote of the person who works with his brain – we could say, works with his wealth – must be several times the vote of his worker or employee (in fact he is also talking about peasants). This is a thread which Losurdo highlights in so-called liberal thought, where unfortunately the word 'liberal' ends up meaning its opposite.

Here we may think of another revered exponent of that current, Benjamin Constant, who had well before Mill served in many trenches, been with Bonaparte and then with Louis XVIII and then with the Hundred Days, and then . . . let us say, he was a liberal running out of breath. In his best-known text, *The Liberty of Ancients Compared with That of Moderns*, Constant theorises another perhaps more disturbing aspect. This is that, even at an electoral level, there must be a distinction between people who have nothing to lose in terms of their assets – for example, professors – to whom we give a modest vote, as compared to those who have a lot to lose, and so must be given more space in the electoral conflict to conquer a parliamentary majority. Not to mention the most acute representative of this current, perhaps the one to whom Losurdo is dialectically most linked – reading him, holding him in esteem, and rightly criticising him – namely Tocqueville. There is a private note of Tocqueville's – published long after his death in a fine volume by Bollati Boringhieri – on a sheet of paper, which happened to be saved, which he had written while he was a member of parliament in the Second French Republic in 1848. Tocqueville was a little bored by the parliament's interminable debates, and so wrote these notes to himself containing his thoughts. He says that, caught amid the battle between equality and liberty, I reject equality – I am a man of liberty. So, this is, if you like, the most explicit and honest characterisation of a current of thought that has always had a hostile relationship with equality and suffrage for all.

In his work of excavation, Losurdo not only studies the historical stages of universal suffrage, but also rightly points out that the so-called extension of suffrage due to Giovanni Giolitti in 1912 was in fact only partial. It is curious that, in the current vulgate, Giolitti passes for being the man who established universal suffrage in Italy. Of course, even the partial extension that did take place was only for men, as it remained in 1919 when the franchise was extended for real after the war. While this vulgate continues to spread, in reality there were considerable limitations to the granting of suffrage, which, Losurdo notes, are well described in an excellent entry on Suffrage in the *Enciclopedia italiana*, a text which is, moreover, full of surprises for those who examine it carefully.

This does not take away from the fact that this idea of a Giolitti extending suffrage to all has established itself in the historiography. This leaves in the shadows another factor which also concerns liberals' doubts over universal suffrage and equality, if not outright hostility towards them. By that I mean the strong doubts nurtured by Benedetto Croce. He was a close friend of Giolitti's; he had already been a senator appointed by the royal family well before the Giolitti government which took that decision, and he warned Giolitti that this extension of suffrage would be a colossal, capital error.

This is the real, concrete history of that conflict, which Losurdo discusses in a fine essay he gave us an account of in one of the courses he held in San Marino. The history of the *ancien régime*'s long endurance, he says, perhaps ended in 1918 with Year One of the October Revolution in Russia: the caesura with the *ancien régime*. Lest we forget that in liberal Britain, plural suffrage – in which some groups had more votes than others – persisted until the first majority Labour government after World War II.

In this discussion on the fundamental conflict of the nineteenth century, democracy against liberalism and vice versa, Losurdo repeatedly crossed paths with an interlocutor with whom he also had lively polemics, ones from which I think he emerged victorious, namely Norberto Bobbio. I do not know if Bobbio has already become a *Pater Patriae*; he was a character who had great self-restraint and capacity for self-criticism, even if his followers have tried to canonise him. The clash between the two revolved around, emerged and was expressed in the newspapers on the occasion of the first Gulf War, when Bobbio supported the thesis of the just war – the war that should be supported. Developing over time, this led to the catastrophe which we are today living through, of which the war in Iraq was the most serious detonator.

But Losurdo also rightly notes the stages in Bobbio's rather wobbly path, for instance dedicating many pages to the book published by Einaudi – *Politics and Culture* – in which Bobbio brought together his long-distance discussion with Palmiro Togliatti. By then, Einaudi was rather out of step with the cultural policy of the Italian Communist

Party, whereas, in the immediate post-war period, the relationship had been so close that it wanted Togliatti to give it texts by Zhdanov to publish. Togliatti said it ought to ask Giancarlo Pajetta . . . and did not publish them. But at the time, Losurdo reminds us, Bobbio had theorised that basically the socialism achieved in the USSR was already almost a complete, positive system; Bobbio said there only needed to be a 'drop' of greater freedom in that system. So, this was the moment of the closest relations, let us say, between the former militant of the Action Party and the Italian Communist Party.

Bobbio was a sensitive man, honest in his way; when there were the revelations about the ugly page of his compromises with Fascism, the only one who rejected the ad hoc, self-serving defences was Bobbio himself. He wrote a very short article in the Turin *La Stampa* that rejected adulation that was instrumental and ill-founded, or founded on lowly motives. Well, Bobbio in 1975 – I think it is right to remember this – abandoned his minimum theory of democracy as the rules of the game (and that alone) on an important occasion, namely the event marking the thirtieth anniversary of the Liberation, held at the University of Milan between January and April 1975. For this important occasion, Feltrinelli produced a collection including texts by Lelio Basso, Umberto Terracini, Ezio Franceschini and Bobbio himself.[3] Here, Bobbio returned to the theme of the definition of democracy and – mindful, we might say, of the content of the key articles of our Constitution – he wrote that the content of democracy is social justice, not the rules of the game, which are merely externalities. It is striking that, as time went on, with the crisis in the workers' movement and the communist movement in Italy and beyond, Bobbio then returned to his positions holding that democracy is the rules of the game. This oscillation is symptomatic, because it shows that this is a problem with which liberal thought is unable to fully come to terms.

The other volume I wanted to touch on for a moment is *Liberalism: A Counter-history*. I think that this volume, among many important works of Losurdo's, is always rich in concrete documentation, and never mere rhetoric. At first, with a little self-mockery, he tries to justify this somehow journalistic and combative title by saying, rightly, that he is taking

3 *1945/1975 Italia. Fascismo antifascismo Resistenza rinnovamento* (Milan: Feltrinelli, 1975).

his cue from the first page of Tocqueville's *The Old Regime and the Revolution*. In this, his most profound work, Tocqueville says that, to understand France on the eve of 1789, it is not enough to focus on the great figures that represent it on the level of culture, political power and religion. It is necessary to observe the social functioning of the conflict among classes. Losurdo says: I, *si parva licet*, intend to do the same with respect to the gap between abstract liberal thought and the concrete practice of real-life states, which historically have been led by liberal elites and which have found themselves confronted with conflicts that have been resolved in a way that restricted freedom – what he calls a disemancipation. To get to the substance of this rich book, I think it is worth recalling the concluding pages, in which he somehow comes to terms also with himself. For example, there is a part I appreciate very much in that book where he says that liberalism has tried to take on the lesson of its antagonist – forced by history, naturally, forced by conflict – but it has not retreated, and perhaps its antagonist could have done likewise, but did not. In those same pages, Losurdo advances a consideration that I believe is the substance of the whole book. He says that it is true that, in the states led by liberal elites, there was a process of accepting – albeit under the urgent pressure of conflict – the affirmation of the principle of equality, in its various aspects. But this process developed at the same time as the planet-wide consolidation of colonialism, meaning the projection, outside the states led by these same elites, of slave-type dependency and exclusion from full citizenship. Thus, colonial empires and the enlargement of suffrage in the metropole go hand in hand – emancipation and a disemancipation.

For Losurdo, this greatly limits the credit owed to liberalism. It understood the lesson that its antagonist imparted to it, but in that same context arrived at a question that I believe is the crucial one we have before us. If, at the end of this long cycle, we can conclude that liberalism has assimilated this lesson and incorporated the principles of equality within its horizons, its answer is also full of doubts. I believe we can go further with regard to the fundamental question Losurdo raises over those we could call the victors of the conflict that exploded at the end of the twentieth century. I often say this, but I think it is not superfluous to repeat it: today, profit needs slavery. Slavery is back on the planet in a big way, not only in far-off worlds which are thus invisible or easily concealed, but inside the metropole itself. So, the turn we have before us is a dramatic one, posing not only empirical problems but also ethical ones. The enslavement of human beings is no longer a relic of history but a fundamental part of profit in all its aspects, of which financial capital is in a sense the pillar. For the money that comes from the various arenas of slavery – such as trafficking, war, the huge drug trade, and so on – is laundered through the major banking institutions, and so financial capital is the place where the holy grail of profit is protected. I think that this is the problem we face.

The last point, on the vast output of this man of whom I am trying to provide an outline portrait here, is that here we are evidently talking about an eminently critical scholar, not prone to self-indulgence or concealment when he poses the problem of the crisis of socialism. A crisis or else a transformation – I am very much in accordance with this focus of his. I believe that the weight of the history of the countries where socialist-type revolutions took place inevitably constituted the clay, the coarse earth that was to be kneaded with ideal intentions. History alters those intentions, and those intentions are in turn a yeast that can change the weight of that history. So, it does not move in a straightforward way. I think that Losurdo brilliantly captured this with a metaphor he used in a fine text entitled 'Marx, Columbus and the October Revolution'. Here, he poses the question:

> Did the October Revolution fail? There is no doubt that the goals it pursued or proclaimed were not achieved. Think of Lenin and the leaders of the International who saw the World Soviet Republic already taking shape with the disappearance, in the final analysis, of classes, of states, of nations, of the market, of religions. Not only was the objective not approached, but there was no march in that direction. So, are we faced with a failure? In truth, the gap between programmes and results is a property of all revolutions. The French Jacobins did not achieve or restore the ancient polis. The American revolutionaries did not produce the society of small farmers and producers without a polarisation of wealth and poverty, without a standing army, without a central power. The English Puritans did not bring back to life the biblical society they mythically transfigured. The story of Christopher Columbus who set off in search of the Indies but discovered America can serve as a metaphor for understanding the objective dialectics of revolutionary processes.

1

The Fight for the Vote: A Tortuous and Still-Unfinished History

Benjamin Constant and Property Qualifications

If we want to understand the genesis of modern democracy and the problems that it poses, we need to turn back to the era of the French Revolution. The highest praise for this Revolution came in an objective statement from an authoritative exponent of the liberal tradition. After jeering at the idea that suffrage is a 'natural, absolute right' – a conception he deemed 'peculiar' to France alone – and emphasising how alien such a ruinous and strange notion of politics was to Britain and the United States (countries which he admired), this, in many ways, classic thinker concluded: 'It would take the French Revolution for something resembling universal suffrage to be found in Europe.'[1]

Indeed, it was through the radicalisation of this revolution that the demand arose for a more or less universal and direct suffrage (albeit one limited to the male population). This was especially the case after the events of 10 August 1792, which marked the birth of the revolutionary Commune in Paris. This radicalisation put into question not only the distinction between active and passive citizens but also the institution of intermediate bodies of 'electors' and the two-tier suffrage which had been maintained by the legislative Assembly, even if on a

1 Édouard Laboulaye, *Histoire des États-Unis* (Paris: Charpentier, 1866), vol. 3, pp. 319, 322.

temporary basis. The Jacobins, instead, argued that 'the sovereign people must alienate its sovereignty as little as possible'.[2] While the elections to the Convention had still been held on the basis of the two-tier electoral system, from which domestic servants were excluded, the Constitution of 24 June 1793 stipulated universal, direct (male) suffrage.[3] Of course, the concrete conditions in which the elections to the Convention were held, with the shadow of the Terror already looming, did not guarantee a fully free or secret vote, and dramatic developments both domestically and internationally prevented the ratified Constitution from ever coming into effect.[4] Yet, this first radical challenge to discrimination based on property remains a fact of great historical importance.

Corresponding to the transformations which further democratised the electoral system, in the period of the Jacobin radicalisation of the Revolution there were also incisive state interventions on the economic terrain. Made through such means as progressive taxation, it enacted measures which we would today define in terms of income redistribution. Tellingly, Maximilien Robespierre – who condemned the restriction of political rights on the basis of property qualifications, deeming this in contravention of the Declaration of the Rights of Man – at the same time theorised the right to life as the first among 'man's inalienable rights'.[5]

After Thermidor, the liberal bourgeoisie faced a dilemma. While it clung to the representative system, in an anti-absolutist and anti-feudal key, it also had to stop political representation granting any overly powerful influence to the popular masses. Hence the return to a policy that tightly restricted political rights based on property qualifications: indeed, the critique of the Jacobins' social policy went hand in hand with the critique of the democratic electoral system. Progressive taxation was a particular target for opposition, being denounced as

2 Alphonse Aulard, *Histoire politique de la Révolution française* (Aalen: Scientia, 1977), pp. 256ff.

3 Edmond Villey, *Législation électorale comparée des principaux pays d'Europe* (Paris: Larose-Pedone, 1900), pp. 4ff.

4 Jean-François Fayard, 'Elections', in Jean Tulard, Jean-François Fayard and Alfred Fierro, *Histoire et dictionnaire de la Révolution française 1789–1799* (Paris: Laffont, 1987).

5 Maximilien Robespierre, *Textes choisis* (Paris: Éditions Sociales, 1958), vol. 1, p. 140, and vol. 2, p. 85.

synonymous with 'land reform' and thus with attacks on property rights. Boissy d'Anglas asserted the need to exclude non-property owners from political rights: in the absence of such restrictions, 'they will establish, or have established, harmful taxes'.[6] This was also Benjamin Constant's view: he insisted that measures involving tax exemptions or favourable fiscal treatment for the poor not only unjustly penalised 'the comfortably-off' but ended up treating 'poverty as a privilege', instituting 'a privileged caste in the country' – a caste surprisingly composed not of nobles or the rich but rather of *les misérables*.[7] This was a remarkable text, if for no other reason than the fact that it arrived at a moment in which – according to the authoritative accounts of Madame de Staël and Mallet du Pan – the combined effect of shortages and inflation were reducing 'the bottom class of society to the most miserable condition', inflicting 'unheard-of hardships' upon this class including death by 'malnutrition'.[8] But, for the liberal tradition, the important thing was to neutralise these masses politically, even in their conditions of destitution or literal famine.

What was the most appropriate means for achieving this goal? The post-Thermidorian bourgeoisie reintroduced both the restriction of political rights on the basis of property qualifications (even if in a softer form than had been set out in the 1791 Constitution, swept aside by the insurrection of 10 August 1792) and a two-tiered electoral system, as a further means of imposing social filters on representative bodies and keeping them at one remove from plebeian or popular contamination.[9] But, from Constant's point of view, this latter clause of the electoral system made it difficult, if not impossible, for the mass of the people to identify with its representatives. For it reduced, rather than expanded, the margin of consensus and risked opening up a gulf surrounding the government and legislative organisms.[10] Hence the

6 Georges Lefebvre, *La France sous le directoire 1795–1799* (Paris: Éditions Sociales, 1984), pp. 28ff.

7 Henri Guillemin, *Benjamin Constant muscadin 1795–1799* (Paris: Gallimard, 1958), pp. 76ff.

8 Anne-Louise-Germaine Necker Staël-Holstein, *Considérations sur les principaux événements de la Révolution française* (Paris: Tallandier, 1983); Guillemin, *Benjamin Constant muscadin*, p. 37.

9 Lefebvre, *La France sous le directoire*, p. 34.

10 Benjamin Constant, *Principles of Politics Applicable to All Governments*, transl. Dennis O'Keeffe (Indianapolis: Liberty Fund, 2003), pp. 329–30.

property qualification now imposed itself even more drastically than it had in the past. To prevent *les misérables* transforming into a 'privileged caste' – that is, taking advantage of political power, or the influence they exercised upon it, to force through income redistribution and somehow improve their own material conditions – the exercise of political rights had to be the exclusive privilege of the wealthy classes; otherwise, the existing social order would be exposed to intolerable risks.

Tocqueville and the Rejection of Direct Universal Suffrage

Constant's preoccupations were shared by Tocqueville. The latter is today erroneously presented as a theorist of democracy, when he should instead be counted among its critics – at least so long as we consider direct universal suffrage to be an integral part of democracy. The author of *Democracy in America* was motivated by the same social preoccupations that we have already observed in the liberal tradition he had behind him: he was sharply opposed to political authorities intervening on the economic terrain, to any suggestion of income redistribution, and, in consequence, to any electoral system liable to favour such deplorable eventualities. As against any bid to put 'the foresight and wisdom of the state in the place of individual foresight and wisdom', Tocqueville proclaimed that 'nothing can authorise the state to interfere in industry'.[11] This was part of his famous 12 September 1848 speech, insisting that the Constituent Assembly should reject the demand for the 'right to work' which had already been bloodily stamped out in the June Days. Tocqueville's laissez-faire approach went as far as to place the legal regulation (and thus reduction) of the working day ('le travail de douze heures') in the basket of 'socialist doctrines', on which grounds he ruthlessly condemned any such legislation.[12]

But this danger was now confronted in a different manner to that which Constant had preferred. The latter had maintained that it was preferable

11 Alexis de Tocqueville, *Œuvres complètes*, ed. Mrs De Tocqueville and G. Beaumont (Paris: Michel Lévy Frères, 1864–67), vol. 9, pp. 551ff.

12 Alexis de Tocqueville, *Œuvres complètes*, ed. J. P. Mayer (Paris: Gallimard, 1951), vol. 16, p. 126.

to neutralise the popular masses politically by setting property qualifications that restricted political rights, rather than by resorting to an electoral system based on different tiers. The author of *Democracy in America* instead declared himself in favour of this second option, invoking the example of the country he had visited and taken as a model. Notwithstanding the wide extension of suffrage, the United States enjoyed an enviable political and social stability because it had left great room for the two-tier electoral system. Thus, without having to take recourse to sweeping forms of discrimination often perceived as odious, the United States also succeeded – indeed, all the more effectively – in keeping representative bodies at a distance from the influence, or at any rate the excessive influence, of the popular masses. This, at least, was Tocqueville's interpretation, as he provided a telling comparison between the House of Representatives and the Senate (which in this period, it should be remembered, was elected by the legislatures of the individual states):

> When you enter the House chamber in Washington, you feel struck by the vulgar aspect of the great assembly. Often your eye searches in vain for a celebrated man within the assembly. Nearly all its members are obscure persons, whose names bring no image to mind. They are, for the most part, village lawyers, tradesmen, or even men belonging to the lowest classes. In a country where instruction is nearly universal, it is said that the representatives of the people do not always know how to write correctly . . .
>
> Two steps from there opens the Senate chamber, whose narrow enclosure contains a large portion of the famous men of America. You notice hardly a single man there who does not evoke the idea of recent celebrity. They are eloquent lawyers, distinguished generals, skilled magistrates, or known statesmen. All the words that issue from this [august] assembly would do honor to the greatest parliamentary debates of Europe.
>
> What causes this bizarre contrast? Why is the nation's elite found in this chamber rather than in the other? Why does the first assembly gather so many vulgar elements, while the second seems to have a monopoly of talents and enlightenment? . . . What causes such an enormous difference? I see only a single fact that explains it. The election that produces the House of Representatives is direct; the one producing the Senate is subject to two stages.

He concludes:

> It is easy to see a moment in the future when the American republics will be forced to multiply the use of two stages in their electoral system, under pain of getting miserably lost among the pitfalls of democracy.
>
> I will have no difficulty in admitting it; I see in indirect election the only means to put the use of political liberty within reach of all classes of the people. Those who hope to make this means the exclusive weapon of one party, and those who fear this means, seem to me to be equally in error.[13]

We need hardly emphasise here that the French liberal's predictions for America's future proved radically mistaken; its future would, in fact, be marked by the triumph of the direct universal suffrage that both he and Constant considered so harmful to – indeed, incompatible with – social and political stability. Both men rejected the idea of an autonomous political representation of the 'vulgar elements' – that is, the 'men belonging to the lower classes' who made their baleful influence felt in the House of Representatives in Washington, in that legislature where access was barred neither by the property qualifications so dear to Constant nor by the two-tier electoral system so dear to Tocqueville. The latter's private comments on direct election were, truth be told, even more bitterly hostile to it than the stances he took publicly would lead us to believe. That is, at least, what we would conclude from a letter in late 1835, in which, after he pointed to 'multiple-degree elections' (thus allowing even more than two tiers) as the only 'remedy to the excesses of democracy', Tocqueville added that, given the dominant ideological climate, it was necessary to present 'with great prudence' an argument that he had himself expressed only cautiously in public, blunting its sharp edges.[14]

As confirmation of why we should not rush to hail the author of *Democracy in America* as a champion of democracy, we should bear in mind that the Legitimists were also promoters of a universal or very

13 Alexis de Tocqueville, *Democracy in America*, ed. Eduardo Nolla, transl. James T. Schleifer (Indianapolis: Liberty Fund, 2012), vol. 1, pp. 320–1.

14 Tocqueville, *Œuvres complètes*, vol. 15: I, p. 57.

broad suffrage, albeit one again expressed on the basis of the two-tier electoral system.[15] Moreover, as we shall see, immediately after Louis Bonaparte's coup d'état, Tocqueville briefly maintained contacts with the latter. It is worth bearing in mind that, in 1789, the elections for even such a typical institution of the *ancien régime* as the *États-géneraux* were far from characterised by rigid property-based discrimination. Rather, they took place on the basis of a 'near-universal suffrage', which however filtered the Third Estate through successive elections so as to remove, without too much trouble, 'the illiterates who had survived the first assemblies'.[16] One thing is for certain: while a stance in favour of the two-tiered electoral system could be filled with rather diverse social and political contents,[17] in his case, Tocqueville looked to this principle as a means of politically neutralising the popular classes and socially purging representative bodies – that is, the same function Constant had instead entrusted to the monopolisation of political rights by the propertied.

Moreover, also telling is the concrete attitude that Tocqueville adopted in the course of the struggles that developed in France in opposition to discrimination based on property. It has been noted that the author of *Democracy in America* 'kept aloof from the agitation to extend the franchise during the July Monarchy'.[18] In his *Memoirs*, Tocqueville would write that this was a movement that committed the imprudence of appealing 'to the people', and which he feared might escape – as indeed happened – the leadership and control of the 'middle class', i.e. the bourgeoisie.[19] But perhaps the liberal theorist's attitude towards these struggles was not just 'distant', but, rather, diffident and hostile. It is true that, in his political writings from this period, we can find one statement in which he deemed opportune 'the gradual extension of the circle of political rights, going beyond the confines of the middle class, such as to make public life more varied and more fertile, interesting the lower

15 Stéphane Rials, *Révolution et contre-révolution en France au XIX siècle* (Paris: Albatros, 1987), pp. 153–5.

16 Ran Halévy, 'États géneraux', in François Furet and Mona Ozouf, eds, *Dictionnaire critique de la Révolution française* (Paris: Flammarion, 1988), p. 80.

17 Domenico Losurdo, *Hegel e la libertà dei moderni* (Rome: Editori riuniti, 1992), §§ 6.6, 12.5.

18 Seymour Drescher, *Tocqueville and England* (Cambridge, MA: Harvard University Press, 1964), p. 10.

19 Tocqueville, *Œuvres complètes*, ed. Mayer, vol. 12, p. 43.

classes in political questions in a regular and peaceful manner'.[20] But this extension of the right to vote was meant to concern only individual elements, or a very limited layer of those who had been excluded. The French liberal stood so far from the idea of universal suffrage and the democratic participation of the broad masses in political life that, in a transparent polemic against the 'reform banquets', he declared: 'The people should not be wooed, and they should not be recklessly and wastefully bestowed with more political rights than they are capable of exercising.'[21] In recompense, the legislative organs elected on the basis of property qualifications should display a 'philanthropic' concern for the 'needs of the poor man', such as to bind the people to institutions and 'reconcile it with the fact that it cannot make laws, by constantly making it see that the legislator is indeed thinking of it'.[22] But we should be clear: Tocqueville continued to consider intolerable any legislative intervention in the sphere of the economy and private property. There was a reason why he spoke of 'philanthropy' – 'charity' – or even of 'public charity' and 'Christian charity as applied to politics'.[23] If Robespierre subsumed voting rights and the right to life under the general category of the rights of man, for Tocqueville the former was a question of political expediency and the latter was simply inconceivable, given that 'human miseries' were the work of 'Providence' and not of 'laws', thus making it absurd to imagine 'being able to get rid of poverty by changing the social order'.[24]

Lastly, Tocqueville does not seem to have opposed the *coup de main* of 31 May 1850, which removed the (male) universal suffrage that had been introduced by the revolution of February 1848. The reservations that he did express in a letter to a friend concerned nothing more than the question of how politically expedient it was to attack a principle that had now taken root in the consciousness of the day, especially given that the new legislation – while drastically reducing the electorate and thus producing understandable irritation – 'does not seem to me to give more serious guarantees of order, given that it still stands faced with a crowd

20 Ibid., vol. 3: II, p. 737.

21 Ibid., p. 727.

22 Ibid.

23 Ibid.; Tocqueville, *Œuvres complètes*, ed. Tocqueville and Beaumont, vol. 9, pp. 537, 571.

24 Tocqueville, *Œuvres complètes*, ed. J. P. Mayer, vol. 12, p. 84.

and its emotions'. Rather, the new legislation might even have counter-productive effects, given that it 'str[uck] hard but blindly', to the point of erasing from the electoral lists in the countryside 'the men who most depend on the propertied and the clergy and are more easily directed by them'.[25]

It is true that, in the wake of the coup d'état by Louis-Napoleon, who was already posturing as the vindicator of trampled-upon universal suffrage, Tocqueville seemed to understand the pressing need to revisit or abrogate the law of 31 May.[26] But such a bid to rethink the legislation again started out from the political preoccupations we have noted already, and certainly not from any principled attachment to universal suffrage. Moreover, just a few weeks after the 2 December 1851 coup, the liberal philosopher entered into contact with Legitimist circles and wrote directly to the Bourbon pretender, the Comte de Chambord, calling on him to fight for a constitutional monarchy which would provide for a 'sincere representation of the nation' within the terms of a robust 'traditional power founded on the nation's moral and upper classes'.[27] Would universal suffrage have survived the success of such an attempt, had it come to pass? Or would this instead have given rise to a disemancipation, perhaps camouflaged through the introduction of a two-tier electoral system?

Europe and America

When he wrote *Democracy in America*, Tocqueville had in mind the period that had begun with Andrew Jackson's rise to the presidency in 1829. This was a period that saw a powerful democratisation process within America's white community, which seemed destined to wipe out the property qualifications that still remained all-dominant in Europe. But if we examine the history and the situation that had prevailed in this country in the immediately previous decades, we see the alternating use, or indeed combination, of the same instruments for erasing or filtering popular suffrage that were also discussed and used in France.

25 Ibid., vol. 15: II, pp. 29ff.

26 André Jardin, *Alexis de Tocqueville 1805–59* (Paris: Hachette, 1984), p. 436.

27 Rials, *Révolution et contre-révolution*, pp. 164ff.

The delegates to the Philadelphia Convention of 1787, from which the draft Federal Constitution emanated, were 'appointed by the states'; it should be added that 'a majority of the states placed direct property qualifications on the voters, and the other states eliminated practically all who were not taxpayers'; and, therefore, in this case, the second-degree electoral system was intertwined with property qualifications, and sometimes with religious discrimination. This meant that, in states such as New Hampshire and Georgia, in order to be entitled to political rights, one had to be of the Protestant religion and thus, in practice, belong to the oldest group of inhabitants.[28] As for the Conventions in the individual states, in order to ratify the proposed new Constitution, they certainly did not rest on a very broad popular base. Indeed, among a population of around 3.5 million, the voters amounted to 160,000 – a proportion lower than that in France in the election of the Estates General under the *ancien régime*.[29]

The ideology called upon to legitimise discrimination on the basis of property also had clear similarities on both sides of the Atlantic. As for Constant, for Gouverneur Morris, manual labourers could be counted among the ranks of 'children', who did not and could not vote because they had no autonomous will.[30] This was also Hamilton's view.[31] Above all, we see the same social preoccupations at work in America as in Europe. Madison observed that, if elections in England were opened up to all classes of the people, this would bring the immediate introduction of an agrarian law, thereby endangering landed property. It is true that America's social composition was different – freeholders had far greater weight in US society. But it was also necessary to have some foresight and think about the future, in which the opposition between classes and the contradictions between rich and poor would have further developed, as had already taken place in European countries. It was thus

28 Charles Beard, *An Economic Interpretation of the Constitution of the United States* (New York: Macmillan, 1914), pp. 67–72.

29 Marie-France Toinet, '"Americanizzazione" o "europeizzazione": lo studio attuale dei partiti americani nel processo politico', in Maurizio Vaudagna, ed., *Il partito politico americano e l'Europa* (Milan: Feltrinelli, 1991), pp. 123ff.

30 Samuel E. Morison, *Sources and Documents Illustrating the American Revolution and the Formation of the Federal Constitution 1764–1788* (Oxford: Clarendon, 1953), p. 276.

31 Charles E. Merriam, *A History of American Political Theories* (New York: Kelley, 1969), p. 84.

necessary to take measures in the present, in order to keep the people at bay. For Hamilton, far from the people being 'God's voice' as was commonly believed and pretended, they were 'turbulent and fickle', envious, and thus inclined to attack property.[32]

As in the European case, it was sometimes considered possible to confront the popular threat by way of indirect elections. Some delegates to the Philadelphia Convention proposed that this method be applied to the House of Representatives and not only to the Senate. Interesting, in this regard, is Madison's response. After having begun by stating that he was himself in favour of the system of 'a series of filters' on the vote, he noted that, in some states, legislative power was already the result of indirect election, for which reason there was also the danger of pushing 'too far' along this path, at the risk of compromising the 'necessary sympathy' between people and government, and thus reducing the latter's base of consensus and stability.[33] As we can see, this is the same argument to which Constant also later resorted in his polemic against the two-tier electoral system. There are thus obvious analogies with Britain and Restoration France and, even more so, with the France of the July Monarchy: within the country's bicameral system, before Jackson's day the American lower house was also based on the restriction of political rights by way of property qualifications. The upper house, conversely, was sheltered from the popular masses' political influence: in Europe by way of the monopoly guaranteed to hereditary peers, and in America – where the feudal aristocracy was practically nonexistent – by way of two-tier elections. Not by accident, in Philadelphia the proposal that the Senate should not be directly elected from below, but rather by the legislatures of the individual states, was advanced with the explicit intention of constituting an upper house as similar as possible to the British House of Lords. It would thus be made up of members who were already distinguished by their 'rank', ensuring the unchallenged predominance of the 'sway of property'.[34] It should be added that, in the United States, the Supreme Court functions in practice as a third house called upon to serve as the 'guardian of property against the power of numbers'. It was

32 Morison, *Sources and Documents Illustrating the American Revolution*, pp. 263–5, 259.

33 Ibid., pp. 238–40.

34 Ibid., p. 244.

precisely in this guise that in the nineteenth century the Court strongly impeded the development of democracy, the organisation of trade unions, progressive income taxes, the prohibition of child labour, and so on.[35]

For these reasons alone, it is unsustainable to attempt to recast the history of the United States by bathing it in the aura of a supposed 'exceptionalism' characterised by democracy and equality. Rather, as we shall see, discrimination based on property would prove particularly dogged in the United States, even into our own times. Without doubt, within the white community, this discrimination was strongly put into question during the Jackson presidency. It was precisely in the wake of this broad extension of suffrage that Tocqueville's *Democracy in America* paid tribute to a two-tier electoral system that had such egregious success in reserving the Senate to the 'nation's élites' while keeping 'obscure characters', 'vulgar elements', and above all 'men belonging to the lower classes' at bay. Such an unambiguously clear-sighted description of the 'two-tier' system, with no mention of possible qualms, seemed to suggest that this system should be introduced also for the House of Representatives, as had indeed already been proposed in Philadelphia by the right wing of the forces arrayed in the Convention.

Property-Based Discrimination and Racial Discrimination

But here it is worth dwelling on the interpretation of post-Jacksonian America as a land in which discrimination in political rights on the basis of property had substantially disappeared. This is all the more important, given that Tocqueville's opinion was also shared by the young Marx, who saw 'the property qualification for the right to elect or be elected abolished' in many American states: in this view, property qualifications no longer constituted a legal condition for the exercise of political rights and eligibility for elected posts: the unpropertied would thus, at least in theory, have become legislators over the proprietors, too, and thus *politically* 'the state annuls . . . private property'.[36] Even so, for Marx,

35 Harold J. Laski, *The American Democracy: A Commentary and an Interpretation* (Fairfield, NJ: Kelley, 1977), pp. 20, 30ff.

36 *Marx-Engels Collected Works* (*MECW*) (London: Lawrence & Wishart, 1975–

in the very moment in which wealth was declared to be without political significance – as a fact that exclusively pertained to the private sphere – it could exercise its influence and its domination undisturbed. In this sense, as *On the Jewish Question* put it, America appeared to be the land of 'complete political emancipation', or, as the *German Ideology* had it, '[t]he most perfect example of the modern state', ensuring the bourgeoisie's rule without a priori excluding any class from the enjoyment of political rights.[37]

Truth be told, both Marx and Tocqueville were mistaken to interpret the United States in this way. They generalised a certain tendency and raised it to an absolute level – and, while this tendency really was operational, they overlooked the episodes of resistance to it. In Virginia before 1851, 'between a third and half of white men were denied suffrage'.[38] But what requires the most urgent emphasis is the fact that, in America, far from discrimination based on property having disappeared, it was expressed through ethnic and racial discrimination. In this form, it would prove far more stubborn in America than it would in Europe. Marx displayed his understanding of this aspect of the question during the War of Secession, when he defined the rebels defending the institution of slavery as the 'nobility of the Confederation' (*Konföderientenadel*), thus establishing an implicit comparison with the France of the *ancien régime*. The Republic was no longer taken as exemplary of a particularly advanced modern state. This is also clear from the fact that Marx considered Lincoln as the continuator of Washington's work: as the figure who was somehow bringing to completion in the United States the bourgeois-democratic revolution that had already triumphed in the more developed European countries. Did not the enemies of the Southern secessionists and slave owners often call them 'Bourbons'? As for Tocqueville, he himself noted that the highest value for the white masters of the South was *oisiveté*, from *otium* (idleness), whereas 'work merges with the idea of slavery'.[39] Labour was thus deprived of civil as well as political rights. In the North, it is true, blacks were free and, in theory, they were not excluded from suffrage, either; but, as the French liberal

2004), vol. 3, p. 153.

37 Ibid., pp. 151, 90.

38 William Cooper Jr, 'L'arena della politica sudista (1828–1956)', in Loretta Valtz Mannucci, ed., *Gli Stati Uniti nell'età di Jackson* (Bologna: Il Mulino, 1987), p. 258.

39 Tocqueville, *Democracy in America*, p. 558.

himself observed, if 'in nearly all the states where slavery is abolished, the Negro has been given electoral rights . . . if he presents himself to vote, he risks his life'.[40]

Blacks made up an essential aspect of a more general reality. It has been noted that the 'United States imported its working class by sailboat and steamships'. This did not only apply to slaves: 'European migration before the American War of Independence also included many people who accepted the temporary bondage of indenture in the hope of establishing themselves in the New World; these indentured laborers may have comprised as many as two-thirds of all early migrants'.[41] Who were these 'apprentices'? Let us listen to a contemporary US historian. They were the so-called 'indentured servants', in practice 'semi-slaves', at least for the duration of their 'contract' (which was, moreover, often arbitrarily prolonged by their master upon various pretexts). They were bought and sold on a regular market, which was also advertised in the local press, and if they fled or unduly wandered from their place of work they were hunted down.[42] Sieyès defined this as a 'legal slavery', recommending its extension to France in order to regulate the social and economic position of 'the lowest class, made up of men who have nothing but their hands'.[43] Sieyès would elsewhere define this class as that set of 'passive citizens' to whom it would be absurd to grant any role in political life.

These realities do not relate only to the earliest history of the United States. Rather, even in the nineteenth century, that country imported considerable masses of Chinese workers – for instance, the 'coolies' employed to build the continuous rail line designed to consolidate the conquest of the Far West.[44] To understand the social and juridical status of these immigrants, we need only reflect on the fact that Nietzsche took them as a possible model as he underlined the need to introduce a 'new slavery' to Europe and the Western world – a 'new type of slave relation' such as could be realised through 'a massive introduction of barbarian

40 Ibid., p. 554.

41 Eric R. Wolf, *Europe and the People Without History* (Berkeley: University of California Press, 2010), p. 363.

42 Marcus W. Jernegan, *Laboring and Dependent Classes in Colonial America, 1607–1783* (Westport, CT: Greenwood, 1980).

43 Emmanuel-Joseph Sieyès, *Écrits politiques* (Paris: Éditions des archives contemporaines, 1985), pp. 76ff.

44 Wolf, *Europe and the People Without History*, p. 377; Allan Nevins and Henry S. Commager, *America: The Story of a Free People* (Oxford: Clarendon, 1947).

Asian and African populations', in particular the Chinese, who 'would bring the way of living and thinking appropriate to industrious ants'. Similarly – albeit making a clearly different and opposed value judgement – Engels spoke of the 'camouflaged slavery of the Indian and Chinese coolies'.[45]

Thus, even beyond blacks, there was another important category of US society excluded from political rights and even, in large part, from civil rights. In seeking to justify discrimination based on property, to the disadvantage of wage workers, Constant assimilated the latter (among other things) to 'foreigners' lacking an interest in the 'national prosperity, with whose elements they are not familiar', and in which they had next to no share.[46] Yet this metaphor became a reality in the United States, where a workforce largely imported from across the oceans continued to be alien until the moment of naturalisation – a moment that could easily be deferred during crisis situations. Such was the case of the Naturalization Act of 1798, when the residency period necessary to achieve naturalisation was increased from five to fourteen years.[47] We could even ask whether, when Constant resorted to the metaphor of foreigners, as well as to the metics of Classical antiquity, he was not thinking precisely of America, which he repeatedly invoked and sometimes referred to as a 'great example'.[48]

Excluded from Democracy

If Tocqueville took explicit interest in immigrants to the United States, it is interesting to examine the particular terms in which he did so. With the gathering of the storm clouds that would, within a few years, lead to the War of Secession, the French liberal attributed the worsening crisis to 'the rapid introduction of men foreign to the English race into the United States', a factor that was making America run 'the greatest

45 Domenico Losurdo, 'Le catene e i fiori. La critica dell'ideologia tra Marx e Nietzsche', *Hermeneutica* 6 (1986), pp. 87–143.

46 Constant, *Principles of Politics*, p. 166.

47 Henry S. Commager, *Documents of American History* (New York: Appleton-Century-Crofts, 1963), vol. 1, p. 175.

48 Domenico Losurdo, *Hegel e la libertà dei moderni*, § 8.8.

danger'.[49] Tocqueville tirelessly warned his American friends and correspondents about this threat: 'Unfortunately, every day brings you so many foreign elements that soon you will no longer be yourselves: all the reasoning that could once be made on your nature will become ever more uncertain. Indeed, mixed with so many races as you are today, who can today say what your nature is?' And further: 'What I find alarming is this prodigious number of foreigners, which is turning you into a new people.'[50] It is probably excessive to state that Gobineau, the theorist of racial inequality, was 'not so far removed from Alexis de Tocqueville, at one time his mentor and superior, as might be supposed'.[51] All the same, it is senseless to paint as a champion of democracy an author who denounced the US ruling class's lack of opposition to mass immigration (and the consequent bastardisation of the original American population) as one of its 'great faults' – an author, that is, who seems to have shared the arguments later used by American nativists in their campaign to deny political rights to immigrants (above all, those extraneous to the Anglo-Protestant 'race') and even to subject them, as we shall see, to a process of disemancipation.[52]

The fact is that Tocqueville never thought about democracy in truly universal terms. This alone explains the paradox through which, at the same time as he lucidly described, without indulgence, the inhuman treatment imposed on the Native Americans and blacks, he also insisted that the United States was the only true model of democracy. The Native Americans were subjected to the 'dreadful evils' that accompanied 'forced emigrations' (that is, the successive waves of deportations imposed by the whites) and were now close to being wiped from the face of the Earth.[53] As for blacks, the French liberal recognised the catastrophe that was their situation, and not only in the South. He observed: 'Racial prejudice seems to me stronger in the states that have abolished slavery than in those where slavery still exists, and nowhere does it appear as intolerant as in the states where servitude has always been unknown.'[54] However, this did not stop Tocqueville from

49 Tocqueville, *Œuvres completes*, ed. Mayer, vol. 8: III, p. 229.
50 Ibid., vol. 7, pp. 177, 182.
51 Ernst Nolte, *Three Faces of Fascism* (New York: Mentor, 1969), p. 635.
52 Tocqueville, *Œuvres completes*, ed. Mayer, vol. 7, p. 177.
53 Tocqueville, *Democracy in America*, p. 526.
54 Ibid., p. 553.

celebrating America as the only country in the world in which democracy prevailed,

> Living, active, triumphant . . . There you will see a people among whom conditions are more equal even than they are among us [French]; among whom the social order, customs, laws, everything, is democratic; among whom everything emanates from and belongs to the people and where, even so, every individual enjoys a fuller independence, a greater freedom, than in any other era or in any other clime on Earth.[55]

The fate of the Native Americans and blacks never rears its head to cast a shadow on this shining example. There is something quite incredible about the programmatic declaration which the French liberal sets at the beginning of his chapter dedicated to the problem of the 'three races that inhabit the territory of the United States': 'The principal task that I had set for myself has now been fulfilled; I have succeeded, at least as much as I could, in showing what the laws of the American democracy were; I have made its mores known. I could stop here.'[56] Only to avoid the possibility of disappointing his reader does Tocqueville speak of the relations between the three races: 'These topics touch on my subject, but do not enter into it; they are American without being democratic, and above all I wanted to portray democracy.'[57] In the course of his polemic against the Jacobins, Constant reproached them for having forgotten the fact that ancient democracy, which they purported to take as a model, was in fact based on slavery. But it was he himself who ran into even more remarkable amnesia, or absent-mindedness, when, in his text dedicated to illustrating and celebrating modern freedom, he asked what 'the word freedom' (among others) meant 'to an inhabitant of the United States of America', as if that country had nothing to do with the institution that cast such a shadow over the freedom of the ancients.[58] What Constant had forgotten or overlooked became a sort of programmatic declaration in Tocqueville, who clearly asserted that the fate of the

55 Tocqueville, *Œuvres complètes*, ed. Tocqueville and Beaumont, vol. 9, pp. 544ff.

56 Tocqueville, *Democracy in America*, p. 515.

57 Ibid., p. 516.

58 Benjamin Constant, 'De la liberté des anciens comparée à celle des modernes', in *De la liberté chez les modernes* (Paris: Hachette, 1980), p. 494.

blacks (and Native Americans) was a question external and extraneous to the essence of American democracy. Even where slavery was cited as an explanation and condemnation of ancient democracy, the liberal tradition could lightmindedly ignore it when the task at hand was to counterpose American democracy to the violence and plebeian turbulence of the French revolutionary tradition. The development of US democracy, celebrated as peaceful and orderly, in fact rested on the fetters which shackled the 'dangerous classes' even in the sites of production themselves.

Property, Culture and Political Rights in John Stuart Mill

In seeking to neutralise the popular masses politically and defuse democracy's tendency towards income redistribution, Constant looked to the restriction of political rights based on property, whereas Tocqueville – misunderstanding and remoulding the US model – recommended recourse to indirect elections. For his part, John Stuart Mill, proceeding by way of an appraisal of traditional methods and a somehow more modern, seductive reformulation of them, above all drew attention to what he recommended as a new method. For now, we can concentrate on the first aspect. The second-tier electoral system so dear to the English liberal's friend and interlocutor Tocqueville appeared to Mill himself as scarcely practicable, even if only for the fact that it was difficult to export it to a country without a federal structure:

> The case in which election by two stages answers well in practice is when the electors are not chosen solely as electors, but have other important functions to discharge, which precludes their being selected solely as delegates to give a particular vote. This combination of circumstances exemplifies itself in another American institution, the Senate of the United States . . . These members are not chosen by the population, but by the State Legislatures, themselves elected by the people of each state.[59]

59 John Stuart Mill, *Considerations on Representative Government* (New York: Henry Holt, 1873), pp. 200–1.

It is also worth bearing in mind that the two-tier electoral system began to prove a fiction even where it did formally remain in force: only 'nominally' was the United States' system for electing a president 'indirect'; in reality, the members of the Electoral College were elected with a mandate binding them to a specific candidate and him alone.

What could be done? In Mill, we can see a fresh preoccupation which had not hitherto emerged in the liberal tradition. In the meantime, universal (male) suffrage had established itself for good in France, and, even if it was 'regulated' and frustrated by the Bonapartist regime, it had become ever more difficult to challenge it on grounds of principle. The English author himself realised as much; it was 'absolutely necessary' that suffrage should be 'widely expanded', or rather, become 'universal'.[60] But, after this recognition of principle, the same old preoccupation immediately resurfaced: 'the great majority of voters in most countries, and emphatically in this, would be manual laborers, and the twofold danger, that of too low a standard of political intelligence, and that of class legislation, would still exist in a very perilous degree.'[61] In seeking to confront this danger, there again emerged the traditional remedy of restricting political rights on the basis of property:

> It is also important that the assembly which votes the taxes, either general or local, should be elected exclusively by those who pay something towards the taxes imposed. Those who pay no taxes, disposing by their votes of other people's money, have every motive to be lavish and none to economise. As far as money matters are concerned, any power of voting possessed by them is a violation of the fundamental principle of free government, a severance of the power of control from the interest in its beneficial exercise . . . in some of the great towns of the United States, [their having such a power] is known to have produced a scale of local taxation onerous beyond example, and wholly borne by the wealthier classes. That representation should be coextensive with taxation, not stopping short of it, but also not going beyond it, is in accordance with the theory of British institutions.[62]

60 Ibid., p. 179.
61 Ibid.
62 Ibid., p. 176.

Here, it becomes clear that the principle of 'No taxation without representation' so dear to the liberal tradition also – and perhaps above all – means that those too poor to be taxed have no right to autonomous political representation ('No representation without taxation'). Moreover, this was the sense in which this principle – 'the most fundamental principle of British freedom' – would be interpreted by Lecky a quarter of a century later.[63] For Mill, there could in any case be no doubt that

> the receipt of parish relief should be a peremptory disqualification for the franchise. He who cannot by his labour suffice for his own support, has no claim to the privilege of helping himself to the money of others. By becoming dependent on the remaining members of the community for actual subsistence, he abdicates his claim to equal rights with them in other respects. Those to whom he is indebted for the continuance of his very existence may justly claim the exclusive management of those common concerns to which he now brings nothing, or less than he takes away. As a condition of the franchise, a term should be fixed, say five years previous to the registry, during which the applicant's name has not been on the parish books as a recipient of relief.[64]

But ever wider layers of the population came to consider odious the granting (or denial) of political rights based on income. Hence, discrimination on the basis of property qualifications strove to present a more modern, acceptable face: 'I regard it as wholly inadmissible that any person should participate in the suffrage without being able to read, write, and, I will add, perform the common operations of arithmetic.'[65] Some years later, the process of rolling back the emancipation of blacks and poor whites in the United States was also imposed by way of an exam that sought to ascertain the elector's level of literacy and education.

Telling, in this regard, is the argument to which Mill resorted as justification for the exclusion of the illiterate from political rights: to give 'the suffrage to a man who could not read' would be like

63 William H. Lecky, *Democracy and Liberty* (Indianapolis: Liberty Classics, 1981), p. 29.

64 Mill, *Considerations on Representative Government*, pp. 177–8.

65 Ibid., p. 174.

'giving it to a child who could not speak'.[66] Here returns the same metaphor that had served Constant in discriminating against '[t]hose whom poverty holds in endless dependence and condemns from childhood to labouring work' who are thus no 'more informed than children as to public affairs'.[67] Considered illiterates or infants, these creatures whose hard toil impeded them from access to culture and mature citizenship were the same social class to which both liberal authors denied political citizenship. Writing a few decades after Constant, Mill seemed inclined to loosen the binds of property discrimination, proving less intransigently opposed to the 'opinions and wishes of the poorest and rudest class of labourers' being 'one influence among others on the minds of the voters, as well as on those of the Legislature', even though 'it might be highly mischievous to give them the preponderant influence, by admitting them, in their present state of morals and intelligence, to the full exercise of the suffrage'.[68] Citizens traditionally considered 'passive' could now take the initiative of communicating their opinions to 'active' ones, though the latter would remain the sole holders of political rights in the strict sense.

But what did this mean for 'universal suffrage', even if it was indeed affirmed on grounds of principle? For it to be realised in concrete terms, it was necessary to take steps such that 'taxation, in a visible shape, should descend to the poorest class' and 'the means of attaining these elementary acquirements' of understanding required for political rights 'should be within the reach of every person'.[69] Clearly, for Mill, universal suffrage was conjugated in the future tense – put off until the point at which illiteracy had disappeared and there would no longer be individuals so poor as to need public assistance and not be subject to even a minimal level of taxation – whereas the exclusions dictated (whether immediately or in more mediated fashion) by property were conjugated in the present tense. In reality, the philosopher, who also had the merit of raising question-marks over – and condemning – the exclusion of women from political rights, did not manage to overcome the logic of

66 Ibid.
67 Constant, *Principles of Politics*, p. 166.
68 Mill, *Considerations on Representative Government*, pp. 214–15.
69 Ibid., pp. 177, 174.

property-based discrimination, notwithstanding some formal tributes paid to the principle of universal suffrage.

Plural Voting

And there is more. As the English liberal directed his attentions to the rising movement that demanded the extension of political rights, he pointed to another method of neutralising or limiting the popular classes' political influence as far as possible:

> When two persons who have a joint interest in any business differ in opinion, does justice require that both opinions should be held of exactly equal value? . . . if the institutions of the country virtually assert that they are of the same value, they assert the thing which is not. One of the two, as the wiser or better man, has a claim to superior weight.[70]

Hence, even when it is conjugated in the future tense, universal suffrage cannot, in any case, be equal for all: legislative means will be used to ensure the best and brightest a greater influence on political life. But is not this discrimination itself odious? Mill does not think so: 'Every one has a right to feel insulted by being made a nobody, and stamped as of no account at all. No one but a fool, and only a fool of a peculiar description, feels offended by the acknowledgment that there are others whose opinion, and even whose wish, is entitled to a greater amount of consideration than his.'[71] But how is it possible to ascertain the electors' level of intelligence, so that it would be possible to assign multiple votes to those who deserve them? For the English liberal, there is one immediately obvious way of telling:

> An employer of labour is on the average more intelligent than a labourer; for he must labour with his head, and not solely with his hands . . . A banker, merchant, or manufacturer is likely to be more intelligent than a tradesman, because he has larger and more

70 Ibid., pp. 179–89.
71 Ibid., p. 181.

> complicated interests to manage . . . two or more votes might be allowed to every person who exercises any of these superior functions.

And similar privileged treatment might be reserved for the 'liberal professions'.[72] We hardly need to emphasise that the property-based discrimination that had been chased out of the door here storms back in through the window. At least in one case, it does not even need to avoid the main entrance or to don any deceptive disguise. For Mill explicitly proposes plural voting, based on the elector's property ownership, for elections to local bodies: as he puts it, 'the honest and frugal dispensation of money forms so much larger a part of the business of the local than of the national body, that there is more justice as well as policy in allowing a greater proportional influence to those who have a larger money interest at stake.'[73]

At this point, the theorist of plural voting was forced to polemicise – even in vigorous tones – against the land which his friend and interlocutor Tocqueville instead took as a model. After all, the United States was based on equal universal suffrage, however much this was filtered through a two-stage electoral system. Thus, for the English liberal,

> The American institutions have imprinted strongly on the American mind that any one man (with a white skin) is as good as any other, and it is felt that this false creed is nearly connected with some of the more unfavourable points in American character. It is not a small mischief that the constitution of any country should sanction this creed; for the belief in it, whether express or tacit, is almost as detrimental to moral and intellectual excellence as any effect which most forms of government can produce.[74]

As we see, it is also mistaken to make a champion of democracy out of Mill. He himself openly recognised his distrust towards such a political system, given his dread of 'the ignorance and especially the

72 Ibid., p. 183.
73 Ibid., p. 290.
74 Ibid., p. 189.

selfishness and brutality of the mass'.[75] Rather, at the end of the nineteenth century, the liberal or liberal-conservative Lecky was quite correct to identify – as he advanced his own denunciation of the ruinous effects of the collapse of all property discrimination – with the teachings of Mill, who was 'not insensible to the danger and injustice of dissociating the power of voting taxes from the necessity of paying them, and to the fact that unqualified universal suffrage leads plainly and rapidly to this form of robbery'.[76]

The history of plural voting deserves one further point of reflection. It had been adopted on a limited scale in France during the Restoration, at the moment in which the noble and clerical reaction most strongly made itself felt. Through a curious turn of events, the electoral system proposed by Mill in order to reconcile the extension of suffrage with the hegemony of the cultured and property-owning classes would, in practice, preside over each of the attempts to roll back emancipation which developed over the subsequent decades. This happened after the Paris Commune, in Italy immediately after the March on Rome, and again in France after the fall of the Third Republic and Pétain's arrival in power.[77] All that needs adding is that, even in America today, there are those who have proposed, following in Mill's footsteps, the introduction of a system of proportional representation that grants weight to each man's vote in relation to his demonstrated capacity to make intelligent choices. The article in question, by Joseph Farkas – published on the 'op-ed' page of the *New York Times* – bears the rather telling title, 'One Man, ¼ Vote'![78]

Property Discrimination as a Principle of Legitimacy

The obstinate, variegated and multiform character of the resistance to the principle of universal suffrage is a major disturbance to the argument dear

75 John Stuart Mill, *Autobiography*, in *Collected Works*, vol. 1 (Toronto: University of Toronto Press, 1981), p. 238.

76 Lecky, *Democracy and Liberty*, p. 232.

77 Edmond Villey, *Législation électorale comparée des principaux pays d'Europe* (Paris: Larose-Pedone, 1900), p. 10; Raymond Huard, *Le suffrage universel en France 1848–1946* (Paris: Aubier, 1991), p. 357.

78 Cited in Arthur M. Okun, *Equality and Efficiency. The Big Tradeoff* (Washington: The Brookings Institution, 2015 [1975]), p. 8.

to those who more or less openly seek to reduce property discrimination to a sort of accident along the liberal tradition's way. It was not, in fact, a youthful indiscretion that was overcome through the spontaneous maturation of this tradition, without the need for external pressure and conditioning.[79] In reality, this tradition showed so little openness towards the extension of suffrage to the popular classes that it considered such a move – insofar as it was pregnant with ruinous attacks on property – as a violation of the rules of the game, which even ought to be combated by violent means. For Montesquieu, the abolition of the hereditary house of peers and its veto right over the 'initiatives of the people' (and thus of laws propounded by a somehow popular branch of parliament) is already synonymous with despotism, and even with 'slavery', given that it would give rise to legislation wholly or mostly directed against the privileged layers.[80] For his part, the Thermidorian Boissy d'Anglas took up the standpoint of the bourgeoisie more than of the nobility. Having warned against the 'harmful taxes' that the legislature would inevitably impose once it fell prey to the propertyless, or else came under their influence, he added that a country 'governed by the propertied is under a social order, whereas one in which the unpropertied govern is instead in the state of nature'.[81] In the absence of a juridical order and legal norms, clearly weapons would have the decisive say. Constant expressed himself in similar terms, albeit using more cautious language:

> The necessary purpose of the propertyless is to manage to become propertied. All the resources you give them they will use for this purpose. If you add to the freedom for their talents and efforts, which you do owe them, political rights, which you do not, these rights, in the hands of the vast majority of them, will infallibly be used to encroach on property . . . Put the unpropertied class in charge of the State, however well intentioned they may be, and the anxiety of the propertied will hem in all their measures. The wisest laws will be suspected and hence disobeyed.[82]

79 Salvatore Veca, *Cittadinanza. Riflessioni filosofiche sull'idea di emancipazione* (Milan: Feltrinelli, 1990), p. 27.

80 Charles-Louis de Secondat de Montesquieu, 'Esprit des lois', in *Œuvres completes* (Paris: Gallimard, 1949–51), Book 11, Chapter 6.

81 Lefebvre, *La France sous le directoire 1795–1799*, p. 35.

82 Constant, *Principles of Politics*, pp. 170–1.

Which is to say, these laws would be – legitimately, or understandably – ignored or broken. It was on the basis of similar considerations that French liberal circles participated in the organisation of the coup d'état of 18th Brumaire, or – at least at the outset – greeted it warmly.

The scenario is no different if we move from France to Britain – which, moreover, already provided a model for Montesquieu. For Locke, the very purpose of society was the 'preservation of property'; and it followed from this not only that 'Hence it is a mistake to think, that the Supream or Legislative Power of any Commonwealth, can do what it will, and dispose of the Estates of the Subject arbitrarily, or take any part of them at pleasure', but also that the composition of the legislative power could not be changed, for instance by moves to undermine the House of Lords and the hereditary succession that operated therein.[83] Even if it was mediated by the legislative power's intervention, the intrusion or 'invasion' of non-property owners within the sphere of property would always be an arbitrary act, an act of pillage, and one that the party under attack could thus legitimately resist by force. This was also the opinion of John Stuart Mill himself: any 'power of voting' in the hands of non-taxpayers is 'a violation of the fundamental principle of free government'; to grant political rights and thus a share in legislative power to poor citizens not subject to taxation 'amounts to allowing them to put their hands into other people's pockets for any purpose which they think fit to call a public one'.[84]

At the end of the nineteenth century, Lecky adopted Constant's thesis according to which non–property owners who had political rights would inevitably be led to pursue 'predatory and anarchic purposes' and even to 'break up society'. On this basis, he portrayed 'a system of veiled confiscation – one class voting the taxes which another class was compelled to pay', which thus effectively stripped the wealthy of political rights.[85] That is, the undue political emancipation of the popular classes would effectively disenfranchise the only classes up to the task of leading the country. As we can see, the thesis of a spontaneous maturation of liberal thought as it gradually opened up to an ever-wider extension of

83 John Locke, *Second Treatise of Government*, paras 138, 243. In *Two Treatises of Government*, edited by Peter Laslett, Cambridge: Cambridge University Press, 1988, p. 361.

84 Mill, *Considerations on Representative Government*, p. 176.

85 Lecky, *Democracy and Liberty*, pp. 24, 4.

suffrage is nothing but an apologetic myth. Moreover, even up to our own time, authors like Mises and Hayek have identified in universal suffrage the ultimate cause of the despotic and totalitarian measures to redistribute wealth that have emanated also from the welfare state in the West.

Emancipation and Its Reversal

But the thesis advanced by the liberal tradition's apologists is unsustainable, and not only because it overlooks the gigantic political and social struggles waged by the popular masses excluded from political rights. It is also because it confers a linear character on the historical process of the conquest and extension of suffrage, which does not at all correspond to the reality. Already the first electoral reform carried out by liberal Britain, which began to introduce the constitutive elements of the modern representative system, displayed contradictory traits: 'the franchise in many boroughs was democratic, more democratic before than after 1832; and while the great reform bill mitigated many abuses and swept away some anomalies, it disfranchised numbers of poor electors, and created a grievance which fostered the Chartist movement.'[86]

Here, we see how emancipation for some was interwoven with a loss of freedom for others. We could also advance similar considerations about France. After 1789, the liberal bourgeoisie introduced a discrimination based on property, harsher than that which had existed in past elections to the Estates General. As we have seen, the latter had operated on the basis of a 'quasi-universal suffrage', albeit one controlled – in the case of the Third Estate – by way of a multiple-level electoral system. As in Britain, in France, too, the onset of the modern representative system was characterised by the intersection of emancipation and its reversal.

This system's subsequent historical development saw the closely interwoven succession of demands for emancipation (and measures to this effect) and attempts (and measures) to roll it back. The events of 10 August 1792 imposed a quasi-universal male suffrage that was subsequently cancelled out by Thermidor. Something similar took place after

86 Albert F. Pollard, *The Evolution of Parliament* (London: Longmans, Green & Co., 1920), p. 164.

the revolution of 1848, which itself sanctioned universal (male) suffrage. But, in May 1850, the liberal bourgeoisie did not hesitate in trampling on the Constitution to which it had sworn its loyalty two years previously. This document had affirmed (in its article 25): 'All Frenchmen aged 21, and in the enjoyment of their civil and political rights, are electors, without property qualifications of any kind.' Yet, with a sort of 'parliamentary coup d'état', the political emancipation that had only just been won was stripped from those who could not show a stable residency certificate, because they were instead forced to move constantly in search of employment.[87] As a result, '3 million out of 9 and a half million voters' were excluded. Those deprived of their emancipation were the 'vile multitude' unworthy of political rights; this, at least, was the opinion of Thiers, who then added – not without a certain cynicism – 'Universalism does not mean for all, but for the greatest possible number in the spirit of the Constitution', and thus – on closer inspection – in the spirit of the existing social order.[88]

In his own efforts to win popular support, Louis-Napoleon reintroduced universal male suffrage, though he also controlled it from above within a regime whose characteristics we will go on to analyse over subsequent chapters. As we have seen, there was no lack of attempts to replace the Bonapartist regime with a liberal-Legitimist one that would not likely have left direct universal suffrage standing. Just as after the Jacobin experience and the revolution of 1848, again after the Paris Commune, direct universal suffrage would be strongly challenged and put in question by liberal circles themselves. The most diverse proposals flourished – whether they envisaged plural voting to the advantage of the 'most intelligent', or suffrage based on multiple grades, or even a return to explicit property qualifications. This last option immediately appeared either rather perilous or wholly impractical, given the popular reactions it might produce. It was no longer possible, or in any case advisable, openly to put the principle of universal suffrage into question. If anything, it was a question of 'regulating it, imposing morals on it, purifying it', as

87 Victor Pierre, *Histoire de la République de 1848* (Paris: Plon, 1878), vol. 2, pp. 366, 322.

88 Alfred Cobban, *A History of Modern France* (Harmondsworth: Penguin, 1965), vol. 2, p. 155; Huard, *Le suffrage universel en France*, p. 11.

Thiers would put it (perhaps referring to the law of 31 May 1850, of which he had been one of the promoters), albeit hesitating to give the impression that he wanted to reintroduce discrimination based on property. But even this apparently easy way out seems rather problematic, and all the more so given that the Bonapartists continued to posture as the defenders of universal suffrage. The electoral law of the Third Republic thus settled for implementing a first-past-the-post system that designated the constituencies on the basis of criteria that 'distorted the equality in citizen representation, to the advantage of the rural *départements*'.[89]

The United States is the classic homeland of thwarted emancipation, where this phenomenon prevailed with particular breadth and tenacity. At the end of the nineteenth century, an articulated movement developed to roll back emancipation, made up of three distinct processes (though they were doubtless also interwoven). The first victims, of course, were blacks: emancipated from slavery and admitted into the community of political rights after the War of Secession, at first they even achieved a certain presence within local and state representative bodies.[90] But their situation rapidly worsened – indeed, drastically so – after the withdrawal of Federal troops and the 'reconciliation' between North and South. 'Before the twentieth century was a decade old the constitutional disfranchisement of the Negro was a fact throughout the South'; what the ruling class saw as the 'unworkable principle of universal suffrage had been frankly discarded'.[91] As we shall see, in this period, many whites were also stripped of political rights. But here we are also dealing with a dis-emancipation process that specifically affected blacks, as demonstrated by the targeted legislation enacted by multiple Southern states and by Louisiana's reinterpretation of the Literacy Test. In 1898, it introduced the 'grandfather clause', by which a citizen was exempted from having to undergo the reading and writing test if he could prove that he had voted before 1 January 1867, or was the child or grandchild of someone who had: thanks to this expedient, the

89 Huard, *Le suffrage universel en France*, pp. 108–17.

90 Frances F. Piven and Richard A. Cloward, *Why Americans Don't Vote* (New York: Pantheon, 1988), p. 79.

91 Paul H. Buck, *The Road to Reunion, 1865–1900* (Boston, MA: Little, Brown, 1937), pp. 286–7.

electoral lists were purged of all coloured voters while they included 'all' – or almost all – 'classes of whites'.[92]

The evolution of immigrants' political status was especially complex and tormented. The Naturalization Act of 1798, which we have already had cause to mention, in practice entailed a disemancipation, given that it denied citizenship to many immigrants who had, up to that point, been entitled to it. They were also stripped of certain civil rights, for this law was also the pretext for others that immediately followed, which granted the president discretionary powers regarding the 'arrest and deportation' of foreigners.[93] Subsequently, immigrants would also benefit from the general emancipation process that came about in the decade following the War of Secession, and which seemed intended to destroy all political discrimination: in some states, immigrants could vote 'on condition that they had been residents for several years and/or expressed the intention to seek naturalization', even if they had not formally achieved citizenship. At the moment of the greatest extension of political citizenship, immigrants had the right to vote in the majority of states (twenty-two out of thirty-seven). But, from 1875, there began a disenfranchisement process: in 1900, only eleven states granted such voting rights, and by 1925 Arkansas was the only state still to do so: 'in 1928, for the first time since the country's origins, not even one non-American participated in an election, be it at the federal, state or local level.'[94]

Poor whites were also subject to disemancipation measures through the poll tax and the literacy test. In many cases, the disemancipation was officially enshrined: 'most of the Southern States' made constitutional revisions 'requiring that the electors shall be able to read or even explain the text of the constitution'.[95] At the federal level, conversely, 'registration laws' were issued which offloaded onto the individual citizen the

92 Ibid. p. 286.

93 Woodrow Wilson, *A History of the American People* (New York: Harper & Brothers, 1902), vol. 3, p. 152.

94 Walter Dean Burnham, *Critical Election and the Mainsprings of American Politics* (New York: Norton, 1970), pp. 71–90; Marie-France Toinet, 'La Participation politique des ouvriers américains à la fin du dix-neuvième siècle', in Marianna Debouzy, ed., *À l'ombre de la statue de la liberté. Immigrants et ouvriers dans la République américaine 1880–1920* (Vincennes: Presses Universitaires de Vincennes, 1988), pp. 294ff, 299.

95 Moisei Ostrogorski, *Democracy and the Organization of Political Parties* (New York: Macmillan, 1902), vol. 2, pp. 174–5.

responsibility for registering on the electoral roll, and made this task ever more laborious and costly, with the result (and indeed the intention) of discouraging the poorer classes from electoral participation. In fact, there was a sudden slump in turnout. The year 1896, which saw the definitive defeat of the populist movement and the acceleration of reactionary initiatives by the still-frightened ruling classes, marked a turning point that can even be defined as a 'counter-revolution', albeit one that proceeded by peaceful means.[96]

The Denial of Political Rights, the Labour Market and Slave Labour

Just as the dogged restriction of political rights based on property was no accident or 'mistake' for the liberal tradition, the rolling back of emancipation was no chance error or youthful folly of this tradition. The counter-revolution in question had obvious social implications. We can begin by analysing the consequences it had for immigrants and white Americans. In numerous states, working-class and popular pressure had succeeded in winning social legislation which limited and regulated women's and child labour, and imposed certain general safety measures in factories and workplaces. Although this legislation was widely disregarded and often cancelled out by the courts in the name of freedom of contracts, the ruling classes nonetheless felt it to be a threat, and connected it with the faults of universal suffrage and the political influence wielded by what they considered the dangerous classes. It was thus necessary to take decisive measures to limit their influence, such as could impede or throw up as many obstacles as possible to the advent of the social state: and the 'counter-revolution' at the end of the nineteenth century was the main factor behind the United States' backwardness on this terrain.[97]

As for immigrants, the extra obstacles posed to their naturalisation and achievement of citizenship came in a period in which a frenzied racist campaign against them was taking root, including cases of the

96 Piven and Cloward, *Why Americans Don't Vote*, pp. 48ff.
97 Ibid., p. 9; Toinet, 'La Participation politique des ouvriers américains', pp. 291ff.

lynching of Chinese people.[98] And it was no accident that this was a minority often locked into semi-servile employment relations. It has been aptly observed that 'Racial terms mirror the political process by which populations of whole continents were turned into providers of coerced surplus labor.'[99] Other ethnic minorities who had been stripped of their emancipation or denied the possibility of access to citizenship, and who were racially 'stigmatized', were relegated to the 'lower levels' of the employment market.[100]

Yet clearer is the relationship between political and social disemancipation in the case of blacks. Not a few studies emphasise the fact that in the South 'the suppression of blacks' right to vote was a condition of the stability of the plantation economy and the servile labour on which it was based'.[101] The presence of black political representatives at the local and state level threw up obstacles to the re-establishment of the 'caste labor system'.[102] Thus, slaves who had already been emancipated and accepted into citizenship again became 'foreigners', inferior by nature and by race, and thus destined to 'work for the whites' in a condition 'comparable to serfdom'.[103] This brought a 're-enslavement' of blacks, whose starvation wages were imposed not by the market but by the brute force of the white masters.[104]

The Liberal Tradition, Property-Based Discrimination and the Racialisation of the Excluded

At this point, we can better understand the significance of the property-based discrimination that has been a pervasive complement to the liberal tradition throughout its history. Theorising the distinction

98 Thomas F. Gosset, *Race: The History of an Idea in America* (New York: Schocken, 1963), p. 290.

99 Wolf, *Europe and the People Without History*, pp. 380–1.

100 Ibid.

101 Frances F. Piven, 'Regole, partiti e atteggiamenti politici: l'assenteismo elettorale americano in prospettiva comparativa', in Maurizio Vaudagna, ed., *Il partito politico americano e l'Europa* (Milan: Feltrinelli, 1991), p. 243.

102 Piven and Cloward, *Why Americans Don't Vote*, p. 79.

103 Buck, *Road to Reunion*, pp. 284–6.

104 John H. Franklin, *From Slavery to Freedom: A History of Negro Americans*, 6th edn (New York: Alfred A. Knopf, 1988).

between active citizens and passive ones, Sieyès considered it a condition for peace that the 'uneducated multitude' should be obliged to conduct 'forced' labour which was thus 'lacking in freedom'. As we have noted, he proposed the formal introduction of slave or semi-servile labour in France, to which the passive citizens (or 'labouring machines' – the two categories sometimes coexisted unproblematically) ought to be subjected.[105] The spokesman of France's Third Estate and liberal bourgeoisie not only referred to *machines de travail* but spoke of the 'greater share of men' as 'human instruments of production' or as 'bipedal instruments', ultimately resorting to the same category which Aristotle had used to define slave labour.[106]

If we turn from France to Britain, we see that Burke – the English Whig still so dear to liberal authors like Hayek and Dahrendorf – subsumed the farm labourer and wage labourer under the category of *instrumentum vocale*, used in classical antiquity to designate and classify the slave.[107] And it is easy to understand this; even Locke had held the view that 'the greatest part of mankind' must necessarily be subject to living and working conditions in which it is 'enslaved'.[108] In turn, Mandeville, another classic thinker of the liberal tradition, identified the 'meanest indigent Part of the Nation', 'the working slaving people', destined forever to carry out 'dirty slavish Work', in which context educating them could only be considered a force for disturbance.[109]

As we can see, discrimination based on property went hand in hand with a division of labour that pushed so far as to justify slave or semi-servile labour. The destitute condemned to such work were then described in terms which justified their use as simple instruments of production, and somehow represented as beings who lacked fully human characteristics. What sense would it have to grant political rights to those who, as Locke put it, remain at the level of a 'Pack-horse, who is driven constantly forwards and backwards in a narrow Lane, and dirty

105 Sieyès, *Écrits politiques*, pp. 81, 236.

106 Ibid., pp. 89, 75, 81.

107 Edmund Burke, *Thoughts and Details on Scarcity*, in *The Works of the Right Honourable Edmund Burke* (London: Rivington, 1826), vol. 7, p. 383; Domenico Losurdo, *Hegel e la libertà dei moderni*, § 6.4.

108 John Locke, *An Essay Concerning Human Understanding* (Oxford: Oxford University Press, 1975), p. 707.

109 Bernard Mandeville, *The Fable of the Bees* (London: Penguin, 1989), pp. 144, 306.

Road, only to Market', and were separated from the men of the upper classes by 'a greater distance . . . than between some Men and some Beasts'?[110] Similar was the attitude taken by Burke, who spoke of the greater share of men – that which derived its means of subsistence from hard daily toil – as a 'swinish multitude', and that of Sieyès, who denied the possibility of 'finding men', at least in the full sense of the word, among the 'immense crowd of bipedal instruments lacking in liberty, lacking in morality and lacking intellectual life'.[111] The foundation and justification of discrimination on the basis of property was an anthropology and an ontology, or – to invoke a category today at the centre of sociological study and political debate – a racialisation process which made those excluded from citizenship totally extraneous to the active citizenry and the dominant elite.[112]

It has been observed that in England between 1660 and 1760 there developed 'an attitude towards the new industrial proletariat noticeably harsher than that general in the first half of the seventeenth century, and which has no modern parallel except in the behaviour of the less reputable of white colonists towards coloured labour'.[113] This observation is owed to two orders of considerations. First, it throws utterly into crisis the evolutionist schema so dear to the apologists of the liberal tradition. Just as they ignore the multiple intersections between emancipation and disemancipation, they overlook the connection characteristic of the onset of liberal England, which connected discrimination based on property to the racialisation of those who were discriminated against – a connection that can, indeed, also be observed in other countries. For instance, it is obvious that, in the French case, it would be difficult to find in authors like Bodin or Bossuet the same harshness that Sieyès displayed towards those he defined as 'bipedal instruments'.

The second order of considerations springs from a connection established by Tawney, who compared the attitude that proto-liberal England

110 Locke, *Essay Concerning Human Understanding*, p. 709.

111 Sieyès, *Écrits politiques*, p. 81.

112 Pierre-André Taguieff, *La force du préjugé. Essai sur le racisme et ses doubles* (Paris: La Découverte, 1987); Étienne Balibar, 'Racisme et nationalisme' and 'Racisme de classe' in E. Balibar and I. Wallerstein, eds, *Race, nation, classe. Les identités ambigües* (Paris: La Découverte, 1988).

113 R. H. Tawney, *Religion and the Rise of Capitalism* (New Brunswick: Transaction, 1998), p. 269.

adopted towards the industrial proletariat to the racist attitude towards colonial or ex-colonial populations that remains very widespread even in our own time. Indeed, we can find Locke directly stating that a day-labourer is 'no more capable of reasoning than almost a perfect natural'; neither has reached the level of Christian, rational creatures.[114] And, in the liberal France of the July Monarchy, the Lyons silkweavers' revolt appeared to Saint-Marc Girardin as the 'new barbarian invasion'; and after the workers' revolt of June 1848, Tocqueville evoked the spectre of 'Vandals and Goths', even as he described the collective emotions of the time.[115] But, already in Sieyès, we can read that a 'great nation is necessarily composed of *two peoples*', in a sense two races, of essentially different value. After all, on the one hand, there are the real 'producers' or the 'chiefs of production' and, on the other, the 'human instruments of production'; on the one hand are 'intelligent persons' or 'honest people', and on the other 'the workers who have only a passive force', and are simple 'instruments of toil'.[116]

Hence, we can better understand the sense of the metaphor that hangs like a shadow over the history of the liberal tradition even into our own time, comparing those excluded from citizenship to 'foreigners'. This is a metaphor we can find even before Constant; in a sense, it is already there in Sieyès, for whom, among this 'immense crowd of bipedal instruments', there is 'not one capable of entering into society' and making up part of the restricted circle of the truly 'civilised' (*policés*).[117] Here, 'manual labourer' is synonymous not only with 'foreigner' but also with 'extraneous to civilisation' – in a sense, a member of a lower race. It is telling that this same metaphor had already been used by Locke, in this case referring to 'another sort of servants, which by a peculiar name we call slaves, who being captives taken in a just war . . . and being in the state of slavery, not capable of any property; cannot in that state be considered as any part of civil society; the chief end whereof is the preservation of property'.[118]

114 John Locke, *Of the Conduct of the Understanding* (Oxford: Clarendon Press, 1881), p. 21.

115 Volker Hunecke, 'Tendenze anticapitalistiche nella rivoluzione francese', *Società e storia* I (1978), pp. 143–65 (cited from p. 164); Tocqueville, *Œuvres complètes*, ed. Mayer, vol. 12, p. 93.

116 Sieyès, *Écrits politiques*, pp. 75, 89 – emphasis in original.

117 Ibid., p. 81.

118 Locke, *Two Treatises of Government*, p. 323.

Whether the metaphor in question was applied to the outright slave or to the manual labourer carrying out semi-servile work, it in any case played an important role in the denial of political rights. It was also important to certain laws rolling back emancipation, such as the 31 May 1850 law in France (which, in stipulating specific residency requirements, ended up considering the workers forced to follow a certain trade from one location to another as 'foreigners'). Such was also true of the laws in the United States that lengthened the period of residency, or in any case added to the hurdles immigrants had to overcome to achieve naturalisation and be admitted into citizenship.

The relationship between discrimination based on property and the racialisation of the excluded also jumps out from another – apparently more innocuous – metaphor which the liberal tradition employed in order to define and justify the exclusion of wage labourers from citizenship. Forced to work day and night, the latter remained in a condition of 'endless dependence' and were thus akin to 'children', albeit ones endowed with the particular characteristic of never being able to become adults.[119] Moreover, according to Locke, the waged servant became part of 'the family of his master, and under the ordinary discipline thereof'.[120] It should be borne in mind that slaves also made up part of the *oikos*, the ancient Aristotelian *familia*, and this reference again takes us back to the 'barbarians' from whose ranks came the 'slaves by nature' of which the Greek philosopher spoke. And Mill, who theorised despotism over 'barbarians' or members of 'backward societies', specified that in this case 'the race itself may be considered as in its nonage'.[121] Moreover, Sieyès, who divided society into two clearly distinct and opposed peoples, also defined the one destined to provide the 'human instruments' – or better, 'bipedal' ones – of production as the 'multitude of eternal children'.[122]

In the United States, the process of racialisation within the white community was impeded by the fact that the instruments of labour – the bipedal machines – were identified with blacks and subsequently, in the second half of the nineteenth century, with immigrants from outside

119 Constant, *Principles of Politics*, p. 166.

120 Locke, *Two Treatises of Government*, p. 322.

121 John Stuart Mill, *On Liberty, Utilitarianism and Other Essays* (Oxford: Oxford University Press), 2015, p. 13.

122 Sieyès, *Écrits politiques*, p. 80.

Europe, or southern and eastern Europe, and, in any case, not the stock of authentic Americans of old vintage. But at the Philadelphia Convention there were also those who defended property's monopoly on suffrage with the argument that such a precious and delicate right could certainly not be extended to the 'bipeds of the forest', to barbarians and savages.[123] Above all, it highlighted the characterisation in which, as against the 'mass of the people' made up of 'mechanics' – people in any case lacking in culture and 'liberal education' – Hamilton and John Quincy Adams came from the members of the dominant elite, 'rich and well-born'.[124] Also evident in this definition is the tendency toward the naturalisation, and thus, to some extent, the racialisation of the social differences that existed within the white community itself. This language is all the more significant in that it makes us think of that used a few decades later by Nietzsche, who celebrated the 'better developed' (*wohlgeraten*) who made up part of the 'conquering *master race*, that of the Aryans', as against the plebeian-democratic mass and all that which is 'degenerate' and 'parasitic'.[125]

The workers and the popular classes fighting for the recognition of their right to association and for their political rights became aware that the discrimination against them was closely intertwined with an anthropology which – considering them foreign not only to the community in which they lived, but also, in the last analysis, to civilisation – relegated them to a lower race, denying them their full human dignity. For this reason, in Paris immediately after the July Revolution, the working-class newspapers reproached the 'bourgeois nobles' for insisting on seeing the workers not as 'men' but as nothing other than 'machines' called on to produce only for the 'needs' of their bosses.[126] A category dear to two liberal authors like Burke and Sieyès was thus identified and attacked with some precision. It is interesting to note that, after the February Revolution in France, popular songs celebrated the achievement of

123 John F. Jameson, *The American Revolution Considered as a Social Movement* (Princeton, NJ: Princeton University Press, 1968).

124 Morison, *Sources and Documents Illustrating the American Revolution*, p. 259; Merriam, *History of American Political Theories*, pp. 130, 132, 140.

125 Friedrich Nietzsche, *On the Genealogy of Morality* (Cambridge: Cambridge University Press, 2008), pp. 15, 95 – emphasis in original; Friedrich Nietzsche, *The Birth of Tragedy* (Cambridge: Cambridge University Press, 1999).

126 William H. Sewell Jr, *Work and Revolution in France: The Language of Labor from the Old Regime to 1848* (Cambridge: Cambridge University Press, 1980), p. 198.

universal suffrage as the proof that even the individuals of the humblest layers had begun to be raised up 'to the rank of men'.[127]

Beyond such spontaneous expressions from among the popular classes, if we want to find a critique of racialisation processes, we certainly ought not to look for it in the classical liberal tradition. There is a fragment of Rousseau in which the slaves fighting against their 'master' reproach him for considering and treating them as mere 'machines', 'instruments of labour' or 'utensils'.[128] From this text there springs an objective indictment against the liberal tradition which, in defining wage labour, continues to make use of the categories that had already been used in classical antiquity in reference to the slave who was denied full human dignity. If Locke compared the day labourer to a 'pack horse' and Burke inveighed against the 'swinish multitude', Rousseau reproached the upper classes for their tendency to reduce the 'unfortunates oppressed by unending labours' to 'oxen' or pets.[129] Lastly, the metaphor (so dear to Constant and implicitly present even in Sieyès) assimilating wage labourers to foreigners or members of a people different and inferior to that constituted by the ruling classes was criticised in advance by the Geneva philosopher, when he underlined that in a well-ordered state no one should be able to feel 'foreign'.

Robespierre considered himself a disciple of Rousseau. For him, unlike in the case of the absolute monarchy and the aristocracy, where one or a few individuals could say that they had a *patrie*, whereas all others were stateless, the 'democratic regime' is that in which 'the State is truly the *patrie* of all individuals', who are all accepted on an equal footing into the 'fullness of the rights of the citizen'.[130] It is certainly no accident that in Marx the starting point of the critique of capitalist society was a denunciation of the fact that, in this society (as the *Communist Manifesto* put it), the working class are 'instruments of labour, more or less expensive to use, according to their age and sex'.[131]

127 Huard, *Le suffrage universel en France*, p. 53.

128 Rousseau, *Œuvres complètes*, ed. B. Gagnebin and M. Raymond (Paris: Gallimard, 1959), vol. 4, p. 1726.

129 Rousseau, *Œuvres complètes*, ed. M. Launay (Paris: Seuil, 1971).

130 Robespierre, *Textes choisis*, vol. 3, pp. 114ff.

131 *MECW*, vol. 6, p. 491.

From Liberalism to Democracy?

The myth dear to Norberto Bobbio, that liberalism spontaneously developed in the direction of democracy, does not stand up to historical scrutiny.[132] The fact is that the very countries with the most well-consolidated liberal tradition behind them are the very ones that were considerably slower to arrive at political emancipation: 'the United States was not a democracy, in the elementary sense of an effective universal suffrage, during the twentieth century'.[133]

We can even leave aside the case of the Native Americans, or better, the ones that survived: in theory, they were afforded political rights from 1887 onwards.[134] But, in reality, they were recognised as American citizens by Congress only in 1924, after a long series of back-and-forth moves – and, in any case, 'States like New Mexico and Arizona refused them the right to vote until 1948'.[135] As for another racial minority, still after World War II we can see how the ruling classes in the South condemned attempts to abolish the poll tax and force through the electoral registration of blacks 'regardless of their intelligence and capacities . . . as a criminal attack on the best "Anglo-Saxon heritage", and an attempt to reduce real Americans to a 'mongrel, inferior race'.[136] Not only blacks but also poor whites continued to be subject to restrictions based on property 'until the 1960s–1970s'.[137] The Supreme Court rulings that declared unconstitutional norms requiring a certain level of literacy and a poll tax as prerequisites for the recognition of the right to vote date only to 1966; the ruling that declared unconstitutional the norm, which then still applied in Texas, which subordinated one's right to election to the payment of a sum proportional to the importance of the office one

132 Norberto Bobbio, *Il futuro della democrazia. Una difesa delle regole del gioco* (Turin: Einaudi, 1984), pp. 6ff.

133 Piven and Cloward, *Why Americans Don't Vote*, p. 9.

134 Arthur Meier Schlesinger, *The Rise of Modern America, 1865–1951* (New York: Macmillan, 1951).

135 Philippe Jacquin, *Histoire des Indiens d'Amérique du Nord* (Paris: Payot, 1976), p. 214.

136 Arthur Meier Schlesinger, *The History of US Political Parties* (New York: Chelsea House & Bawker, 1973), pp. 3409, 3416–17.

137 Toinet, '"Americanizzazione" o "europeizzazione"', pp. 123ff.

intended to stand for, dates to 1972.[138] However, electoral registration laws which effectively undermine the participation of the poorest classes and thus, according to some authors, constitute a new indirect and camouflaged form of property discrimination, continue to apply today.[139] This, in what continues to behave, up to the present, as the West's leading country. Moreover, still in 1988 the Democratic Party's electoral platform called for a fight – with reference to electoral registration laws – against 'any dilution of the principle "one man one vote" '.[140]

Similar considerations can be advanced with regard to the other classic homeland of the liberal tradition, Great Britain, with its historical delay in terms of political emancipation and the conquest of universal suffrage. It is hardly worth mentioning that, throughout the eighteenth century, up to the Reform Act of 1832 – that is, a century and a half after the liberal Glorious Revolution – 'both houses of parliament were appanages of the highest class of society', namely the aristocracy. Yet more important is the fact that, for a long time, almost up to our own day, 'feudal traditions' continued to shape the very idea of representation: 'Representation, in fact, was nowise regarded as a means of expressing individual right or forwarding individual interests. It was communities, not individuals, who were represented.'[141] In 1788, the *Federalist* – anything but an Anglophobic publication – summarised voting rights in the former homeland as follows:

> The number of inhabitants in the two kingdoms of England and Scotland cannot be stated at less than eight millions. The representatives of these eight millions in the House of Commons amount to five hundred and fifty-eight. Of this number, one ninth are elected by three hundred and sixty-four persons, and one half, by five thousand seven hundred and twenty-three persons. It cannot be supposed that the half thus elected, and who do not even reside among the people at large, can add any thing either to the security of the people against the

138 Liliane Kerjan, *L'égalité aux États-Units: mythes et réalités* (Nancy: Presses Universitaires de Nancy, 1991), pp. 67–70, 123–7.

139 Piven and Cloward, *Why Americans Don't Vote.*

140 Patrick Gérard, *George Bush président: histoire d'une élection* (Nancy: Presses Universitaires de Nancy, 1989).

141 Pollard, *Evolution of Parliament*, pp. 164, 155.

> government . . . On the contrary, it is notorious, that they are more frequently the representatives and instruments of the executive magistrate, than the guardians and advocates of the popular rights.[142]

The situation that existed a few decades later was described by Ostrogorski: 'According to a table prepared about 1815, the House of Commons contained 471 members who owed their seats to the good-will and pleasure of 144 peers and 123 commoners, 16 Government nominees, and only 171 members elected by popular suffrages.'[143] But what did 'popular suffrage' mean here?

> The voters simply represented the personal following of the rivals who fought the electoral duel; they were their retainers or sold themselves to them on the polling-day for money. In the counties the tenant followed his landlord . . . The rural freeholders, who were more independent, generally gravitated in the orbit of the great nobleman who irradiated the neighbourhood. Of the boroughs, several were directly dependent on territorial magnates, who owned them as private property or exerted a hereditary influence over them. Most of the other towns sold themselves at the elections, wholesale or in lots . . . The members who had secured election through the territorial influence or that of their patrons, or who bought their seats for ready money, were practically independent of their constituencies.[144]

To understand how far this independence really went, it is worth remembering that 'when Palmerston entered the House in 1807, his patron posed a single condition: that he should never set foot among the electorate'. A condition that doubtless helps to identify similarities between his spell as an MP and that of Robert Peel, who in his decades as a parliamentarian 'never participated in an electoral contest'.[145]

An English liberal of the nineteenth century, singing the praises of his country's constitution, observed that the lower and upper houses were

142 *Federalist* 56 (1788). The text of this and other cited issues of the *Federalist* are taken from the Library of Congress website, guides.loc.gov.

143 Ostrogorski, *Democracy and the Organization of Political Parties*, p. 20.

144 Ibid., pp. 135–6.

145 Mauro Calise, *Governo di partito. Antecedenti e conseguenze in America* (Bologna: il Mulino, 1989), p. 39.

each long subject to the monopoly of, or strict control by, the Lords, who also decided the composition of the Commons: both houses of parliament were thus in effect the prerogative of the aristocracy.[146] This 'representation', which had not managed to shake off the burden of the medieval tradition that lay behind it, considered suffrage not as a right, or even a right reserved to the members of a given income class, according to a somehow general rule, but rather as a mark of distinction or a privilege that was graciously conceded and passed on via heredity to certain communities, layers or orders. This 'representation' knew nothing of the modern individual as an autonomous subject endowed with rights; rather, it involved the full 'subordination of the individual to society'.[147] This peculiar 'representation' did not much differ, in the eighteenth century at least, from that of the Estates General of France's *ancien régime*, and it was targeted for criticism by Rousseau. In his *Social Contract*, after emphasising that representation was rooted in 'feudal government', he concluded that 'the English people believes itself free, but is greatly mistaken', and condemned the representative system *as such* as contrary to freedom.

With the electoral reform of 1832, the House of Commons did become increasingly open to the presence and influence of the bourgeoisie. Bagehot warmly advised the 'plutocracy' and 'aristocracy' to avoid fighting among themselves and to work harmoniously to keep parliamentary institutions at arm's length from the mass of the people. Each of the two Houses had to remain the monopoly of one of the two upper classes that held the country's wealth.[148] Without doubt, the two subsequent electoral reforms in 1867 and 1884–85 brought a considerable extension of the franchise. But this was still far from (even male) universal suffrage, given that, even with this latter reform, instigated by Gladstone, it was 'homeowners' who enjoyed the right to vote, whereas there continued to be 'considerable disadvantage[s]' to 'the lower class of voters, who might frequently change their place of residence' on account of their work.[149] As Lenin noted during World War I, citing a German author, 'the electoral

146 Walter Bagehot, *The English Constitution: Introduction to Second Edition*, in *Collected Works*, ed. N. St John-Stevas (London: Economist, 1974), vol. 5, p. 175.

147 Ostrogorski, *Democracy and the Organization of Political Parties*, vol. 1, p. 13.

148 Bagehot, *English Constitution*, pp. 175–9.

149 E. J. Feuchtwanger, *Democracy and Empire: Britain, 1865–1914* (London: Edward Arnold, 1985), p. 175.

system' in Great Britain was still 'sufficiently restricted to exclude the lower stratum of the proletariat proper'.[150] In this same period, Weber observed that, had the electoral system in force in Britain up to the war (and the October Revolution) applied in Germany, the number of Social Democratic MPs in the Reichstag would have been halved, to the obvious disadvantage of the subaltern classes.[151]

But even more important than the persistent restrictions based on property was the fact that, in Great Britain, there endured a fundamentally premodern idea of representation. At least until the reform of 1918, leading figures from the privileged classes 'contended that the number of a man's votes should be proportionate to his possessions'.[152] Indeed, plural voting would continue in this country for some decades. One contemporary historian summarised its difficult path to democracy in the following terms: 'The British electoral system reached theoretical democracy only in April 1928 . . . One adult, one vote was at last attained except for the business and university franchises which together gave about half a million people (mainly males) a second vote until they were abolished in 1948.'[153]

Bobbio has observed that 'Individualism is the philosophical basis of democracy: one person, one vote. As such, it has always been counterposed, and will always stand counterposed, to holistic conceptions of society and history, from wherever they might issue.'[154] If the authoritative liberal philosopher wanted to take seriously the principle which he here articulates, he would have to completely rewrite the history of individualism and democracy that has emerged from his writings thus far. He would have to recognise that the classic homeland of the liberal tradition which he so celebrates (or himself transfigures) was itself seriously late in arriving at either individualism or democracy. He would, likewise, have to recognise the fundamental contribution that a quite different political tradition made to the victory of the democratic and

150 V. I. Lenin, *Imperialism: The Highest Stage of Capitalism*, in *Selected Works in Three Volumes* (Moscow: Progress, 1970), vol. 1, p. 246.

151 Max Weber, 'Parliament and Government in Germany under a New Political Order', in *Political Writings* (Cambridge: Cambridge University Press, 1994), p. 210.

152 Pollard, *Evolution of Parliament*, p. 165.

153 A. J. P. Taylor, *English History 1914–1945* (Oxford: Oxford University Press, 1992), p. 262.

154 Norberto Bobbio, *Il terzo assente. Saggi e discorsi sulla pace e la guerra* (Turin: Sonda, 1989), pp. 122ff.

individualist principle (one person, one vote) – indeed, a tradition that the most recent of Bobbio's works have dismissed far too lightmindedly. The (English) historian of the British parliament we have already repeatedly cited paid objective homage to this tradition when he observed, in remarks from 1920 on the debate then taking place in his country, that 'Vast inroads have . . . been made on feudal theory by ideas of universal suffrage, and the real issue with regard to representation is whether the individual or the family is the unit to be represented. Modern socialism tends to make the state the sole form of society and to weaken every other bond of association; and parliament, instead of representing communities or families, is coming to represent nothing but individuals.'[155]

To speak of socialism, at this moment, also meant speaking about the October Revolution and the demands and agitation that took their cue from it, influencing and setting conditions for the entire workers' movement.

The Three Stages of the Conquest of Universal Suffrage

Indeed, on closer inspection there were three fundamental milestones in the conquest of equal universal suffrage: 10 August 1792, the revolution of February 1848, and the revolutionary upheavals of the Russia of 1917. All three dates are extraneous to the liberal tradition, which instead looked upon these happenings with diffidence, if not outright hostility.

Looking at the first case, it is notable that the theorists of property restrictions in the France of the time invoked precisely the example of liberal England. Robespierre himself noted as much. Far from allowing himself to be impressed by the model brandished by his adversaries, he compared exclusion from political rights to the condition of the slave in classical antiquity.[156]

As for the second of these milestones, it is interesting to reread the statements made by authoritative liberal spokesmen in the years that preceded the outbreak of the 1848 revolution. Polemicising against the

155 Pollard, *Evolution of Parliament*, p. 165.
156 Robespierre, *Textes choisis*, pp. 75, 69.

movement that demanded the widening of suffrage, Thiers observed that, yes, it was true that '32 million men are governed by the vote of 240,000. There are 240,000 men who command and 32 million who obey.' This may seem, and perhaps was, 'an appalling disproportion'; but, in reality, the concession of political rights had already gone too far (or rather, too low down the social order), having 'already gone down to a class that does not have sufficient free time, culture or property to take an interest in political questions'.[157] Even in 1847, Guizot declared: 'The dawn of universal suffrage will never come: the day in which all human beings without distinction can be called on to exercise political rights will never arrive.'[158] It was no accident that Tocqueville looked on at the revolution of 1848 with dismay, seeing it – already in February – as 'exclusively waged outside and against the bourgeoisie', as a revolution whose 'philosophy' was inspired by 'socialist theories' in which the 'bourgeois' would be the 'true and only defeated' side.[159] Denounced even in our own time by Hayek as the inauspicious prologue to ' "social" or totalitarian democracy', it was a revolution that sanctioned universal (male) suffrage. And, as we have seen, even this was immediately trampled on and suppressed by the liberal bourgeoisie, as soon as the latter felt itself secure and protected from the pressure of the popular and plebeian masses in the streets.

Lastly, we get to the third milestone. It could be objected that, in a country like Italy, universal (male) suffrage had been achieved already before the October Revolution. Indeed, Italy did not pass through a Jacobin period either, and, in any case, no revolutionary process as radical as the one that took place in France. But even apart from the fact that, in this case too, one can hardly overlook the influence and pressure exerted by the workers' and socialist movement, it is worth noting that, contrary to the widespread myth, the electoral reform of 1912 did not in reality provide for universal suffrage even among men. An important section of the population – that between twenty-one and thirty years old – continued, in a sense, to be subject to the bond between 'property' (or 'qualifications of culture and honour') and its

157 Adolphe Thiers, *Discours parlementaires* (Paris: Calman Lévy, 1879), vol. 2, pp. 484ff.

158 Huard, *Le suffrage universel en France*, p. 19.

159 Alexis de Tocqueville, *Œuvres complètes*, ed. Mayer, vol. 12, pp. 92, 94f.

'electoral capacity'.[160] The press of the time spoke of 'expanded suffrage'.[161] Lenin was right to note (with a certain mocking tone) that Giolitti's reform had 'introduced "almost" universal suffrage'.[162]

Even if we acknowledge that the Chamber of Deputies was elected without any discrimination based on property, it ought not to be forgotten that it was, in any case, neutralised by a Senate composed as follows: 'there were the princes of the House of Savoy, who, being prerogative members, gave this assembly its royal imprint.' This was not only an assembly monopolised by the upper classes, but one 'weighted with a substantial feudal element'. At this point, we can advance the more general consideration that the 'Italian Senate shared many family resemblances with all [the other] upper chambers' in Europe, which, with the exception of the French case, were not elected; 'everywhere there was a mix of heredity and royal appointment'. Even the Senate of France's Third Republic, which had behind it an uninterrupted series of revolutionary upheavals culminating in the Paris Commune of 1871, was constituted in such a way as to 'guarantee the wanton overrepresentation of the villages and towns over Paris and the major cities', to the advantage of 'the large farmers and small peasants'.[163] The historian here cited saw the Europe of 1914 as still considerably dominated by the *ancien régime*, which was then swept aside not only by the world war itself but also by the Russian Revolution. A year after 1917 in Russia, there broke out the revolutions that marked the end of the Hohenzollern dynasty in Germany and the Habsburgs in Austria – and, indeed, the end of upper houses that had been a prerogative of the bourgeoisie and of a nobility still in some senses linked to the *ancien régime*. Egalitarian universal suffrage now necessarily became part of the overall political order in these countries, though it would be a long time before it came to Great Britain and the United States.

Thus far, we have spoken of universal male suffrage, leaving aside women, who, upon the eve of World War I, were excluded from political

160 Manfredi Siotto Pintor, 'Storia del regime elettorale', subentry in 'Elezione', *Enciclopedia italiana* (Rome: Treccani, 1932), vol. 13; Giovanni Corso, 'Elezioni amministrative', subentry in 'Elezione', *Enciclopedia italiana*.

161 Luigi Lucatelli, 'La Federazione degli Insegnanti Medi e le candidature Salvemini', in Gaetano Salvemini, *Il ministro della mala vita* (Rome: La Voce, 1919).

162 V. I. Lenin, 'Imperialism and Socialism in Italy' (1915), in *Lenin Collected Works*, vol. 21, (Moscow: Progress, 1974), pp. 357–66, available at marxists.org.

163 Arno J. Mayer, *The Persistence of the Old Regime: Europe to the Great War*, (London: Pantheon, 1981), pp. 160–2.

rights in practically the entire world. Only in 1920 did the US Constitution integrate the amendment that issued a federal ban on any discrimination in voting rights based on 'difference of sex'. The achievement of this important objective, by women's own efforts, cannot be understood without bearing in mind both their mass integration into production during World War I and the profound influence of the upheavals that had taken place in Russia. Speaking of the constitutional amendment just mentioned, one illustrious American historian explained the speed with which conservative resistance was overcome by invoking the fact that 'European countries' were now catching up and overtaking the United States in this field, and that President Wilson would not allow 'democratic America' to 'fall behind'.[164] It is clear that – consciously or otherwise – Schlesinger is here referring also to revolutionary Russia, the country that had opened the way to the total removal of gender discrimination in the enjoyment of political rights, and for precisely this reason exerted considerable force of attraction on the feminist movement in France, as elsewhere.[165] It should be added that, while the October Revolution marked the beginning of a worldwide campaign for the full social and political emancipation of women, in the West there was an active tradition of thinking which, while asserting the need for female suffrage, primarily did so because it saw it as a conservative counterweight to the growing influence of the social and ethnic groups it wanted to contain. Indeed, at the end of the nineteenth century, the latter were excluded from political citizenship in the United States, even as women began to gain it. Traces of this conservative attitude were probably present also within the commitment to female suffrage exhibited by President Wilson from World War I onwards. Indeed, he also imposed segregation against blacks in federal civilian offices, including for bathrooms and cafeterias, and showed himself likewise racially prejudiced against immigrants from Eastern Europe.[166]

Naturally, the notes of caution we have sounded regarding the effects of 10 August 1792 and the Jacobin movement also apply to the October Revolution. In each case, what we see is a principle proclaimed with greater or lesser radicalism at the same time as there also flared up a

164 Schlesinger, *Rise of Modern America*, p. 309.

165 Huard, *Le suffrage universel en France*, p. 223.

166 Gosset, *Race*, pp. 279, 284.

state of exception that the political leaders of the time were unable to move beyond. This failure was owed either to the extreme difficulty of the objective situation or to the fact that their own grave political and theoretical shortcomings led them to pursue ideals that could not be realised, and thus served only to block a return to normality – from the Jacobins' ideal of the ancient community to the Bolsheviks' idea of the withering away of the state. Yet this takes nothing away from the historical importance of the assertion of the right of each individual to participate in political life without discrimination of class, race or sex, and indeed to do so on the egalitarian basis of one person, one vote.

2

A New Tutor for the 'Childlike' Multitude

Universal Suffrage and Bonapartism

Louis-Napoleon re-established the universal suffrage that had been abolished by the liberal bourgeoisie's *coup de main*. Together with the liberal bourgeoisie, Bonapartist propaganda shared a common hatred and disdain for those it dismissed as 'demagogues', the 'egalitarians', the 'detestable dreamers of the speculative doctrine'.[1] The extension of political rights was linked not to a project of social emancipation, but rather to a particular political concern. Already before the coup d'état of 2 December 1851, in explaining the position he had taken against the law of 31 May 1850 the prince-president observed:

> I asked myself if, in the presence of the delirium of passions, the confusion of doctrines, the division between parties, when everything seemed to combine to detract any prestige from morality, justice and authority, it was really necessary to overturn or impair the only principle that Providence has kept standing to keep us united. Once universal suffrage had reconstructed the social edifice, through the very fact of having replaced a revolutionary feat with a law, was it perhaps wise to seek to further restrict its base? Lastly, I asked myself

1 Frédéric Bluche, *Le bonapartisme. Aux origines de la droite autoritaire (1800–1850)* (Paris, Nouvelles Editions Latines, 1980), p. 357.

> if this would not have meant compromising in advance the new powers called upon to preside over the country's fate, in providing a pretext for challenging their origin and disregarding their legitimacy.[2]

Without doubt, Louis-Napoleon showed a political intelligence superior to that of his liberal adversaries. In France, but gradually also in other countries, universal suffrage was now becoming *the* principle of legitimacy. The violation of this principle fed and intensified opposition: far from consolidating the existing social order, such a violation would end up pushing it into seriously troubled waters.

But, even looking beyond popular reactions, the disemancipation measures which the liberal bourgeoisie decided to push through proved counterproductive even at a straightforwardly technical level:

> In its application the law of 31 May went beyond the objective it thought it would serve: no one had foreseen the removal of millions of voters, two-thirds of whom are made up of peaceable countryside-dwellers. What was the result? This vast exclusion served as a pretext for the party of anarchy, which cloaks its detestable designs under the cover of a violated right that is to be reconquered.[3]

The path of explicit disemancipation appeared impracticable or ruinous, in its pretence to exclude from political citizenship those who had earlier been granted it. Rather, other paths needed to be taken, realising once and for all that since 'public opinion [is] queen of the universe', universal suffrage constituted a new principle of legitimacy which it was unwise to row back from.[4] The programme set out by the president-by-coup was clear: it sought to establish a political regime 'that would be strong through the fact of being popular'.[5] Discrimination on the basis of property was inadmissible: 'Today, the reign of castes is over, one can govern only with the masses'; 'it is necessary that the mass be . . . the

2 Napoléon III, *Œuvres* (Paris: Plon-Amyot, 1861), vol. 3, pp. 259ff.

3 Ibid., p. 261.

4 Ibid., vol. 1, p. 370.

5 Gisela Geywitz, *Das Plebiszit von 1851 in Frankreich* (Tübingen: Mohr Siebeck, 1965), p. 258.

constant force from which all powers emanate'.[6] If, as we have seen, at the moment of the suppression of universal suffrage, Thiers expressed his full disdain for the 'vile multitude', and if liberal or liberal-conservative circles continued to manifest their aristocratic disgust towards the 'populace' or the 'rabble' (*canaille*), Louis-Napoleon always spoke of the 'people' or 'mass', without assigning even this latter term any negative connotation, though he also referred pejoratively to the 'passions of the crowd'.[7]

But what was this people whose support he wanted to win? Certainly not one autonomously organised in parties or trade unions. Louis-Napoleon presented himself not as a 'party representative' but, rather as the interpreter of the nation and its best traditions, as the figure who sought to 'govern in the interest of the masses and not in the interest of a party'.[8] As early as 1848, Bonapartist propaganda insisted that 'between the people and its sovereign there must be no intermediary that arrogates itself the right to substitute for either'.[9] On the eve of the coup d'état, a pamphlet that seems to have been partly the work of Louis-Napoleon himself attacked the existing constitution for setting up 'voting by list as the means of election, a misleading method that takes away any freedom and any choice from the people and transfers power over the election to the newspapers and committees'.[10] Organised political groups and parties and the press organs corresponding to them were attacked as instruments of coercion and of the suffocation of the electorate's spontaneous will, which must be 'liberated' from all this so that it could instead be entrusted to the direct and subaltern link to the local chief and, at the national level, to the nation's own unchallenged charismatic leader.

In the appeal to the people issued shortly after 2 December 1851, the president-by-coup went back to thundering against 'list voting', which he again condemned as an instrument for polluting and falsifying the free will of the people. This judgement was repeated and solemnly

6 Napoléon III, *Œuvres*, vol. 2, p. 122; vol. 1, p. 381.

7 Geywitz, *Das Plebiszit von 1851 in Frankreich*, pp. 261ff; Napoléon III, *Œuvres*, vol. 1, p. 9.

8 Napoléon III, *Œuvres*, vol. 3, pp. 140ff, 37.

9 Geywitz, *Das Plebiszit von 1851 in Frankreich*, p. 261.

10 Adolphe Granier de Cassagnac, *La révision de la Constitution* (Paris: Plon, 1851), p. 6.

ordained in the preamble to the Constitution of 1852, and indeed in the Constitution itself: 'Choosing each candidate in isolation, the people can more easily evaluate the merits of each of them.'[11] The single-member constituency that had been abolished by the revolution of 1848 was thus reintroduced.[12] By this point, the reasons for his preference for this electoral system are very clear. Examining the situation immediately prior to the coup d'état, Marx observed that the Constitution still then in force ended up

> abrogat[ing] itself once more by having the President elected by all Frenchmen through direct suffrage. While the votes of France are split up among the 750 members of the National Assembly, they are here, on the contrary, concentrated on a single individual. While each separate representative of the people represents only this or that party, this or that town, this or that bridgehead, or even only the mere necessity of electing some one of the 750, where neither the cause nor the man is closely examined, he is the elect of the nation and the act of his election is the trump that the sovereign people plays once every four years. The elected National Assembly stands in a metaphysical relation, but the elected President in a personal relation, to the nation.[13]

If there was anything that could cloud the skies for a president who had decided to strike the posture of the single and direct interpreter of the nation, as the charismatic chief standing clearly above the petty squabbles and personal rivalries that divided MPs and those who aspired to seats in parliament – if there was something that could throw up obstacles to such a plan – it came from the existence of nationally organised parties capable of addressing the people. That is to say, parties which addressed the people in order to invite its vote not for this or that individual, but rather for a specific programmatic platform, the focus of a debate whose importance far transcended the individual constituencies, and which in so doing broke the presidential monopoly on appealing to the people. The success and the consolidation of the Bonapartist

11 Napoléon III, *Œuvres*, vol. 3, pp. 274, 292, 308.

12 Edmond Villey, *Législation électorale comparée des principaux pays d'Europe* (Paris: Larose-Pedone, 1900), p. 113.

13 *Marx-Engels Collected Works* (*MECW*) (London: Lawrence & Wishart, 1975–2004), vol. 11, pp. 116–17.

project thus required the dissolution or marginalisation of the parties – and thus the liquidation of an electoral system based upon them, which introduced a troublesome filter between the president and his popular investiture or acclaim.

With the twentieth century already well underway, a great political scientist observed: 'The single-member district election makes possible a personal relationship between the electorate and a recognized leader', who is 'acclaimed through the election. The system of proportional representation, by contrast, eliminates the personal relationship', such that 'the power of the party organizations becomes stronger'.[14] But precisely this strengthening of party organisation was irreconcilable with the nature of the Bonapartist regime and its modes of functioning. Once this regime felt itself secure it could, indeed, concede a certain space of individual liberty; but in no case could it tolerate independent and autonomously organised political and social organisations. From this point of view, the single-member constituency offered three advantages: 1) it personalised the electoral contest, and thus dissolved each party into its constituent individuals; 2) at the level of each constituency, this system reproduced the relation between the charismatic leader and the amorphous and fragmented mass; 3) precisely because it made each individual MP the representative of a local constituency or the interests prevalent therein, rather than the representative of the nation or exponent of a political programme of claimed national scope, it allowed the president-emperor – the chief, in the proper sense – to stand clearly above the rest as the sole interpreter of the nation, who responded to it alone.

The attitude which Napoleon III took towards the trade-union movement responded to this same logic. Of course, in the period of the revolutionary crisis and that of the new institutions' initial weakness, the Bonapartist regime harshly repressed the movement, in this sense moreover moving in continuity with the policy previously pursued by the liberal bourgeoisie.[15] Yet in its 'liberal' phase, when it felt sufficiently solid and secure, the new regime did not hesitate to

14 Carl Schmitt, *Constitutional Theory*, transl. Jeffrey Seizer (Durham, NC: Duke University Press, 2008), p. 348.

15 William H. Sewell Jr, *Work and Revolution in France: The Language of Labor from the Old Regime to 1848* (Cambridge: Cambridge University Press, 1980), p. 272.

legalise strikes: the workers were allowed to coordinate their common action with a view to any single economic demand or protest, but what did remain severely prohibited was any permanent bond of association.[16]

In light of these considerations, we can advance a reinterpretation of the claim, already seen above, that 'the reign of castes is over, one can govern only with the masses'. Louis-Napoleon continued: 'It is necessary, then, to organise [the masses] so that they can formulate their will, discipline them so that they can be directed and enlightened as to their true interests.'[17] Unlike in the previous liberal tradition, the multitude was no longer considered 'vile', but continued to be 'childlike' and unable to articulate any autonomous political discourse or representation of its own. Among this multitude, 'the heart feels before the mind is able to conceive anything'; 'feelings come before . . . reason' and play a decisively greater role. But the multitude, or indeed the 'masses' and 'peoples' could be led along and guided by the 'influence of a great genius [which], in this sense similarly to the influence of Divinity, is a fluid that spreads like electricity; it inflames imaginations, makes hearts palpitate, and enchants because it affects the soul even before it persuades'! Such an influence is a stabilising factor, for it serves 'not to shake society but, quite the opposite, to reorder and reorganise it': the 'masses' were as if harnessed and tamed by a higher personality and a higher force of attraction.[18]

Clearly, the task of the tutor of the 'childlike' multitude was no longer to be taken on by property owners and nobles, but rather by the single supreme representative of the nation. Precisely because he clearly stood above classes and social conflict, he could listen and take note of the voices and needs even of the humblest layers of the population, or at least posture as the only figure competent and prepared to do so. For this reason, according to Louis-Napoleon himself, 'aristocracy has no need for a chief, whereas it is in the nature of democracy to be personified in a man'; 'in a government whose basis is democratic, only the leader has the power [*puissance*] to govern', and with this power is

16 Hendrik N. Boon, *Rêve et réalité dans l'oeuvre économique et sociale de Napoléon III* (The Hague: Nijhoff, 1936), p. 150.

17 Napoléon III, *Œuvres*, vol. 2, p. 122.

18 Ibid., vol. 1, pp. 12ff.

accountable to the nation itself, given that 'everything directly goes back to him, be it hatred or love'.[19]

In the 'appeal to the people' issued immediately after the events of 2 December 1851, the president-by-coup asked to be appointed in the name of the 'great mission' incumbent upon him, namely that of 'putting an end to the era of revolutions, satisfying the people's legitimate needs and protecting it against subversive passions'. This mission had not only national dimensions. Already several years previously, Louis-Napoleon had said of his great uncle that if, at the beginning, his mission had been a merely French one, it then came to concern 'all humanity', seeking to enlighten 'the nations' and spread the advances that had already been made by France.[20] On the eve of the coup d'état, the Bonapartist press insisted on one central point: 'The President of the Republic is not only the man who enjoys our sympathies but also the man who, in our view, represents a great idea, and specifically the mightiest one in the body of our civilisation, the idea of strength, the idea of order, of enthusiasm, of initiative and of probity in government.'

This idea could all the more easily be upheld as a model and exported around the world given that the figure who embodied it was, at the same time, the heir to France's 'military splendour'.[21] Clearly, here we are dealing with a new model for the political and social control of the masses, within which universal suffrage is neutralised by the absolutely pre-eminent position of the president of the republic or the chief of the executive. On the one hand, the latter seeks to ingratiate himself with those classes considered dangerous by making some limited concessions (the development of public works, ceilings on rent in the big cities, and so on). On the other, he tries to channel and divert discontent towards the outside, raising the standard of France's mission in the world. Already in a pamphlet written at a young age, Louis-Napoleon had appealed to the unity of 'all good Frenchmen', without distinction of party or any other kind, in order to present 'Europe with the imposing spectacle of a great people that comports itself without excesses and proceeds in a freedom without disorder. If the powers that want to carve up France were to make war on us, they would then

19 Ibid., pp. 37n, 56.
20 Ibid., vol. 3, p. 273; vol. 1, pp. 368, 29.
21 Bluche, *Le bonapartisme*, p. 358.

see a free people rise up united like a giant amidst the pygmies that wished to attack it.'[22]

The novelty of this political regime seemed to disorientate the traditional liberal elite. Tocqueville was scandalised by its economic interventionism: though recognising the great 'poverty' that weighed down on the 'lower classes', he condemned Napoleon III's measures as 'socialism pure and simple', even more radical than that of Ledru-Rollin. The liberal theorist added, in this regard, that, in a peasant's house, he had seen the portraits of the revolutionary and the emperor facing one another; from this he drew confirmation of the essential identity between Jacobin socialism and Bonapartism.[23] Napoleon III would himself give the lie to such reasoning three years later, when, now solidly established in power, he issued a far-reaching and almost general amnesty that made a single exception for Ledru-Rollin personally.[24] In reality, the new regime was the – critical – heir to the liberal tradition far more than the Jacobin one: notwithstanding the changed conditions, it continued to seek to guarantee the security of property and of the private sphere from the intrusion of an overbearing political power fed by the *pathos* of the *citoyen* and the social demands of the popular classes.

The 'Childlike' Multitude and the Charismatic Leader

The line of continuity suggested here appears all the more clearly if we turn from France to other countries where no such radical and indeed radically democratic and plebeian revolution had taken place, but where power was also increasingly personalised. In the wake of the second electoral reform in Britain, Bagehot sung the praises of his country's political system as based not on the division of powers and the theory of 'checks and balances', as commonly believed, but rather on the concentration and indivisibility of sovereign power in the hands of the prime minister: the 'efficient secret of the English Constitution may be described as the close union, the nearly complete fusion of the executive

22 Napoléon III, *Œuvres*, vol. 1, pp. 386ff.

23 Tocqueville, *Œuvres complètes*, ed. J. P. Mayer (Paris: Gallimard, 1951), vol. 15: II, p. 182.

24 Alfred Cobban, *Dictatorship: Its History and Theory* (New York: Haskell, 1971), p. 105.

and legislative powers'.[25] This personalisation of power proved all the more necessary following the considerable widening of the franchise that took place in 1867. What use was to be made of political rights by an ignorant mass who 'have no time to improve themselves, for they are labouring the whole day through', and are in absolute need of leadership?[26] The aforementioned theme of the 'ever-childlike multitude' was clearly taken up by the Victorian English liberal. He, too, deployed the metaphor of the 'child', of which the behaviour of the 'working men' of Leeds was so reminiscent when at the same meeting they heartily applauded both the conservative and the 'blatant radical' speaker, inclined as they were to be led along 'without much thinking' by any brilliant speech.[27] The fact is that '[t]he common ordinary mind is quite unfit to fix for itself what political question it shall attend to'.[28] Bagehot also took up a position in continuity with the earlier liberal tradition when he expressed the wish that the multitude continue to defer to 'wealth and rank, and to the higher qualities of which these are the rough symbols and the common accompaniments'.[29]

The crown played a fundamental role in this sense: the veneration and splendour surrounding it and the 'mystical' role attributed to it contributed to keeping the 'plebs' at bay. It helped ensure that the 'miserable creatures' immersed in a life of hardships would content themselves with their lot and, faced with a queen who had become such 'by the grace of God', would bend their knee with a sentiment of 'mystical reverence', 'religious obedience' and child-like deference. Thus far, we are still within the terms of a liberal society – after all, the crown did not hold any effective power, or at least only a very limited one. Yet this was also a society in which the ideology, customs and ruling classes of the *ancien régime* nonetheless continued to bear considerable weight. The problem of keeping a lid on the lower classes appeared an easily solved one, for the latter seemed to accept their lot as a natural event or as something

25 Walter Bagehot, *The English Constitution: Introduction to Second Edition*, in *Collected Works*, ed. Norman St John-Stevas (London: Economist, 1974), vol. 5, pp. 344–66, 210.

26 Ibid., pp. 169–70.

27 Walter Bagehot, *Physics and Politics or Thought on the Application of the Principles of 'Natural Selection' and 'Inheritance' to Political Society*, 2nd edn (London: Henry S. King, 1873), pp. 91–2.

28 Bagehot, *English Constitution*, p. 172.

29 Ibid., p. 170.

inherent to a mysterious providential design. But as the mobility and secularisation proper to industrial society developed, the problem became rather more complex. In a certain sense, what now needed doing was to extend the sacred aura and charisma of the crown such that it also imbued those who held and exercised real power and who, thanks to the extension of suffrage, now found themselves in the front line of relations with the 'plebs'.

As compared to the previous liberal tradition, a new element that began to emerge in Bagehot was the cult of the 'leading statesman', bathed in an aura which, in the masses' eyes at least, seemed to set him at a higher level. This was a cult of great statesmen who lead humanity and 'by a great speech or two, determine what shall be said and what shall be written for long after'. It was no longer traditional notables but these leaders who were called upon to 'guide the new voters in the exercise of the franchise'. They should guide them not with 'argument', still less with a 'formal exposition of that argument', but rather through the 'manly utterance of clear conclusions', perhaps with 'humorous illustrations'.[30] Unable to examine the general political questions related to the 'nature of a constitution, the action of an assembly, the play of parties', these masses could identify only with 'the action of a single will' and 'the fiat of a single mind'.[31] The crown, in its effect of bathing power in a sacred aura, made this a painless transition. But it was now clear that, while the mass remained childlike, it was now changing its tutor, henceforth entrusted not to the care of notables but increasingly that of a charismatic leader endowed with an orator's 'impulse', a '*nature*, as Coleridge might have said, towards his audience', which he did not so much convince as 'excite'. This leader did not communicate his understanding: rather, he proved that 'if they only knew what he knows, they would feel as he feels, and believe as he believes. And by this he conquers.' His power is based on 'this living faith, this enthusiasm, this confidence'.[32] The liberal writer's warm and at points enthusiastic description, most notably with regard to the model provided by Gladstone, brings to mind Louis-Napoleon's indulgent celebration of

30 Ibid., pp. 171–3.

31 Bagehot, *English Constitution*, p. 226.

32 Norman St John-Stevas, ed., *Walter Bagehot: A Study of His Life and Thought Together with a Selection from his Political Writings* (London: Economist, 1958), pp. 402–3.

his peerless uncle, the 'great genius' capable of harnessing and taming the masses, cited above.

Naturally, for such an outcome even to be possible, it is necessary that the masses be ready to succumb to this genius's seductive power. They must therefore be kept at bay from 'metaphysical questions', from a 'spirit of doctrine that destroys any vital seed', from discussions of political and social principle that might agitate them, distracting their attention with party struggles and disturbing a state of mind in which they would otherwise be disposed to faithful expectation in the captivating leader called on to lead them.[33] But this was, in the last analysis, also Bagehot's opinion. For him, it was necessary to ban 'isms' and topics liable to 'excite the lower classes' from political debate – or, better, from electoral competition.

Not only does the charismatic leader *not* communicate understanding, but we would more rightly say that he should steer well clear of so doing: he must, in any case, avoid raising 'questions which will excite the lower orders of mankind' and 'bind the poor as a class together' against 'the rich'.[34] The 'metaphysical' themes that needed to be banished from the stage certainly did not include such ideas as 'military splendour' and national glory. We have seen as much in the case of Louis-Napoleon, and will soon see that the same also applied to the English liberal. Indeed, the latter explicitly specified that such an idea must be systematically wielded in order to combat the propaganda and activity of those seeking to connect the hardships of the masses to the existing social order and, on the basis of such critical claims and analysis, to organise the lower classes in society on an autonomous footing.

The ruling classes could thwart such a threat with a show of moderation, avoiding any competition between individuals for this or that public post from turning into a generalised political struggle and direct confrontation. Already in the *Communist Manifesto*, Karl Marx had observed: 'Altogether collisions between the classes of the old society further, in many ways, the course of development of the proletariat.'[35] This was also the English liberal's view, as he called on the 'aristocracy' and 'plutocracy' who controlled the upper and lower houses respectively

33 Napoléon III, *Œuvres*, vol. 1, pp. 10, 375.
34 Bagehot, *English Constitution*, p. 172.
35 *MECW*, vol. 6, p. 493.

to be careful to abstain from such in-fighting and polemics as would end up undermining the multitude's traditional deference to the upper classes and encourage 'a political combination of the lower classes, as such and for their own objects'. For Bagehot, this is to be considered an evil of the first magnitude', as 'a permanent combination of them would make them (now that so many of them have the suffrage) supreme in the country'.[36] The task of breaking the autonomous political organisation of the popular classes (who had obtained or were beginning to obtain political rights) had earlier been entrusted to notables, but now began to become a demand upon the charismatic leader himself.

It was necessary for the latter's purposes that he should be faced with an amorphous mass, not organised in trade unions or workers' or people's parties. Tellingly, the first bill passed to extend suffrage beyond the confines of the aristocracy and the bourgeoisie coincided with the introduction of severe limitations on trade-union rights. The courts condemned several trade unions as 'imposing restrictions on trade', and they were thus denied the rights they had enjoyed since 1825, from the moment that workers' 'combination' was legalised.[37] Intervening in the debate that preceded the passing of the Second Reform Bill, the great critic Leslie Stephen asked:

> how far is the remedy of excluding [the working] classes from any solid share of influence sound or satisfactory? Does not the fact of excluding them from legislative influence, teach them to look to other means . . .? We have constantly had the tyrannical practices of Trade Unions dinned into our ears, as though they supplied a conclusive reason against allowing workmen to have the suffrage. To me, it seems equally conclusive the other way . . . [T]he exclusion of workmen from the franchise tends, if anything, to spread [Trade Unions] faster.[38]

It is true that this legislation, striking a blow against the trade unions, was later repealed. Yet it was symptomatic of the tendency to associate

36 Bagehot, *English Constitution*, pp. 174–9.

37 George M. Trevelyan, *British History in the Nineteenth Century 1782–1901* (London: Longmans, Green & Co., 1922).

38 Albert Hirschman, *Shifting Involvements: Private Interest and Public Action* (Princeton, NJ: Princeton University Press, 2002).

political emancipation with a rolling-back of trade-union freedoms, with the latter serving as the necessary condition for atomising a mass who were now to be delivered, unarmed, to the power of attraction exerted by the charismatic leader.

The transformation that took place with respect to the traditional regime of notables was well captured by Hannah Arendt. As she put it, from this moment onwards, 'the great men, not the aristocrats, were the true representatives of the nation, in whom the "genius of the race" was personified'.[39] Indeed, Disraeli tirelessly repeated that the great man is 'the personification of race, its choice exemplar'.[40] The Tory prime minister's great adversary was Gladstone, who further expanded suffrage with the reform of 1884–85. Yet – for good reason – the latter became the model whom he especially looked towards when he celebrated the leader endowed with an exceptional human rapport thanks to his ability to exert a magnetic attraction over the masses. There took form a kind of 'popular Caesarism': the leader was now 'a general in command of an army. He barely consults his staff, the front bench, and practically confines his confidences to an inner circle of a few lieutenants. All the rest of the army simply receives marching orders.'[41]

In France, the Bonapartist propaganda condemning election by lists demanded the introduction of single-member constituencies. Yet these had always existed in England: the very limited traces of any other electoral system were definitively wiped out by Gladstone – indeed, in direct combination with the new law he passed to extend the franchise.[42] The victory of the single-member constituency system was all the more total given that it stood in perfect harmony with the argument so dear to Bagehot – which now set the tone – for which the 'childlike' multitude, unable to analyse general political questions, could only express its choice between two particular individuals, one of whom would think on its behalf about political questions that stood beyond its reach. The English liberal continued to assert the thesis so dear to the liberal

39 Hannah Arendt, *The Origins of Totalitarianism* (New York: Harcourt Brace, 1973), p. 180.

40 Ibid.

41 Moisei Ostrogorski, *Democracy and the Organization of Political Parties* (New York: Macmillan, 1902), vol. 1, p. 607.

42 Jean-Paul Laffitte, *Le paradoxe de l'égalité et la représentation proportionnelle* (Paris: Hachette, 1910), pp. 221, 259.

tradition according to which *otium* (leisure) and property are the prerequisites of political participation. It was only natural, then, that the masses should be excluded from politics given that they are characterised by 'a life of labour, an incomplete education, a monotonous occupation, a career in which the hands are used much and the judgment is used little'.[43] In the new conditions created by the extension of the franchise, this traditional argument was reinterpreted in a new and different sense: the 'miserable creatures' weighed down by labour and their hardships would remain at the margins of political life, but would nonetheless be granted a local or national-level choice between two leaders, within the context of an electoral system founded on the two-party system and single-member constituencies – or, more precisely, on the competition between two candidates. Bagehot was decidedly critical of proportional representation, which would encourage the development of parties programmatically inclined to agitate over questions that ought absolutely to be avoided, or even to aid the autonomous organisation of the lower classes of society.

Hero Worship and the Personalisation of Power

The personalisation of power and the celebration of the charismatic leader also found expression in the philosophy of history, as there began to make itself heard the cult of the solitary hero and the genius standing above the general mediocrity and banality – the genius compared to whom the masses were so much raw material. The sun had now set on that diffuse, chorus-like heroism which had refused to isolate an exceptional individual from the people and the epoch of which he was the product and expression. Such had been the democratic heroism which we can see in Robespierre's writings, the other face of a profession of faith in democracy. In illustrating his plan to establish national fêtes that would celebrate heroes and at the same time galvanise the unity of the people, the Jacobin leader outlined an ideal pantheon in which there was ample space for figures from everyday life, and so, too, for many names 'still wrapped in darkness' and yet 'worthy of being written into

43 Bagehot, *English Constitution*, p. 380.

the feasts of history'.[44] This heroism finds its most exceptional interpreter in Michelet: 'the chief actor is the people' far more than 'those brilliant, powerful speakers, who expressed the thoughts of the masses'.[45] This vision, born of the French Revolution, still held on strong even in the Napoleonic era: as Talleyrand stated as he paid tribute to the victorious general returning from the stunning Italian campaign, the glory of Bonaparte 'belong[ed] to the Revolution', to the institutions that it produced, to all those who had first made possible this colossal historic upheaval and then defended it with such ardour; it 'belong[ed] to those valiant soldiers whom freedom has made into invincible heroes', and lastly 'to all Frenchmen worthy of the name'.[46]

In Hegel, an admirer of the French revolution and Napoleon, we find the statement that the great historical personalities 'seem to draw exclusively from themselves', to carry out a work that is only 'theirs'; but, in reality, they prove to be great to the extent that they know how to bring to light 'the truth of their time and their world'.[47]

In any case, as far as the philosophy of history is concerned, we can measure the distance that now separated the protagonist of the coup d'état of 2 December 1851 – seeking a political regime willing to recognise the superior merits of the 'transcendent geniuses'– from the French Revolution.[48] Not by chance, this Revolution had been indicted by conservative and reactionary publicists as inspired by hatred towards 'genius' and a lack of 'respect for great personalities'.[49] In Carlyle, too, the hero-cult is accompanied by a discomfort towards the egalitarian tendencies of modernity – a discomfort which takes on an increasingly explicit and virulently anti-democratic meaning. After 1848, Engels was fully aware of this; polemicising with the Scottish writer, he mocked an ideology that sought to cast the ruling class as 'privy genius' and to

44 Maximilien Robespierre, *Textes choisis* (Paris: Éditions Sociales, 1958), vol. 3, p. 177.

45 Jules Michelet, *History of the French Revolution* (Chicago: University of Chicago Press, 1967), p. 12.

46 Luigi Mascilli Migliorni, *Il mito dell'eroe. Italia e Francia nell'ètà della Restaurazione* (Naples: Guida, 1984), pp. 14, 9–10.

47 G. W. F. Hegel, *Werke in zwanzig Bänden*, ed. E. Moldenhauer and K. M. Michel (Frankfurt: Suhrkamp, 1969), vol. 12, p. 46.

48 Napoleon III, *Œuvres*, vol. 1., p. 382.

49 Friedrich Gentz, 'Über die Moralität in den Staatsrevolutionen' (1793), in *Ausgewählte Schriften*, ed. W. Weick (Stuttgart-Leipzig: Rieger, 1837), vol. 2.

justify the condition of the oppressed class on account of its being 'excluded from genius'.[50] The cult of genius went hand-in-hand with discrimination on the basis of property. But the anti-democratic implications of Carlyle's view of history had already been observed by Mazzini, who commented in a long review dedicated to the Scottish writer:

> I protest against these ideas in the name of the democratic tendencies of our age. History is not the biography of the rarest and most powerful of intellects . . . The great minds are but the milestones of the path that Humanity follows . . . There is always something greater and more divinely mysterious than great individuals, and it is the Earth that sustains them, the human race that includes them, the thought of God that stirs in them, and that only the collective work of all can translate into a political fact and norm of life . . . The inspiration of the Genius belongs half to heaven, half to the multitude of mortals over whose life He rises.[51]

After 1848, the not only anti-democratic but also pro-Bonapartist content of the hero-cult began to emerge clearly. Polemicising against the revolution and the universal suffrage it sanctioned, Carlyle complained that the subversive wave put into doubt and swept away every lordship or leadership – or rather, every Dux or Duke. The subversive upheavals were increasingly contrasted not with the old society of aristocrats and nobles based on 'lords' and 'dukes', but with a new regime led by a 'leader' or 'duce'. This was so much the case that the Carlyle essay here quoted concluded with the invocation of a 'Real Captain' who would finally take the place of that 'Phantasm Captain' bequeathed by the wretched wave of 'universal democracy'.[52]

Significantly, John Stuart Mill was an admirer of the anti-democratic writer. In his *Autobiography*, he boasted that, even before the 'common critics' had made themselves heard, he had immediately taken a position celebrating Carlyle's 'epic poem' on – or rather, against – the French

50 *MECW*, vol. 10, p. 310.

51 Migliorni, *Il mito dell'eroe*, pp. 147ff.

52 Thomas Carlyle, *Latter-Day Pamphlets* (1850), ed. M. K. Goldberg and J. P. Seigel (Ottawa: Canadian Federation for the Humanities, 1983), pp. 12ff, 31.

Revolution as 'one of those productions of genius which are above all rules and are a law to themselves'.[53] This is an admiration not confined to the literary sphere. Starting from a denunciation of the modern world and its tendency towards the 'ascendant power of mediocrity' and the excessive power of 'masses', the liberal philosopher expresses a philosophy of history not very different from Carlyle's: 'The initiation of all wise or noble things, comes and must come from individuals; generally at first from some one individual. The honour and glory of the average man is that he is capable of following that initiative.'[54] It is true that Mill pre-emptively defends himself from the accusation that he, too, favours 'hero-worship', but he does so only to provide a less threatening and sugar-coated version thereof – one that, excluding the right to violence, limits itself to claiming for 'the strong man of genius' the 'freedom to point out the way' to the masses.[55]

Unlike Carlyle, the English philosopher declares himself in favour of universal suffrage, but he attaches this wish to a vague and indeterminate future. Indeed, in both men's vision of the philosophy of history, there emerges – albeit in different ways – a cult of the leader and the hero that cannot be separated from the gradual establishment of Bonapartist tendencies in the political field. This is confirmed by Nietzsche, whose 'metaphysics of genius' goes hand in hand with the polemic against any vision of history that 'democratises the rights of genius'.[56] The philosopher who, in polemic against the developments of modernity, continues to hold fast to the view dear to classical antiquity and the liberal tradition that 'the many' are to be regarded as mere 'bearers, instruments of transmission', was such a radical enemy of democracy that he condemned Bismarck and the Second Reich as excessively inclined to 'mediocrity, democracy and "modern ideas"' because of their demagogic recourse to the instrument of plebiscitary approval from below.[57] Yet, especially in his maturity, the philosopher realised

53 John Stuart Mill, *Collected Works*, ed. J. M. Robson (Toronto: Routledge & Kegan, 1965), vol. 20, p. 133; John Stuart Mill, *Autobiography*, in *Collected Works*, vol. 1 (Toronto: University of Toronto Press, 1981), p. 224.

54 John Stuart Mill, *On Liberty*, in *Collected Works*, vol. 18, pp. 268–9.

55 Ibid.

56 Friedrich Nietzsche, *Sämtliche Werke, Kritische Studienausgahe* (Munich: DTV, 1980, vol. 1, pp. 700, 666.

57 Ibid., vol. 12, p. 492; vol. 1, p. 20.

that universal suffrage can be bent in a different and opposite direction to democracy: 'There is no reason to be disconsolate . . . The manipulability [*Dressierharkeit*] of men has become very great in this democratic Europe . . . Those who are able to command find those who must obey: I am thinking for example of Napoleon and Bismarck.'[58]

Historical experience has now shown that it is possible to control universal suffrage, bending it into an instrument of control and domination of the masses by exceptional personalities. In this sense, 'the democratization of Europe is at the same time an involuntary exercise in the breeding of tyrants – understanding that word in every sense, including the most spiritual'.[59] In otherwise such different authors, the cult, or rather the 'metaphysics' of genius, begins to take on a clearly pro-Bonapartist content.

Bonapartism, Liberalism, Liberal Bonapartism

Even on a more strictly political level, the emergence of Bonapartist tendencies was a phenomenon that extended beyond France: Engels went so far as to speak of the Franco-Prussian war as the clash between 'two Bonapartes'.[60] Indeed, there is no shortage of similarities between Napoleon III and Bismarck. Both came to power after the defeat of the revolution of 1848 and played on agrarian and peasant conservatism to thwart and break up the radical-democratic tendencies that had emerged in the course of that essentially urban revolution. After an initial split, the Iron Chancellor succeeded in fully reconciling himself – indeed, from a position of strength – with the liberal or national-liberal bourgeoisie; but this is what Napoleon III also did, or tried to do, in the final phase of his Empire. Partly different was the situation in Britain, which remained immune to the revolutionary wave of 1848. Nonetheless, Disraeli – who, at least as far as foreign policy was concerned, compared Bismarck to Bonaparte – did have some traits in common with the

58 Ibid., vol. 11, pp. 269ff.

59 Friedrich Nietzsche, *Beyond Good and Evil* (Cambridge: Cambridge University Press, 2002), p. 134 (para. 242).

60 In the 1895 introduction to *The Class Struggles in France*: see *MECW*, vol. 27, pp. 506–24.

German chancellor and with Louis-Napoleon himself.[61] Bypassing the liberal bourgeoisie, all three directly addressed the masses, to whom they granted suffrage, to a greater or lesser extent, and whose support they gained or tried to gain by making concessions on the level of economic and social policy, stimulating national and chauvinistic excitement, and on this basis building up the cult of the *super partes* charismatic leader, undisputed interpreter and leader of the nation.

Of course, unlike in France, in other countries Bonapartist tendencies remained confined and limited within the bounds of a more or less liberal regime. And yet, we must also steer clear of hasty and overly sharp contrasts. In the meantime, in 1799, Napoleon Bonaparte's coup d'état had been organised with the important contribution of Sieyès, and with the warm support, at least initially, of Constant, Madame de Staël and liberal circles which had hailed the general who had come to power as the French Washington.[62] But it is especially interesting to examine the attitude taken by Tocqueville after the revolution, or revolutions, of 1848. Just as, in his capacity as foreign minister, he had called on the French troops in Rome to 'strike the demagogic party with terror', in a letter from Frankfurt on 18 May 1849, he wished for 'the victory of the princes' and the Prussian army in Germany, so as also to put an end to an 'excessive decentralisation' which favoured the spread of 'hotbeds of revolution'.[63] This attitude was not so different from the one adopted in this same period by Bismarck, who was subsequently able to build his political edifice precisely on the basis of the victory invoked by the French liberal. As far as France is concerned, after having recommended, on the occasion of the June Days, the shooting on the spot of anyone caught 'in a defensive stance' more than a year after the workers' revolt, when the ruthless repression seemed to have banished the Jacobin and socialist danger forever, Tocqueville still considered it necessary to use an iron fist against the danger from the Left.[64] For Tocqueville, 'palliative' measures could not be enough; to sweep away not only the Mountain, but also 'all the surrounding hills', one must place oneself

61 William Flavelle Monypenny and George Buckle, *The Life of Benjamin Disraeli, Earl of Beaconsfield* (New York: MacMillan, 1914).

62 Guillemin, *Constant muscadin*, pp. 275–9.

63 Alexis de Tocqueville, *Œuvres complètes*, Mayer edition, vol. 15, I, p. 123; vol. 8, II, pp. 133ff.

64 Ibid., vol. 12, p. 176.

'courageously at the head of all those who wish to re-establish order, to whichever shade they belong'; one must not hesitate in resorting to a 'heroic . . . remedy'.[65]

Indirectly suggested here is the need for exceptional measures, with the suspension of constitutional liberties. However, the energetic, compactly organised party of order that was invoked here turned out to be hegemonised by Louis Bonaparte, lead actor in a coup d'état that also marginalised the liberal bourgeoisie. Now came the moment when Tocqueville drew closer to the Legitimists. What regime did he propose, in the letter he addressed to the Comte de Chambord, pretender to the throne under the name Henri V? Certainly, this regime would seek to establish a 'constitutional and representative monarchy' able to guarantee 'individual liberty' and a 'real liberty of the press'. But, at the same time, 'after the anarchy that followed '48', it would have to proceed with 'great caution' on this terrain: 'it is necessary first of all to ensure the monarchical power all the rights that are compatible with liberty, and, in the first stages, not to grant to liberty anything beyond the indispensable rights without which it could not exist'. For example, 'a parliament where discussions are free and whose debates are public seems to me to be a sine qua non condition of constitutional monarchy, but from this it does not necessarily follow that, initially, parliament may not be severely limited in its powers and contained in the duration of its proceedings'.

Freedom of the press is indispensable – but this does not mean that 'no kind of guarantee can or should be made against the abuses of this tremendous freedom'.[66] Was this programme much different from the one that the Second Empire would later realise, in its final phase? The most significant difference perhaps lay in the role that the liberal theorist continued to attribute to the traditional nobility, at least judging by his expressed wish that he would see the primacy of the 'superior and moral classes of the nation' restored. On the eve of Napoleon III's more or less liberal turn, in February 1858 Tocqueville wrote a letter to his friend Beaumont in which he expressed the view that only the consolidation of the existing regime could encourage a political evolution in a liberal-Bonapartist sense: 'Sometimes I think that the only possibility of

65 Ibid. vol. 8: II, p. 53.

66 Stephane Rials, *Révolution et contre-révolution en France au XIX siècle* (Paris: Albatros, 1987), p. 165.

seeing the living taste of freedom reborn in France is in the calm and seemingly final establishment of despotism.'[67] Back in his own day, after Constant overcame the phase of disappointment that followed his initial hopes or enthusiasms aroused by the supposed French Washington, he had ultimately come to identify with the First Empire. Would Tocqueville have ended up throwing in his lot with the liberal Second Empire, in the same way that his fervent admirer Laboulaye later did?

Nor should we idealise the regimes outside France that now increasingly based themselves on a personalisation of power. Having remained immune to the wave of upheavals that marked 1848, Britain rushed to recognise Louis-Napoleon's coup d'état – it was the first among all governments to do so, showing what Marx called 'indecent haste'.[68] Indeed, the Palmerston government did not hesitate to express its sympathy and approval to the French ambassador.[69] This attitude was also shared by distinguished liberal authors. While Bagehot continued, of course, to celebrate the superiority of Britain's institutions, in the French events he saw a confirmation of his theory about the inevitable, and beneficial, tendency of the masses to personalise power. The French people preferred to be governed not so much by an Assembly as by Louis-Napoleon – the single leader whom they were able to envisage concretely.[70] Moreover, it should be remembered that France was going through a serious crisis – and that, for Bagehot, 'the first duty of society is the preservation of society'.[71] It was in the name of this same duty to preserve society, this 'first and fundamental natural law', that Locke had justified the executive's 'prerogative' 'to act according to discretion for the public good, without the prescription of the law, and sometimes even against it'.[72] And – one illustrious English liberal constitutionalist observed at the beginning of the twentieth century – thanks to this prerogative, in moments of crisis in Great Britain, the executive was almost in the position of the 'last of the Tudors and the first of the

67 Tocqueville, *Œuvres complètes*, Mayer edition, vol. 8, III, p. 544.

68 *MECW*, vol. 22, p. 269.

69 William Lecky, *Historical and Political Essays* (London: Longmans, Green & Co., 1910 [1896]), p. 55.

70 Bagehot, *English Constitution*, p. 226.

71 St John-Stevas, *Bagehot: A Study of His Life and Thought*, p. 419.

72 John Locke, *Two Treatises of Government and a Letter Concerning Toleration* (New Haven, CT: Yale University Press, 2003), §159, p. 172.

Stuarts' – that is, it had the power of an absolute monarch, and in any case no less power than Louis-Napoleon had after the coup d'état.[73]

It should be added that, even apart from the state of exception, the coercive element was hardly absent from the popular Caesarism that began to impose itself outside France. This is immediately obvious in the case of Germany, where Bismarck was able to reconcile the concession of universal suffrage with an iron fist against socialists and Catholics. And even the Iron Chancellor's contemporaries compared his regime to that of Disraeli's Britain.[74] No lack of authors have wanted to see in the latter's government an anticipation of certain characteristics of the 'totalitarian regimes of the twentieth century'.[75] More precisely, the mass chauvinistic excitement exerted a psychological and sometimes even physical pressure and intimidation on dissidents, who were isolated and demonised as potential traitors. When we read Disraeli's opponents denouncing the use of the 'rabble' who blocked 'any attempt by the intelligent and honest to make their voices heard', while 'authority' stood by and even applauded, we can only be reminded of the behaviour of the Society of December 10, which Louis-Napoleon recruited from among the underclass; its task was 'to improvise a public for him, stage public enthusiasm, roar *vive l'Empereur*, insult and beat up republicans, of course under the protection of the police'.[76]

If we analyse the respective political situations of France, Germany and Britain in the second half of the 1860s, the analogies are striking. For, in all three cases, we are in the presence of a political regime whose more or less liberal features were balanced by the presence of a strong executive power, in which the concession of political citizenship to large strata of society was neutralised by a Caesarism with a more or less popular face, and which in any case played on the chauvinistic excitement of the masses.

73 James Bryce, *Studies in History and Jurisprudence* (Oxford: Oxford University Press, 1901), p. 146.

74 Bruno Bauer, *Disraelis romantischer und Bismarcks sozialisticher Imperialismus*, 2nd edn (Aalen: Scientia, 1979 [1882]).

75 Ottavio Barié, *Idee e dottrine imperialistiche nell'Inghilterra vittoriana* (Bari: Laterza, 1953), p. 145.

76 Ibid. p. 144; *MECW*, vol. 11, p. 150.

The Personalisation of Power, National 'Mission' and the Externalisation of Conflict

So, let us now focus on Britain. It may seem rather odd that the first appreciable extension of suffrage beyond the aristocracy and the bourgeoisie took place on the initiative not of liberals, but of Disraeli – a figure rightly called a racial or racist thinker. Indeed, Disraeli never tired of repeating that race, rooted in blood, is 'the key to history', that 'all is race; there is no other truth' and that, therefore, the world is inevitably divided between the dominant superior races and the inferior ones, which are either subjugated or have to be subjugated.[77] The prime minister who granted political rights to large sectors of the popular masses was a 'race fanatic' who mocked what he considered the 'pernicious doctrine of modern times, the natural equality of man'; a statesman who, starting from these assumptions, tried to develop a popular Toryism, based on the cult of the Empire and the imperial mission of a British people who constitute the 'aristocracy of nature'. Yes: in the imagination of this British politician of Jewish background, Britain was Israel, the 'chosen' people.[78] The British prime minister's programme is described by one scholar as follows:

> The Conservative Party had to represent all those who were proud to belong to a great country, to an 'imperial country', who wished to maintain its greatness and saw in the old English institutions the primary cause of Great Britain's present position. The working classes had to be represented in worthy fashion therein: they were English to the core and repudiated cosmopolitan and internationalist principles.[79]

All this allowed the silencing, domestically, of all dissenting voices as foreign or hostile to the nation and the British soul – in turn directing against outsiders the activity and the passions of the masses guided by the leader and subjugated by his charisma. Emancipation and disemancipation were closely intertwined, here: when vast popular strata were

77 John Vincent, *Disraeli* (Oxford: Oxford University Press, 1990), pp. 27–30.
78 Arendt, *Origins of Totalitarianism*, pp. 70, 73, 78.
79 Barié, *Idee e dottrine imperialistiche*, p. 139.

admitted to citizenship in Britain, this went hand-in-hand with a colonial expansion involving the imposition of more or less camouflaged slavery or semi-servile forms of labour on subjugated populations.[80] The categories and metaphors that had long been used to designate certain social strata within the capitalist metropole were now reserved exclusively for colonial populations: from this moment on, it was they who John Stuart Mill identified as 'barbarians' or the 'lesser races'. In fact, the English liberal went even further, to the point of placing certain primitive peoples 'very little above the highest of the beasts'.[81] The de-racialisation of the classes in the capitalist metropole gradually admitted to citizenship – no longer considered simply as work machines or vocal instruments – went hand-in-hand with an appalling configuration of the colonial populations in a racialising key. In this period, the vision dear to Kipling, according to which colonial peoples were to be considered half-children and half-devils – i.e. minors in need of tutelage, who were barbarians and even worse if they should refuse such tutelage – was very widespread. Corresponding to the English writer was the American statesman Theodore Roosevelt, who also spoke of the 'inferior races' as 'children', or as 'savages' and 'barbarians'.[82] Once cast in this way, it is clear that the populations subject to European or 'Western' domination were to be totally deprived of political rights, either because they had not yet progressed past the stage of childhood (and freedom – says Mill – applies 'only to human beings in the maturity of their faculties'), or because they are foreign to civilization (and, again according to the English liberal, 'Despotism is a legitimate mode of government in dealing with barbarians').[83] We have seen that, according to Sieyès, 'a great nation is necessarily composed of two *peoples*'. Now this metaphor returned in Disraeli, but in a critical sense. In Disraeli's early novel, which referred to this theme already in its title, it is the Chartist agitator who speaks of England as divided into 'two nations', namely 'the rich and the poor'.[84] This

80 J. A. Hobson, *Imperialism* (London: Routledge, 2020 [1902]).

81 John Stuart Mill, *Considerations on Representative Government* (New York: Henry Holt, 1873), p. 46.

82 Theodore Roosevelt, *The Letters* (Cambridge, MA: Harvard University Press, 1951), vol. 2, pp. 620, 1401; Theodore Roosevelt, *The Strenuous Life: Essays and Addresses* (New York: Century, 1901), pp. 292–4.

83 Mill, *On Liberty*, p. 224.

84 Benjamin Disraeli, *Sybil, or The Two Nations* (Oxford: Oxford University Press, 1988 [1845]), pp. 65ff.

view is, however, rejected by the English conservative politician who contrasts it with the thesis that 'work' is the 'twin brother' of 'property'. The social classes, formerly divided by a somehow racial gulf, now become part not only of the same nation but even of the same family.[85] And yet, rather than fading away, the racialisation of which the working classes were traditionally the victims seemed to be displaced away from Europe and the West. It is no accident that the same youthful novels that so warmly emphasised the bond of 'fraternity' which now united 'the privileged and prosperous English people' obsessively played on the theme of race as soon as they looked beyond Britain and the West.[86]

It may be useful here to establish a comparison between developments in Britain and in the United States. It was not long after the end of the War of Secession that the process of disemancipation began in the United States, also involving limited sectors of poor whites. In Britain, meanwhile, the extension of suffrage, even after the third electoral reform of 1884–85, still left out some sectors of the working classes – namely the most destitute, who were still, in some ways, burdened by the racialisation which had previously affected manual workers in general. On the other side of the Atlantic, disemancipation and the exclusion from rights above all affected, indeed in especially harsh fashion, the black population – subjected, as we know, to forms of semi-servile labour – together with certain non-European immigrants such as the Chinese coolies. As for Britain, its semi-servile labour force was displaced, for it was to be found in the colonies. But identical, or very similar, in both countries was the ideology that racially discriminated against those excluded from citizenship, while integrating or trying to integrate large sectors of the de-racialised and emancipated manual workers. The Disraeli who extended the franchise in Britain would certainly not have been opposed to the process of disemancipation at the expense of blacks in the United States: after all, he was of the view that, if Americans mixed with former slaves, 'they would become so deteriorated that their states would probably be reconquered and regained by the aborigines'.[87]

85 Benjamin Disraeli, *Coningsby, or The New Generation* (London: Longmans, Green & Co., 1904 [1844]), p. 411.

86 Disraeli, *Sybil*, p. 422.

87 Vincent, *Disraeli*, p. 30.

The relationship between the extension of citizenship in the capitalist metropole and the external projection of the racialisation process is also evident in the French case: colonial expansion reached its peak with the Third Republic, founded on universal male suffrage, which did not hesitate to conduct a policy of extermination at the expense of 'unarmed people'.[88] If, with their admission to political rights, the French workers celebrated their elevation to the 'rank of men', for the French army conquering Algeria, 'the Arabs are like evil beasts'. This, at least, according to Tocqueville, who – convinced of the impossibility of treating Arabs 'as if they were our citizens and our equals' – invited his fellow citizens to be careful not to sow 'astonishment and confusion' among 'semi-civilized peoples', filling them 'with erroneous and dangerous notions', such as equality.[89]

Finally, the phenomenon here under examination can also be seen in another liberal country. In the Italian case, already in Orlando – a leading exponent of the liberal ruling class of the time – we come across the acknowledgement of the 'certainly not fortuitous coincidence of such memorable events [the conquest of Libya] with the radical democratic reform of our order' – that is, with the broad extension of political rights sanctioned by the reform of 1912. This was wryly noted by the socialist Filippo Turati, who observed in turn that universal suffrage had been imparted by Giovanni Giolitti – once its 'irreducible adversary' – in order to broaden popular consent for the colonial enterprise.[90] But the deepest analysis of 'Italy's transformation into an imperialist country and the government's agreeing to electoral reform' (to which Giolitti himself, 'prior to the Tripolitanian war', had been 'bitterly opposed') is Lenin. Explaining the change that occurred in the Italian statesman, he makes recourse to a long quotation from Michels:

> Notwithstanding their long-standing theoretical aversion from a colonial policy, the industrial workers, and more so the lower strata, fought against the Turks with perfect discipline and obedience, contrary to all expectations. Such slavish behaviour towards the

88 V. I. Lenin, 'War and Revolution' (14 May 1917), in *Lenin Collected Works* (Moscow: Progress, 1974), vol. 24, pp. 398–421. Text from marxists.org.

89 Tocqueville, *Œuvres complètes*, Mayer edition, vol. 15: I, p. 224; vol. 3: I, p. 324.

90 Filippo Turati, *Socialismo e riformismo nella storia d'Italia. Scritti politici 1878–1932*, ed. Franco Livorsi (Milan: Feltrinelli, 1979), pp. 295–8.

> government's policy merited a reward to induce the proletariat to persevere along this new road. The President of the Council of Ministers declared in Parliament that, by his patriotic behaviour on the battlefield of Libya, the Italian worker had proved to the country that he had reached the highest stage of political maturity. He who is capable of sacrificing his life for a noble cause is also capable of defending the interests of the country as a voter, and he therefore has a right that the state should consider him worthy of full political rights.[91]

Thus, in Italy, the ruling classes were reconciled with the popular classes, now considered participants in civilisation and therefore deserving of admission to political citizenship. Yet, at the same time, the racialisation of the barbarians located outside the capitalist metropole developed to the point of prompting them into a ruthless colonial war of extermination against them, involving the massacre of 'whole families', including 'women and children'.[92] The link between the extension of suffrage and warfare abroad is highlighted by the electoral reform of 1912, which stated that males under thirty but over twenty-one could obtain political rights not only by virtue of census or 'titles of culture and honour', but also by virtue of military service.[93] The disenfranchisement of conscientious objectors for five years in post–World War I Britain had a similar meaning.[94] But let us return to Victorian Britain. A contemporary of Disraeli and of Britain's prodigious colonial and imperial expansion – and an admirer of the great leaders who led such an enterprise, capturing the consent and admiration of the entire nation – was Bagehot. He insisted that the 'childlike' multitude was, indeed, incapable of understanding the 'ends of government', but, if treated properly, could be enthused by great and fascinating enterprises:

91 V. I. Lenin, 'Imperialism and Socialism in Italy' (1915), *Lenin Collected Works*, vol. 21 (Moscow: Progress, 1974), pp. 357–66, available at marxists.org.

92 V. I. Lenin, 'The End of the Italo-Turkish War' (1912), in *Lenin Collected Works*, vol. 18 (Moscow: Progress, 1974), pp. 337–8, available at marxists.org.

93 Manfredi Siotto Pintor, 'Storia del regime elettorale', subentry in 'Elezione', *Enciclopedia italiana* (Rome: Treccani, 1932), vol. 13, p. 781; Giovanni Corso, 'Elezioni amministrative', subentry in 'Elezione', *Enciclopedia italiana*, p. 785.

94 A. J. P. Taylor, *English History 1914–1945* (Oxford: Oxford University Press, 1975), p. 116.

> It is not true the lower classes will be absorbed in the useful; they do not like anything so poor. No orator ever made an impression by appealing to men as to their plainest physical wants, except when he could allege or prove that those wants were caused by the tyranny of some other class. But thousands have made the greatest impression by appealing to some vague dream of glory, or empire, or nationality. The ruder sort of men – that is, men at one stage of rudeness – will sacrifice all they hope for, all they have, themselves, for what is called an idea – for some attraction which seems to transcend reality, which aspires to elevate men by an interest higher, deeper, wider than that of ordinary life.[95]

It was thus necessary to divert the masses' attention from their material problems, avoiding the danger that dissatisfaction – liable to be skilfully exploited by demagogues – would call into question the existing socio-political order. This aim could be achieved by means of some colonial policy adventure: thousands of orators and demagogues – in this case welcome and beneficial ones – would work deftly to stir up the right emotions. The success of such a policy of externalising conflict, with the disappearance, in 'a nation which exploits the whole world', of the opposition even of the working class, now won over to the fascination and advantages of colonial policy – all this was also noted by Engels in some letters that attracted Lenin's attention in the course of World War I, at the tragic moment when, in Bagehot's words, the pursuit of 'some vague dream of glory' led the 'childlike' multitudes of the countries engaged in the conflict to sacrifice 'all they hope for, all they have, themselves' – that is, to die on opposite sides in the bloodsoaked trenches.[96]

From the 'Childlike' Multitude to the 'Psychology of Crowds'

At the end of the nineteenth century, as the extension of the franchise was spreading, the theme of the 'childlike' multitude underwent an

---

95 Bagehot, *English Constitution*, pp. 208ff.

96 V. I. Lenin, *Imperialism, the Highest Stage of Capitalism*, in *Essential Works of Lenin* (New York: Dover, 2012) Chapter 8, 'Parasitism and Decay of Capitalism', see p. 252.

important alteration. Gustave Le Bon mounted an implacable indictment against the 'crowds' that he saw as stuck at 'inferior forms of evolution' in the manner of 'savages and children'.[97] Despite the noticeably different language and cultural climate, there was a re-emergence of the categories of the eternal 'child' and the 'foreigner' (a member of a race considered more or less explicitly inferior), on which basis the liberal tradition excluded wage workers from political rights. Even the assertion that 'crowds are everywhere distinguished by feminine characteristics' echoed an argument drawn from that same tradition, which, starting from the fact – considered obvious and uncontroversial – of the exclusion of women from political citizenship, sought to exclude also wage workers, whose level of maturity could certainly not be held to be superior.[98]

The psychology of crowds – a term we saw used in a pejorative sense already by Louis-Napoleon – emerged at the end of the nineteenth century, at a time when universal suffrage either had been or was being implemented. This was the direct heir of the psychology of the 'childlike' multitude, developed and upheld in a historical period in which discrimination by property qualifications still predominated.

Le Bon deals explicitly with the ongoing extension of political rights:

> No doubt the weak side of universal suffrage is too obvious to be overlooked. It cannot be gainsaid that civilisation has been the work of a small minority of superior intelligences constituting the culminating point of a pyramid . . . The greatness of a civilisation cannot assuredly depend upon the votes given by inferior elements boasting solely numerical strength. Doubtless, too, the votes recorded by crowds are often very dangerous.[99]

Like the liberal tradition, whose representatives (Tocqueville, Macaulay, Spencer) he often cited, Le Bon connected the extension of suffrage to the spread of socialist ideas. By violating 'economic laws', the latter purported to 'regulate the conditions of labour and wages', spreading 'a

97 Gustave Le Bon, *The Crowd: A Study of the Popular Mind* (New York: Macmillan, 1896), p. 17.

98 Ibid., p. 21.

99 Ibid., pp. 198–9.

superstitious confidence in the State, whom it regards as a sort of Providence', and the expectation that a supposed social question would be resolved through legislative intervention in property relations. All this had already had ruinous effects, and threatened further ones: 'it is probable that the vagaries of popular sovereignty will cost us still more dearly'.[100] Was it, then, necessary to return to property qualifications, or to promote a distribution of political rights that would privilege the educated classes? Writing in France – the country that had, before any other, starting already in the period that ideologically prepared the outbreak of the revolution, seen the emergence of the *engagé* intellectual – Le Bon did not share Mill's illusions about the positive effects that could derive from electoral privileges for the more educated classes:

> Must it be believed that with a restricted suffrage – a suffrage restricted to those intellectually capable if it be desired – an improvement would be effected in the votes of crowds? I cannot admit for a moment that this would be the case, and that for the reasons I have already given touching the mental inferiority of all collectivities, whatever their composition. In a crowd men always tend to the same level, and, on general questions, a vote recorded by forty academicians is no better than that of forty water-carriers . . . In consequence, were the electorate solely composed of persons stuffed with sciences their votes would be no better than those emitted at present. They would be guided in the main by their sentiments and by party spirit. We should be spared none of the difficulties we now have to contend with, and we should certainly be subjected to the oppressive tyranny of castes.[101]

Constant had already excluded from political rights, along with wage-labourers, intellectuals without property who, in pursuit of 'chimerical' and subversive theories, were inclined to 'disdain conclusions drawn from facts and to despise the real and sensible world, to reason fanatically about the welfare state'.[102] In the Taine for whom he so showed such extraordinary admiration, Le Bon may have read his

100 Ibid., pp. xxi, 87.

101 Ibid., pp. 200–1.

102 Benjamin Constant, *Cours de politique constitutionelle*, 3rd edn (Brussels: Société Belge de Librairie, 1837), pp. 106ff.

indictment against intellectuals *à la* Rousseau, 'the man of rancour', and of the stirring up of the masses. In these years, Nietzsche expressed himself similarly, dedicating a chapter of *Thus Spoke Zarathustra* to denouncing those poisonous 'tarantulas' that were the revolutionary or subversive intellectuals.[103] In turn, the French sociologist lamented the fact that the school system in his country, so little attentive to practical and professional training, continuously produced 'anarchists', 'an army of the discontented ready to obey all the suggestions of utopians and rhetoricians'.[104] It thus made no sense to seek to reverse back down the path that had led to mass or universal suffrage – especially since it had 'exercised for a long time but little influence' and been easily directed. It had become ungovernable starting with the spread of socialist ideas and the organisation of the 'crowds' into trade unions and parties, based precisely on these ideas.[105] And intellectuals played an important role within the union or socialist movement. So, what could be done about this? For Le Bon, the solution that needed to be explored was a different one. Crowds are unable to argue logically, but this fact, which is apparently an obstacle, is in fact the prerequisite for the solution of the problem: 'The type of hero dear to crowds will always have the semblance of a Cæsar. His insignia attracts them, his authority overawes them, and his sword instils them with fear.'[106]

But how should this hero, or Caesar, seek to play the crowds? Not on the basis of rational arguments. The late-nineteenth-century sociologist fully shared in the distrust expressed a few decades earlier by Louis-Napoleon for 'metaphysical questions' and by the liberal Bagehot for ideologies and 'isms'. It would make no sense to try to use the tools of those intellectuals who had exercised and continued to exercise such a ruinous influence on the masses. Such instruments risked being counterproductive; they would end by stirring political interest among the masses, who might then be led to agree with demagogues who blamed politics for the lower classes' hardships. For Le Bon, '[t]he idea that institutions can remedy the defects of societies, that national progress is the consequence of the improvement of institutions and governments',

103 Domenico Losurdo, *Hegel and the Freedom of Moderns* (Durham, NC: Duke University Press, 2004), pp. 183–5.

104 Le Bon, *The Crowd*, p. 97.

105 Ibid., p. xvi.

106 Ibid., p. 41.

was superstition. In denouncing this 'grave delusion' that had taken hold since the French Revolution, of which 'philosophers and historians have endeavoured in vain to prove [the] absurdity', the psychologist of crowds was in agreement with Tocqueville, whom he cited repeatedly.[107] But his suggested remedy was quite different, for it did not lie in a second-degree electoral system or any other device to limit or contain direct universal suffrage. Rather, the latter had to be brought to completion so that the leader, unhindered by barriers and diaphragms, could exert sway over the masses by resorting to the instruments of persuasion. Le Bon describes these tools as follows:

> Affirmation pure and simple, kept free of all reasoning and all proof, is one of the surest means of making an idea enter the mind of crowds. The conciser an affirmation is, the more destitute of every appearance of proof and demonstration, the more weight it carries. The religious books and the legal codes of all ages have always resorted to simple affirmation. Statesmen called upon to defend a political cause, and commercial men pushing the sale of their products by means of advertising are acquainted with the value of affirmation.
>
> Affirmation, however, has no real influence unless it be constantly repeated, and so far as possible in the same terms. It was Napoleon, I believe, who said that there is only one figure in rhetoric of serious importance, namely, repetition. The thing affirmed comes by repetition to fix itself in the mind in such a way that it is accepted in the end as a demonstrated truth[108]

So, here, the sociologist and psychologist of crowds summons up a Caesar or Napoleon, their 'insignia', and the dreams of imperial glory to which Bagehot had already referred. But Le Bon also imagined the propaganda deemed suitable for the Caesarist or Bonapartist regime he had in mind – and did so on the model of commercial advertising:

> To this circumstance is due the astonishing power of advertisements. When we have read a hundred, a thousand, times that X's chocolate is the best, we imagine we have heard it said in many quarters, and we

107 Ibid., p. 79.
108 Ibid., pp. 126–7.

end by acquiring the certitude that such is the fact . . . If we always read in the same papers that A is an arrant scamp and B a most honest man we finish by being convinced that this is the truth, unless, indeed, we are given to reading another paper of the contrary opinion, in which the two qualifications are reversed.[109]

As we have seen, at the very origins of the political regime based on a more or less accentuated personalisation of power, its theorists celebrated the magnetic qualities of the charismatic leader, and his ability to charm the masses, independently of any concrete political programme. The sociologist and psychologist of the crowd Le Bon continued to nurture mistrust towards 'abstract' ideologies and theories, organised parties based on programmes, the autonomous political representation of the subordinate classes, and intermediate bodies that might hinder the direct relationship between the atomised masses and the leader. But, alongside these elements of continuity, an evident novelty emerged, here: personal charisma was now replaced by the hidden persuasion of commercial advertising. The 'thousands of orators' called upon by Bagehot to ignite the chauvinistic passions of the masses were here replaced by a centralised advertising apparatus able to penetrate far more widely and intensively.

Elements of continuity remained. From the point of view of society and civilisation as a whole, the inability of the 'childlike' multitude to reason and argue rationally was not, for Bagehot, a negative factor: only thanks to this could it be dazzled by the religious charisma of the queen or the heroic charisma of the nationalist leader who agitated around the 'vague dream of glory'. Only in this way, for Bagehot, could the multitude lose its potential dangerousness and meekly accept its proper place, as required by the interests of society (and of the ruling class). Le Bon's attitude was not very different: 'Should it be regretted that crowds are never guided by reason? We would not venture to affirm it.'[110] In fact, it is beneficial that they 'may be fired with enthusiasm for glory and honour'. 'Doubtless a crowd is often criminal, but also it is often heroic'; only they are capable of that 'heroism[,] without doubt somewhat unconscious', of which 'history is made. Were peoples only to be

109 Ibid. p. 127.
110 Ibid. p. 115.

credited with the great actions performed in cold blood, the annals of the world would register but few of them.'[111]

The propaganda and advertising apparatus called upon to arouse the crowds' or the 'childlike' multitude's enthusiasm for 'glory' (to which both the English political scientist and the French sociologist and psychologist refer, as well as Louis-Napoleon himself) would reveal all its impressive power starting above all from World War I. It was then that, after a long gestation period, the Bonapartist regime faced and brilliantly overcame its baptism of fire. But, before analysing its triumphal march, it is appropriate to probe further into the genesis and historical development of what seems to be the political regime of our time.

111 Ibid., pp. 14–15.

3

An Alternative to Property Qualifications: The Origins of Bonapartism, from America to France

French Bonapartism and the American Model

We have already seen that it is reductive to seek to confine the emergence and development of the Bonapartist tendencies of the nineteenth century exclusively to France. It should be added that, in this country, the protagonists and ideologists of Bonapartism often liked to evoke the example of the United States. When the coup d'état was carried out, Napoleon was hailed in liberal circles as a sort of 'new Washington'. A few months later, on 9 February 1800, it was the First Consul himself who presided over a great ceremony at Les Invalides in honour of the first president of the United States, whose death had just been announced, declared national mourning, and sent his troops a message with a stirring homage to the dead statesman: 'Washington is dead. This great man fought against tyranny. He consolidated the freedom of his country.'[1] Was this skilful, self-interested political propaganda? No doubt. But perhaps there is another aspect that it would be unfair to overlook. In his exile on St Helena, Napoleon returned to this theme:

> Once I was in power, some would have liked me to have been a Washington . . . If I had been in America, I would gladly have been a

1 Jean-Denis Bredin, *Sieyès. La clé de la Révolution française* (Paris: Éditions de Fallois, 1988), pp. 464, 496.

> Washington, and I would also have had little merit in so doing, because I do not see how it would have been reasonably possible to do otherwise. But if he had found himself in France, faced with internal dissolution and external invasion, I would have challenged him to be what he was, and if he had wanted to be so, he would have been nothing but a simpleton and would have done nothing but prolong great misfortunes. In what concerns me, I could only be a *crowned Washington*.[2]

For now, without discussing this further, let us limit ourselves to taking note of the thesis Napoleon formulated in his testament from St Helena, comparing himself to the first US president as far as the strengthening of executive power was concerned, while adding that this inevitably took different political and institutional forms, owing to the different situation of the two countries.

The reference to the US model reappears with even greater vigour in Louis-Napoleon, who stayed in that country for a few months in 1837, after being forced into exile by the July Monarchy following a failed attempt at insurrection. We do not know whether it is really true that, thanks to 'his knowledge of the institutions of various European countries', Louis-Napoleon was really 'admirably prepared to observe and study in depth the United States and its government', or whether he really 'later implemented in France some of the ideas with which he had become acquainted in the United States'.[3] What is certain is that he visited the republic on the other side of the Atlantic a few years after Tocqueville, at a time when General Jackson, setting himself on a collision course with the old notables, had largely abolished property qualifications within the white community, while also encouraging the mission of expansion into the Far West, in the context of a policy that greatly strengthened presidential powers.

Indeed, Louis-Napoleon spoke of the mission that 'Providence has entrusted to the United States of America . . . to populate and gain for civilisation all that vast territory that extends from the Atlantic to the South Seas, and from the North Pole to the Equator'. Along with Russia,

2 Frédéric Bluche, *Le bonapartisme. Aux origines de la droite autoritaire (1800–1850)* (Paris: Nouvelles Éditions Latines, 1980), p. 354.

3 Hendrik N. Boon, *Rêve et réalité dans l'oeuvre économique et sociale de Napoléon III* (The Hague: Nijhoff, 1936), pp. 15ff.

America was one of the two countries that, unlike the 'old European centre', advanced 'without hesitation, towards perfection'. The difference was that, while the former did so 'by the will of one man', the latter did so 'by freedom' – that is, by 'putting into practice the old adage *laissez faire, laissez passer* to favour the irresistible instinct that drives the peoples of America toward the West'. This passage clearly echoes a judgement of Tocqueville, who is explicitly quoted at another point.[4] In *Democracy in America* we read:

> Today there are two great peoples on earth who, starting from different points, seem to advance toward the same goal: these are the Russians and the Anglo-Americans . . .
>
> The one combats the wilderness and barbarism; the other, civilization clothed in all its arms. Consequently the conquests of the American are made with the farmer's plow, those of the Russian with the soldier's sword. To reach his goal the first relies on personal interest, and, without directing them, allows the strength and reason of individuals to operate. The second in a way concentrates all the power of society in one man. The one has as principal means of action liberty; the other, servitude.[5]

Perhaps Louis-Napoleon or one of his ideologues may have read in Tocqueville's work that the American president, 'the one and only representative of the executive power of the Union', 'possesses some nearly royal prerogatives'.[6] What is certain is that Bonapartist propaganda for the revision of the Constitution, before the coup d'état, explicitly and repeatedly referred to the American model, declaring its wish to draw inspiration from it as regards 'the position of the head of state'. The French Constitution suffered a serious contradiction insofar as, while it had a president elected through universal suffrage, thus considering him somehow the representative of the nation, it then placed him in a 'subordinate position' with respect to the legislature.[7] But in France, too,

4 Napoléon III, *Œuvres* (Paris: Plon-Amyot, 1861), vol. 1, pp. 24ff, 98.

5 Alexis de Tocqueville, *Democracy in America* (Indianapolis, IN: Liberty Fund, 2012), pp. 655–6.

6 Ibid., pp. 202, 209.

7 Adolphe Granier de Cassagnac, *La révision de la Constitution* (Paris: Plon, 1851), pp. 25, 8.

it was argued, the head of the executive must have 'real, serious, effective power'. The new institutional framework being demanded was summarised in the following terms:

> On the one hand, a government committed to acting and not to speaking, to administering and not to legislating, can devote all its time, all its forces to the public good, instead of using them in miserable agitations and struggles. On the other hand, the legislative power, being engaged only by making laws, and not in making and unmaking governments, will at last find itself in the ordinary conditions of calm, wisdom, and patriotism which befit a deliberative body.[8]

The legislative power should stop overstepping its own competences: it is there to 'examine, discuss, control, moderate, but not direct'.[9] It was, conversely, up to the president of the republic to direct and govern, to ensure obedience to the laws, and to represent the unity of the nation, and it was he who would independently choose his ministers – his 'necessary agents': 'Guardians of his thought and organs of his will, it is indispensable that they depend on him and be devoted to him.'[10]

The American Federalists' 'Coup d'État'

The American model was followed quite closely here, as can be deduced also from the fact that the main target of this polemic was 'the parliamentary regime, its predominance and the oblivion of the executive authority's role'.[11] Was this not also the enemy of the protagonists of the Philadelphia Convention, which gave rise to the US Constitution? Given the reference made to the United States and its Constitution by those stressing the need for a strong executive power in France – indeed, from the 1799 coup d'état onward – it is worth taking a closer look at this document and its historical genesis.

The decisive event behind the US Constitution was the uprising mounted by poor and indebted peasants in Massachusetts in 1786–87.

8 Ibid., pp. 23, 40ff.
9 Ibid., p. 46.
10 Ibid., p. 25.
11 Ibid., p. 8.

Led by Daniel Shays, a retired colonel from the Continental Army that had defeated Britain, they rebelled against the auctioning-off of their land and property at low prices and against the imprisonment of debtors. On this point, the American legislation was harsh and ruthless. A few decades later, Tocqueville observed that in the United States the poor were imprisoned even for absolutely insignificant debts: it could be calculated that, in Pennsylvania, 7,000 individuals annually were arrested for their debts; if we add to this figure the number of those condemned for more serious crimes, the result was that more or less one in every 144 inhabitants ended up in prison each year.[12]

But let us return to the developments of the American Revolution. Although harshly repressed with the intervention of the militia, the agitation and revolt of the poor peasants threw the landowning classes into panic. The looming 'catastrophe' made John Jay (signer of the peace treaty and scion of a rich family of New York traders) 'more restless and more worried than during the war' against the English, and he communicated these worries to George Washington. The now retired general also received a letter from another interlocutor, who portrayed a dramatic dilemma: either 'submit to the horrors of anarchy and licentiousness' promoted by the 'lower order' of the population and by a 'class whose desperate fortunes are remediable only by the ruin of society', or else put an end to 'weak and feeble governments' once and for all. This latter option would demand the immediate imposition of 'a permanent capable government' provided with 'that power which is indispensably necessary to chastise evil and reward virtue'. Such was the picture painted by Henry Lee, delegate of Virginia, in a letter also addressed to Washington.[13] General Knox had just returned from Massachusetts, where he had been sent by Congress in order to quell the revolt in which were involved – he reported with alarm – 'a body of about 12 or 15,000 desperate & unprincipled men' recruited 'chiefly of the young & active part of the community', prey to strange and monstrous ideas of land redistribution, of 'agrarian laws' and even of 'common property'.

12 Alexis de Tocqueville, *Œuvres complètes*, Mayer edition, vol. 4: I, pp. 323ff.

13 Angela and Willi Adams, *Die Amerikanische Revolution und die Verfassung* (Munich: DTV, 1987), pp. 309ff [TN: Text of 8 September 1786 letter from founders.archives.org].

General Washington, in turn, communicated the 'melancholy accounts' from Knox to Madison, together with the conclusion he had drawn from it. For Washington, to escape 'anarchy & confusion' it would take 'a liberal & energetic constitution' and some 'alteration in our political creed'.[14] It was necessary to abandon – he had already observed in a letter to Jay – 'too good an opinion of human nature', unaware of the need for a strong central power to curb vice and evil inclinations.[15] The sense of the political turn taking place in America was well grasped by the French envoy, who reported back to Paris that this was a matter of establishing on solid bases 'the clear predominance of the rich and the big landowners'. In order to achieve this objective, it was necessary to liquidate definitively the aspirations to 'perfect democracy', to 'absolute freedom', to 'the abolition of the Senate', and to measures in favour of poor and indebted peasants claimed by the 'people' or the 'lower people'. Indeed, in order to neutralise, and eventually tame, the latter, a strong 'executive authority' was now called for.[16] Its strengthening was invoked not only, or not even mainly, to overcome the limits of a confederation continually exposed to the risk of disintegration, so much as to avert the feared popular and plebeian threat. The great goal of the construction of a nation-state on a federal basis was thus set under a clearly conservative hegemony.

Indeed, because of the political climate we have seen already, the Convention that met in Philadelphia was composed of men 'overwhelmingly conservative in their general philosophy of politics', who, working in strict secrecy – and going far beyond their mandate, which only foresaw a reform of the 'Articles' of Confederation – drafted a totally new constitutional text which enormously strengthened the central power: 'If Napoleon had done such a thing, it would have been pronounced a coup d'état.'[17] In this case, the comparison between Washington and the protagonist of Brumaire was not so much made by Napoleon III himself,

14 US State Department, *Documentary History of the Constitution of the United States of America* (Washington, DC: Department of State, 1905), p. 34.

15 To John Jay from George Washington, 15 August 1786, available at founders.archives.org.

16 In Samuel Eliot Morison, ed., *Sources and Documents Illustrating the American Revolution and the Formation of the Federal Constitution 1764–1788* (Oxford: Oxford University Press, 1965), pp. 220–5.

17 Allan Nevins and Henry S. Commager, *America: The Story of a Free People* (Oxford: Clarendon, 1947), pp. 106, 108.

but rather by two contemporary American historians. Such an assessment is implicitly bolstered by the analysis advanced, already long before them, by a historian who would himself ascend to the presidency of the United States. From a legal point of view, Woodrow Wilson points out, the original Constitution could have been modified only on the basis of the unanimous consent of the signatory states; even if, as an exception to legality, there could 'have been a counting of heads the country through, a majority would have been found opposed to the [new] constitution; yet the protagonists of the Philadelphia Convention had 'not taken measures to please, but measures to save the country'.[18] That is to say, the political-constitutional turn was legitimated neither by the existing legal system nor by the appeal to popular sovereignty, but by the absolute necessity of sparing the country from the looming threat of attacks on property, anarchy and chaos.

This is the same principle usually used to provide legitimacy to coups; and tellingly, the spectre of the coup, or its danger, was evoked already by contemporary opponents of the new Constitution.[19] The protagonists of this political turn were dominated by the concern to develop the most effective instruments for repressing eventual popular uprisings. We find this as we leaf through *The Federalist Papers*: there is recurrent reference to Shays' Rebellion, to the 'civil war' in Massachusetts and to the need to constitute an authority able to 'break and control the violence of faction' (no. 10) and 'rescue us from impending anarchy' (no. 15).[20] There was a constantly lurking danger of 'wars and rebellions'; to 'guard the body politic against these two most mortal diseases of society' (no. 34), it was necessary to build up 'bod[ies] of troops', first and foremost required because of the threat coming from within the country, as demonstrated by the well-known case of Massachusetts, as well as Pennsylvania, where even the most hesitant had been convinced of the need for a standing army, at least 'as long as there is any appearance of danger to the public peace' (no. 25).

To be prepared for any eventuality, it was an absolute necessity to have a government with 'energy' (no. 37), a 'vigorous executive' (no. 70)

18 Woodrow Wilson, *A History of the American People* (New York: Harper & Brothers, 1902), vol. 3, pp. 80, 70.

19 Adams and Adams, *Die Amerikanische Revolution*, p. 361.

20 TN: All texts from *The Federalist Papers* are here cited from the Library of Congress website.

also able, if necessary, to challenge the 'displeasure' of 'the people' and able to 'act his own opinion with vigor and decision' (no. 71), an executive in a position to command all armed bodies in a centralised manner – including, if need be, the 'militia of the several States' (no. 69). So, we can well understand the arguments of those who have seen in the Philadelphia Convention not only a 'peaceful coup d'état' – indeed, such an interpretation is quite commonplace – but a coup d'état which, in its obedience to the 'model of the Leviathan-state', represented 'the victory of Hobbes over Locke'.[21]

France and America: How to Leave the Revolution Behind

This is an excessive judgement and, as we shall see, also misleading. It is worth reflecting, first of all, on the characteristics of the political regime baptised by the new Constitution, starting from a comparison with the events in France that concluded with the triumph of Napoleon Bonaparte. The upheavals in late-eighteenth-century America and Europe have sometimes been spoken of as a single 'Western, or more precisely, Atlantic, revolution'.[22] But, if such a definition is a judicious one, we immediately have the problem of comparing not only the beginnings of the different revolutions and the manner of their unfolding, but also their conclusion: if the French Revolution ended, albeit temporarily, in 1799, the American one ended, definitively, in 1788–89, with the passing of the new Constitution. In both countries, an acute social crisis led to the rise to power of a general bathed in glory. Domestically, in each case, the concern was to reabsorb or crush the radical tendencies that had emerged in the course of previous upheavals. 'The revolution is over', Napoleon proclaimed as he presented the project for a new Constitution, immediately after the coup. *The Federalist* expressed itself in similar terms as it illustrated the results of the Philadelphia Convention: 'It was a thing hardly to be expected that in a popular revolution the minds of men should stop at that happy mean' (no. 26); it was

21 Hans Wehler, *Grundzüge der amerikanischen Außenpolitik 1750–1900* (Frankfurt: Suhrkamp, 1984), p. 58.

22 Jacques Godechot, *La grande nation: l'expansion révolutionnaire de la France dans le monde de 1789 à 1799* (Paris: Aubier, 1956), p. 6.

now time to bring a close to a period (made up of 'universal ardor for new and opposite forms') that had left its mark on 'all the existing constitutions' in the single states (no. 49).

With his usual lucidity, and with greater frankness, the French envoy summarised in the following terms the conclusions reached by the 'most enlightened patriots' following the 'unpleasant event' that was Shays' Rebellion: 'It has become clear to them that, at the time when the Constitutions arose, when they urgently needed the support of the lower people, they had to make more concessions to the latter than is compatible with the stability of public order, the security of the citizenry, and the agility of the government's functioning'; it was now necessary to place the emphasis on 'tranquillity and public order' rather than on liberty and participation.[23]

The same problem presented itself in France, indeed in more dramatic terms, in a country where the strength of the popular masses was felt far more acutely, and where first Thermidor and then Brumaire were greeted even in liberal circles as a liberation from the threat of the 'populace' or rabble, which could now, finally, be militarily and politically neutralised. This helps us understand the violent polemic against 'brute democracy' that Sieyès and the press outlets close to him unleashed immediately after the 1799 coup d'état, as well as the related clarification that the representative regime simply consisted of the delegation of full powers to a 'representative elite' – a 'class of representatives' which the people had no right to disturb, not even by petition, once it had taken power.[24] But in America, too, *The Federalist* took care to make clear that 'the republic' differed from democracies (which had 'ever been spectacles of turbulence and contention'), insofar as the former, founded on the 'system of representation', consisted in the 'delegation of the government . . . to a small number of citizens elected by the rest', also in this case with the substantial exclusion of any autonomous space for popular initiative (no. 10). Both the build-up to the Philadelphia Convention and its work were dominated by the preoccupation – again inspired by the Massachusetts 'rebellion' – to put an end to 'anarchy' and 'the excesses of democracy' and to the agitation of demagogues or 'pretended

23 In Morison, *Sources and Documents*, p. 221.

24 Bredin, *Sieyès*, pp. 468, 475n.

patriots'.[25] In turn, opponents of the new Constitution denounced it as an indirect instrument to establish the political monopoly of the upper classes, who considered themselves the 'natural aristocracy of the country': the very low number of deputies and senators envisaged therein would also make it difficult for exponents of the lower and poorer social classes to secure election.[26] It is interesting to see how these criticisms were rebutted by the protagonists of this same political turn: *The Federalist* replied that it was only natural that 'representative bodies' should be exclusively composed of 'landholders, merchants, and men of the learned professions. But where is the danger that the interests and feelings of the different classes of citizens will not be understood or attended to by these three descriptions of men?' Rather, it was clear that the 'opulent landowner', having at heart the fate of agriculture as a whole, would also be able to interpret the will of the 'middling farmer', whereas 'artisans and manufacturers' (i.e. manufacturing workers) would 'commonly be disposed to bestow their votes upon merchants and those whom they recommend', obviously interested in promoting and guaranteeing the well-being of the economic activities with which their own wealth was connected. Besides, why should artisans and workers elect other artisans and workers, as if there were no reason for competition between them? It was more feasible and more logical for them to have a merchant represent them. Lastly, the exponents of the learned professions, enjoying a 'neutrality to the rivalships between the different branches of industry', offered a further guarantee for the respect of the 'general interests of the society' (no. 35).

More or less radical critics of the new Constitution objected to the political monopoly of representative bodies by those with the privilege of *otium*; were they not ignorant or distant from the 'common concerns of the people'?[27] Hamilton retorted that, because members of the lower classes were conscious that their 'habits in life', consisting of hard toil, meant that they lacked the 'talents' necessary to serve any worthy role in a representative assembly, they instead relied with full confidence on the superior knowledge of the upper classes (no. 35). For Hamilton, indeed,

25 Max Farrand, *The Records of the Federal Convention of 1787* (New Haven, CT: Yale University Press, 1911), vol. I, pp. 18ff, 48.

26 Adams and Adams, *Die Amerikanische Revolution*, pp. 362, 381ff.

27 Ibid., p. 383.

they were right to do so. Speaking at the New York Assembly for the ratification of the new Constitution, the Federalist leader went even further, as he observed that, on the moral as well as the intellectual level, 'the advantage of character belongs to the wealthy. Their vices are probably more favorable to the prosperity of the state, than those of the indigent; and partake less of moral depravity.'[28]

In America, as in France, *otium* continued to be considered the indispensable condition for acquiring the knowledge and probity necessary to be capable of participating in the community's political leadership. Meanwhile, the idea of the popular classes having autonomous representation and political initiative was dismissed as the height of absurdity. On both sides of the Atlantic, about a decade apart, the two coups d'état (with or without quotation marks) carried out at the end of the two revolutions aimed to neutralise the radical and plebeian drives that had characterised them. As General Washington put it, this meant sweeping away 'anarchy and confusion' and guaranteeing the 'life, liberty and property' of citizens within the framework of a 'liberal & energetic constitution'; or, in the words of the aforementioned two proclamations by General Bonaparte, it meant completing the 'dispersal of factious elements' and establishing a 'representative government' endowed with 'strong and stable' powers, which would thus be capable of defending 'the sacred rights of property, equality, and liberty'. Similar social and political concerns were brewing on either side of the Atlantic: while the Philadelphia Convention reassured creditors frightened by the agitation among indebted peasants, Napoleon abolished the progressive income tax, which the propertied had denounced as a form of robbery.[29] If we abstract from the religious situation, the American Federalists expressed positions very close to those of the 'French bourgeoisie that had become conservative and to its extreme interpreter, Sieyès'.[30]

Even the language was quite similar. Just as the 'Proclamation du général en chef Bonaparte' of 19 Brumaire associated 'conservative' and 'liberal' ideas, on the eve of the Philadelphia Convention, General

28 Alexander Hamilton, *The Papers*, vol. 5: *June 1788–November 1789* (New York: Columbia University Press, 1962).

29 Alfred Cobban, *Dictatorship: Its History and Theory* (New York: Haskell, 1971), p. 87.

30 Georges Lefebvre, *La Révolution française* (Paris: Presses Universitaires de France, 1951), p. 606.

Washington coined a sort of advertising motto – 'liberal & energetic' – in order to illustrate and propagandise for the Constitution called upon to put off the danger of social subversion once and for all. In each case, liberal was synonymous with conservative, as counterposed to the now restless and troubling world of mechanical labour, servile and distant from the liberal arts.[31] A few years earlier, Sieyès, not accidentally among the inspirers of Napoleon's coup, had celebrated those classes whose 'affluence' enabled them to 'receive a liberal education'.[32] Washington similarly contrasted those familiar with the 'liberal arts' with 'mechanics'.[33] In the moment of Brumaire, Madame de Staël hoped for the definitive consolidation of the power of the well-to-do and wealthy, of the *gens de biens* or *honnètes gens*; in America, we have seen Hamilton and John Quincy Adams speak of the ruling elite as the 'rich and well-born', as opposed to the 'mass of the people', composed of 'mechanics' and others devoid of culture and 'liberal' education.[34]

Immediately after Shays' Rebellion, Washington reported to Jay that influential figures also favoured a 'monarchical form of government'.[35] Hamilton's monarchical sympathies were known to be shared by other delegates, such as Dickinson (from Delaware), though the latter was well aware of the impracticality of such an 'experiment', unfortunately alien to the 'spirit of the times'.[36] Indeed, the 'British option' faced overwhelming and perhaps insuperable unpopularity at a time when memories still burned of the war against the England of George III, whom the Declaration of Independence had cast as a tyrant who had shown 'Cruelty & perfidy scarcely paralleled in the most barbarous ages, and totally unworthy the Head of a civilized nation'. Nonetheless, the former homeland continued to inspire the search for instruments to control popular pressure and social tensions. In January 1788, Washington

31 Department of State, *Documentary History of the Constitution*, vol. 4, pp. 34ff.

32 Emmanuel-Joseph Sieyès, *Écrits politiques* (Paris: Éditions des archives contemporaines, 1985), p. 133.

33 George Washington, *A Collection*, ed. W. B. Allen (Indianapolis, IN: Liberty Classics, 1988), pp. 397, 455.

34 Henri Guillemin, *Benjamin Constant muscadin 1795–1799* (Paris: Gallimard, 1958), pp. 182ff.

35 To John Jay from George Washington, 15 August 1786, available at founders.archives.org.

36 Charles C. Tansill, *Documents Illustrative of the Formation of the Union of the American State* (Washington, DC: Government Printing Office, 1927), p. 143.

received a letter from Knox who, informing him that in Massachusetts the upper classes were overwhelmingly in favour of the project for a new Constitution launched in Philadelphia, added that 'many of them would have been still more pleased with the new Constitution had it been more analagous [*sic*] to the british [*sic*] Constitution'.[37] Already at the Philadelphia Convention, Dickinson had spoken out explicitly in favour of the creation of a House of Lords; Hamilton also leaned towards this, holding that a senate made up of lifetime members was necessary to protect 'the few', namely 'the rich and well born', from the envy and possible assault of 'the many'.[38] But even the introduction of an upper chamber on the English model appeared problematic in a country that, with little or no feudal tradition behind it, could not easily invent hereditary life peers endowed with a centuries-old prestige.

France had to confront similar difficulties: although the nobility had been decimated by the colossal political upheavals and the civil war, it remained possible to set up a House of Lords even if, due to the break represented by the Revolution, it could not count on the prestige deriving from an interrupted tradition, as in the British case. Putting aside the now discredited Bourbon dynasty, it was even possible to mount a search for a new dynasty. But, as the brief experience of the July Monarchy had shown, even this solution had serious drawbacks. For, while it did not placate the republican opposition, it divided the royalist front, and could thus no longer count on the sacred aura in which, according to Bagehot, the Crown had the gift of bathing power itself.

The Shadow of Ancient Roman Dictatorship

In conclusion, the two coups d'état on either side of the Atlantic sought to re-establish the traditional political monopoly held by wealth and *otium*. But, also under the pressure of the objective situation, the political regime called upon to achieve this objective ended up assuming new traits – ones that went beyond the consciousness and intentions of the protagonists and would only gradually come to light through

37 To George Washington from Henry Knox, 14 January 1788, available at founders.archives.org.

38 Morison, *Sources and Documents*, p. 259.

subsequent historical development. We can take our cue from the above-cited letter of January 1788, in which Knox informed Washington that the upper classes of Massachusetts would have preferred a British-style constitution, and in any case favoured the 'most vigorous government'.[39] In fact, some went even further: after the debtors' rebellion, Jay observed in June 1786 that the 'better kind of people' (i.e. the richest families) had begun to be entirely indifferent to the 'charms of liberty', while they were ready for any remedy that would put an end to the 'insecurity of property', guaranteeing 'quiet and security'.[40] Thus, there was no lack of elements of the ruling class attracted by the idea of a more or less open dictatorship. But, much like the monarchical option, the latter solution was very problematic in a country that had just come out of a revolution that had raised the banner of liberty, and on this basis managed to rouse the enthusiasm necessary to defeat the British troops.

The Philadelphia Convention instead opted for a strong executive. But what form should this take? In contrast to France, from the outset there was a widespread and clear awareness in American ruling circles that this power must be embodied in a single person: it was imperative to avoid paralysing signs of discord or uncertainty emerging from within its ranks. *The Federalist* observed: 'In the conduct of war, in which the energy of the Executive is the bulwark of the national security, every thing would be to be apprehended from its plurality.' The decisive argument was war, be it civil or international (no. 70). The powers conferred upon the president were so broad that he appeared, to the opponents of the new Constitution, as not unlike the crowned heads of old Europe. Given the still vivid passions stirred by the struggle against the 'tyrant' George III, a mark of shame threatened to hang over the supreme magistracy; but *The Federalist* levelled an accusation of 'deliberate imposture and deception' against those who evoked 'the gross pretense of a similitude between a king of Great Britain and a magistrate of the character marked out for that of the President of the United States' (no. 67). There were, doubtless, differences. Yet in a later article demonstrating the full consonance of the 'vigorous Executive . . . with the genius of republican government', this same author tellingly referred to another institution:

39 Department of State, *Documentary History of the Constitution*, vol. 4, p. 442.
40 Morison, *Sources and Documents*, p. 215.

> Every man the least conversant in Roman story, knows how often that republic was obliged to take refuge in the absolute power of a single man, under the formidable title of Dictator, as well against the intrigues of ambitious individuals who aspired to the tyranny, and the seditions of whole classes of the community whose conduct threatened the existence of all government, as against the invasions of external enemies who menaced the conquest and destruction of Rome (*The Federalist*, no. 70).

Evident in this description is a certain sympathy, or at least understanding attitude, towards the Roman dictatorship: and we should not forget that, for *The Federalist*, republican ancient Rome was synonymous with freedom (no. 41). But what deserved imitation was not the consulate as an institution; indeed, because of the division of executive power, this had brought Rome many 'mischiefs', from which negative lessons could and must be drawn: 'That unity is conducive to energy will not be disputed. *Decision*, *activity*, *secrecy*, and *despatch* will generally characterize the proceedings of one man in a much more eminent degree than the proceedings of any greater number' (no. 68).

We might reflect on the nouns used here, which I have italicised, and on the fact that the subject of the decisive, active, secret, rapid action here desired is a single person who does not have to share power with any colleague or collaborator. Clearly, here we are looking at a state of exception, deriving from internal or international conflict. And the figure of the president was ever-liable to transform into that of the dictator of republican Rome. Contemporaries of the Philadelphia Convention expressed deep concern over the fact that the Constitution explicitly provided for the suspension of the 'Privilege of the Writ of Habeas Corpus . . . when in Cases of Rebellion or Invasion the public Safety may require it' (art. 1, section 9, clause 2). From Paris, Jefferson protested that he would like to see the enshrinement of 'the eternal and unremitting force of the habeas corpus laws' and the absolute inviolability of a bill of rights that the Constitution ought to have carefully specified.[41] Similar protests arising in Pennsylvania and elsewhere were immediately countered by the Federalist Noah Webster, who asked in a defiant, sarcastic tone, 'Do you really mean to say that it is never lawful to

41 Jefferson to Madison, 20 December 1787, available at founders.archives.gov.

suspend *habeas corpus* and the rights of liberty?'[42] Rather, in emergency situations, the powers granted to the federal authority

> *ought to exist without limitation*, BECAUSE IT IS IMPOSSIBLE TO FORESEE OR DEFINE THE EXTENT AND VARIETY OF NATIONAL EXIGENCIES, OR THE CORRESPONDENT EXTENT AND VARIETY OF THE MEANS WHICH MAY BE NECESSARY TO SATISFY THEM. The circumstances that endanger the safety of nations are infinite, and for this reason *no constitutional shackles can wisely be imposed on the power* to which the care of it is committed . . . *there can be no limitation of that authority which is to provide for the defense and protection of the community*, in any matter essential to its efficacy (*The Federalist*, no. 23).

The sort of dictatorship here theorised was legitimate and necessary whenever the 'preservation of the public peace' was in danger, whether threatened by 'internal convulsions' or 'external attacks'. It is true that the Constitution does not grant the ability to suspend habeas corpus exclusively to the president. But given that it is, in any case, up to the president to 'preserve, protect and defend' the Constitution itself, to direct all the armed forces, and to 'take Care that the Laws be faithfully executed' (art. 2, sections 2 and 3), it is clear that he, as the subsequent history of the United States was to show, would be in an absolutely privileged situation to decree a state of emergency and assume full powers. A new political regime was being born: and it certainly had little to do with monarchy (here, Hamilton was perfectly right), or indeed with the traditional rule of gentlemen and the 'well-born' so dear to Hamilton, John Adams and many of the architects or supporters of the new Constitution. The extraordinary breadth of powers placed in the hands of the so-called 'supreme Magistrate of the United States' did not stand in contradiction with popular investiture. *The Federalist* offered a telling description of a famous figure of ancient Greece: 'Solon, according to Plutarch, was in a manner compelled, by the universal suffrage of his fellow-citizens, to take upon him the sole and absolute power of new-modeling the constitution' (no. 38). While this discourse was articulated in the terms of the past, what it described was the operation of a regime

42 Adams and Adams, *Die Amerikanische Revolution*, p. 366.

tending towards Bonapartism, combining a very broad investiture from below with an extremely extensive – in emergency situations, even absolute – exercise of power.

The Liberal Tradition, the State of Exception and the US Constitution

However, it would be equally misleading to say that the Philadelphia Convention represented the victory of Hobbes over Locke. It should, moreover, be noted that reflection on the state of exception and on dictatorship has accompanied all modern thought. It is present, for example, in Rousseau, who also foresaw, in situations of particularly acute crisis – again, invoking the ancient Roman example – the recourse to a dictatorship of 'very short' duration, which should not be liable to extension under any circumstances.[43] Reflection on this theme plays an important role in the liberal tradition. Montesquieu had no doubt that it is part of the 'custom of the freest peoples that have ever been on earth' to 'put a veil over freedom for a moment, just as the statues of the gods are hidden'.[44] For Locke, the state of distress provoked by an attack, of whatever form and origin, against private property justifies the recourse not only to exceptional measures but also to a sort of total war. So much so, indeed, that its perpetrators deserve to be treated 'as any other wild beast, or noxious brute, with whom mankind can have neither society nor security'.[45]

The peculiarity of the liberal tradition lies in the fact that the internal state of exception is conceived with reference to the attacks that can be made on the existing political-social order not only or mainly by the Crown or by the executive, but also and above all by the legislature.[46] Montesquieu puts this in unequivocal terms when, having denounced the 'delirium for liberty' that led the plebeians of ancient Rome to strip the patricians of their 'share in legislative power' and to subject them to the

43 Rousseau, *The Social Contract*, Book 4, Chapter 6, in *The Social Contract and The First and Second Discourses* (New Haven, CT: Yale University Press, 2002), p. 244.

44 Charles-Louis de Secondat de Montesquieu, 'Esprit des lois', in *Œuvres completes* (Paris: Gallimard, 1949–51), Book 12, Chapter 19.

45 Locke, *Two Treatises of Government*, p. 383, §§171–2.

46 Ibid., §§201, 226.

'legislative power of another body of the state', he exalts another 'admirable institution': namely, the dictatorship thanks to which the sovereign people was forced to 'lower its head and the most popular laws were kept silent'.[47] Behind warnings against the possible prevarications of the legislature was the historical experience of the first English revolution and the Levellers' movement. The lesson provided by the two liberal philosophers – as mediated by the distress caused by Shays' Rebellion and by the manifestation, also on American shores, of what Madison calls the 'leveling spirit' – had a profound effect on the Philadelphia Convention.[48] Many delegates agreed with James Wilson on the need to confront, above all else, the danger of 'legislative despotism'; and many agreed with Gouverneur Morris in thinking 'the public liberty in greater danger from Legislative usurpations than any other source': 'Emissions of paper money, largesses to the people – a remission of debts and similar measures' were especially to be feared.[49] Claims as to the danger of 'unjust and pernicious laws' and 'pernicious measures' being introduced, especially in individual states, recurred obsessively in a whole series of interventions.[50]

So, the inspirers and authors of the US Constitution were not only thinking of a state of exception caused by a war or by a violent popular uprising. If, in the columns of *The Federalist*, Madison referred primarily to the possibility of a victorious popular rebellion in a single state, in the confidential debates in Philadelphia he expressed the view that an 'emergency' could arise even with the simple formation of a parliamentary majority that imposed 'unjust laws' through which 'debtors defrauded their creditors'. Again, we see the shadow of Shays. This danger was all the more concrete given that, with demographic increase, America, too, was bound to see a rise in the number of the 'poor', i.e. those who 'labour under all the hardships of life, & secretly sigh for a more equal distribution of its blessings'.[51] Even a moderate redistribution of income through legislation ought to be seen as an attack on property, which called for, or could call for, the state of exception.

47 Montesquieu, 'Esprit des lois', Book 11, Chapter 16.

48 Tansill, *Documents Illustrative of the Formation of the Union*, p. 280.

49 Farrand, *Records of the Federal Convention of 1787*, vol. 1, p. 261.

50 Tansill, *Documents Illustrative of the Formation of the Union*, pp. 425, 427, 450. See also Alberto Aquarone, *Due costituenti settecentesche. Note sulla Convenzione di Filadelfia e sulla Assemblea nazionale francese* (Pisa: Nistri-Lischi, 1959), pp. 29–43.

51 Ibid., pp. 163, 280.

Present, at a latent level, already in representative bodies, the danger for owners and the 'few' that they would be isolated or fall into a minority was even graver in society at large. Yes, Shays' Rebellion was a minority affair, but, what if a new popular uprising rallied 'a majority of PERSONS, by the accession of alien residents, of a casual concourse of adventurers, or of those whom the constitution of the State has not admitted to the rights of suffrage?' And this is not to mention blacks, that 'unhappy species of population abounding in some of the States, who, during the calm of regular government, are sunk below the level of men; but who, in the tempestuous scenes of civil violence, may emerge into the human character, and give a superiority of strength to any party with which they may associate themselves'. Given this potentially explosive mix of poor Americans, immigrants and black slaves, it should be concluded that social subversion could prevail, even if just in a single state; and one of the most important 'advantages' of the federal union – Madison observes, quoting Montesquieu – is 'that should a popular insurrection happen in one of the States, the others are able to quell it' (*The Federalist*, no. 43).

As we can see, alongside Locke, here is another liberal author who helps us to think about the state of exception. Particular attention was bound to be paid to this question in a country like the United States, whose population has developed through successive waves of importing black slaves or white semi-slaves. Especially in the case of the former, revolt has always been (or has always been considered to be) lurking, with each international conflict stoking the fear of an internal front emerging, fed by the complicity or conspiracy of America's enemies. Indeed, it is not possible or easy to distinguish between internal and external enemies, between civil war and war proper, when a considerable mass of 'aliens' already live within the homeland.

The Constitution that emanated from the Philadelphia Convention inherited and further radicalised the attention that the liberal tradition had directed towards the state of exception, with an eye to the feared prevarications of the legislature. But the remedy was no longer to be found in a hereditary House of Lords with veto rights over the more or less popular branch of parliament, as in Locke and Montesquieu. Rather, it now lay in a strong executive concentrated in the hands of a single person – namely a president susceptible to transformation at any moment into a dictator, in the Roman sense of the term.

France Between Imperial Presidency and Presidential Empire

On both sides of the Atlantic, the revolution ended in the rise of Bonapartist tendencies. But there is a further reason not to isolate Brumaire from its international context: if the revolution was 'Western' or 'Atlantic', so too was the struggle against it, or at least its radical and plebeian tendencies. A year before Napoleon's coup d'état, the Alien and Sedition Acts were passed in the United States, imposing severe restrictions on constitutional freedoms, and particularly striking at the American-based followers of French revolutionary ideas. Already a few years earlier, in 1794, Britain had suspended habeas corpus: 'troops occupied most of the industrial areas as if they were conquered territory . . . Pitt, backed by a large share of public opinion, relentlessly persecuted all those who showed themselves favourable to liberal ideas or otherwise inclined to French ideas.'[52]

Is there a relationship between these events and, in particular, the events in the two countries that had just come out of two great revolutions? As we have seen, Napoleon invoked the name of Washington: the propaganda aspect of this move is obvious; indeed, it has often been emphasised. Yet it seems worth asking whether the powers of the First Consul were really more extensive at this time than those of the president of the United States, who could now count on the very wide margin of discretion granted to him by the Alien and Sedition Acts. These Acts had been issued also with the agreement of Washington – indeed, it was he who would direct the mighty army which had been put together in the meantime, more with an eye towards the internal enemy than any external foe.[53] The old American general and statesman's support for 'these extraordinary laws' can be explained by the fact – Woodrow Wilson would later observe – that he 'so passionately . . . love[d] order, hate[d] faction, and fear[ed] for the safety of the new Union'.[54] But does not such a motivation also apply to the French case? Was the danger of Jacobinism and 'anarchy' less acute in this country than in America?

52 Jean-Marie Poursin and Gabriel Dupuy, *Malthus* (Paris: Seuil, 1972), pp. 61–4.

53 Bernard Bailyn and Gordon Wood, *The Great Republic: A History of the American People* (Lexington, MA: Heath, 1985), p. 244.

54 Wilson, *History of the American People*, vol. 3, p. 152.

It is true: while Washington retired from public life after completing his term in office, in 1802 Napoleon became consul for life. But it should not be forgotten that, even within the Philadelphia Convention, voices were raised in favour of a presidency or a supreme magistracy for life – and that Hamilton himself was inclined towards such a solution. Even the establishment of the hereditary empire was motivated in Napoleon by an ideological concern and a persuasion common to authors such as Burke, Necker and 'monarchical and also liberal' culture, for which 'power must be inseparable from an imposing apparatus of majesty that unleashes its power on the people's imaginations'.[55] In fact, here we are in the presence of a debate that would continue well into the nineteenth century. Bagehot explains the grandeur and stability of British institutions by citing the fact that, while effective power belongs to the unity of the executive and the legislature – as realised in the cabinet and in the person of the prime minister – the Crown, too, carries out a decisive function, despite being at a remove from the concrete action of governing and directing the country. For, in bathing power in a sacred aura, the Crown not only stimulates the filial submission of the lower classes but also legitimises, transfigures and consecrates the armed force necessary for the maintenance of order – the 'armies' which others are then called upon to direct and employ. Two distinct functions are thus entrusted to two different organs – the priestly-ideological one, so to speak, as well as the properly political-military one.[56]

Similar problems and preoccupations emerged in the debate that developed on the other side of the Atlantic, during the Philadelphia Convention and already in the build-up to it. Reporting on the mood among the most influential circles in the United States, the French envoy observed that their concern was not only to strengthen 'executive authority' drastically, but also to give it a different image and a greater capacity to grip the masses; it was necessary to put an end to 'political leaders' modest manner of presenting themselves to the multitude', which 'drew them its disdain' given that 'it judges only by its senses'. Hence, for America's rulers to enjoy the necessary 'respect', they would

55 François Furet, *La Révolution de Turgot à Jules Ferry 1770–1880* (Paris: Hachette,1988), p. 250.

56 Walter Bagehot, *The English Constitution: Introduction to Second Edition*, in *Collected Works*, ed. N. S. John-Stevas (London: Economist, 1974), vol. 5, p. 206.

also need to be provided with an external 'documentation of power, arms and soldiers'.[57] There was a widespread view in US ruling circles and among the most influential personalities that the central authority must avoid humble, unassuming tones and instead vaunt its 'imperial dignity'; Washington reported this opinion as commonplace, and indeed seemed to share in it.[58] In 1791, he would make a triumphant and 'elaborate tour of the country in the manner of a king' to seal the end of the crisis and a new beginning for the United States, endowed with a strong central authority led by the general-president.[59] In the absence of a monarchical tradition or of a king (or queen) who was also the head of the Anglican Church, the roles that the British Constitution kept distinct and entrusted to different bodies tended, in the United States, to be unified in the figure of the president. The latter would concentrate in his own person not only the strictly political-military function, but also the priestly-ideological function that was his responsibility as head and interpreter of a nation invested with a religious mission, and constituted, according to Puritan ideology, by the divinely elect.

The British model, as described by Bagehot, was no longer feasible in France, where, after the caesura of the Revolution, there was no uncontested dynasty capable of bathing power in a sacred aura. Moreover, the American solution was also impracticable, given the different religious tradition that lay behind it: in the Catholic world, the sacred is embodied in the Church and its hierarchy, and can only legitimise and transfigure political power to the extent that it is consecrated by the Church. In France, the identification of the priestly-ideological function and the political-military function was unimaginable, and, to the extent that it could take place, it would require the mediation of a Church (and an ecclesiastical hierarchy) that traditionally consecrated the old monarchical dynasties and that now, following a hard-won compromise with the new France, consecrated the new dynasty founded by Napoleon also for these reasons.

If Washington sealed the new Constitution and the creation of an absolutely pre-eminent presidency with a triumphal procession styled in the manner of a king, in France the establishment of the Empire was

57 Morison, *Sources and Documents*, p. 221.
58 To John Jay from George Washington, 15 August 1786.
59 Bailyn and Wood, *Great Republic*, p. 243.

sealed by a 'last homage to the republic' – that is, by a plebiscite even more massive than that which had ratified the Brumaire coup d'état.[60]

After a long parenthesis, Bonapartism reappeared in France upon the revolutionary crisis of 1848. Much as after Brumaire, the bourgeoisie was called not only to confront the proletarian agitation, but to fight on two or more fronts. Even taking for granted the need to strengthen the executive – a necessity felt both in France in 1799 and in the United States from Shays' Rebellion to the Philadelphia Convention – there was also the immediate question of choosing between republic and monarchy. We have seen Tocqueville briefly entertain the idea of a Bourbon restoration under the banner of a meekly liberal legitimism. This, even after the coup d'état was already completed. But, immediately after the collapse of the July Monarchy, the liberal bourgeoisie believed it could identify the French Washington in General Cavaignac, renowned as a republican hero for having 'saved' the republic from the workers' revolt of June and the Red danger. The new Constitution clearly cast an eye across the Atlantic. While it renounced the fiction of the electoral college, it provided for a popularly elected president who would, for this very reason, be invested with a legitimacy of his own, independent from the Legislative Assembly. This would allow the president to resist, as circumstances demanded, a chamber like the Jacobin Convention, too permeable to popular and plebeian pressures.[61]

But Cavaignac was defeated by Louis-Napoleon, who, at least initially, also wielded the US Constitution as a model. Here, it is worth looking back to the pamphlet circulated immediately before the coup. Granier de Cassagnac started from a premise that has its own precise logic: the situation in France could not be compared to that of Britain, where the aristocracy, far from being liquidated, continued to play a leading role. Britain's parliamentary system did not represent abstractly political individuals or parties, but rather expressed full-bodied social forces, 'the clergy, the nobility, the Commons . . . three orders united in sovereign assemblies', to which 'the monarchical power clearly finds itself subservient'.[62] The two houses of parliament thus exercised a function similar to that of the Estates General in France, where the situation had

60 Furet, *La Révolution*, p. 250.

61 Ibid., pp. 404–7.

62 Granier de Cassagnac, *La révision de la Constitution*, pp. 12ff.

changed radically on account of the anti-aristocratic moves taken by the Revolution, and even before that by the absolute monarchy. In Britain, the stability and solidity of the parliamentary system was guaranteed by the presence of 'three great bodies so ancient, so national, so strong, so intelligent, so united, so conservative, so liberal'. Conversely, 'in a country like France, where all the great bodies have been broken up or annihilated', where there was no longer any room for 'the great traditional and permanent interests', parliamentary majorities fluctuated in a vacuum, leaving them precarious and ever-exposed to the whims and ambitions of individuals and groups.[63] Under such conditions, the only possible counterweight to democracy and to the instability and prevarications of the legislature would be a strong executive, just as in the republic across the Atlantic.

For this reason, ministers would have to depend exclusively on the executive, of which they would be the 'necessary agents': thanks to such an arrangement,

> by electing a president for four years, the United States know in advance what system they will bring to power, and they then have the certainty that this system will be loyally followed and experimented for four years, without any obstacle being set in the way of the ministers charged with applying it, moreover applying it whatever this system may be, whether it be peace, or war, or banks, or freedom, or slavery, or the annexation of a new state.

Nor was there reason to fear that this would hand the president overweening powers, for 'the national representation, armed with its immense rights, having the budget in its hands, is always able to moderate, to contain this system, and to put up a dam against its invasions, should it become contrary to the real and evident interests of the country'; all this, once again, according to the US model.[64]

Bonapartist propaganda had no hesitation in invoking the *Spirit of Laws* – 'the best-known modern French book in America' – and, indeed, Montesquieu, the author particularly dear to *The Federalist*, without whom, it has been said, it is inconceivable that the US Constitution

63 Ibid., pp. 16–19.
64 Ibid., pp. 25ff.

could have taken the form that it did.[65] Yet, the pamphlet I have repeatedly cited observes that 'Montesquieu calls the division and independence of powers the very principle of liberty. And he adds that, if in any society, the man, the assembly, or the caste that makes the law also has the power to enforce it, then we have despotism, disorder, and anarchy.' It was thus necessary 'completely to separate the executive power from the legislative power': it hardly needs adding that the principle of the separation of powers invoked here was perfectly functional to the affirmation of an 'elevated central power, free and strong', unhampered by the legislature and by 'parliamentary omnipotence'.[66] Was this not also the US Constitution's approach?

Earlier on, we saw Bagehot championing the unity of the executive and the legislature; the American Federalists, as well as French Bonapartist propaganda, instead insisted upon the independence of the executive. But, despite the differences of language, in each case we see a common concern at work: namely, that a strong legislative power heavily under the sway of the popular masses would pose serious risks to property and to existing economic and social relations. The counterweight to what authoritative delegates to the Philadelphia Convention condemned as 'legislative despotism' and what Louis-Napoleon's ideologist branded 'parliamentary omnipotence' was identified – in Britain as in France and the United States – in the drastic personalisation of power, which was to be entrusted to a leader capable of neutralising the multitude politically. The liberal bourgeoisie in France had already started to move in this direction right after the February revolution, but in a series of alternating phases. In order to reduce the size of the legislature and exorcise the spectre of the Jacobin Convention, they had the president elected directly by the people on the basis of universal (male) suffrage, before then abolishing the latter in order to make way for a barely disguised property qualification, now called upon to perform the function of guarantor of private ownership. Bonapartist propaganda deftly exploited all this, not only playing on the frustrations of the now-disenfranchised classes, but also pointing out the contradictions in which the

65 Robert R. Palmer, *The Age of the Democratic Revolution: A Political History of Europe and America, 1760–1800* (Princeton, NJ: Princeton University Press, 2014), p. 46; Henry S. Maine, *Popular Government* (Indianapolis, IN: Liberty Classics, 1976 [1885]), p. 218.

66 Granier de Cassagnac, *La révision de la Constitution*, pp. 31, 37ff, 47.

liberal-moderate bloc was enveloped. Indeed, by having the president elected by the people but then making his ministers accountable to the legislature, Tocqueville showed that he had not learned much from his study of America – that is, he had not assimilated 'the feeling of that provision so simple and so sensible' that characterised the US Constitution.[67]

As we can see, in France it was Louis-Napoleon's party that presented itself to the people with a programme of American-style reforms, addressing it as follows in the appeal issued the day after the coup d'état:

> Convinced that the instability of power and the preponderance of a single Assembly are permanent causes of disorder and discord, I submit to your suffrage the following fundamental bases of a new constitution that the Assemblies will subsequently develop:
>
> 1) A responsible head elected for ten years;
> 2) Ministers that depend only on the executive power . . .;
> 4) A legislative body, debating and voting on laws, elected by universal suffrage, without list voting which would falsify the elections.[68]

Immediately striking, here, is the length of the presidential term. But it must not be forgotten that, at the Philadelphia Convention, authoritative voices had pushed in this same direction, even envisaging a presidency for life.

Of course, the imperial presidency evoked by the Bonapartist party in France then turned into a hereditary empire. Granier de Cassagnac had already left a door open to this when he wrote that 'in democratic countries, whatever the name given to the head of the executive, the spirit of obedience can only derive from the head himself, given that everything around him is mobile, variable, transitory'.[69] In fact, in striving to specify 'how the position of the president of the United States differs from that of a constitutional king in France', Tocqueville himself had set down a significant methodological premise: 'In this comparison, I will attach little importance to the external signs of power; they fool the observer more

67 Ibid., p. 27.
68 Napoléon III, *Œuvres*, vol. 3, pp. 273ff.
69 Granier de Cassagnac, *La révision de la Constitution*, p. 24.

than they help.'[70] On the other hand, in a youthful text of 1832, Louis-Napoleon had formulated a project of political and institutional reforms explicitly based on 'entirely republican principles'. Here, the people was to be represented by the two chambers and the emperor, whose ascent to the throne should in any case be subject to 'popular sanction', even at the moment of succession.[71] It is true that Napoleon III would later drop this point; but the fact remains that, in the text we have just examined, we have a project for a sort of presidential empire: it rests on the principles of the 'representative' system, and is subject, as far as the choice of the sovereign is concerned, to a sort of referendum or plebiscite. We might even say that Jackson's United States – at that time committed to eliminating discrimination based on property qualifications within the white community – was taken as a model by the prince, if one obviously adapted to French conditions as well as to his own ambitions. In the state envisioned by the young Louis-Napoleon, 'there shall be no more distinction either of rank or of fortune; every citizen shall compete equally in the election of deputies'. If the lower house was to be directly elected by the people, the upper house was to be – like the US Senate – the result of second-degree elections via 'electoral colleges'. In a country like France, without a federal structure, these electoral colleges would be filled by citizens who had distinguished themselves at the national level for their services to the *patrie*. In the United States, if the Electoral College normally expected to elect the president is not able to produce the qualified majority required by the Constitution, it passes the question over to the House of Representatives; in Louis-Napoleon's youthful project, the two chambers would 'propose a new sovereign' in the event that the one they had earlier designated did not obtain the necessary popular approval.[72]

Worth adding to this picture are the later comments by Édouard Laboulaye, an authoritative theorist and representative of French liberalism, who was an admirer of the United States. Condemning the 1848 revolution as guilty of seeking to 'debase the executive power' and of having forgotten that 'an energetic authority . . . is the first guarantee of liberty', he expressed his views on the regime with which he ended up throwing in his lot, albeit with a certain critical distance:

70 Tocqueville, *Democracy in America*, p. 205.

71 Napoléon III, *Œuvres*, vol. 1, pp. 382–5.

72 Ibid., vol. 1, pp. 384ff.

> The Constitution of 1852 has preserved universal suffrage: it is the very principle of our government. The Empire is a democracy, with a hereditary head and representative institutions. It is a new political system which has no precedent in history . . . The novelty of a form of government does not seem to me at all an objection against it; and perhaps the alliance of an energetic power and representative guarantees answers very well to the character and temperament of the French.[73]

America and France: Similarities and Differences

Of course, I have no intention here of wishing away the differences between France and America, which are as numerous as they are evident. But, if we do not want to settle for facile and lazy anthropological explanations (dear, moreover, to many liberal publicists, starting at least with Tocqueville) holding that the French political tradition was weighed down by a sort of original curse that incurably infected it with statism and despotism, then we must problematise and question certain stereotypical counterpositions. In both countries, there was a similar aspiration to control or liquidate the radical impulses that had emerged during the revolution. This was a much simpler endeavour in a country like the United States, which was 'overwhelmingly rural' with a 'sparse' population: only five cities had a population above 8,000, and only 2 or 3 per cent of the entire population lived in them.[74] France, on the other hand, was characterised by the presence of urban centres with a high population density and a considerable potential for social explosions. In the US case, the task, at the time of the passing of the Constitution, was to control about 160,000 voters out of about 3.5 million inhabitants; in the French case, the problem was more serious and complex, simply because of the much larger size of the electoral body.

Moreover, France did not have a Wild West to use as a pressure valve for the discontent of the poorer classes and social conflicts. These

73 Édouard Laboulaye, *L'état et ses limites suivi d'essais politiques* (Paris: Charpentier, 1863), p. 45; Édouard Laboulaye, *Le Parti libéral. Son programme et son avenir* (Paris: Charpentier, 1863), p. 150.

74 John F. Jameson, *The American Revolution Considered as a Social Movement* (Princeton, NJ: Princeton University Press, 1926), p. 41.

struggles were less bitter on the other side of the Atlantic, also for a reason already cogently identified by Hegel: 'America is hitherto exempt from this pressure, for it has the outlet of colonization constantly and widely open, and multitudes are continually streaming into the plains of the Mississippi. By this means the chief source of discontent is removed, and the continuation of the existing civil condition is guaranteed.'

To draw a purely ideological contrast between France and the United States, overlooking the different material conditions of life in each country, was thus senseless: 'North America will be comparable with Europe only after the immeasurable space which that country presents to its inhabitants shall have been occupied, and the members of the political body shall have begun to be pressed back on each other.' This is why Hegel goes so far as to say: 'Had the woods of Germany been in existence, the French Revolution would not have occurred' – or at least that it would not have shown the radicalism and the successive waves and lacerations that characterised its development.[75] In turn, Engels points out that in 'North America . . . class contradictions are but incompletely developed; every clash between the classes is concealed by the outflow of the surplus proletarian population to the west.'[76]

This analysis finds indirect confirmation among the protagonists of the American Revolution themselves. When Jefferson, struck by the spectacle of destitution in Paris, expressed the view that the remedy could be found in the distribution among the poor of uncultivated lands or lands left uncultivated by the nobility, Madison objected that such a measure would be incapable of solving the problem: 'A certain degree of misery seems inseparable from a high degree of populousness.'[77] And it was Madison himself who invited the Philadelphia Convention not to forget that, 'in process of time', in America as in the 'states and kingdoms of Europe', 'the number of landholders shall be comparatively small'. On that same occasion, Gouverneur Morris pointed out that '[n]ine-tenths of the people are at present freeholders', but that it would not be long until 'this country will abound with mechanics and manufacturers who

75 G. W. F. Hegel, *Lectures on the Philosophy of History* (London: G. Bell & Sons, 1914), pp. 89–90.

76 *Marx-Engels Collected Works* (*MECW*) (London: Lawrence & Wishart, 1975–2004), vol. 10, p. 333.

77 Edmund S. Morgan, 'Slavery and Freedom: The American Paradox', *Journal of American History* 59: 1 (June 1972), p. 11.

will receive their bread from their employers', and who would inevitably pose a challenge to the stability and orderly functioning of US institutions.[78] The various delegates discussed – and sometimes divided over – the measures that needed to be taken in the present in order to confront the dreaded future. But they were in agreement that this was a question of erecting a political and institutional dam against the onslaught of the 'many' and the poor. After much discussion, this dam was finally found in the very wide powers granted to the executive and the president. If it was France's fate to construct and experiment with a new political regime in the course of a social storm that was already underway, the United States had the advantage of being able to set its line of march in a situation of relative tranquillity. Having crushed Shays' Rebellion, it acted with a view to a future which, in the French case, was already happening in the present.

Here, the harshness of social conflict was intertwined with the complexity of the political contradictions. In the wake of the 1848 revolution, not only – as in the earlier case of Brumaire – did the challenge to the established order come from two opposing directions (plebeian radicalism and royalist agitation), but the royalist front was itself divided between followers of the Bourbons and the Orléans, not to mention the Bonapartists. This latter problem was absent in America: forced to flee, Crown loyalists took refuge in Canada, and even England, from where they did not return, which considerably aided the stabilisation of their country of origin.[79] Those few loyalists who remained in or returned to the United States, even if they 'regretted separation' from their homeland, resigned themselves to the de facto situation and sided with the new federal Constitution, which provided solid guarantees of the 'centred and efficient government' they admired.[80]

One last factor worth keeping in mind is the radically different international context. Tocqueville himself notes that while, in the course of the War of Independence, the Americans were favoured by being '[s] eparated from their enemies by 1,300 leagues of ocean', France, conversely, was 'the object of attacks from the whole of Europe, without

78 Morison, *Sources and Documents*, pp. 264, 276.

79 George Trevelyan, *A Shortened History of England* (Baltimore, MD: Pelican, 1959 [1942]), p. 438; Palmer, *Age of the Democratic Revolution*.

80 Wilson, *History of the American People*, vol. 3, p. 79.

money, credit, allies', and was, moreover, forced to face the 'conflagration that devoured its bowels' from within. But, in celebrating the Federal Constitution and American democracy as a whole, the liberal author proceeds as follows: 'what is new in the history of societies is to see a great people, warned by its legislators that the gears of government are grinding to a halt, turn its attention to itself, *without rushing and without fear*; sound the depth of the trouble; *keep self-control for two whole years*, in order to take time to find the remedy.'[81] Here, we need not dwell on the rose-tinted hues of Tocqueville's description of US events: not once does he mention Shays' Rebellion, which dominated the debate at the Philadelphia Convention! From this point of view, we can only agree with the argument that *Democracy in America* 'is not so much a political study as a work of edification' and, in this sense, should be compared to Arendt's essay glorifying the American Revolution and the Founding Fathers, which also completely ignores the revolt of the Massachusetts farmers and debtors.[82] But, returning to the French case, it is clear that, given the objective situation described by Tocqueville, it could hardly have afforded itself the course of conduct I have italicised in the citation above, which the liberal author exclusively credits to a US democracy fortunately free from infection by the Jacobin bacillus.

Over the subsequent years and decades, while the United States could pursue its imperial mission (an essential element of Bonapartism) in the Western Hemisphere without excessive difficulty, spreading into the territories taken from the poor Native Americans and, in the mid nineteenth century, from a weak country like Mexico, the period from the Revolution to the Restoration saw France locked in struggle with the great European and world powers, and engaged in a militarisation process that was inevitably also felt on a more directly political level. We can read in this sense Marx's observation that the First Empire was 'the offspring of the coalition wars of old semi-feudal Europe against modern France'.[83] But militarisation was also the result of explosive internal political and social conflicts. Here, again, we can take a cue from Marx,

81 Tocqueville, *Democracy in America*, p. 189.

82 James Bryce, *Studies in History and Jurisprudence* (Oxford: Oxford University Press, 1901), p. 325; Domenico Losurdo, 'Hannah Arendt e l'analisi delle rivoluzioni', in Roberto Esposito, ed., *La pluralità irrappresentabile. Il pensiero politico di Hannah Arendt* (Urbino: Istituto Italiano per gli Studi Filosofici – QuattroVenti, 1987).

83 *MECW*, vol. 22, p. 329.

who notes how the military apparatus developed by the bourgeoisie for an anti-working-class function ends up engulfing society as a whole, and the ruling class itself; with the repression of the workers' revolt in June, General Cavaignac (dear to the liberal bourgeoisie) exercised 'the dictatorship of the bourgeoisie by the sabre' – which, however, ended up turning into the 'the dictatorship of the sabre over bourgeois society'.[84] Obsessed by the 'Red' working-class threat, the ruling classes were

> bound not only to invest the executive with continually increased powers of repression, but at the same time to divest their own parliamentary stronghold – the National Assembly – one by one, of all its own means of defence against the Executive. The Executive, in the person of Louis Bonaparte, turned them out. The natural offspring of the 'Party-of-Order' Republic was the Second Empire.[85]

The French Washington, first sought and identified in General Cavaignac, ended up taking on the more troublesome form of Napoleon III.

So, while there were clear differences between the American and French cases, this should not lead us to overlook the points of contact. The concern to contain popular and plebeian claims did not lead in either case to a reassertion of rule by the nobility. But – even going beyond the aspirations and subjective intentions of the protagonists themselves – it did lead to a new political regime, in which a strong or very strong executive found its legitimacy in a popular investiture that was expressed either by plebiscite or by an electoral suffrage that was broad and, in any case, considerably more extensive than in the past. This new political regime proved especially effective in America because it was able to combine the rapidity, strength and unity of the decision-making centre with competition and turnover among different leaders and, in normal conditions, with citizens' enjoyment of their rights to freedom. In this sense, America produced a soft Bonapartism, albeit one which – thanks to the wide powers conferred on the president – could painlessly turn into a hard war-Bonapartism able to rule with an iron fist whenever a crisis situation required or seemed to require this. In France, conversely, Bonapartism would appear only in this latter form, and it

84 *MECW*, vol. 10, p. 76.
85 *MECW*, vol. 22, p. 330.

thus proved incapable of giving rise to a stable regime based on an orderly and peaceful succession.

Bonapartism as an Alternative to Property-Based Discrimination

If, in France, it was Louis-Napoleon who reintroduced universal suffrage, in America each development in the direction of Bonapartism was accompanied or preceded by a debate which ended in the defeat of the tendencies or aspirations – matured in conservative and more traditionalist circles on the occasion of more or less acute crises – to restrict suffrage or to contain it as far as possible. This had happened already at the Philadelphia Convention: at this moment, discrimination by property qualifications was widely prevalent, yet the horror that Shays' Rebellion evoked among the upper classes pushed right-wing elements to ask for a further turn of the screws. This was the sense of Gouverneur Morris's interventions: he believed that federal political rights should be explicitly confined to freeholders, to avert the future dangers to the social order that could derive from the inevitable growth, also on American soil, of the 'mechanics' and the turbulent world of industry and the city. The acceptance of this proposal would have resulted in a narrowing of suffrage, at least in those states where its extension beyond the ranks of the propertied had occurred already; and a further disenfranchisement would have resulted from the lengthening of the necessary residence period for the naturalisation of immigrants, as also sought by Gouverneur Morris. But, as several delegates at Philadelphia noted, such disenfranchisement measures would have sparked popular discontent, which would have been all the more powerful, Franklin observed, because such restrictions would have affected people who had actively participated in the War of Independence and who certainly did not want to be deprived of their political rights, even though they had given a great proof of patriotism and attachment to the common cause. All this would have made the approval of the new Constitution difficult and problematic.[86] Leaving unaltered the existing property-based discrimination at the level of the individual states – and leaving up to the latter the legislation concerning the necessary requirements for

86 Morison, *Sources and Documents*, pp. 274–9.

suffrage – the Philadelphia Convention ultimately decided to confront the new dangers highlighted by Shays' Rebellion not with explicit disenfranchisement measures, but instead with a drastic strengthening of the federal executive.

The period leading up to the extension of political rights that came with Jackson's ascent to the presidency was characterised by a fresh, lively debate on suffrage. A few years earlier, in 1820, the liberal-conservative Daniel Webster declared: 'There is not a more dangerous experiment than to place property in the hands of one class, and political power in those of another . . . If property cannot retain the political power, the political power will draw after it the property.'[87] Especially telling is the fact that, the following year, it was Van Buren – subsequently the architect of Jackson's electoral victory – who declared in favour of maintaining the link between property and political rights, so as to block access 'to the most sacred sanctuary of the constitution' of 'a violent and disorganising mob or riffraff like the French Jacobins'.[88] Once Jackson had become president, he did grant political rights to practically all Americans, so long as they were white males: but the other side of the coin was a decisive step forward in strengthening the powers of the executive and the missionary and charismatic role of the figure of the president.

The period of the Civil War, which was to lead to the abolition of slavery and, temporarily at least, to the extension of political citizenship to blacks, saw a symptomatic divergence between the respective political systems in the North and in the South. Even though the secessionist Confederacy based itself on a constitutional text that very much referred back to the model provided by the Founding Fathers, also in force in the Union, the Southern president Jefferson Davis assumed a much more limited set of powers than his antagonist: 'It cannot be ruled out that the Confederate system would have approached a parliamentary one, if it had been allowed to last longer.'[89] The institution of slavery – with the big proprietors' control of labour-power at the site of production,

87 Arthur Schlesinger, Jr, *The Age of Jackson* (New York: Little, Brown & Co., 1945), p. 269.

88 Mauro Calise, *Governo di partito. Antecedenti e conseguenze in America* (Bologna: il Mulino, 1989), pp. 89ff.

89 Klaus von Beyme, *Vorbild Amerika? Der Einfluß der amerikanischen Demokratie in der Welt* (Munich: Piper, 1986), pp. 53ff.

practically without legal limitations – made possible a richer democratic life among the ruling class. Insofar as the lower classes broke or wore away the shackles of slavery, the ruling class resorted to greater precautions, first among them the strengthening of the executive, in order to keep these 'dangerous' classes at bay.

In the postbellum Union, the powers of the executive and the presidency were reduced, and the 'government of Congress' was established, in years in which – not by chance – a general disemancipation process developed to the detriment not only of blacks, but also of immigrants and poor whites. The young Woodrow Wilson looked kindly on such tendencies, and, in a diary entry in 1876 – the hundredth anniversary of the proclamation of US independence – he noted: 'The American *Republic* will in my opinion never celebrate another Centennial. At least under its present Constitution and laws. Universal suffrage is at the foundation of every evil in this country.'[90] In an essay published three years later he reiterated that 'universal suffrage is a constant element of weakness, and exposes us to many dangers which we might otherwise escape.' But what was the remedy? A rising tide of public opinion demanded that representative bodies be purged of 'their ignorant elements'.[91] This was also the opinion Wilson expressed in a public speech in 1880.[92] We should put in this same context the letter addressed to the future US president in April 1879 by his father, Joseph Ruggles Wilson, who posed the dilemma facing the country in the following terms:

> Either a limitation of suffrage or anarchy in twenty-five years or sooner. I do not refer to Negroes any more than to the ignorant Northern voters. The true principle unquestionably is: the owners of a country ought to be its rulers. That is, let there be property qualification – and all the more, because, ordinarily, property and intelligence go together. The Statesman who shall find an effectual and yet peaceful remedy for universal suffrage will be the foremost leader in the U. States.[93]

90 Woodrow Wilson, *The Papers of Woodrow Wilson, 1856–1880*, ed. Arthur S. Link (Princeton, NJ: Princeton University Press, 1966), p. 143. Emphasis in original.

91 Ibid., p. 494.

92 Ibid., p. 481.

93 Ibid., p. 477.

At first glance, the author of the letter speaks like Constant or the other exponents of classical liberalism, in expressing the view that political representation must necessarily be monopolised by the propertied. But, between the lines, a new concern also emerges, here: namely, that it could be risky to challenge the principle of universal suffrage openly. So, rather than being removed outright, it would have to be hollowed out and neutralised. Historical experience also weighed in favour of such a solution: the law of 31 May 1850, which in France had disenfranchised one-third of the previous electorate, was very careful not to openly reintroduce property-based discrimination, forbidden by the Constitution and by now disagreeable and odious to popular consciousness. The 1850 law instead preferred to rely on residency requirements. The disemancipation process developed in a similar way in the United States at the end of the nineteenth century: while the exclusion of blacks was so taken for granted and uncontroversial that it could be declared more or less openly and imposed even outside any legality, immigrants were deprived of political rights as they became 'aliens' again, and poor white Americans primarily insofar as they were humiliatingly forced to run the gauntlet of literacy tests and registration laws. Was this the 'effectual and yet peaceful remedy' suggested in Wilson's father's letter? In fact, already in his own 1879 essay, a different alternative began to rear its head: yes, universal suffrage played a harmful role, but it was not solely responsible for the country's ills; the omnipotence of the legislature and the related weakness of the executive must also be hauled into the dock.[94] Hence, the American politician who had begun by advocating a restriction of suffrage would end up granting the vote to women as well, but within a political regime that revealed ever more clearly Bonapartist aspects.

It is interesting to note the continuity between the ideology with which the liberal tradition justified the exclusion of the 'childlike' multitude from political rights, and the arguments Wilson uses to underline the absolute necessity of the concentration and personalisation of power: a 'very numerous . . . class of persons', indeed the 'majority of the nation', if capable of thinking at all, can do so only 'in concrete forms', faced with in-the-flesh individuals, while it remains incapable of rising to 'generalizations' and thus of choosing between political ideas and

94 Ibid., p. 494.

programmes.[95] This is a theme we have already seen in Bagehot, of whom the future US president was a reader and admirer. From Constant to Wilson, via the Victorian English liberal who already identified the strong executive led by a charismatic leader as the antidote to the extension of suffrage, the multitude continues to be 'childlike'. From this perspective, it would not be wise or prudent to deny or take away the masses' political rights, but it is appropriate to limit the exercise of these rights to the ability to choose from among individuals placed in a clearly superior sphere and endowed with very broad powers. What has, in more recent times, been called the 'imperial presidency' was the real alternative to a disemancipation process that, if pursued too openly, could have provoked sharp and even violent reactions.[96]

Bonapartism and the Imperial Mission

The two victorious generals who assumed power at the end of a period of revolutionary upheaval, in 1789 and 1799 respectively, were charged not only with maintaining order at home but also with ensuring and building their countries' power and glory in the world. As the protagonists of the Brumaire coup submitted the new constitution for popular approval, they mounted an indictment against the previous regime, primarily for the 'uncertainties' it had brought in the 'Republic's external relations and in its internal and military situation'. Meanwhile, *The Federalist* denounced the fact that, in the absence of a strong central authority, America had 'reached almost the last stage of national humiliation', as it had not been able to recover the 'valuable territories and important posts' that belonged to it by right. The strong executive invoked here was essential both for the 'protection of property' and for the 'protection of the community against foreign attacks' (no. 70). It should be borne in mind that the Philadelphia Convention was made up, as we have seen, of 'overwhelmingly conservative' and 'overwhelmingly nationalist' figures.[97] They set out primarily to ensure the nation's

95 Woodrow Wilson, *Congressional Government: A Study in American Politics* (New York: Meridian, 1959), p. 57.

96 Arthur Schlesinger, Jr, *The Imperial Presidency* (Boston, MA: Houghton Mifflin, 1973).

97 Nevins and Commager, *America*, p. 106.

commercial and mercantilist expansion of the nation.[98] But how would 'our commerce' be defended, and 'by what right' – James Wilson asked – 'can we expect our flag will be respected, if we are incapable of firing even a cannon shot in our own defense?'[99] *The Federalist* had no hesitation in issuing a prophecy in this regard: 'We have heard much of the fleets of Britain, and the time may come, if we are wise, when the fleets of America may engage attention' (no. 4). A strong executive was all the more necessary – as James Wilson had emphasised – for a country that was destined to conquer a leadership position at least on a cultural level; for a country – Hamilton observed in 1795 – that was 'a great empire in embryo' and that, already at the moment of its foundation and even before gaining independence, liked to present and celebrate itself as 'a new empire'.[100] William Henry Drayton, scion of a family of wealthy planters and later a delegate to the continental congress in Philadelphia, explained that this empire 'with the Lord's blessing, promises to be the most glorious of all time', giving rise 'to the most important epoch in history, not of a nation but of the world'.[101]

Integral to Bonapartism is not only an imperial consciousness, but one ideologically transfigured into the terms of religious, moral or political mission. In this way, the sense of belonging to a particular community is powerfully reinforced, attention is diverted from internal conflicts, and dissent is marginalised or silenced, and criminalised. It is well known that the Great French Revolution brought out – or, harkening back to an earlier tradition, altered and further strengthened – a kind of missionary consciousness in the nation that was its protagonist. Carlyle remarked sarcastically upon the French considering themselves 'the chosen "soldiers of liberty"' and 'a People whose bayonets are sacred, a kind of Messiah People, saving a blind world in its own despite, and earning for themselves a terrestrial and even celestial glory'.[102] But, even outside its borders, France was celebrated, by enthusiastic liberals and democrats, as the chosen

98 Wehler, *Grundzüge der amerikanischen Außenpolitik*, p. 57ff.

99 Adams and Adams, *Die Amerikanische Revolution*, p. 354.

100 Ibid. p. 355; Piero Bairati, *I profeti dell'impero americano. Dal periodo coloniale ai nostri giorni* (Turin: Einaudi, 1975), p. 100.

101 Bairati, *I profeti dell'impero americano*, p. 77.

102 Thomas Carlyle, *Latter-Day Pamphlets* (1850), ed. M. K. Goldberg and J. P. Seigel (Ottawa: Canadian Federation for the Humanities, 1983), p. 8.

people or country of the 'new religion' of liberty, the 'vanguard fighter' of the cause of liberty, i.e. the country or people outside or against which there would be no salvation (*nulla salus*)![103] This ideological theme was cleverly exploited by Bonapartist propaganda (from Napoleon I to Napoleon III), which presented the (actually accomplished or hoped-for) expansion of France as a contribution to the cause of civilisation and human progress. Indeed, it was on this basis that it summoned all Frenchmen to gather around a commander, both civilian and military, already garlanded by prestige and glory on account of the salvific task he was called upon to achieve at the international level.

But consciousness of the nation's imperial mission played a much more important role in America, where it was furthermore experienced in explicitly religious terms. It was impossible, *The Federalist* claimed, to understand the success of the American revolution without taking into account 'that Almighty hand which has been so frequently and signally extended' in support of the colonists engaged in the struggle for independence (no. 37). John Adams had no doubt that his country was destined 'for the illumination and the emancipation of the slavish part of mankind all over the earth'.[104] His was no isolated voice: countless personalities and authors tirelessly repeated that the new republic, that intrepid standard-bearer of the cause of freedom, was destined to exercise and ' "extend" its benign influence to savage, enslaved, and benighted nations', and that America thus represented the chosen people and even a 'chosen race', invested with a providential role.[105] If consciousness of the nation's imperial mission was a constitutive element of Bonapartism, as we have seen with Disraeli and Bismarck as well as the two Napoleons, it is also worth bearing in mind that in the American case this played an unparalleled role in unifying the nation, and in overcoming or concealing political differences. Jefferson was an opponent of the Federalists, but shared with them the view that the United States was destined, also by means of the eventual annexation of Cuba and Canada, to 'possess

103 Domenico Losurdo, *Tra Hegel e Bismarck. La rivoluzione del 1848 e la crisi della cultura tedesca* (Rome: Editori Riuniti, 1983), pp. 93ff.

104 Harold J. Laski, *The American Democracy: A Commentary and an Interpretation* (Fairfield: Kelley, 1977 [1948]), p. 8.

105 Albert K. Weinberg, *Manifest Destiny: A Study of Nationalist Expansionism in American History* (Chicago: Quadrangle, 1963), pp. 18, 39ff.

such an empire for liberty as [the world] has never surveyed since the creation.'[106]

With perhaps a touch of self-irony, Heine celebrated the France that emerged from the revolution as the 'new Jerusalem'.[107] Jefferson proposed, in all seriousness, that the coat of arms of the United States should portray the children of Israel led by a beam of light.[108] One nineteenth-century author spelled out the argument according to which the '*Anglican* race' (first and foremost that which had taken root in the United States) had the task of 'carr[ying] *Anglican* principles and liberty over the globe', like a 'missionary'.[109] It is worth pausing for a moment to consider the adjective repeatedly used here (the one I have italicised), by an author still today dear to important American cultural and political circles. In this, we see a wholesale fusion of race, national community, and religion; that is, the emergence of a sort of national religion that legitimises and transfigures the imperial mission, bathing in an avowedly sacred aura the man called upon to lead it, the president of the United States. The latter thus somehow becomes both a political and religious leader at the same time, a charismatic leader in the full sense of the term. If the idea of an imperial mission generally contains a religious element, albeit a secularised one, we can say that in the American political tradition it took the form of an explicitly declared and professed religion.

The US President as Interpreter of His Nation's 'Mission'

The consciousness of France's national mission that emerged or consolidated after 1789 had an inherent limitation, precisely because the Great Revolution represented a moment of serious laceration that was not easily healed. Moreover, this consciousness was first seriously weakened

106 Cited in Piero Bairati, *I profeti dell'impero americano*, pp. 104ff [TN: English-language citation retrieved from *The Papers of Thomas Jefferson: Retirement Series*, ed. J. Jefferson Looney, Robert F. Haggard, Julie L. Lautenschlager and Ellen Hickman (Princeton, NJ: Princeton University Press, 2004), vol. 1, p. 168].

107 Losurdo, *Tra Hegel e Bismarck*, pp. 93ff.

108 Weinberg, *Manifest Destiny*, pp. 18, 39ff.

109 Francis Lieber, *On Civil Liberty and Self-Government* (Philadelphia, PA: Lippincott, 1859), p. 21.

with Waterloo, and then suffered a decisive setback with Sedan and defeat in the war against Prussia. The history of the United States is different: deeply rooted in the religious conscience – or rather, representing one of its constituent elements – the idea of mission seems unshakable. As US imperial expansion developed at an irresistible march, this sense of mission was increasingly consolidated; at the same time, tendencies towards a soft Bonapartist regime were strengthened. We can already observe this phenomenon at the moment of the passing of the new Constitution, called upon to overcome the weaknesses of the old Confederation, which 'could not find sufficient resources to stand up to the Indian nations'; and it was no accident that the first president of the United States was not only a general (Washington), but a general who had 'a large amount of fluid capital which he judiciously invested in western lands', expecting their 'large appreciation with the establishment of stable government and the advance of the frontier.'[110] As we have already seen, a constitutive element of Bonapartism is the externalisation of social conflict, and this succeeds all the more easily when accompanied by an expansion that reinforces consciousness of the peculiar mission of one's own country. And this combination is especially characteristic of the history of the United States, of which expansion was a constituent element from the outset, and which is the more susceptible to ideological transfiguration because of its ability to assume the peaceful appearance of a progressive shifting of the 'frontier', fulfilling a mission of freedom and civilisation. The protagonists of this mission – those who lead the movement bringing forward the frontier of freedom and civilisation – end up garlanded by a halo that is not only military in character: 'It is natural enough to an American that a successful general should, like Jackson or Taylor, Harrison or Grant, go to the White House.'[111] The figure who led the first substantial broadening of presidential powers was Andrew Jackson, a general who conquered the highest office in 1828 thanks to his 'military fame': he was an 'Indian-fighter' lifted to the rank of a 'great national leader' also for having achieved the only American success during the war against Britain in 1812–1815.[112]

110 Tocqueville, *Democracy in America*, p. 188; Charles Beard, *An Economic Interpretation of the Constitution of the United States* (New York: Macmillan, 1914), p. 123.

111 Laski, *American Democracy*, p. 12.

112 Schlesinger, Jr., *Age of Jackson*, p. 36; Nevins and Commager, *America*, p. 175.

This fighter 'for the military supremacy of the United States' had not demonstrated his energy on the battlefield alone: he had not hesitated to have 'English meddlers hanged in Spanish Florida' and to order 'the execution of an unruly teen-age [American] soldier'.[113] Jackson was a Democrat who asserted his intention to prevent the formation of 'a moneyed aristocracy dangerous to the liberties of the country'.[114] But the development of democracy does not concern either Native Americans or blacks: the president, 'a wealthy slave owner', became a popular hero and won mass approval, even 'giv[ing] voice to the West's demand for territorial expansion as a way to ensure economic opportunity'.[115] Potential social conflict was channelled and directed outwards – if not out of the United States, then at least out of the white community; the Democratic president even supported the citizens of Georgia in their campaign to exterminate the Cherokee people.[116] The general who had now ascended to the supreme magistracy proved to be 'the most forceful and aggressive president since Washington', 'exert[ing] his dominance over Congress with an unprecedented use of vetoes', and 'treat[ing] his cabinet in the manner of the army's commander in chief', relying on a group of informal advisors whom he hired or fired at will. The extension of President Jackson's powers went so far that one of his opponents, Daniel Webster, attacked 'King Andrew' as 'a reincarnation of the French monarch Louis XIV'.[117] While the 'old aristocracy' warned against the new Caesar, 'the newly enfranchised and chauvinistic masses regarded the military hero with wild enthusiasm', allowing Jackson to make 'the presidency more powerful than it had ever been before'.[118]

The strengthening of presidential powers was particularly evident in foreign policy and at the most important stages of the expansionist process. Here, we can rely on the reconstruction offered by an exceptional historian who, having himself ascended to the highest office in the United States, would in turn give great momentum to the development of the imperial presidency. When, in 1836, the American farmers

113 Bailyn and Wood, *Great Republic*, p. 375.

114 Schlesinger, Jr, *Age of Jackson*, p. 36.

115 Bailyn and Wood, *Great Republic*, p. 373.

116 Peter Carroll and David Noble, *The Free and the Unfree: A New History of the United States* (New York: Viking, 1977), p. 191.

117 Bailyn and Wood, *Great Republic*, pp. 373–4, 380.

118 Schlesinger Jr, *Age of Jackson*, pp. 38, 276.

who had, for decades, trespassed into Texas declared the independence of that province – thereby dropping their previous assertions of loyalty to the Mexican government – President Jackson proceeded to a prompt recognition. He took the decision – one that risked taking America to war with Mexico and perhaps even with Britain – having consulted 'neither with Congress nor with any one except the friends of Texas herself'. In deciding on the annexation of this territory in 1844, President Tyler met with opposition from the Senate (which was diffident or even hostile, on domestic-policy grounds); but Texas was 'too vitally connected with the mastery of the continent, too plainly a thing which lay at the heart of western plans, to be put aside by vote of the Senate'. Annexation was formally approved in December 1845, and Democratic president Polk ordered General Taylor to advance towards the Rio Grande, threatening the city of Matamoros. The Mexicans demanded the withdrawal of the US troops, only to meet with a stern refusal. Border clashes ensued, and 'Mexico' – the president told Congress – 'passed the boundaries of the United States . . . and shed American blood upon American soil. War exists, and exists by the act of Mexico herself.' But President Polk 'had not consulted Congress [which was in session] before he ordered General Taylor forward to the Rio Grande and brought this momentous matter to a head'. Wilson added: 'War indeed existed – but by whose act Congress was no longer at liberty to inquire.'[119]

US presidents have been able to proceed all the more nonchalantly and at their own discretion, the more they have been in in tune with what the Democratic journalist John L. O'Sullivan termed Manifest Destiny – that calling which summons the United States 'to overspread the continent allotted by Providence for the free development of our yearly multiplying millions'.[120] This missionary consciousness was to fall into crisis with the War of Secession, which drew attention to the terrible reality of slavery – especially since Lincoln, himself a veteran of the wars against the Native Americans, which had also involved the 'merciless' massacre of 'men, women and children', was rather reticent on the question of blacks.[121] In 1858, before his ascent to the

119 Wilson, *History of the American People*, vol. 4, pp. 106, 101, 117.
120 Weinberg, *Manifest Destiny*, p. 112.
121 Nevins and Commager, *America*, p. 203.

presidency, he had declared that he had absolutely no intention of granting them political rights or access to public office, and that he was against mixed marriages: 'there is a physical difference between the white and black races' that 'forbid[s] the two races living together on terms of social and political equality'; it was therefore natural that the white race's superiority should be acknowledged.[122] Even after the emancipation of the slaves, the president entertained the idea of having them deported to Liberia or Latin America.[123] Yet, the blood shed in the struggle to crush the slavers' secession was interpreted by Lincoln as the definitive confirmation that the United States was indeed God's 'favored land', and that he had appointed it to represent eternally on earth the cause of freedom and government 'of the people, by the people, and for the people'.[124]

Even when the president has not been a general, on no few occasions he has been a personality who could boast of his military and patriotic merits. Theodore Roosevelt cited Jackson's example, celebrating this 'military genius' and 'really good general' able to 'face even the English regulars, then the most formidable fighting troops in the world'.[125] And Roosevelt, whose own 'popularity grew most rapidly as a result of his Spanish war service', further boosted Bonapartist tendencies.[126] Not by chance, he liked to boast of the very broad independence he enjoyed in the field of foreign policy: 'The biggest matters, however, such as the Portsmouth, peace, the acquisition of Panama, and sending the fleet around the world, I managed without consultation with anyone; for when a matter is of capital importance, it is well to have it handled by one man only.'[127] The president was called upon to be a 'very strong man' capable of unhesitatingly wielding the power that comes with a 'very powerful office', superior to that exercised by

122 Abraham Lincoln, *The Collected Works* (Springfield, IL/New Brunswick, NJ: Rutgers University Press, 1953), vol. 3, pp. 145–6.

123 Thomas F. Gosset, *Race: The History of an Idea in America* (New York: Schocken, 1963), p. 255.

124 Lincoln, *Collected Works*, vol. 4, p. 271; vol. 7, pp. 20–1.

125 Theodore Roosevelt, *Gouverneur Morris* (Boston, MA: Houghton Mifflin & Co., 1888), p. 349.

126 Richard Hofstadter, *The American Political Tradition and the Men Who Made It* (New York: Knopf, 1973), p. 273.

127 Theodore Roosevelt, *Letters*, selected and ed. Elting E. Morison (Cambridge, MA: Harvard University Press, 1951), vol. 6, p. 1498.

the magistracy 'in any great republic or constitutional monarchy of modern times'.[128]

Interpreting the president's role in a vigorous key, Roosevelt repeatedly declared his intention to follow in the footsteps of Jackson and Lincoln.[129] But, along with elements of continuity, there was no shortage of new developments. The president was now the 'steward of the people', authorised to proceed 'actively and affirmatively', without waiting for a 'specific authorization' and without letting himself be hobbled by a 'narrowly legalistic point of view': the president alone was the interpreter of the 'public welfare' and the 'common well-being of all of our people' and was answerable to the people alone. The figure of the 'guide' – the *condottiero* and *duce* of his people – emerged in the United States before it did in Europe, albeit obviously within a political framework characterised by respect, at least in normal conditions, for precise rules of the game. It was these rules that would be swept away in countries like Italy and Germany, given both the particular harshness of the Second Thirty Years' War in these countries and their lack of any rooted tradition of guarantees akin to the American one. But, in Theodore Roosevelt, we see a direct relationship beginning to be established between the people and their president, beyond any mediation or hindrance by the legislature. The president now acted as the solitary interpreter of the 'public welfare', not only in absolutely exceptional situations like the War of Secession, but even in his day-to-day political action – which, moreover, was increasingly studded with moments of crisis or sensitivity, as the United States' march towards its great-power role and its global hegemony progressed.

Together with the strengthening of the executive, the consciousness of the American imperial mission also took a further step forward. The United States and its president-interpreter are not called upon only to maintain order and spread civilisation based on law throughout the Western Hemisphere. Rather, they also have – in a now explicit and immediate way – a much broader and more ambitious task ahead of them: 'We have done our duty to ourselves, and we have done the higher duty of promoting the civilization of mankind.' This was a mission that

128 Ibid., pp. 1136, 1086.

129 Theodore Roosevelt, *An Autobiography* (New York: Scribner's, 1920 [1913]), pp. 357ff.

began with the conquest of the Far West, calling on Americans to 'put down savagery and barbarism' everywhere so as to 'bring light into the world's dark places'.[130] It was a mission developed in the war against the 'medieval tyranny' of Spain and the 'savage anarchy' of the newly conquered Philippines. Ultimately, it was a mission without boundaries: the United States had the 'great and righteous task' of bringing civilisation to every corner of the world, and it was still 'warring against the existence of evil'; it had the 'privilege of playing a leading part in the century that has just opened'.[131]

Woodrow Wilson had in 1888 lamented what he deemed the excessive might of Congress – contrasting it with the example of countries like Britain and Germany, with their very strong executives and personalisation of power in charismatic leaders like Gladstone and Bismarck.[132] In the 1900 introduction to his *Congressional Government*, he explained that the 'greatly increased power' bestowed upon the president was to be connected with the fact that the United States had now 'plunge[d] into in international politics and into the administration of distant dependencies . . . When foreign affairs play a prominent part in the politics and policy of a nation, its Executive must of necessity be its guide'; and Theodore Roosevelt was in a pre-eminent position 'as no president, except Lincoln, has been since the first quarter of the nineteenth century, when the foreign relations of the new nation had first to be adjusted'.[133] The admiring remarks Wilson had earlier dedicated to Germany, where the figure of the 'imperious and domineering chancellor' far surpassed the Reichstag on which he theoretically depended, now also held true for the United States, and would apply even more so over the course the following years and decades.[134]

130 Theodore Roosevelt, *The Strenuous Life: Essays and Addresses* (London: Grant Richards, 1903), pp. 292–4.

131 Ibid., pp. 9, 294, 26, 287.

132 Wilson, *Congressional Government*, p. 58.

133 Ibid., p. 22.

134 Ibid., p. 58.

Normality and the State of Exception

In celebrating the English political system in contrast to the American one, Bagehot reproaches the latter for its 'want of elasticity'. Elected for a four-year term, even a dull and mediocre president cannot be replaced by another energetic one, equal to a crisis situation that has developed in the meantime: in this sense, the US Constitution is negatively characterised by 'the impossibility of a dictatorship, the total absence of a revolutionary reserve'.[135] By taking for a general rule the particular crisis caused by Lincoln's assassination, and the accidental rise in his place of a vice president absolutely lacking in quality, the English liberal here falls into a colossal error of judgement. As we have already seen, the conception of the US Constitution constantly bore in mind the state of exception and the ancient Roman model of dictatorship that intervened to deal with crises without permanently altering the institutional framework.

The history of the years immediately following the Philadelphia Convention is highly instructive here. We might say that the 'Founding Fathers' sought a baptism of fire for the new Constitution. In 1794, a modest farmer's rebellion in western Pennsylvania against the hated whisky tax provided the occasion for the national government to proceed with a spectacular display of force by recruiting some 15,000 militiamen: before this, declared Washington, 'we had given no testimony to the world of being able or willing to support our government and laws'. Hamilton added that 'government can never [be] said to be established until some signal display has manifested its power by military coercion'.[136]

A few years later, with the onset of a political crisis (acute tensions with revolutionary France – a country which enjoyed some sympathy also in the United States) which certainly did not call into question the social order or national independence, there was a drastic limitation of constitutional freedoms. The Sedition Act of 14 July 1798 criminalised any writing deemed 'scandalous' or even simply 'malicious' towards the government, one or other house of congress, or the president of the United States, and stipulated jail sentences for not only the authors of such writings but also anyone who should 'print, utter or publish' it or

135 Bagehot, *English Constitution*, pp. 223ff.
136 Bailyn and Wood, *Great Republic*, p. 244.

assist any of these operations.[137] Those convicted under this law included several Jeffersonian journalists, and even a member of Congress.[138] It is interesting to read in this regard the comment of Wilson who, as a historian, shows himself to be rather critical, but who later, having become president himself, would go much further with repressive measures. But we read: 'The Sedition Act cut perilously near the root of freedom of speech and of the press. There was no telling where such exercises of power would stop. Their only limitations and safeguards lay in the temper and good sense of the President and the Attorney General.' Even more significant were the Alien Acts (25 June and 6 July 1798), which granted very wide discretionary powers to the highest authority of the State for the arrest and deportation not only of foreigners as such, but also of immigrants awaiting naturalisation; male citizens or those coming from countries considered enemies could even be deported, from age fourteen upwards. In this case, too, it may be useful to read the comments of Wilson, who observes that, in this way, foreigners and immigrants were deprived of all rights 'on [the president's] own suspicion, without accusation, without jury, without public trial, without confrontation of the witnesses against him, without having witnesses in his favour, without defence, without counsel'.[139] In fact, in the name of 'public safety', 'public peace or safety' or the 'peace and safety of the United States', the president was authorised to intervene harshly against those whom he had 'reasonable grounds to suspect' might be dangerous to national security.[140] The Alien and Sedition Acts seemed to give concrete form to the figure of the dictator of ancient Rome, evoked by *The Federalist* already ten years beforehand.

Hence, the president would be liable to turn into a dictator at any moment. For the moment, let us leave the Civil War to one side and instead look at the end of the nineteenth century. Faced with the tensions emerging within the white community itself, as populist and working-class agitation developed, we see how normality was always on the verge of turning into a state of exception. The head of the

137 Henry Commager, *Documents of American History* (New York: Appleton-Century-Crofts, 1963), vol. 1, pp. 177ff.

138 Marie-France Toinet, *Le Système politique des États-Unis* (Paris: Presses universitaires de France, 1987), p. 568.

139 Wilson, *History of the American People*, vol. 3, pp. 152, 336.

140 Commager, *Documents of American History*, vol. 1, pp. 176–8.

executive was able to order or threaten to send in federal troops when faced with strikes considered harmful to national interests: Cleveland used military force to crush a transport strike which the high-bourgeois press denounced as an act of 'war against the government and against society' – as an action likely to provoke, or which had already brought about, a state of exception that had to be confronted with exceptional methods. The president at the forefront of this enterprise immediately appeared as a national saviour, while his antagonist, the trade unionist Eugene V. Debs, was denounced by the big press outlets even before his arrest as an enemy not only of the country but also 'of mankind', who must in any case be got rid of as soon as possible.[141] The immersion of the nation's leader-interpreter in an aura of patriotic sanctity went hand in hand with the externalisation of conflict and the criminalisation of dissent, in the sense that dissenters were considered alien not only to America, but also to civilisation and even to mankind.

Cleveland's action was deemed 'excellent' by Theodore Roosevelt, who, having appointed himself to the highest magistracy, boasted in turn of 'keeping order in Nevada' by intervening energetically against 'the Federation of Miners [which] threatened anarchy', and of having succeeded, at the same time, in bringing to book the 'big corporations' and even the 'plutocracy'. The president who called for a 'strong executive' posed as a leader *super partes* who used 'every ounce of power' in his office to save social peace, in the higher interest of the nation of which he is the privileged and sole interpreter. But it is not difficult to grasp the real political and social content of what Roosevelt termed '*progressive* conservatism'.[142] The Bonapartist or tendentially Bonapartist regime that was being constituted here might well proceed with some limited concessions from above to the subordinate classes, as per the model of Louis-Napoleon, Disraeli and Bismarck; but it could not tolerate their autonomous organisation and activity. As has been observed, Roosevelt's 'mind was a single track when it came to strikes, and that track always carried troops to the scene of the dispute'. Indeed, throughout his long political career – from member of the New York state

141 Foster Rhea Dulles, *The United States Since 1865* (Ann Arbor: University of Michigan Press, 1969), p. 85.

142 Roosevelt, *Letters*, vol. 1, p. 391; vol. 6, pp. 1087ff, 1369.

assembly to police chief, governor, undersecretary of the Navy, vice president, and finally president – Roosevelt repeatedly proclaimed the executive's right to use the iron fist: even during labour unrest, order had to be 'kept at whatever cost. If it comes to shooting we shall shoot to hit. No blank cartridges or firing over the head of anybody'; 'I like to see a mob handled by the regulars, or by good State-Guards, not over-scrupulous about bloodshed.' Significant in these statements is not only their brutality, but also, and above all, Roosevelt's awareness of how easy it was, in the American political and constitutional order, to move from normality to a state of exception: 'The sentiment now animating a large proportion of our people can only be suppressed as the Commune in Paris was suppressed, by taking ten or a dozen of their leaders out, standing . . . them against a wall, and shooting them dead. I believe it will come to that.'[143]

The passage from normality to a state of exception at the level of the individual states revolved around the governor and, at the federal level, the president. When speaking of a state of exception, our minds naturally turn to the War of Secession. Lincoln proceeded with a general mobilisation and a powerful build-up of arms, suspended habeas corpus, decided on the arrests he considered opportune, suppressed the hostile or 'disloyal' press, and affirmed his right to proclaim martial law in the rear. The introduction of conscription in the North prompted an uprising by the mass of poor immigrants in New York, especially the Irish: 'It was necessary to march an army corps against the city, and after several days of terror and fires the revolt was suppressed.'[144] All these extraordinary measures, necessary if the slavers' secession was to be crushed, were taken 'without a declaration of war by Congress'. And so easy, for the American president, is the state of exception that in a sense one need not even proclaim it. Bagehot, who lamented the supposed 'impossibility of a dictatorship' within the American constitutional system, was objectively answered by Lincoln's secretary of state, who boasted to the British ambassador: 'I can touch a bell on my right hand and order the imprisonment of a citizen of Ohio; I can touch a bell again and order the imprisonment of a citizen of New York; and

143 Hofstadter, *American Political Tradition*, pp. 282–4.

144 Raimondo Luraghi, 'Introduzione', in *La guerra civile americana* (Bologna: Mulino, 1978), p. 53.

no power on earth, except that of the President, can release them. Can the Queen of England do so much?'[145]

But there are other considerations to be made. Lincoln's opponents accused him of Jacobinism for imposing 'military governments' and 'military courts', interpreting 'the word "law"' to mean 'the will of the president', and habeas corpus as the 'power of the President to imprison whom he pleases, as long as he pleases'.[146] Indeed, as the Jacobins had invoked *le salut public*, so too did Lincoln appeal to public safety – 'the laws of necessity, of self-preservation, of saving our country' that required the amputation of a 'limb' in order to save the body as a whole.[147] But this comparison captures only one side of things, for it overlooks the fact that, at least formally, the Jacobin dictatorship is not in the hands of an individual, but those of a committee of public safety, invested by the legislature and answerable to it. So, reversing Bagehot's judgement, we can say that the particular flexibility of the American constitutional and political system consists in the fact that its president, who already holds very broad powers in times of peace and normality, is able seamlessly to turn into a dictator who wields (near-)absolute powers in managing a crisis, without there being any institutional shocks. In the first decades of the US Constitution's life, such a transformation was achieved through the mediation of Congress, but, over time, it increasingly took a back seat. The novelty, highlighted above all by the War of Secession, lies in the dictator who has, in a sense, invested himself with his powers.

Bonapartist Regime, Soft Bonapartism, War Bonapartism

To understand this last point properly, it is worth returning for a moment to the war against Mexico. This war confronted Congress with a fait accompli, to the great perplexity of Abraham Lincoln, at that time a little-known member of the House of Representatives: if the president was authorised to invade the territory of another country by invoking the need to 'repel' an invasion pre-emptively, and if he was the '*sole*

145 Schlesinger Jr, *Imperial Presidency*, pp. 58–9.

146 Arthur Schlesinger Jr, *History of US Political Parties, vol. 2: 1860–1910: The Gilded Age of Politics* (New York: Chelsea House, 1980), pp. 915–21.

147 Schlesinger Jr, *Imperial Presidency*, pp. 25, 59.

judge' of this alleged need, then a president with the power to 'make war at pleasure' is, in fact, placed in the traditional position of monarchs, and indeed exercises 'the most oppressive of all Kingly oppressions'.[148] This objection put its finger on a sore point by evoking a classic question of political philosophy: *quis judicabit*? But Lincoln would provide an unequivocal answer to this question in the course of the War of Secession. The judge is, without doubt, the president who has sworn to 'preserve, protect and defend' the Constitution of the United States and the country itself – the president whom the Constitution calls on to 'take Care that the Laws be faithfully executed' (art. 2, sections 1 and 3).

This was a crucial turning point: the president considered that he was recognised as having the right effectively to decide not only on the launching of war operations, but on war operations that also entailed the drastic limitation of constitutional freedoms domestically, as would indeed happen in the course of both world wars. If the 'sovereign is he who decides on the exception', the supreme magistrate of the United States is sovereign twice over, for after deciding on the state of exception he is then called upon to manage it.[149] Contrary to what Bagehot thought, the transition to dictatorship is more complicated in the British case: recourse to the royal prerogative is not possible without the consent of the Crown, which does not itself manage the state of exception. In the American constitutional and political system, there is room not only for a dictator, but for a dictator who ultimately invests himself with powers that Hamilton and *The Federalist* (no. 23) explicitly declare to be 'without limitation' and without 'constitutional shackles'. Moreover, given the US system's unification of the priestly-ideological function and the political-military one, in the moments of most acute crisis – when the destiny of the American nation, endowed with its special religious mission, seems to be at stake – its head and interpreter, the president-dictator, is more than ever immersed in a sort of sacred aura that makes it easier to exercise the powers required by the state of exception.

In this sense, in the United States we see the development of a political regime at least tending towards Bonapartism. Clearly, such a definition is not contradicted by the fact of popular investiture, which, as we

148 Lincoln, *Collected Works*, vol. 1, pp. 451–2.

149 Carl Schmitt, *Political Theology: Four Chapters on the Concept of Sovereignty*, transl. George Schwab (Chicago: Chicago University Press, 2005), p. 5.

have seen, is constitutive of Bonapartism as a phenomenon: the plebiscite for Louis-Napoleon expressed a real and very broad consensus, and the form of electoral consultation also allowed for the expression of opposition, given that 'thanks to the reintroduction of the secret ballot, everyone had the possibility of voting no without suffering any disadvantage'. It could be objected that the bombardment of propaganda made any possibility of choice null and void; but the scholar cited here also points out that the 'propaganda campaign that was conducted remained within limits which were rather narrow compared to the full array of present-day means of propaganda'.[150]

But, even leaving aside today's realities, we can also look at the case of the 1896 electoral campaign, which saw the triumph of McKinley and Theodore Roosevelt (destined to succeed the former as president after his assassination). This race was marked not only by the chorus-like mobilisation of the press or by the flood of dollars and propaganda material that the victors had at their disposal, but also by a full-scale campaign of intimidation. This was not limited to denouncing the Democratic-populist candidate Bryan as 'anarchist' and 'crazy'; rather: 'Manufacturers made contracts contingent upon McKinley's victory, and wage earners were told that otherwise the factories would close and their families starve. The Democratic national chairman charged that "with scarcely an exception" the great corporations were "engaged in a concerted effort to coerce their employees to vote against their convictions"'.[151]

The definition which I have here proposed of a regime at least tending towards Bonapartism may seem to stand in contradiction with the fact that, in the United States, there is a choice between several candidates and an orderly succession. Yet, we can speak of a 'regime' precisely when the succession process is orderly – and, given the ideological presuppositions on which Bonapartism rests, this succession must necessarily be regulated by universal suffrage. While, in France, we can see the establishment of more or less Bonapartist dictatorships, these did not succeed in turning into a genuine regime, also on account of the development of a sort of permanent state of exception. But a political regime

150 Gisela Geywitz, *Das Plebizit von 1851 in Frankreich* (Tübingen: Mohr Siebeck, 1965), pp. 248ff.

151 Arthur Meier Schlesinger, *The Rise of Modern America, 1865–1951* (New York: Macmillan, 1951).

demonstrates its solidity not only through its capacity to endure over time by defining rules of succession, but also through its ability to pass relatively painlessly from normality to a state of exception and back again. Here it may be useful to turn back to Theodore Roosevelt, a great admirer not only of Jackson, but also of two other US presidents, Washington and Lincoln, as well as of Oliver Cromwell, considered 'not only . . . one of the great generals of all time, but . . . a great statesman who on the whole did a marvellous work'. He did, however, have a limit: 'his making himself a dictator was unnecessary and destroyed the possibility of making the effects of that particular revolution permanent'.[152] It is worth noting that dictatorship was here criticised for not being *time-limited*; 'in the great days of the Roman republic, no harm whatever came from the dictatorship, because great tho [*sic*] the power of the dictator was, after a comparatively short period he surrendered it back to those from whom he gained it'. One should not, therefore, be alarmed at the extraordinary breadth of the prerogatives of the highest magistracy of the United States: the great presidents of its history are those who 'cannot be accused of weakness or timidity' and who have proved to be 'quite as strong' as Cromwell and Bismarck, and 'very much stronger than the Louis Napoleon type'; the important thing is that their term of office should not last too long: 'it is not well that a strong executive [which is also absolutely necessary] should be a perpetual executive'.[153] So, here, Theodore Roosevelt ascribes the presidency very wide powers and a right of solitary decision-making, especially as regards foreign policy; but, at the same time, he realises that such an institution can become permanent only within the framework of a regime capable of ensuring an orderly and painless succession. US political reality thus sets us in front of a sort of soft Bonapartism which can, however, easily transform into an explicit war-Bonapartism, as need be, before returning to normality once the state of exception is considered surpassed.

Indeed, this is a political regime that, after brilliantly passing the test of fire of World War I, has racked up one victory after another, up to the present. But before analysing its irresistible rise, it is worth pausing for a moment to dwell on one of its assumptions, which has thus far remained in the shadows.

152 Roosevelt, *Letters*, vol. 2, pp. 1327, 1047.
153 Ibid., vol. 6, pp. 1086–7.

4

The Trumpets of the Ruling Classes and the Bells of the Subaltern

The Representative Regime and the Armed Forces

At the end of the nineteenth century, Engels repeatedly took stock of the historical period that had begun with the French Revolution. For Engels, the era of barricades and popular uprisings that had played such an important role up to the Paris Commune had now passed: weapons had become too precise and powerful, and it was impossible to match up to the overwhelming firepower in the hands of the state and its armed forces. Engels sometimes seems to blame this radically changed situation above all on developments in military technology: 'Up to 1848 it was possible to make the necessary ammunition oneself out of powder and lead'; now this was no longer possible, or posed great difficulties, and in any case the rudimentary weapons the people could muster were now 'far from being a match for the magazine rifle of the soldier, even in close fighting'. The army's powerful weapons were now able to sweep away every obstacle and every barricade.[1] The state monopoly of armed force was a fait accompli; but this outcome also had to do with the political action of the bourgeoisie, whose 'first aim', in the France following the February Revolution, had been 'to disarm the workers'.[2]

1 *Marx-Engels Collected Works* (*MECW*) (London: Lawrence & Wishart, 1975–2004), vol. 27, p. 519.

2 Ibid., p. 181.

But perhaps this last observation can be radicalised. Rarely has proper attention been paid to the fact that a fundamental stage in the history of the representative regime was the narrowing of the electoral sphere, which had in a certain period also encompassed the armed forces and their leadership. One of the first acts of the French revolutionary bourgeoisie consisted of counterposing to the royal troop – controlled from above by an officer corps composed exclusively of nobles – a National Guard whose officers were elected, though within its ranks there applied the same property-based discrimination as in political life in general. In the period of the greatest radicalisation of the Revolution, the elective principle, which had now broken free of the previous exclusion of 'passive citizens', also established itself within the army proper.[3] At this point, the whole of the armed forces was subject to some form of control from below, and the process of elevating the nation's military leaders did not differ in principle from that for its political leaders.

Such a situation was fraught with danger for the bourgeoisie, whose subsequent action was inspired by the concern to secure itself a monopoly of armed force. This problem was also much in the minds of the delegates to the Philadelphia Convention. Yet, in their very different institutional framework, they were easily able to resolve this issue by submitting even the militias of the individual states to presidential authority in moments of crisis.

Political Control and Economic Control of the Means of Information

We might ask whether a process analogous to the one affecting the military field did not also occur – by different routes and over much longer timescales – in the control of the press and the means of information. The important mobilising role played by newspapers during the French revolution is well known: it is calculated that between 1789 and 1800

3 Albert Soboul, *The French Revolution, 1787–1799: From the Storming of the Bastille to Napoleon*; transl. Alan Forrest and Colin Jones (New York: Vintage, 1975), p. 251; Jean-François Fayard, 'Elections', in Jean Tulard, Jean-François Fayard and Alfred Fierro, *Histoire et dictionnaire de la Révolution française 1789–1799* (Paris: Laffont, 1987).

more than 1,350 separate titles were published.[4] Indeed, 'in Paris in the year 1789 every marginally prominent politician formed his club, and every other founded his journal; between February and May alone 450 clubs and over 200 journals sprung up'; this was a time when the journals of even 'the tiniest political groupings and associations' mushroomed.[5] Given the still artisanal stage of printing and publishing, and the relatively low production costs, the popular classes had fairly easy access to these instruments of agitation and mobilisation. Initiatives to stabilise power and the existing social order needed not only to disarm the working classes, but also to heighten control of the propertied over the means of information and political agitation. If the *ancien régime* had sought to control the press by means of pre-emptive censorship, a different instrument would now have to be used – one that resulted from the interconnection of politics and economics.

Already in the years of the Restoration, the monopoly of political life by the propertied was achieved both through property-based discrimination, which directly excluded the popular masses from exercising political rights, and through the obligation to pay a security deposit when registering a press organ. It is interesting to note that the law of 9 June 1819 staggered the level of the deposit according not only to the periodicity of the given press organ but also its place of publication, imposing the highest sum on newspapers that published more than three issues per week and that were published in Paris and in the three neighbouring *départements*.[6] That is, it sought to strike at – and silence – the sheets most likely to 'stir up' the popular masses, and especially the Parisian popular masses who played such an important and radical role in the course of the Great Revolution.

As directly political control of the press declined and the property-based restrictions on political rights were relaxed, the use of the security deposit as an instrument for excluding the popular masses from political life became ever more important. The July Revolution abolished censorship, but, as has been rightly observed, this 'did not mean that the government was powerless in its relations with journalism. Political

4 Fayard, 'Élections'.

5 Jürgen Habermas, *The Structural Transformation of the Public Sphere* (Cambridge, MA: MIT Press, 1989), pp. 183–4.

6 *MECW*, vol. 10, p. 703.

journals had still to deposit a substantial sum as caution money.'[7] After the assassination attempt on Louis-Philippe in July 1835, 'the atrocious September laws against the press' not only criminalised propaganda or incitement to hatred against the existing property relations, but also burdened press outlets with even higher security deposits.[8] Immediately after the 1848 revolution, Blanqui took stock of the policy pursued first by the governments of the Restoration and then by the July Monarchy:

> For thirty years, only the counter-revolution has spoken to France. Gagged by the fiscal laws, the press has penetrated the surface of society. The education of the masses has been done solely by oral teaching [i.e. by the Church], which has always belonged and still belongs to the enemies of the republic. Especially in the countryside, it is only the notables of the defeated factions [i.e. in the February revolution] who attract the people's attention, while men devoted to the democratic cause are unknown to them.[9]

Blanqui hoped that the collapse of the July Monarchy would also bring an end to the monopoly of the press and information that the conservative bloc had managed to achieve thanks to the suffocation of popular newspapers through the deposit laws. But this institution instead became even more important in the new situation which, for the moment at least, provided for universal male suffrage and, in any case, a considerable extension of the enjoyment of political rights. The ruling bourgeoisie resorted to a new press law that not only upped the rate of the caution money, but sought to strike at 'all publications appearing weekly or monthly up to a certain number of sheets' and even the 'feuilleton novels' – that is, any literary product likely to circulate among the popular masses and express their mood, however episodically.[10]

As a further guarantee of the media monopoly of the propertied, regulations were enacted which stipulated 'enormous fines' for any infractions against the press laws. In this way, 'the revolutionary press

7 Alfred Cobban, *A History of Modern France* (Harmondsworth: Penguin, 1965), vol. 2, p. 105.

8 *MECW*, vol. 22, p. 520.

9 Raymond Huard, *Le suffrage universel en France 1848–1946* (Paris: Aubier, 1991), pp. 34ff.

10 *MECW*, vol. 10, p. 137.

disappeared altogether. It had long fought up against persecution: week by week, paper after paper and pamphlet after pamphlet, were accused, fined, suppressed. The middle-class sat in the jury-box, and they crushed the working-man's press.'[11]

This last point deserves further reflection. Already in the days of the July Monarchy, 'offering an affront to the king or holding the government up to contempt might bring a fine of 1,000 francs, accompanied by a term of imprisonment for the editor'. Yet, 'though juries were chosen only from the wealthy class which possessed the right of franchise', they tended 'to acquit journalists charged with press offences'.[12]

So, why did the courts become markedly stricter after 1848? It was not only because the danger of social revolution and the overthrow of existing property relations seemed to have become more concrete and immediate. There is also another reason that needs bearing in mind. In the years of the July Monarchy, the bourgeoisie, whose most radical sectors were still engaged in the struggle against the landed aristocracy and the feudal nobility, was internally divided, since a part of it was still excluded from the enjoyment of political rights, access to which was barred by a rather high property threshold. The unity of the propertied classes had not yet been achieved, and the laws on the press, the deposit and the related fines did not only strike against the popular sheets, as would be the case after 1848. This was why, in the years of the July Monarchy, the jurors could show indulgence towards the accused, with whom they were sometimes linked by multiple threads of social belonging and political solidarity.

After the February Days – and what the horrified Tocqueville called a 'socialist' revolution – the administration of justice took on a clearly and unequivocally classist configuration, at least as far as press offences were concerned. Even after the fall of Napoleon III, the new government led by Thiers introduced a tax 'of two sous on each copy of any publication', leading Marx to bewail the inauspicious continuity with the laws of September 1835, in which Thiers had himself already played a prominent part.[13] That the institution of the deposit was a new way of reintroducing property discrimination in a regime of universal (or at least

11 Ibid., p. 569.

12 Cobban, *History of Modern France*, p. 105.

13 *MECW*, vol. 22, p. 520.

greatly widened) suffrage, did not escape the most attentive political observers of the time. We have seen Marx lamenting the fatal blow dealt against the 'working-class press'. On the opposite side, we see a lucid German conservative, Stahl, counting 'the property bar for representation' and 'deposits for the press' among the 'politico-legal distinctions in favour of the well-off' to which the bourgeoisie organised in the 'liberal party' resorted in order to 'dominate public life [and] complete and consolidate their material satisfaction by means of political satisfaction', while keeping at bay 'the class of the unpropertied'.[14]

The Editor, the Newspaper and the Party

It may be useful at this point to cite a very famous passage from the *German Ideology*:

> The ideas of the ruling class are in every epoch the ruling ideas: i.e., the class which is the ruling material force of society is at the same time its ruling intellectual force. The class which has the means of material production at its disposal, consequently also controls the means of mental production, so that the ideas of those who lack the means of mental production are on the whole subject to it.[15]

In the course of the bourgeois revolution, the division of the propertied classes and of 'material power' corresponds to the division of 'mental power'. In this phase, the newspaper played an eminently subversive role; it represented the instrument with which the Third Estate as a whole could oppose the *ancien régime*, which could count on the Church's extensive organisation and ideological influence. This was the sense in which, on the eve of July 1830 – that is, of the uprising that would definitively overthrow the Bourbon monarchy – after underlining that even 'having the Paris newspapers near at hand' made the 'petty tyrants fearful', Stendhal wondered: 'Can the daily newspaper ever

14 Friedrich J. Stahl, *Die gegenwärtigen Parteien in Staat und Kirche. Neunundzwanzig akademische Vorlesungen* (Berlin: Hertz, 1863), pp. 72ff.

15 *MECW*, vol. 5, p. 59.

replace the priest?'[16] Hegel's aphorism from more than two decades earlier should be read in this same sense: 'Reading the morning newspaper is the realist's morning prayer. One orients one's attitude toward the world either by God or by what the world is. The former gives as much security as the latter, in that one knows how one stands.'[17]

At this moment, there were two instruments of conscience and opinion formation, and they each referred to different and opposing classes and social blocs. The last time the newspaper and the priest faced each other at the head of two opposing camps had been on the occasion of Louis-Napoleon's rise to the presidency, and then to dictatorship. He had been able to make use of the support and the very wide influence of the Church to neutralise the press and sweep away the weak and vain resistance of the liberal bourgeoisie – which, moreover, had already silenced the working-class clubs and papers during the June Days.

With the liberal stabilisation of the Second Empire, and even more so with the Third Republic, there was a substantial unification of the propertied classes, with their respective instruments of public-opinion-formation converging towards a common objective, namely the consolidation of the existing social order. Nonetheless, the propertied classes failed to gain a total monopoly over the media: a subversive press continued to make its presence felt, though it was now reduced in size. It should be remembered that while, during the Great Revolution, the newspaper had been the instrument of the Third Estate, the latter was already traversed by acute contradictions. Within the Third Estate, the weight of the popular classes – owing to the concrete modalities of the process of material and mental production and its consequent ease of access to the means of information – was, from the bourgeoisie's perspective, excessive and dangerous. We can thus understand the denunciation Comte made of 'newspapers' even before the revolution of 1848, which cast them as one of the major vehicles for the spread of the revolutionary and 'metaphysical contagion . . . among the lower classes'.[18]

16 Stendhal, *Red and Black* (New York: W. W. Norton, 1969), p. 158.

17 G. W. F. Hegel, *Werke in zwanzig Bänden* (Frankfurt: Suhrkamp, 1969), vol. 2, p. 547; translation from *Miscellaneous Writings of G.W.F. Hegel*, translated by Jon Bartley Steward (Evanston, IL: Northwestern University Press, 2002), p. 247.

18 Auguste Comte, *A Discourse on the Positive Spirit* (London: Reeves, 1903), p. 143.

The thesis in the *German Ideology* thus came at the beginning of the process by which the bourgeoisie concentrated the means of information in its own hands. That is, it was formulated at a time when it was only partially true, given that full control of material production did not yet automatically entail full control of mental production. These were, as we have seen, years in which the bourgeoisie was forced to resort to additional political expedients (the imposition by law of onerous taxes and deposits on the publication of press organs) in order to reduce the ideological influence of the subaltern classes to a minimum, or eliminate it altogether. What is more, in this as in similar cases, as Marx outlines a basic tendency of bourgeois society, he also suggests the conduct and methods by which the subaltern classes can counteract it – that is, he stimulates the real historical movement which tends to falsify the thesis which he himself enunciates. Organised and sustained by the enthusiasm and spirit of self-sacrifice of the social classes who hope in this way to achieve their emancipation, the political party with a popular and working-class social base undermines and challenges the bourgeois-proprietor monopoly over the media. Such a party itself develops as a means of mental production – indeed, a powerful one – with its newspapers, its intellectuals and its functionaries capable of exercising extensive ideological and political influence. This is why, in 1882, Engels praised the German social-democratic workers who had been 'read[ing] newspapers to a far greater extent and far more regularly'.[19] On the other side of the political spectrum, Treitschke denounced the nefarious influence that social democracy exerted on the masses, 'through the exhibition of the power of its newspapers'; its officials and 'bureaucracy' could proliferate only thanks to the 'proceeds of newspaper sales' (*Zeitungseinnahme*).[20] These were years in which conservative publicists accused the partisans of the 'social revolution' of unscrupulously using the 'means of modern culture' and 'newspapers'; years in which Bismarck came to point to newspapers as the 'instruments of the Antichrist', presumably with a particular view to the social-democratic and oppositional press.[21]

---

19 *MECW*, vol. 24, p. 458.

20 Heinrich von Treitschke, *Der Socialismus und der Meuchelmord* (Berlin: Reimer, 1878), pp. 6ff.

21 Christoph Luthardt, 'Die modernen Weltanschauungen und ihre praktischen Konsequenzen, Vorträge', in Karl H. Hoefele, *Geistund Gesellschaft der Bismarckzeit*

In this period of history, the foremost philosopher and poet of this demonisation of the political and party press was Nietzsche, who lamented how 'the newspaper takes over from the daily prayers'.[22] This was the same counterposition we have already seen in Stendhal and Hegel, but now with the value judgement reversed: in an era when even the priest's sermon came in more useful than ever, in opposition to working-class and social-democratic agitation, the philosopher of the Antichrist looked with disappointment upon the disappearance of the dull, muffled tranquility of the masses in the shadow of the bell tower and its replacement by the 'newspaper'. For the latter went hand-in-hand with 'petty politics', or even the *furor politicus* that resulted from daily newspaper reading.[23] Perhaps behind this there was also the vague memory of the experience of the 1848 revolution (which Nietzsche had painted in dark hues in his autobiography), when newspapers, periodicals and party sheets sprang up like mushrooms even in Naumburg (where the philosopher's family was then located), where they were daily devoured by readers in the grip of political passion, eager to follow and influence events.[24] What is certain is that, after the turning point that traumatic year represented for the whole of European conservative culture, the theme already seen in a philosopher as radically anti-Christian as Nietzsche could be found in Italy in a liberal Catholic philosopher such as Vincenzo Gioberti, who also expressed the conviction that 'the press and newspapers', spreading among the 'people', contributed powerfully to 'increase the feeling of its ills and its desire to redeem itself from them'.[25] A year before Gioberti's comments, in 1850, *Civiltà Cattolica* had thundered against 'journalism', explicitly pointing its accusing finger against 'revolutionary France', the land of incessant political upheaval, where journalism had proved more clearly than ever to be 'an instrument of perpetual

(Göttingen/Berlin/Frankfurt: Mutterschmidt, 1967 [1880]), pp. 157ff; Benedetto Croce, *Storia d'Europa nel secolo decimonono* (Bari: Laterza, 1965), p. 219.

22 Friedrich Nietzsche, *Sämtliche Werke, Kritische Studienausgahe* (Munich: DTV, 1980), vol. 13, p. 123; vol. 11, p. 68ff.

23 Friedrich Nietzsche, *Beyond Good and Evil* (Cambridge: Cambridge University Press, 2002), p. 102; Nietzsche, *Sämtliche Werke*, vol. 1, p. 409.

24 Domenico Losurdo, 'Le catene e i fiori. La critica dell'ideologia tra Marx e Nietzsche', *Hermeneutica* 6 (1987), p. 134.

25 Vincenzo Gioberti, *Del rinnovamento civile degli italiani* (Bari: Laterza, 1911–12 [1851]), vol. 1, p. 116.

agitation among peoples', and where the spectre of socialism had also recently appeared.[26]

For Nietzsche, the newspaper symbolised the massification of the modern world and all that the philosopher of 'inactuality' condemned therein. But, first and foremost, he saw it as the instrument and expression of the revolt of the masses. The condemnation of the newspaper is the other side of the celebration of the torpor of the popular strata, and of the beneficial character of ideological opium. In the German philosopher, the polemic against the newspaper, the workers' movement, universal suffrage, the advent of the masses onto the scene of politics and history, and the involution of the world all come together. A posthumous fragment identifies 'parliamentarianism' and the 'press' (*Zeitungswesen*) as 'the means by which the herd animal makes itself master', whereas *Beyond Good and Evil* depicts a bleak future in which the despotism of the masses is illustrated by 'the requirement that every man read his newspaper over breakfast'.[27] The fact remains, however, that Nietzsche's indictment of the vulgar and dangerous element of the press is conducted primarily with the spectre of socialism in mind – that is, the dreaded seizure of power by the 'herd animal'.

Newspapers, Organised Parties and the Subaltern Classes

Thus, the denunciation of the newspaper was accompanied by the denunciation of the party. For Nietzsche, the latter institution was itself characterised by its 'demagogic character' and 'intention to appeal to the masses', seeing as it had the either objective or deliberately pursued effect of challenging the masses' traditional subalternity and passivity.[28] The party in question here is not so much the bourgeois-liberal 'party of opinion', but mainly the social-democratic party seeking to organise the masses; it is no accident that the philosopher warns the workers against

26 Gennaro Lerda, 'La schiavitù e la guerra civile nelle pagine della "Civiltà Cattolica" (1850–1865)', in *Italia e America dal Settecento all'età dell'imperialismo*, ed. Giorgio Spini et al. (Venice: Marsilio, 1976), p. 233.

27 Nietzsche, *Sämtliche Werke*, vol. 11, p. 480; Nietzsche, *Beyond Good and Evil*, p. 101.

28 Friedrich Nietzsche, *Human, All too Human: A Book for Free Spirits* (Cambridge: Cambridge University Press, 1996), p. 161.

listening to the 'piping of the Socialist rat-catchers', or in other words 'the newspaper'; the latter is also condemned as an integral part of the 'culture of the big cities', where the phenomenon of mass revolt and elite decline is most evident and frightening.[29] In his lucid reactionary hatred, Nietzsche clearly identifies the socially subversive – even before it is politically subversive – character of the newspaper and the workers' party. To the extent that the latter organises itself independently, it represents the threatening emergence of social strata hitherto incapable of playing a real political role. In Marx's language, by acting as an autonomous centre of intellectual and mental production, such a party undermines or breaks the property-owners' monopoly on such production.

At this point, it is worth returning to the historical balance sheet set out by Engels: in the period up to 1848 – or, at the latest, up to 1871 – given the relative ease with which civilians and the masses could gain access to arms, the relationship between the bourgeois state and the subordinate classes had been characterised by a potential dualism of military power. Yet, the repression of first the June Days and then the Commune put a definitive end to such a situation. This was the moment for the workers' party to abandon the romanticism of the barricades without delay – and also without regret, especially given that, in the different objective situation that had now come about, new instruments of struggle had emerged, no less effective than the old ones. In the first place, this meant universal suffrage, which German social democracy – Engels points out – was able to use wisely, in turn providing a potential model for the other workers' parties. The German was the 'strongest, most disciplined' workers' party: it knew how to engage in a patient work of propaganda and to conquer the masses, thanks to its press and the use of parliament itself as a 'platform'.[30]

But how could universal suffrage be a tool of emancipation, rather than serving the plebiscitary acclamation of a Bonapartist government? Was this not what had happened in Louis-Napoleon's France, and what Bismarck himself hoped to do in Germany when he introduced universal suffrage for the Reichstag elections as 'the only means of interesting the mass of the people in his plans', to gain his coveted Caesarist

29 Friedrich Nietzsche, *The Dawn of Day* (London: George Allen & Unwin, 1924), p. 21; Nietzsche, *Sämtliche Werke*, vol. 13, p. 93.

30 *MECW*, vol. 27, pp. 516–17.

legitimacy? The question is little more than incidentally touched upon, but, even so, Engels does make clear that German social democracy could neutralise Bonapartist manoeuvring insofar as it managed, thanks also to its organisation and its press, to force 'all parties to defend their views and actions against our attacks before all the people'.[31] That is to say, in a situation of dualism or pluralism of the centres of intellectual and mental production, every election is transformed into a great national political debate, in which the people are enabled to make an informed judgement, thanks to the absence of any monopoly on the means of information.

There was thus a historical period in which the trumpets of the bourgeoisie and the propertied classes were challenged, as it were, by the bells of the popular classes. Bourgeois domination would not be sufficiently solid and guaranteed until the monopoly of armed force was complemented by the monopoly of mental production. This would mean marginalising both those means of information and those parties which, because of their organisation and their link with social classes antagonistic to the dominant ones, took the form – or were likely to take the form in crisis situations – of an alternative authority. Regarding the first point, the bourgeoisie is favoured by objective economic and industrial developments. Tocqueville describes the fascinating spectacle of press freedom in the United States, where 'there are no licenses for printers, no stamps or registration for newspapers; the rule of surety bonds is unknown'. Even this contrast with the practice of government controls and harassment in old Europe, including in the liberal country which emerged from the July Monarchy, is not without its stereotypical elements: while, in France, the authorities had to confront a lively and combative popular and even working-class opposition press, born in the wake of the Great Revolution – or, rather, to a revolutionary process that showed no sign of ending – in America, the social and political control of the 'dangerous classes' was primarily assured by the institution of slavery. And we must not forget that, in a crisis moment such as 1798, even in the United States the authorities had not hesitated to take crude measures to gag the press. Tocqueville, however, continues as follows:

31 Ibid., pp. 515–16.

> the creation of a newspaper is a simple and easy undertaking; a few subscribers suffice for the journalist to cover his expenses. The number of periodical or semi-periodical writings in the United States therefore surpasses all belief. The most enlightened Americans attribute the little power of the press to this incredible scattering of its forces . . . in the United States newspapers cannot establish those great waves of opinions that rise up or overwhelm the most powerful dikes. This division of the forces of the press produces still other no less remarkable effects. Because the creation of a newspaper is so easy, everyone can do it. On the other hand, competition means that a newspaper cannot hope for very great profits; this prevents great industrial talents from getting involved in enterprises of this type.[32]

It goes without saying that this picture no longer bears any correspondence to today's reality, characterised by a vast concentration process that has in fact secured the big bourgeoisie's monopoly over the press, and even more so over the mass media, which require even greater capital and investment. By wiping out the working-class and popular press – or decisively contributing to this outcome – economic and technological development has rendered obsolete and superfluous the additional political means of coercion and conditioning of the freedom of the press – a freedom now to be considered juridically complete in normal times, also in the European case. Yet it would be mistaken to believe that the present situation – with the bells of the subaltern classes vanishing, and the uncontested domination of the ever more disproportionately powerful trumpets of the class which, as Marx put it, controls the 'material means of production' – is the exclusive result of a merely economic process.

Parties, Trade Unions and Repressive Individualism

In reality, the development of the working-class and popular press in the nineteenth century cannot be separated from the history of the political and trade union organisation of the subaltern classes, and the

32 Alexis de Tocqueville, *Democracy in America*, ed. Eduardo Nolla, transl. James T. Schleifer (Indianapolis, IN: Liberty Fund, 2012), vol. 2, pp. 295–6.

ruling-class reaction to this process. Particularly instructive in this regard is the evolution that took place in the United States:

> In 1885, the labour press comprised seventeen monthlies, 400 weeklies and a few dailies (including the socialist *Volkszeitung*, the *Irish World* and the *American Industrial Liberator*). Despite the attempts of the bosses, who tried in every way to limit its sway, above all by firing workers caught reading it, the influence of this press was far from negligible. It was owed especially to the libraries and reading rooms opened in this era by trade unions and political movements or circles: the workers kept up with contemporary debates.[33]

But, together with the political organisations that supported it, or of which it was one expression, at the end of the nineteenth century this press became the target and the victim of a developing conservative reaction that resulted in a disemancipation process. Thus, the disappearance of the party and union newspapers was owed not only to the objective economic process, but a specific political action. While these newspapers had allowed the subaltern classes to express themselves with at least some autonomy, they were now supplanted by a press that boasted of its independence, but in reality was controlled by big proprietors.[34] These were years in which, as we know, the principle of universal suffrage was itself under indictment, held guilty of opening the doors of representative bodies to the classes of the destitute and uncultured, drowning the 'government of the best', and sanctioning domination by the ignorant populace and, even worse, by immigrants. The party press – counterposed to the 'independent' press – was denounced as an instrument of this new barbarian invasion, as were the parties themselves, some even going so far as to call for their outright suppression.[35]

33 Marie-France Toinet, 'La Participation politique des ouvriers américains à la fin du dix-neuvième siècle', in *À l'ombre de la statue de la liberté. Immigrants et ouvriers dans la République américaine 1880–1920*, ed. Marianna Debouzy (Vincennes: Presses Universitaires de Vincennes, 1988), pp. 291–2.

34 Walter Dean Burnham, *Critical Election and the Mainsprings of American Politics* (New York: Norton, 1970), p. 76.

35 Arnaldo Testi, '"Questi partiti selvaggi e voraci" James Bryce, Moisei Ostrogorski e l'immagine del partito americano. Le loro fonti nel contesto della lotta politica negli Stati Uniti di fine Ottocento', in *Il partito politico americano e l'Europa*, ed. Maurizio

In the same European authors who, starting from the experience of the United States, systematise the conservative critique of the party system, it is possible to perceive the echo of the attitude, which was widespread among the American upper classes, of hostility towards the extension of political rights to the 'Southern negroes' or to 'city-dwelling immigrants' (a source only of disasters, or at least of 'unwelcome results').[36] Even without going this far, it is telling that, in the denunciation of parties committed to the 'oppression of numbers', essentially it was the classic arguments of the polemic against universal suffrage and democracy that re-emerged.[37]

In a period when, even before the enactment of laws sanctioning their disemancipation, blacks in the South were deprived of political rights by whites through 'force and fraud'; in a period in which trade unions were pushed, as we shall see, into illegality or to the fringes of legality, the federal army intervened to crush strikes, and workers caught reading the trade-union and party press risked being fired – and with this, an irreversible sentence to unemployment and the blackest misery, given the use of 'black lists' drawn up by the employers to keep agitators out of the workplace – in this same period, conservative publicists in America and Europe denounced the organised party as a 'school of servile submission' and an instrument of intimidation that repressed and trampled on the 'individual'.[38] That is, in effect, conservative publicists indiscriminately indicted the only possible forces capable of opposing organised resistance to the violence of the ruling classes and the ruling authorities. Efforts to denounce the party as a 'machine' zoned in on the hateful figure of the political 'boss'. However, the other side of the picture unintentionally, but objectively, emerges from the observation that blacks forced to suffer the whites' vexations were beginning to resign themselves to their fate also because they were 'losing faith in their former bosses'. The latter were indeed now retreating from the

---

Vaudagna (Milan: Feltrinelli, 1991), pp. 59, 62; 'Introduzione', in *L'età progressista negli Stati Uniti*, ed. Arnaldo Testi (Bologna: Mulino, 1984), pp. 40ff.

36 James Bryce, *The American Commonwealth* (London: Macmillan, 1888), vol. 3, pp. 357, 674.

37 Moisei Ostrogorski, *Democracy and the Organization of Political Parties* (New York: Macmillan, 1902), vol. 2, p. 630.

38 Bryce, *American Commonwealth*, vol. 2, p. 364; Allan Nevins and Henry S. Commager, *America: The Story of a Free People* (Oxford: Clarendon, 1947), p. 328; Ostrogorski, *Democracy and the Organization of Political Parties*, vol. 2, p. 636.

South, leaving the terrain free for a civil society and a power that did not need parties to sanction undisputed domination by a 'superior race'.[39]

Even apart from blacks, it becomes clearly apparent who the concrete targets of the campaign against parties are, when we see the accusation levelled against the militants who 'witness the disorders of public life unmoved, because these disorders are covered by the flag of their party'.[40] Clearly targeted, here, are the political, trade-union and social organisations (in the broadest sense of the term) of the lower classes which, in order to be able to put up a minimum of resistance to the government and employers, are obliged to appeal to the cohesion and the spirit of solidarity of their members (to whom they sometimes provide political education and instruction). For this, they are condemned as a sort of 'Church, which takes charge of all the spiritual needs of man'.[41] Moreover, it is a Church that dangerously confuses the ideas of its flock:

> Now, the intellectual vision and the power of attention of the average man are very limited, it is hardly possible for him to apply them to a large area or to a highly diversified prospect; he can only follow action confined to a restricted sphere, like that of the parish, or extending beyond it, but with a single object clearly visible to all and entailing only a temporary duty. Once these limits are exceeded, his sight becomes dazed, his attention is divided and wearied, and if he continues to follow the course prescribed, he does it in a passive manner. The members of a political association pursuing a variety of objects are, therefore, units simply placed side by side.[42]

Here emerges the classic theme of the 'childlike' multitude which the organised party claims to elevate to conscious political life, but which it thereby transforms into a mass of manoeuvre and an army of soldiers accustomed to blind obedience. In this sense, such a party, based on 'passive co-operation' and 'esprit de corps', prevents 'the emancipation of the individual'.[43] It is possible to outline a social history of the party

39 Bryce, *American Commonwealth*, vol. 2, p. 35.
40 Ostrogorski, *Democracy and the Organization of Political Parties*, vol. 2, p. 628.
41 Ibid., p. 615.
42 Ibid., p. 621.
43 Ibid., pp. 616, 621.

form. The organised political party arose on the wave of the subaltern classes' movement demanding their emancipation. It is *these* classes that need as extensive and intensive as possible an organisation – and not those classes that already have at their disposal the apparatus of state and government and private wealth, as well as the social influence that immediately flows from it. That is why, throughout a whole historical period, the bourgeois party of *opinion* stood in contrast with the *organised* workers' or people's party. We have seen Bagehot reflect on techniques to prevent the class organisation of 'miserable creatures' who are satisfied with their lot, either because they are induced into an attitude of filial submission by the charisma of a queen who rules over them 'by the grace of God' or because they are dazzled by the 'vague dream of glory' stirred up by chauvinist leaders. It is the subaltern classes who need enduring, organised efforts to elaborate an autonomous culture and political vision, to 'constitute their own group of independent intellectuals' in the course of a process that is often broken up 'by the [political and ideological] activity of ruling groups'.[44] This is why, for a whole historical period, the at least apparently de-ideologised bourgeois party stood opposed to a workers' or people's party that sought to achieve a greater or lesser degree of internal cohesion, including ideological cohesion. A party formed on such a basis constitutes a strong centre of autonomous mental production. In certain circumstances, especially in situations of acute crisis, the ruling classes have themselves sought to place themselves on this terrain, going beyond the purely opinion-based party form. But it is clear that, from their point of view, the ideal solution lies in the disappearance of parties that offer an ideological and organisational alternative to their own system of power.

Such parties represented the emergence on the political scene of social classes previously considered as a set of 'work instruments' or 'bipedal machines', which now begin to claim recognition of their dignity as men and individuals. But, from Ostrogorski's point of view, the parties that organise these subaltern classes are to be blamed for trampling on individualism. Indeed – using arguments not dissimilar to those used later by conservative publicists against parties, especially workers' parties – the 1791 Le Chapelier law in France banned workers'

44 Antonio Gramsci, *Selections from the Prison Notebooks* (London: Lawrence & Wishart, 1971), Q16, §9, p. 392; Q25 §2, p. 55.

coalitions which, in their pretence to adopt an organisational structure that would defend 'supposed common interests', trampled on the individual's freedom to work. The nascent trade-union movement was long pounded and strangled in the name of this repressive individualism. Even after the July revolution, upon the occasion of a protest against piecework, the authorities of liberal France ordered: 'If the workers of Paris have well-founded claims to raise, these should be presented individually and in a regular form to the competent authorities', and in any case without hurting the 'principle of the liberty of industry' and 'liberty of labor'.[45] Such repressive individualism was also very much alive in the United States in years that saw a developing campaign against organised parties: the Sherman Antitrust Act (1890) was 'applied first and most effectively to labor' – the workers evidently being deemed guilty of gathering in union 'monopolies' with scant respect for individual initiative and freedom.[46]

Adam Smith was also against coalitions of any kind, again in the name of the market and individual choice. But at least he honestly acknowledged that the prohibition, even if formulated in general terms, would end up striking in only one direction: 'The masters, being fewer in number, can combine much more easily . . . Masters are always and everywhere in a sort of tacit, but constant and uniform combination, not to raise the wages of labour above their actual rate [or] to sink the wages of labour even below this rate.'[47]

Of course, the dissolution, or drastic downsizing, of organised political parties also ends up working in the same way as the ban on coalitions. The conservative campaign that grew in America and Europe at the end of nineteenth century sometimes advanced the thesis that to eliminate 'permanent parties with power as their end' would 'enable opinions to come forward with more freedom and to assert themselves with more sincerity'.[48] Exactly the opposite is true: the weakening or dissolution of organised parties allows for the means of mental

45 William H. Sewell, Jr, *Work and Revolution in France: The Language of Labor from the Old Regime to 1848* (Cambridge: Cambridge University Press, 1980), p. 196.

46 Nevins and Commager, *America*, p. 318.

47 Adam Smith, *An Inquiry into the Nature and the Causes of the Wealth of Nations* (Chicago: University of Chicago Press, 2012 [1904]), p. 99.

48 Ostrogorski, *Democracy and the Organization of Political Parties*, vol. 2, pp. 658, 664.

production to be monopolised by a small, privileged circle that no longer faces any organised resistance to its work of manipulation. Late-nineteenth-century conservative critics sometimes declared themselves convinced that the weakening of parties would raise the level of public debate, as there would be 'less inducement to resort to those sensational practices which aim at the emotions and the senses'.[49] Yet, in reality, what followed was a startling decline in the level of political debate. The atomisation of the masses created the conditions for the triumph of Bonapartism, based on the unequal relationship between a leader – who could appeal to the most powerful means of communication and the most refined techniques of covert persuasion and manipulation – and a multitude which was now truly 'childlike', because it was increasingly stripped of any autonomous organisation or means of expression.

The denunciation that Bryce and Ostrogorski levelled against parties and trade unions, accusing them of stifling free individuality, was contemporary to Le Bon's indictment of the 'era of crowds' – that is, the era of trade unions and more or less socialist parties:

> The progressive growth of the power of the masses took place at first by the propagation of certain ideas, which have slowly implanted themselves in men's minds, and afterwards by the gradual association of individuals bent on bringing about the realisation of theoretical conceptions. It is by association that crowds have come to procure ideas with respect to their interests which are very clearly defined if not particularly just, and have arrived at a consciousness of their strength. The masses are founding syndicates before which the authorities capitulate one after the other; they are also founding labour unions, which in spite of all economic laws tend to regulate the conditions of labour and wages. They return to assemblies in which the Government is vested, representatives utterly lacking initiative and independence, and reduced most often to nothing else than the spokesmen of the committees that have chosen them.[50]

49 Ibid., p. 66.

50 Gustave Le Bon, *The Crowd: A Study of the Popular Mind* (New York: Macmillan, 1896), pp. xvi–xvii.

The crowds are therefore the subordinate classes that organise themselves autonomously in parties and trade unions. And it is these organisations whose strength must be broken, so that the individuals thus atomised are consigned defenceless to the charms of the Caesar, who can now subjugate them with the tools of commercial advertising.

5

The Bonapartist Regime's Baptism of Fire

Italy and the United States: How to Force the 'Childlike' Multitude into War

World War I gave renewed vigour to Bonapartism's onward march. We have seen Theodore Roosevelt boasting of his entirely solitary foreign policy decisions, including those involving US military engagement abroad. But Woodrow Wilson, a Democrat, agreed: 'The initiative in foreign affairs, which the President possesses without any restriction whatever, is virtually the power to control them absolutely.'[1] This philosophy inspired Wilson's attitude during World War I, from the initial declaration of neutrality to the ultimate decision to intervene. At this point, it may be useful to make a comparison between Italy and the United States. Neither country was immediately drawn into the conflict, and each of their governments prepared to join the war once the mass enthusiasm of summer 1914 had already largely dissipated. They thus were forced to overcome a broad resistance on the part of public opinion and especially of the popular classes, who had by now grasped the full horror of the enormous carnage that was underway.

In the Italian case, to break the pro-neutrality majority in parliament, and the even larger such majority in the country, a sort of coup

1 Peter Carroll and David Noble, *The Free and the Unfree: A New History of the United States* (New York: Viking, 1977), p. 309.

d'état was needed. This involved the participation of the Crown (which rejected the resignation of Antonio Salandra's minority government) and the unleashing of street forces (tolerated or encouraged by the police) which intimidated and threatened opponents of Italian intervention. In these years, many philosophers and intellectuals conferred legitimacy on the interventionist coup d'état, explicitly theorising the right of the elite to impose their will on backward 'masses' who – as Gaetano Salvemini observed – 'moved by negative instincts and not by positive doctrines' were therefore inclined to avoid 'suffering and pain'.[2] Instead, according to Guido Dorso, 'a daring and brilliant minority is needed to drag this mob of mules and cowards by the throat, to die as heroes or win as victors'.[3] Later, Benedetto Croce himself, who had initially shown hesitation over the merits of Italian participation in the conflict, wrote: 'The opponents of the war . . . were certainly many in number (in Italy as elsewhere), and perhaps "masses", but they did not count, because here we are talking about those who thought, spoke and acted politically' – these masses of men gripped by the 'fear of war, closed in their comfort and selfishness', certainly ought not to be indulged.[4] In a land with a parliamentary regime, such as Italy, the 'childlike' multitude could be forced into self-sacrifice and a sense of duty only through street violence and the Crown's coup against parliament – that is, only through a laceration of the constitutional fabric, thus constituting the beginning of the crisis that led to the establishment of the Fascist dictatorship.

Rather different was the situation in the United States. Upon the outbreak of war, Wilson not only proclaimed American neutrality, but launched an appeal to the country for parties, associations, newspapers and all individual citizens to refrain from partisan and passionate judgements on the conflict and its participants, so as to fully observe a strict neutrality, in 'thought' as well as in 'action'. But a few months later this same president authorised and promoted a loans policy favouring

2 Gaetano Salvemini, *Come siamo andati in Libia e altri scritti dal 1900 al 1915* (Feltrinelli, Milan, 1963), p. 448.

3 Enzo Forcella, 'Prefazione', in Enzo Forcella and Alberto Monticene, *Plotone d'esecuzione. I processi della prima guerra* mondiale (Bari: Laterza, 1972), p. xii.

4 Benedetto Croce, *Storia d'Italia dal 1871 al 1915* (Bari: Laterza, 1967), p. 266.

Britain and France.[5] And, yet, still in 1916, the Democratic Convention in St Louis – reconfirming Wilson's candidacy by acclamation, with only one dissenting vote – drew up an electoral platform, largely the incumbent's own work, in which he was commended to the 'American people' for his 'splendid diplomatic victories' (which had preserved 'the vital interests of our Government and its citizens'), and especially for the fact that 'He kept us out of war'. But Wilson preferred not to commit himself quite so strongly, remaining more cautious and also more ambiguous. As even one rather sympathetic biographer observes, rather than refer to the campaign slogan 'He kept us out of war', Wilson merely insinuated or asserted that, unlike him, many Republicans did wish to intervene in the global conflict.[6] One year later, he sought congressional authorisation to arm merchant ships destined to operate in war zones; but, in the Senate, opposition and obstructionism from pacifists led to the bill's rejection. This was not enough to stop the president who, availing himself of his executive powers, ordered the immediate execution of this same measure.

We can conclude with the words of two American historians:

> The great power of the Presidency in foreign affairs had made it possible for Wilson to place the United States on the verge of war without the knowledge of the average voter. These voters had re-elected Wilson because they believed he would preserve peace. The strong peace movement among women had rallied for Wilson. Many German-Americans and Irish-Americans who hated English imperialism also backed Wilson. A number of midwestern WASP 'progressives' . . . saw the Republican party in 1916 as pro-English and prowar and supported Wilson . . . By March 1917, Wilson had involved the United States in a shooting war with Germany.[7]

Clearly, out of the two countries we are comparing here, the decision for, or imposition of, intervention was more difficult in the Italian case, where the signs of property-based discrimination were clearly visible.

5 Yves-Henry Nouailhat, *L'Amérique puissance mondiale 1897–1929* (Nancy: Presses Universitaires de Nancy, 1987), pp. 130, 132.

6 Leon Canfield, *The Presidency of Woodrow Wilson: Prelude to a World in Crisis* (Rutherford, NJ: Fairleigh Dickinson University Press, 1966), pp. 78–81.

7 Carroll and Noble, *The Free and the Unfree*, pp. 311–12.

This was in any case true of the Italian Senate, which continued to be not only a monopoly of the propertied classes, but also heavily under the sway of the *ancien régime*, as consecrated by the Crown. In the United States, conversely, the traces of property-based discrimination had all but disappeared within the white community (alone empowered to decide); in some states, women had already won the right to vote. But a US president endowed with far-reaching powers could still force the 'childlike' multitude to undergo the sacrifices and horrors of war in a disciplined manner, more easily and more elegantly than Crown and parliament could do in Italy.

A Political Regime Well-Suited to the State of Exception

This first demonstration of the superiority of the soft Bonapartist regime, which was by now establishing itself, was followed by other such examples both in the course of the war and in its aftermath. Its development entailed an enormous extension of executive power in all the countries engaged in the gigantic conflagration. Western countries with a more consolidated liberal tradition were certainly not immune to this phenomenon, and in some respects they were even in the vanguard. An English scholar would later observe that 'Woodrow Wilson, Clemenceau, and Lloyd George' were invested 'with an authority which practically amounted to a dictatorship in the Roman sense of the term'.[8] When we look at the culture and the printed press of early postwar Germany, it appears coloured by sheer astonishment at the fact that it was the Western countries that demonstrated a superior capacity for total mobilisation and total, ironclad disciplining of their populations for the war effort. A German professor visiting the United States offered this telling analysis:

> In prewar political discussions, it was always said, by the defenders of the system of government then dominant in Central Europe, that democracy as a form of political life has certain advantages, but that parliamentary democracy especially would be doomed to failure in

8 Alfred Cobban, *Dictatorship: Its History and Theory* (New York: Haskell, 1971), p. 110.

> war. Practical experience has shown the contrary. In terms of political coherence and the disciplined pursuit of objectives, the Western democracies were clearly superior to the bureaucratic system of Eastern and Central Europe. The internal split between military and political leadership, which paralysed the central empires for most of the war period, was overcome by the Western powers through the efforts of politicians conscious of their objectives. The rise of strong personalities endowed with autonomous initiative, which according to the continental conception should have been rendered impossible by democracy, took place unhindered in the Western powers, but not in Russia, Germany or Austria, where the few strong individuals able to impose themselves were exhausted in an endless struggle against bureaucratic-military intrigues.

His attitude somewhere between astonishment and admiration, the German professor continued:

> During the critical periods of the war, the prime ministers of Britain, France, or Italy, and the president of the United States enjoyed a fullness of powers, in comparison with which the power of an Alexander or a Caesar was limited . . . In Western countries, the dictatorial powers conferred were in practice much broader than those that monarchs were able to exercise in Russia and Germany.[9]

Of course, the protagonist of these miracles or misdeeds was not 'parliamentary democracy', but rather a political regime characterised by the personalisation of power, and which had reached or was reaching complete development precisely in the country the German professor visited. Wilson was 'endowed with almost dictatorial powers', or even fully dictatorial ones.[10] It is an irony of history that the man who had considered the emergency legislation of 1798 to be deadly to freedom, now went much further in his use of the iron fist. He proceeded with a use of the state of exception which, by comparison, made the previously

9 Moritz J. Bonn, *Die Krisis der europäischen Demokratie* (Munich: Meyer & Jessen, 1925), pp. 9, 63ff.

10 Canfield, *Presidency of Woodrow Wilson*, p. 109.

criticised legislation appear 'very mild'.[11] The measures taken in the course of World War I aimed 'to wipe out even the slightest traces of opposition'; according to the Espionage Act of 16 May 1918, one could be sentenced to up to twenty years in prison for expressing 'any disloyal, profane, scurrilous, or abusive language about the form of government of the United States, or the Constitution of the United States, or the military or naval forces of the United States'.[12]

While, as far as intervention in the war is concerned, I have made a comparison with Italy, when it comes to questions of mobilising capacity and total regimentation, the United States should be compared above all with imperial Germany. Here, Karl Liebknecht, after voting against the war credits, had the at least temporary opportunity to use parliament as a tribune to denounce the massacre, and even to invite the soldiers to 'lay down their weapons and turn against the enemy'.[13] Arrested in May 1916 after a pacifist and anti-militarist rally, and sentenced to two and a half years' imprisonment, he was pardoned and released in October 1918, in time to participate in the revolution the following month that put an end to both the war and the Hohenzollern dynasty. The fate of the American Socialist leader, Eugene Debs, was harsher: he had been jailed for supporting the transport strike which President Cleveland crushed by sending in federal troops – and, even on that occasion, he was branded an enemy of the fatherland. He was again arrested in June 1918 for an anti-war speech, sentenced to ten years' imprisonment, and released only in December 1921, after spending in jail both the end of the conflict and the electoral campaign in which he was a presidential candidate.[14] It was Harding who reduced his sentence, after Wilson refused to release him.[15]

But, more than the parallel fate of two leaders of the anti-war protest movement, we ought to examine the situation of the socialist parties in

11 Henry Commager, *Documents of American History* (New York: Appleton-Century-Crofts, 1963), vol. 2, p. 325.

12 Arthur Meier Schlesinger, *The Rise of Modern America, 1865–1951* (New York: Macmillan, 1951), p. 290.

13 Ossip Flechtheim, *Karl Liebknecht zur Einführung* (Hamburg: Junius, 1986), p. 55.

14 William Z. Foster, *History of the Communist Party of the United States* (New York: International, 1968), p. 141.

15 Arthur Schlesinger, Jr, *The Age of Roosevelt: The Crisis of the Old Order, 1919–1933* (Boston, MA: Houghton Mifflin, 1957), p. 47.

the two enemy countries. Despite everything, in Germany, pacifist agitation continued to make itself felt, sometimes even through legal means, with the distribution of leaflets in the factories, and with press organs that hailed the October Revolution and published the appeals for immediate peace which flowed from it.[16] Repressive efforts in the United States were far harsher and more vigilant: 'Federal agents systematically prevented supposedly dangerous Socialist activities, censoring and suppressing their newspapers, raiding meetings and prosecuting speakers'.[17]

Although the war represented a far deadlier danger to Germany than to its enemies on the other side of the Atlantic, protected by the ocean, it was undoubtedly in the United States that the iron fist made itself felt with greater force and effectiveness. The important thing was not so much the radical nature of the state of exception – on the eve of the intervention, Wilson declared that the war would mean the end of all 'tolerance' and recourse to 'brutal and ruthless' methods even within the United States – as the painless way in which it was achieved, starting from a constitutional normality that already contained *in nuce* the figure of the dictator.[18]

With his intervention in the conflagration, the American president assumed dictatorial powers not only over economic matters, but also in the field of culture and information: seven days after the declaration of war, Wilson created a Committee for Public Information that provided the press with 22,000 columns of news a week, while withholding anything considered likely to 'help the enemy'.[19] This Committee emerged through a presidential initiative bypassing Congress, and, at least initially, was also financed with presidential funds.[20] Not even high culture escaped regimentation: this same Committee 'mobilized college professors in its scholarship division to write propaganda for the war effort', while the 'federal government encouraged patriotic organizations

16 Walter Ulbricht, *Geschichte der deutschen Arbeiterbewegung*, ed. Walter Ulbricht (Berlin, Dietz, 1966), vol. 5, p. 55; vol. 6, pp. 22–4.

17 Schlesinger, *Rise of Modern America*, p. 291.

18 Canfield, *The Presidency of Woodrow Wilson*, p. 97.

19 Nouailhat, *L'amérique puissance mondiale*, p. 141; Schlesinger, *Rise of Modern America*, p. 290.

20 Peter T. Manicas, *War and Democracy* (Cambridge, MA: Basil Blackwell, 1989), p. 357.

to scrutinize the teaching of American history in high schools and college.'[21] As a scholar of the propaganda techniques adopted during the war, Harold Lasswell, later wrote, the objective for the belligerent countries – achieved with greatest effectiveness in the United States – was to 'fuse the waywardness of individuals in the furnace of the war dance', to 'weld thousands and even millions of human beings into one amalgamated mass of hate and will and hope . . . temper[ing] the steel of bellicose enthusiasm'.[22]

Having brilliantly survived the baptism of fire of the war, soft Bonapartism was further consolidated with the great world economic crisis, acting as a prelude to a gigantic new conflict. In his inaugural address on 4 March 1933, Franklin Delano Roosevelt claimed such broad, extraordinary powers 'as if the United States had been invaded by a foreign enemy'.[23] Influential statesmen and politicians called for a 'national dictator', and urged the new president to show all his energy: he 'becomes a tyrant, a despot, a real monarch. In the World War we took our Constitution, wrapped it up and laid it on the shelf and left it there until it was over.' Enormous expectations were placed in the nation's new leader, defined as 'a providential person' – that is, in the words of Cardinal O'Connell, 'a God-sent man'. The people on the street wrote to and addressed Roosevelt in even more emphatic terms, declaring that they looked to him 'almost as they look to God', and hoped one day to place him 'in the halls of immortals beside Jesus'.[24] Invited to behave like a dictator and a man of Providence, Roosevelt made very extensive use of his executive power as early as the first hours of his presidency. Later, the 1936 Republican platform would declare: 'The powers of Congress have been usurped by the President.'[25]

The country's supreme magistrate increasingly took the form of a charismatic leader – and all the more so, the better he was able to appear as an expression of the common people. Making skillful use of the new possibilities for direct communication offered by the radio, Roosevelt

21 Carroll and Noble, *The Free and the Unfree*, pp. 330–1.

22 Harold E. Straubing, ed., *The Last Magnificent War: Rare Journalistic and Eyewitness Accounts of World War I* (New York: Paragon House, 1989), p. 109.

23 Commager, *Documents of American History*, vol. 2, p. 242.

24 Arthur Schlesinger Jr, *The Age Of Roosevelt: The Coming of the New Deal* (Boston, MA: Houghton Mifflin, 1958), pp. 3–15.

25 Commager, *Documents of American History*, vol. 2, p. 354.

addressed the nation directly with his 'fireside chats'. His message was clear: what mattered was not 'politics', but 'government'. The parties, or rather the two parties proper to 'our American system', could be useful in the task of 'presenting and explaining issues, of drumming up interest in elections, and, incidentally, of improving the breed of candidates for public office'. But, ultimately, their essential function was to select the 'wise political leaders' with whom 'the future lies', through their appeals to the 'great public' not interested in sterile political disputes.[26]

Naturally, the benevolent and affable tone of Roosevelt's remarks did not prevent recourse to the most drastic measures when he was faced with what was considered an emergency. A few months before the intervention in the latest world conflict, which Roosevelt had progressively been preparing even before Pearl Harbor, an 'executive order' of the 'President of the United States and Commander in Chief of the Army and Navy' authorised the military authorities to deport 11,000 Japanese (two-thirds of whom were American citizens), because they were suspected or liable to be suspected of insufficient loyalty.[27] The appeal made to the Supreme Court was rejected, just like the one that had been made on the occasion of the 1918 Espionage Act; the 'public safety' of which the president was the privileged and sole interpreter also authorised him to cancel rights which, even if they were constitutionally guaranteed, could not be invoked during a state of exception.[28] Not by chance, in his inaugural address Roosevelt had celebrated the American Constitution as 'the most superbly enduring political mechanism the modern world has produced. It has met every stress of vast expansion of territory, of foreign wars, of bitter internal strife, of world relations.'[29]

'Mission' and Total Mobilization

Another element of the Western democracies aroused a sort of envious admiration in the German culture of the early post–World War I period. Ernst Jünger observed in 1930 how, by appealing to the watchwords of

26 Franklin D. Roosevelt, *The Public Papers and Addresses, 9: 1940, War and Aid to Democracies* (New York: Macmillan, 1941), pp. 27ff.

27 Commager, *Documents of American History*, vol. 2, pp. 464ff.

28 Ibid., pp. 469, 147.

29 Ibid., p. 242.

'democracy', 'progress' and 'national self-determination', Germany's enemies had developed a mobilising capacity far greater than that of the Central Empires. They had thus managed to master 'the decisive, fideistic [*glaubensmäßig*] element of total mobilisation', and succeeded in passing off their war as a 'crusade of reason' and transforming their soldiers into 'warriors for mankind'.[30] Without doubt, the idea of mission played an important role in the war-propaganda and ideology of Germany's enemies. In 1915 Georges Sorel remarked wryly upon this fact:

> A few days ago, consulting a history of 1870, I saw that Napoleon III provided the publicists of the Entente with their main argument. In his proclamations to the army, he stated, 'The whole of France follows you with its ardent vows, and the universe has its eyes on you. On our success depends the fate of liberty and civilisation.' Just like today, the French army defended civilisation against barbarism and freedom against tyranny.[31]

The French writer was right to make such reference to Napoleon III: the idea of mission, inseparable from the rise of Bonapartism, had its greatest development in the US political tradition, in which it even took on an explicitly religious dimension. In the years before World War I, US leaders launching the war against Spain accused the latter country of unjustly depriving Cuba of its right to freedom and independence, moreover resorting, on an island 'so near our own borders', to measures that 'shocked the moral sense of the people of the United States' and represented a 'disgrace to Christian civilization'.[32] In this extraordinary document, the indirect reference to the Monroe Doctrine and the call for a crusade in the name of democracy, morality and religion were closely intertwined in order to excommunicate, so to speak, this most Catholic country. To all intents and purposes, this granted the character of a holy war to the conflict that would confirm the United States in the role of a great imperialist power – with the

30 Ernst Jünger, *Die totale Mobilmachung*, in *Sämtliche Werke* (Stuttgart: Klett-Cotta, 1978 [1930]), vol. 7, pp. 130–7.

31 Georges Sorel, *'Da Proudhon a Lenin' e 'L'Europa sotto la tormenta': Lettres à Mario Missiroli* (Rome: Edizioni di Storia e Letteratura, 1973), p. 565.

32 Commager, *Documents of American History*, vol. 2, p. 5.

annexation of the Philippines and Puerto Rico and total control of the Caribbean.

This same combination of ideological elements presided over US participation in World War I. On the immediate eve of its intervention, the American ambassador to London, Walter Page, telegraphed his government to suggest: 'Perhaps our going to war is the only way in which our present prominent trade position can be maintained and a panic averted.' But the same American historian who reports this fact also adds: 'The war once joined became a holy crusade.'[33] A crusade that – to use the words with which Wilson announced the intervention – had as its objective 'democracy' and the 'universal dominion of right', its privileged interpreter being 'this great peaceful people' which from its 'birth' had embodied such 'principles'.[34] The United States' repeated military interventions in Latin America did not in the least undermine this good conscience. On the contrary, as already in the war against Spain, again the crusade took on explicitly religious overtones: the American combatants in Europe were not 'merely soldiers', but 'crusaders'; 'there was something in their eyes that . . . had never [been] seen in the eyes of any other army'; not only were they 'crusaders', but 'crusaders' whose 'transcendent achievement has made all the world believe in America as it believes in no other nation organized in the modern world'. Never had 'crusaders' – not even those who had headed 'to the Holy Land in the old ages that we read about' – been 'more truly devoted to a holy cause than these gallant, incomparable sons of America'.[35] The latter was vested with the attributes that the Christian tradition attributes to Christ: given that the United States was 'the light of the world as created to lead the world' and 'the world knows America as the savior of the world', it would be absurd, and indeed sacrilegious, to seek to resist this country's 'mission'.[36] Energetically set in motion by the president, an immense propaganda machine obsessively insisted on explicitly defining the war waged by the United States as 'a holy war, the holiest in all history'.[37]

33 Schlesinger, *Rise of Modern America*, pp. 277, 289.

34 Woodrow Wilson, *War and Peace: Presidential Messages, Addresses and Public Papers (1917–1924)* (New York: Harper, 1927), vol. 1, pp. 14–16.

35 Ibid., vol. 2, pp. 45, 292, 414, 21.

36 Ibid., pp. 504, 202, 219.

37 Stuart Rochester, *American Liberal Disillusionment in the Wake of World War I* (University Park, PA/London: Pennsylvania State University Press, 1977), p. 58.

The United States succeeded, better and more effectively than any other power, in recasting in ideal terms its participation in the gigantic conflict. Pareto had cause to issue sarcastic remarks about the 'mission' the American leaders assigned themselves of ensuring freedom and peace in the world, following in the footsteps of imperial Rome and Napoleon I.[38] In 1919, even John Maynard Keynes went so far as to describe Wilson as 'the greatest fraud on earth'.[39] The fact remains that this idea of mission was extraordinarily effective not only on an international level – this is perhaps the aspect that most struck Jünger and the German culture of the time – but also and above all on a domestic level in the United States. There, it largely silenced dissent, immersing the – now both political and religious – leader of the nation in a sacred aura, and working effectively to externalise conflict.

'Americanism' and Rites of Purification and Expulsion of Evil

Wilson consistently acted as the interpreter of the 'American spirit' (to be considered the real winner of the war), of the 'American principle', of the 'true Americanism'.[40] In 1928, it was the Republican president Herbert Hoover who underlined the absolute peculiarity of the 'spirit' of the American people, of the 'American system', founded on a 'rugged individualism', which 'differs essentially from all others in the world'.[41] As harsh as the competition between the two parties and their leaders may be, it revolves around the way in which Americanism should be interpreted, without ever questioning the latter as a point of reference, and without ever raising doubts as to the United States' privileged and unique role in the history of the world and of mankind, however that might be fulfilled. In the course of the 1936 election campaign, while the Republican platform accused Roosevelt of betraying the 'American system', the Democratic platform itself declared that it sought the

38 Vilfredo Pareto, *Scritti politici*, ed. G. Busino (Turin: UTET, 1974), vol. 2, pp. 828ff; Vilfredo Pareto, *Scritti sociologici*, ed. G. Busino (Turin: UTET, 1966), p. 742.

39 Robert Skidelsky, *John Maynard Keynes*, vol. 1: *Hope Betrayed 1881–1920* (London: Penguin, 1994), p. 372.

40 Wilson, *War and Peace*, vol. 2, pp. 12, 1, 509.

41 Arthur Schlesinger Jr, ed., *The History of US Political Parties* (New York: Chelsea House & Bawker, 1973), vol. 3, pp. 2229–31.

'reestablishment of the American way of living' and 'real Americanism'.[42] Roosevelt himself, who celebrated 'our American system' and criticised Jefferson for being too influenced by French revolutionary theories, called on his fellow citizens to oppose not only communism but also any other 'foreign ism'.[43] Of course, it would be wrong to confuse or assimilate such different personalities and political-cultural environments. The fact remains that the common reference to 'Americanism' and to America's peculiar mission prevented liberal currents from adequately opposing more decidedly conservative and chauvinistic ones.

But our main object of investigation here concerns another point. If one of the characteristics of Bonapartism is the externalisation of conflict, it must be said that this technique reaches perfection in the United States, thanks to the cult of 'Americanism'. For the latter makes it possible to consider unwelcome ideologies and their followers as alien to the soul and spirit of America, and ideally to expel them. This rite of expulsion is all the easier because of the massive presence of immigrants, often of poor and modest conditions, and thus inclined to adhere to protest movements – and, consequently, all the more easily identifiable as pathogenic agents external to American society. In crisis situations, not only do unnaturalised or recently naturalised immigrants end up being considered literally foreigners – so, too, do all those who adhere to ideologies and movements branded as alien to 'Americanism'. Nativism, distrust and hostility towards immigrants, xenophobia – all these factors favoured the development of a witch hunt aimed at expelling 'imported' ideas such as 'socialism and syndicalism'.[44]

In times of acute crisis, this expulsion is not only metaphorical. The sharp tensions with revolutionary France in 1798 led to the enactment of laws authorising the arrest and deportation of foreigners and immigrants, as we have seen. The rite of purification can also take place by meticulously filtering immigrants before they even enter American territory and rejecting possible pathogenic agents at the borders: in 1903, at a time of social tensions related to the growth of the labour movement, groups affected by the ban on setting foot in the United

42 Commager, *Documents of American History*, vol. 2, pp. 354, 358, 361.

43 Roosevelt, *Public Papers and Addresses*, 9, pp. 28, 30.

44 Patrick Renshaw, 'The IWW and the Red Scare 1917–24', *Journal of Contemporary History* 3: 4 (1968), p. 64.

States included 'physical, mental and moral defectives of all kinds, contagious cases, professional beggars, assisted immigrants, polygamists and anarchists'.[45]

The rite of purification and expulsion of Evil developed in full force following the US intervention in World War I. On that occasion, a 'feverish witch-hunt' was unleashed against anything with a German label. The teaching of German was suppressed in many schools, while it became dangerous to play German music; families and even towns with German names rushed to Anglicise them, 'to avoid incidents or to flaunt their patriotic faith'. Of course, these manifestations of xenophobia were common to all belligerent countries, but they were particularly unanimous and effective in the United States because of the cult of Americanism and the celebration of its privileged and unique role in world history. The repression from above against pacifists and dissidents was accompanied by violence from below, both tolerated and controlled by the authorities: in workplaces and schools suspicious elements were isolated and fired; those who did not show 'sufficient patriotic sentiments' were assaulted in the streets. The 'crusade for conformity' unleashed on US soil continued even beyond the end of the conflict: in 1919, the *Washington Post* reported that, when one 'irate citizen shot a critic of a patriotic pageant', the crowd burst into 'cheering and hand clapping'. And the tolerance of the state and government apparatuses towards those responsible for hunting down pacifists also remained unchanged: in Indiana, a jury took 'two minutes to acquit a citizen' for killing a fellow countryman who, disgusted by the chauvinist craze, had dared utter the phrase, 'To hell with the United States'. But even more significant than open and brutal violence was a gesture that appeared charged with symbolic meaning: those suspected of insufficient patriotism had their front doors daubed with yellow paint, as if to mark forever their estrangement from the American nation and Americanism.[46]

The rite of purification and expulsion of Evil perhaps reached its height following the outbreak of the October Revolution: 'Reds, radicals, foreigners, and dissenters of all kinds were harried, persecuted, prosecuted and deported in the years 1917–20'.[47] The operation of

45 Schlesinger, *Rise of Modern America*, p. 169.

46 Ibid.; Carroll and Noble, *The Free and the Unfree*, p. 332.

47 Renshaw, 'The IWW and the Red Scare', pp. 65–6.

expelling external pathogenic agents from the healthy body of the American nation was, also in this case, charged with a strong symbolic value thanks to the deportation of the victims to the very epicentre of Evil, the Soviet Union – even if, for understandable practical reasons, this meant not the Bolshevik-held areas but the ones controlled by the White armies. On a more strictly military level, this stirred the reservations and anxieties of the British Foreign Office which, in April 1919, expressed concern that the 'use of Siberia as a dustbin for undesirable and extremely dangerous Americans' could hinder the military operations of General Kolchak, who was striving with Entente help to overthrow the Bolshevik authorities. On the other hand, Churchill clearly admired and found satisfaction in the fact that 'several thousands of these infected persons, against whom in many cases, let us remember, no definite act of treason could be proved, were rounded up all over the States, and were dispatched, foaming and howling, in a series of "Red Arks" across the Atlantic Ocean to those melancholy regions over which their high priest Lenin bears his sway'.[48]

The political and social turmoil provoked by the October Revolution was a fresh opportunity to test the capacity of the American political system to deal with the state of exception. We have seen Wilson criticise the dangerous extension of discretionary powers under the Alien and Sedition Acts of 1798, and observe that their only 'limitations and safeguards lay in the temper and good sense of the President and the Attorney General'. But it would be hard to speak of moderate 'temper' in connection to the Wilson administration's attorney general, Mitchell Palmer, who

> set in motion widespread raids, breaking into private homes and union meeting halls without warrants to arrest thousands of suspected radicals. The accused were held without bail, denied lawyers, and often beaten after being chained and marched through the streets . . . Palmer helped to deport radicals, arguing that 'we must purify the sources of America's population and keep it pure.' He declared 'I am

48 Alex Schmid, *Churchills privater Krieg. Intervention und Konterrevolution im russischen Burgerkrieg, November 1918–März 1920* (Zürich: Atlantis, 1974), pp. 176ff, 311ff [TN: Original English text from 'The Red Fever', *Illustrated Sunday Herald*, 25 January 1920].

> myself an American and I love to preach my doctrine before 100 percent Americans, because my platform is undiluted Americanism.' He established a special antiradical division, headed by young J. Edgar Hoover, within the Department of Justice. The New York State legislature expelled its five Socialist members despite the legal status of the Socialist party.[49]

'Americanism', at times, led the hunt for 'radicals' – considered foreigners or agents of the foreigner – to the most extreme proportions: 'In Hartford, Connecticut, for example, visitors at the jail inquiring after friends caught in the raid were themselves arrested on the ground that this solicitude was prima facie evidence of Bolshevik affiliation.'[50]

Despite the economic crisis, which did not spare it, the United States emerged triumphant from the upheavals prompted by World War I. It was successful not only in a military sense, but also because of the superior agility demonstrated by its political system (based on the broad powers of the leader qua interpreter of the nation and its sacred mission) in intervening in the war, notwithstanding the pacifist sentiments of the population. It had shown this agility as it passed from normality to a state of exception, proving able to push the latter to the desired degree of harshness and brutality, and as it externalised a conflict conducted in the name of the absolute peculiarity of American values, whose ultimate meaning the US president was again himself called upon to decide.

Perfect and Imperfect Caesarism in the US, Britain and Germany

For all these reasons, we can understand the interest with which defeated Germany looked at the political realities of the victorious countries, but especially those of the republic on the other side of the Atlantic. Of the utmost interest is the conversation between Max Weber and General Ludendorff, after the war had just ended, while the Weimar Republic was still in its infancy:

49 Carroll and Noble, *The Free and the Unfree*, p. 331.
50 Schlesinger, *Age of Roosevelt: The Crisis of the Old Order*, p. 43.

L. Now you finally have the democracy you so celebrated . . .
W. Do you really think I consider the rubbish we have now to be *democracy*?
L. If you talk like that, perhaps we can understand each other.
W. But even the rubbish we had before wasn't a monarchy.
L. So, what do you mean by democracy?
W. In democracy, the people elect as their leader [*Führer*] the one they trust. Once elected, he declares: 'Now shut up and obey'. The people and the parties can no longer interfere in his decisions.
L. Such a 'democracy' could suit me.
W. Subsequently the people can judge, and if the leader has made mistakes, may he be sent to the gallows![51]

Let us leave aside the reference to the gallows, understandable in the climate still dominated by the conflict that had just ended; nor should we be distracted, here, by the fact that Ludendorff would later identify his leader or *Führer* in the Führer himself, namely Adolf Hitler. Weber's position is different: he looks at the Anglo-Saxon model and draws the conclusion that, during the global conflict, it was Germany's enemies who had the most energetic leadership, endowed with the broadest powers, less hampered by internal dissensions and bureaucratic resistance. The experience of the war and the victory of the 'Western democracies' played a decisive role in Weber's political evolution and in his theorisation of Caesarism.

The latter presupposed in any case that the old legislative discrimination in the enjoyment of political rights be swept away: 'the only possible *outcome* of conflicts about suffrage nowadays must be equality of voting rights.'[52] In 1905, upon the bourgeois-democratic revolution in Russia, Weber mocked those who, guided only by good intentions, believed that the introduction of universal suffrage was indispensable for moral reasons, even at the cost of the triumph of an ignorant mob and of the 'most extreme form of ochlocracy', and of the fearsome

51 Marianne Weber, *Max Weber. Ein Lebensbild* (Tübingen: Mohr Siebeck, 1926), pp. 664ff.

52 Max Weber, 'Parliament and Government in Germany under a New Political Order', in *Political Writings* (Cambridge: Cambridge University Press, 1994), p. 233, emphasis in original.

cultural collapse that would follow.[53] Not only on that occasion, but still in 1917, Weber recalled the Social Democrat Bernstein's reservations about universal suffrage, the introduction of which – albeit limited to the formation of the Reichstag – had perhaps been premature in Germany. The latter, it was suggested, would have done better to follow the British model of 'voting arrangements which gave rather more privileges to those sections of society which were economically and socially prominent and (at that time) politically educated'.[54] But, by now, the war had radically changed the terms of the question: 'equality of voting rights' was the logical and inevitable consequence of the equality before 'fate' and 'death' realised in the trenches; upon returning from the war, even the 'lowliest' could and would seek to claim equal participation in the reconstruction of the nation, while disdainfully spurning any short-termist expedient or any other solution.[55] As a 'citizen', the soldier 'is sent to war and to death, without distinction of property or diploma'.[56] This reasoning, which connects to military service and wartime sacrifice political rights which belong more to the soldier than to the citizen in the strict sense, would seem to grant little or no legitimacy to women's suffrage. This, even if, immediately after the November revolution, Weber did agree with the decision by the Weimar Republic's Social Democratic leaders to grant the vote to women.[57]

However, in the new situation created by the war and total mobilisation, not only was there no point in repeating – the German sociologist went on to say – the old cliché that universal suffrage would give free rein to the worst 'instincts of the masses', but it had to be finally realised that it alone could provide a firm basis for the Caesarism also necessary to keep the masses and all subversive tendencies at bay.[58] In Germany, where the hegemonic state, Prussia, was still characterised by an electoral law based on property-based discrimination and class-differentiated representation, 'we have *demagogy and the influence of the rabble*

53 Max Weber, 'On the Situation of Constitutional Democracy in Russia', in *Political Writings*, p. 42.

54 Max Weber, 'Suffrage and Democracy in Germany', in *Political Writings*, p. 81.

55 Max Weber, *Zur Politik im Weltkrieg. Schriften und Reden 1914–1918*, ed. W. J. Mommsen with G. Hübinger (Tübingen: Mohr, 1988), p. 172.

56 Ibid., pp. 95ff, 99.

57 Ibid., p. 345.

58 Ibid., p. 185.

without democracy, or rather, *because we lack an orderly democracy*'.[59] 'Orderly democracy' was contrasted with 'unorganised parliamentary rule [as] in France and Italy', with its love of 'spectacles' such as 'votes of no confidence' and 'denunciations of ministers', and also with 'parliamentary democracy' as such, which, in 'assiduously seek[ing] to exclude the plebiscitary methods of leadership election' dooms itself to a 'many-headed assembly' incapable of truly governing.[60] Much less does 'orderly democracy' have anything to do with the domination of the public square, apparent in the Latin countries not as a consequence of universal suffrage, but as a result of the 'urban form of life' so dear to them, as well as climatic and anthropological factors. The dangers of 'large modern cities' – with the concentrated presence of the 'industrial proletariat', the 'domination of the square' and the influence of 'occasional demagogues' – could only be averted and overcome by a responsible leader capable of imposing *die geordnete Führung der Massen* – that is, the orderly direction of the masses, or the ordering of the masses under a Führer or responsible leader.[61]

A form of Caesarism also existed in Germany, but less as a reality than as a threat to intimidate the bourgeoisie.[62] Bismarck had well understood that 'equality of voting rights' (introduced for Reichstag elections) and 'anti-parliamentary demagogy' – a polemical attitude towards representative bodies, counterposed to the people – all made up the prerequisites for his personal power and Caesarism. However, the latter could not develop fully and adequately because of the institutional framework in which it remained enmeshed: 'The reaction of monarchic hereditary legitimism to these Caesarist forces was apparent in the manner of Bismarck's departure from office.'[63] There was a contradiction between the 'Caesarist regime' and the 'legitimacy of the monarch'; the Iron Chancellor was to be reproached for ignoring or cloaking this with his conduct and his political outlook, which were still too burdened by pre-modern ideological elements and were, in some way, attached to the *ancien régime*.[64] The coexistence and competition between the personal

59 Weber, 'Parliament and Government in Germany', p. 220, emphasis in original.
60 Ibid., pp. 180, 221, 174.
61 Weber, *Zur Politik im Weltkrieg*, pp. 185ff.
62 Ibid., p. 155.
63 Weber, 'Parliament and Government in Germany', p. 221.
64 Ibid., p. 173.

power of the charismatic leader and the legitimation principle of the hereditary monarchy produced a dualism whose baleful effects fatally made themselves felt when Germany was engaged in a life-and-death struggle. Such a dualism, at best, allowed for the emergence of a Caesaristic leader, but not the consolidation of a real Caesaristic regime. From this point of view, not even Britain could really serve as a model. Certainly, here, too, 'Caesaristic traits' were clearly apparent: in fact, 'In relation to the parliament from which he emerged, the position of the leading statesman there [was] becoming ever more dominant', deriving his power from 'the trust of the masses in the country and the army in the field', and certainly not from parliament, which was now substantially irrelevant: 'The entire broad mass of the deputies functions *only* as a following for the "leader" or the small group of leaders who form the cabinet, and they obey them blindly *as long* as the leaders are successful. *That is how things should be*.'[65] Yet, even in this country, a certain dualism made itself felt: 'in democratised hereditary monarchies the Caesarist-plebiscitary element is always greatly tempered', since it is 'as much in tension with the parliamentary principle as (of course) . . . with the legitimism of hereditary monarchy'.[66]

Hence the United States is the country to which we must look in order to best understand the political evolution that was now underway. The despised French parliamentarism was contrasted first and foremost with 'the American president's position of power', a position 'legitimated by (formally) "democratic" nomination and election; the president's superiority in relation to parliament rests on this very fact'.[67]

Weber: Caesarism and the Primacy of Foreign Policy

Bismarck's introduction of universal suffrage for Reichstag elections was also a response to 'foreign-policy reasons'. Yet the latter continued to play an important and even decisive role in the attitude of Weber, a great sociologist but also a fervent chauvinist. He emphasised the necessity of universal suffrage by arguing that it was the only way to guarantee 'the

65 Ibid., pp. 175, 174, emphasis in original.
66 Ibid. p. 221.
67 Ibid.

position of the nation in the world'; it was no accident that, as the example of World War I and the socialist parties' policy of loyal cooperation had shown, 'Democratic parties which *share in government* are bearers of nationalism everywhere'.[68] The link between the theorisation of Caesarism and the attempt to externalise conflict once again emerges, here. Of course, it would be pointless to look in Weber for the emphatic idea of 'mission' and 'manifest destiny' that runs deep through the American political tradition. And with regard to this other essential presupposition of Bonapartism, imperial-Wilhelminian Germany comes across as distinctly 'behind'. Yes, the great sociologist himself spoke of an 'enduring mission' – yet he did so not exclusively with reference to his own country or to the great powers, but also to the 'outwardly small nations'. More significant in this context is Weber's insistence on the 'responsibility for history' that rested primarily with the German people, for its defeat or abdication of this role would have the consequence that 'in the Western half of our planet there would be nothing other than Anglo-Saxon convention and Russian bureaucracy'.[69]

But, unlike the American ideologues whom he accused of hypocrisy, Weber did not conceal what was materially at stake. As far as Germany was concerned, the war was a matter of life and death for the nation as a whole:

> If we were overwhelmed, the consequences would be felt even by the grandchildren in the humblest little room of the lowliest worker. The restrictions, the sacrifices that the resistance in war entails and will entail for hundreds of thousands of people, this same existence made of restrictions, would then become the permanent destiny of the mass of Germans. The world in fact becomes crowded, the advantage of emigration vanishes. With the democratisation of culture, the linguistic community becomes a source of exclusion even for the masses, national contrasts necessarily become more acute, intertwined as they are with the ideal and economic interests of mass literary production in the individual national languages. A Germany ruined economically by defeat in the war would be forced to sell off German goods on

68 Max Weber, 'Suffrage and Democracy in Germany', pp. 86, 82, emphasis in original.

69 Max Weber, *Zur Politik im Weltkrieg*, pp. 76–8.

> the world market, and the German workforce would be reduced to the condition of coolies. That would be the real 'German danger', and it would reduce the Germans to the rank of pariahs. That is what is at stake.[70]

Even without the American emphasis on 'mission' and 'manifest destiny', the externalisation of conflict implicit in the Caesarist programme continues to function quite effectively. Weber countered every expression of anti-war dissent with the thesis that Germany, as a whole, benefited from its position as a major world power, meaning that the pacifist who refused to defend his country in the current deadly clash, while continuing to benefit from its eminent or privileged international position, stood in a position of logical inconsistency and moral hypocrisy:

> He who takes even a penny of income [*Rente*] that others – directly or indirectly – have to pay, he who owns a consumer good or consumes a foodstuff on which there is the sweat of other people's work, not his own: this man derives his livelihood from the mechanism of that soulless and merciless economic struggle for existence which bourgeois phraseology calls 'the peaceful labour of civilisation': another form of the struggle of man against man, into which not millions, but hundreds of millions of men put their bodies and souls.[71]

In the food consumed in the opulent Western metropoles, the sweat of the looted colonial peoples is visible: here, we are objectively brought back to Lenin's analysis of imperialism. And we are also reminded of the revolutionary leader's analysis by another argument of Weber's, dating back to the end of the nineteenth century, according to which, despite its peaceful appearance, the 'economic struggle for life' already implicitly contains the clash between the great powers and inevitably leads to war over the partition of the world:

> Only total political inexperience and naïf optimism can disregard the fact that, after an interlude of apparently peaceful competition, the inevitable aspirations for commercial expansion of all civilised

70 Ibid., pp. 77ff.
71 Ibid., pp. 40ff.

> peoples organised into states are approaching, with absolute certainty, the moment in which might alone will decide on the individual peoples' share in the economic domination of the earth and thus on the profit margin of their populations, and particularly of their working class.[72]

But this realistic, unvarnished landscape of colonial expansion and competition between the European bourgeoisies (unmasked as a latent war destined to result in an armed clash) here serves the externalisation of conflict. For, to be victorious, the German people must be unanimous in defence of the welfare and position of power which it has conquered and still has to conquer. Hence, the very same Weber who emphasises 'the sweat of other people's work' that weighs on every 'consumer good' or 'foodstuff' enjoyed in the developed capitalist world, then calls upon 'German Social Democracy' to cling more tightly than ever to the rest of the nation in order to repel the Entente army of 'Negroes, Ghurkas and all manner of barbarians who have come from their hiding places all over the world and who are now gathered at the borders of Germany, ready to lay waste to our country'.[73] Again in this case, the universal suffrage invoked for all warrior-citizens within Germany, regardless of property or education, goes hand-in-hand with the ever more appalling casting of harshly racialised colonial populations.

We may find a certain humour in the fact that while, in the German case, Weber externalises all conflict, he does not do this with regard to its adversaries, and in particular Russia, including the Russia which eventuated from the February revolution. When it comes to this enemy country, Weber takes a quite different approach: he emphasises that, whereas 'the whole mass of the peasantry is at the front' and unable to assert its desire for peace, the 'reactionaries' left at home compel the continuation of the war by strengthening the military apparatus primarily 'against the enemy within', which they instrumentally denounce as a set of 'secret agents for Germany'.[74] In this case, Weber himself

72 Max Weber, 'The Nation State and Economic Policy', in *Political Writings*, pp. 14, 30.

73 Weber, 'Parliament and Government in Germany', pp. 130–1.

74 Weber, *Zur Politik im Weltkrieg*, pp. 112–14.

demystifies the attempts to externalise the conflict made by the new Russian leadership group, and thus he seems here to arrive at positions similar to Lenin's. However, it hardly needs adding that Weber's emphasis on the essentially internal character of the conflict in Russia serves only to underline the exclusively external character of the conflict faced by Germany (including German Social Democracy, which he calls on to avoid any illusions in Kerensky). In the great German sociologist, more explicitly than in other authors, the theorisation of Caesarism is inextricably bound up with a vision of international politics that never tires of insisting on the 'inevitability' of 'power struggles', of the '*eternal struggle*' between nations. Since, 'as far as the dream of peace and human happiness is concerned, the words written over the portal into the unknown future of human history are: "lasciate ogni speranza" [leave all hope behind]', it is necessary that authoritative and imperious leaders capable of uniting and fascinating their followers be called to direct those nations that do not want to abandon their hegemonic role.[75] Yes, already in the political competition developing within individual countries, it is the 'will to power' that moves leaders or would-be leaders, and only 'the most narrow-minded kind of moralising' can be scandalised by this.[76] Those who successfully assert their will to power internally, and thus obtain a Caesarist plebiscitary investiture, also prove most suited to promoting their country's external projection, in a world not only characterised by inevitable conflicts, but in which the will to power plays a central and decisive role: 'only a politically mature people is a "nation of masters" [*Herrenvolk*] and '*only nations of masters are called upon to thrust their hands into the spokes of the world's development*'.[77] In this sense, the British parliament was 'the place where political leaders were selected who had the ability needed to bring a quarter of mankind under the rule of a tiny, politically astute minority'; in this sense, it was 'the decisive bearer of England's power in the world'.[78]

The bureaucratic regime which long dominated or played a leading role in Germany, and especially in Prussia, had the main fault of penalising or largely excluding from power those (merchants, industrialists,

75 Weber, 'The Nation State and Economic Policy', pp. 16, 13–14.
76 Weber, 'Parliament and Government in Germany, p. 176.
77 Ibid., p. 260.
78 Ibid., p. 181, emphasis in original.

private-sector employees, workers) daily engaged in the 'economic struggle for existence' and, for this reason, best suited to conducting the struggle for life which is the inevitable highest characteristic of international relations.[79] Universal suffrage and the appeal to the people are thus purely instrumental – and Weber had no difficulty admitting this: 'For this writer [i.e. Weber himself], "democracy" was never an end in itself. What alone interested and still interests him is the possibility of a lucid national policy for a strong, united and outward-looking Germany.'[80]

Mussolini, Pareto, the 'Two Democracies' and Bonapartism

The enormous strengthening of the executive that had occurred especially in countries such as France, Britain and the United States also set the tone among circles and personalities that did not identify with democracy, and began to think about the possibility of an alternative political and institutional framework. We have already seen the interest General Ludendorff showed in the regime theorised by Weber, looking above all at the example of Britain and the United States. When Spengler spoke of 'advancing Caesarism', he certainly also had in mind the political evolution of Germany's Western enemies – that is, those countries where, despite the trappings and rhetoric of democracy, the 'old parliamentarism' had definitively disappeared.[81] It had been replaced by 'Lloyd George's [personal] rule' or by the 'Napoleonism of the French military party'; and, as far as the United States was concerned, by a president who had completely broken the old balance with Congress – and done so to his own advantage.[82]

Especially interesting is the case of the young Mussolini, no longer a Socialist even if not yet a Fascist. He was already taking up positions of clear hostility towards the parliamentary regime, if only because it was deemed an obstacle to the energetic or total war policy he hoped for, also on the domestic level: 'One of the conditions for winning the war is

79 Weber, *Zur Politik im Weltkrieg*, p. 97.
80 Ibid. p. 100.
81 Oswald Spengler, *Jahre der Entscheidung* (Munich: Beck, 1933), p. 140.
82 Oswald Spengler, *Der Untergang des Abendlandes* (Munich: Beck, 1980), p. 1081.

this: closing down parliament, sending the deputies packing. Wilson, for example, exercises dictatorship. Congress ratifies what Wilson has decided. The youngest democracy, like the oldest, that of Rome, feels that the democratic conduct of war is the most sublime of human stupidity.'

This was an 'anti-parliamentary' profession of faith, but was not intended to indict democracy as such.[83] The latter was rejected only when, in clinging to 'normality' and to 'parliamentary practice', it proved unequal to the state of exception, to that 'formidable exception' which is war. Mussolini's target was the 'parliament [that] can give you only the democratic conduct of war', thus proving incapable of achieving, as circumstances demanded, a 'democratic dictatorship' or a 'dictatorial democracy'. But it also had to be said that 'there are or there can be two democracies or at least two forms of democracy'.[84] When it can be personalised in the figure of a capable and energetic leader, endowed with ample discretionary powers, democracy brilliantly passes the test of war: it is, rather, the Tsarist autocracy that proves not up to the situation determined by the war crisis:

> Therefore, it is absurd to accuse the democratic regime, as such, of incapacity in the face of war . . . Rather, such a typical democracy as the English one knows how to wage war. The greatest of democracies, the American one, will also know how to wage war . . . Clemenceau is the exponent of healthy, productive, and, when necessary, a warrior democracy . . . Even democratic nations have little by little centralised real power in a few men or in a single man. In a certain sense Lloyd George, Clemenceau and Wilson are three democratic dictators.[85]

The democracy that stirred the young Mussolini's agreement or admiration had clear Bonapartist traits. For this was a democracy that was not only able to be authoritarian and even dictatorial, but also knew how to conduct an energetic and even outwardly imperialist foreign policy: 'Imperialism is not necessarily anti-democratic and democracy is not necessarily anti-imperialist. Lloyd George's policy is democratic but

83 Benito Mussolini, *Opera Omnia* (Florenece: La Fenice, 1951), vol. 10, p. 144.
84 Ibid., pp. 62ff, 144, 415, 517.
85 Ibid., p. 416.

imperialist at the same time.'[86] We might say that the cult of the Duce took its first steps by looking to a leader like Clemenceau. Mussolini deemed the latter a 'pilot with arms and a heart of iron' who, with his 'energy' and 'inflexibility' – and playing on the support of the 'Parisian multitude' – was capable of 'striking at', 'punishing' and having arrested every Frenchman who showed hesitancy or defeatism, including even Caillaux, the 'once powerful French prime minister', now reduced to 'a mere number in the dark cell of the prison which collects all the riffraff specimens of Paris'.[87] The man who was now starting to become the Duce of Fascism could perhaps also have recognised himself in the ruthless energy with which the America of Wilson and his successor proceeded to repress the Communists, their sympathisers and the workers' and popular movement fuelled by the October Revolution.

Where should one look for a way out of the 'present crisis of the representative regime'? This was a problem also posed in Italy by the liberal-conservative Gaetano Mosca. Having ruled out the outright suppression of universal suffrage, which he considered highly unpopular and rather dangerous, Mosca hinted at another possible solution:

> A short period during which a strong, honest government exercises many powers and has a great deal of authority may be considered opportune in some European nations, because it may contribute to preparing those conditions which will make it possible for the representative regime to function normally in the near future. Even in Rome, in the best days of the republic, recourse was sometimes made to dictatorship, for brief periods.[88]

This would be 'a kind of Caesarism', in which parliament would have 'an almost exclusively ornamental function', as it did under Napoleon I and Napoleon III until 1868.[89] The liberal-conservative theorist did not blind himself to the risks of this solution, including even very serious ones; it was thus to be considered only as a transitional measure, perhaps called on to prepare the ground for a political regime similar to that

86 Ibid.

87 Ibid., pp. 377, 240–2.

88 Gaetano Mosca, *Elementi di scienza politica*, ed. Benedetto Croce, 5th edn (Bari: Laterza, 1953), vol. 2, p. 240 notes.

89 Ibid., p. 232 notes.

which developed in France after 1868, with the liberal transformation of the Second Empire.

Vilfredo Pareto, whose pungent sarcasm directed against the 'adherents of Holy Democracy', the 'adherents of Universal Suffrage' and, even more so, of 'beneficial proportional representation', we shall see later on, was clearly thinking of something similar. Intervening in the debate on the institutional reforms or counter-reforms meant to endorse and consolidate the results of the March on Rome, the great sociologist lucidly clarified the real objective that was to be pursued and not lost sight of amid the accumulation of disparate and often contradictory proposals: 'The means are infinite, but there is a single aim, and it is to escape from the democratic ideologies of majority sovereignty. The appearance of this may remain, but the substance must be put in the hands of an elite, since this is objectively for the best.'[90] Pareto strongly insisted on the need to maintain the 'appearance' of democracy: 'The present dictatorship, sooner or later, will bring about a constitutional reform. Better sooner than later. The reform should respect as much as possible the existing forms, renewing the substance.'[91] The fascist coup d'état should thus provide the opportunity to break with democratic mythology while continuing formally to pay tribute to it. What measures would make it possible to achieve this objective? What was at issue was not so much 'the best means of election', but rather limiting and weakening the powers of parliament, however it was elected, to the advantage of the executive. With his characteristic frankness and cynicism, Pareto declared that it was necessary to resort to 'measures of the kind used by Prince Louis-Napoleon' who 'gave the country universal suffrage, reputed to be a democratic measure, and, as a counter-poison, greatly restricted the powers of the chamber'. Here, Bonapartism was an explicitly pursued model. The 'captain of genius' was certainly a constituent part of this model, but so, too, the recourse to popular legitimation through a 'discreet use of the referendum'.

It is true that the great Italian sociologist was later made a senator by Mussolini. Yet it would be wrong to reduce his positions to Fascism. It was no accident that, alongside the example of Louis-Napoleon, Pareto

90 Pareto, *Scritti politici*, vol. 2, p. 800.
91 Ibid., p. 796.

also cited Bismarck, and even Britain, wrongly used as a banner by democrats, given that its 'government, until recently, was essentially the dictatorship of one of the two great historical parties'. But there was also no question of uncritically imitating Bonapartism proper. It would be absurd and counterproductive to seek to resort to indiscriminate repression:

> there are great currents of sentiments that never disappear, even though they may appear to a greater or lesser degree on the surface . . . under the democratic ideology flowed the current of Fascism, which then spread to the surface. Now underneath it the adverse current remains. Beware lest it, in turn, spread! Beware not to give it force by seeking to stop it entirely!

The grave error of the Second Empire had been its bid to suffocate and repress all dissent, rather than isolate and strike at it with a repression targeted only at its concretely subversive manifestations posing real danger to the existing order. It should not be forgotten that 'the worst enemies of an order are those who want to push it to extremes'. In this perspective, the chamber 'is most useful', indeed indispensable – though not as a real decision-making centre, but rather as a barometer of the dissent that might exist in the country. A strong and shrewd power would, in any case, be able to dull, channel and neutralise such dissent, rendering it effectively irrelevant as a political force.[92]

Clearly, Pareto appears to have been looking for a modern Bonapartism, softer and more flexible than that of Louis-Napoleon. Here, the necessary homage to the principle of popular legitimation or universal suffrage would be reduced to a handful of plebiscites. Mosca, in turn, observed that 'perhaps even the new Caesarism will try to constitute a legal basis for itself by means of popular referendum, that is, plebiscites, as the two Napoleonic Caesarisms did'; and Weber also defined 'direct popular elections and referenda, and above all the referendum on removal from office' as 'the specific instrument of purely plebiscitary democracy'.[93]

92 Ibid., esp. pp. 797–800.

93 Mosca, *Elementi di scienza politica*, vol. 2, p. 232 notes; Weber, 'Parliament and Government in Germany', p. 226.

For some time, Italian Fascism, or some of its circles, seemed to be moving in the direction indicated by Pareto. In 1923, Michele Bianchi, a 'quadrumvir' of the March on Rome, pronounced in favour of a legislative government which, once invested with popular consensus, would be immune from any motion of no confidence. All this was advanced in the name of democracy and respect for the will of the people: it was necessary to make it impossible for parliament to skirt around the 'will expressed by the country through the electoral verdict'.[94] But, giving substance to the fears already expressed by Pareto, Mussolini ended up 'pushing to extremes' and thus jeopardising the 'order' suggested by the great sociologist. The Duce of Fascism instead replaced it with an open dictatorship. Certainly, insofar as the Fascist dictatorship was based on personal charisma and paid homage to the principle of sovereignty or acclamation from below through periodic plebiscites and appeals to the people, it did contain elements of Bonapartism. Yet it failed to consolidate itself as a real 'order' capable of lasting over time, of passing from a state of exception to normality and of surviving the disappearance of a single leader. If we want to explain the reasons for this, it is not enough to cite the ambition or the unquestionable, boundless vanity of the man in question. Here, it may be useful to refer to Germany, where the leader or Führer who had been called for from so many quarters came to power having from the outset cultivated a project of military revanchism and total mobilisation so vast as to outclass the winners of World War I and avoid any possibility of a 'stab in the back' on the home front. With its attentions still fixed on the November revolution, which had broken out a year after the October revolution and sealed Germany's defeat, the revanchist foreign-policy programme was closely bound to the determination to use all means in crushing Communist agitation and any threat to the existing social order. Thus, across the whole arc of its development, the Third Reich would take the form of a war Bonapartism, indeed a total-war Bonapartism, under the banner of a permanent state of exception, managed with unprecedented brutality. This explanation may to some extent also apply to Italy, where, as well as the determination to liquidate the danger of social and political subversion once and for all, war Bonapartism and the permanent state of exception were stimulated by a revanchist foreign-policy project. Within this logic, the

94 Renzo de Felice, *Mussolini* (Turin: Einaudi, 1966), vol. 2: i, p. 521.

myth of the 'mutilated victory' led to a policy of military adventurism, from the march on Fiume to the ultimatum to Greece and the occupation of Corfu, passing through Ethiopia and Spain, up to the catastrophe of World War II.

The Communist Movement and the Spectre of Bonapartism

In these years, the spectre of Bonapartism also haunted the ranks of the international communist movement. After the February Revolution, Lenin saw the 'beginning of Bonapartism' taking shape in Kerensky's regime.[95] The latter was determined to re-establish internal order in order to continue the war, and was also ready to denounce any pacifist agitation as the expression of a conspiracy fuelled by Russia's enemies and supported domestically only by elements alien to the authentic national soul.

Gramsci's reflection is of particular interest in this context. He did not fail to notice that governments of a more or less 'Bonapartist-Caesarist' type could also develop within the framework of a representative or formally parliamentary regime, as happened in Germany with Bismarck, in Italy with Depretis, Crispi and Giolitti, and in Britain with Labour's Ramsay MacDonald. When the *Prison Notebooks* then distinguish between 'reactionary Caesarism' and 'progressive Caesarism', they seem to subsume Stalin's Soviet Union under the latter category.[96] Trotsky constantly speaks of that country as dominated by a Bonapartist dictatorship or by 'Bonapartism on a plebiscite basis'. But, at other points, he defines Stalin in quite different terms, as the 'indubitable leader of the Thermidorian bureaucracy'.[97] Clearly, in these definitions, which are difficult to reconcile, the mechanical analogy between the French Revolution and the October Revolution plays an important negative role. Its effect is that the phase of maximum radicalisation and of most intense development of the popular initiative must be followed first by a Thermidor and then by a Brumaire – all this in conformity

95 V. I. Lenin, 'The Beginning of Bonapartism', in *Lenin Collected Works* (Moscow: Progress, 1974), vol. 25, pp. 223–6.

96 Antonio Gramsci, *Selections from the Prison Notebooks*, Q13, §27, pp. 219–22.

97 Leon Trotsky, *The Revolution Betrayed: What Is the Soviet Union and Where Is It Going?* (New York: Pathfinder, 1972), pp. 278, 96.

with the myth of the revolution that will resume its triumphal march once it has managed to get rid of the bureaucrats, Thermidorians and Bonapartists. But Trotsky, too, was suspected of Bonapartist aims and tendencies by his adversaries, who, in the last analysis, also included Gramsci himself, who denounced his theoretical and political platform for its 'anachronistic and anti-natural form of "Napoleonism"'.[98]

Hence, the *Prison Notebooks* seem to subsume both Stalin and his great antagonist under one same category – hardly the most adequate means, this, of understanding the political developments that took place in the land of the October Revolution. Certainly, this category does not apply to Lenin; in his case, Arendt believes we should speak of 'revolutionary dictatorship' and not of Bonapartism or totalitarianism. As she explains, far from creating an atomised and amorphous society (which is the presupposition of personal power), the Bolshevik leader instead broke with Tsarist policy not only by promoting the development of trade unions but also by organising as many nationalities as possible, favouring the emergence of a national and cultural consciousness even among the most 'primitive tribes'.[99]

This is not the place to analyse the category of totalitarianism or totalitarian democracy, save to note that explanations of twentieth-century history often proceed in an aprioristic way, in the sense of claiming to deduce from the thought of a particular author (Marx or, even earlier, Rousseau) the reality of the total regimentation of the individual, while neglecting the macroscopic fact that, in the course of the Second Thirty Years' War, at least in the most dramatic moments of crisis, even the countries with a more consolidated liberal tradition undertook to 'weld thousands and even millions of human beings into one amalgamated mass of hate and will and hope . . . temper[ing] the steel of bellicose enthusiasm'. I have dealt elsewhere with the category in question and its ideological and Manichean use, which completely disregards the concrete history of total institutions in countries with the most diverse political and social regimes.[100] Let us, instead, focus on the

98 Gramsci, *Selections from the Prison Notebooks*, Q14, §68, p. 241.

99 Hannah Arendt, *The Origins of Totalitarianism* (New York: Harcourt Brace, 1973), pp. 318–19.

100 Domenico Losurdo, 'Marx e la storia del totalitarismo', in Alberto Burgio, Gianmario Cazzaniga and Domenico Losurdo, eds, *Massa, folla, individuo* (Urbino: QuattroVenti, 1992). [See also Domenico Losurdo, 'Towards a Critique of the Category of Totalitarianism', *Historical Materialism* 12: 2 (2014), pp. 25–55.]

category of Bonapartism, which is our proper object of investigation here. Is this category adequate for understanding Stalin's USSR? Only in part: it gives an account, undoubtedly, of the extreme personalisation of power and of its most unscrupulous and terroristic use. But we must not lose sight of another aspect of Stalin's USSR: that of the constant reference to the party, to the revolutionary Marxist programme, to an ideology emphasising the role of the class struggle. Even if the praxis stood in clear antithesis with the theory, the fact remains that the theory was itself an obstacle to the full development of Bonapartism. After all, Bonapartism appeals to the personal charisma of the leader and proclaims itself above all parties and social classes, while tirelessly expressing its contempt for those it condemns as doctrinaires clinging to systematic ideas or constructions or to 'metaphysical questions'. From this point of view, the 'doctrinaires' were those in France who continued to hark back to the revolution of 1848 or to the Jacobin tradition; and Stalin and his men would also have appeared as 'doctrinaires', continually engaged as they were, despite their extreme practical unscrupulousness, in wearisome discussions about the realisation of the programme of Marx, Engels and Lenin and the degree of loyalty to the October Revolution.

To the extent that the Kremlin chief could count on popular consensus, he owed this not to his personal charisma, to his ability periodically to take to the streets to immerse himself in the acclaiming crowds, nor even to his skill in mastering the mass media. Rather, it was owed to the activity and the propaganda efforts of thousands or millions of party activists and militants, convinced, rightly or wrongly, that they were fighting, in accordance with the heritage of ideas of a definite revolutionary tradition, for the realisation of a certain model of society. In this context, it is not the radio (or as it would be today, the television) that played the decisive role, but rather the party school. On the other hand, Trotsky himself, who accused Stalin of Bonapartism, provided this telling portrait of him: 'previously unknown to the masses . . . Before he felt out his own course, the bureaucracy felt out Stalin himself. He brought it all the necessary guarantees: the prestige of an old Bolshevik, a strong character, narrow vision, and close bonds with the political machine as the sole source of his influence.'[101] This is certainly not the portrait of a

101 Trotsky, *Revolution Betrayed*, pp. 92–3.

Bonapartist leader: suffice it to think of the sharp contrast Weber rightly established between bureaucratic power and Caesaristic power. If anything, Stalin's victory represented the victory of a party and state apparatus that was becoming radically autonomous from the base it 'represented', and which itself defeated a possible Bonapartist-type alternative. The latter could easily have been embodied in the victorious leader of the Red Army, endowed with a charisma unknown among the other Bolshevik leaders. It was he, more than any other, who seemed to embody the idea of the mission of exporting a superior civilisational and societal model to the rest of the world.

Naturally, the long duration of the Second Thirty Years' War, as well as the expectation of world revolution (itself generating a climate of mobilisation and war), could also stimulate Bonapartist tendencies within the Communist world. We may take the case of Fidel Castro's Cuba, with the country's military, political and economic encirclement; the threats, and the attempts actually made, of invasion; the embargo (a war measure); the permanent state of emergency imposed from outside – all this objectively pushes towards the personalisation of power. But the properly Bonapartist tendencies are also countered by the reference to a well-defined ideology and political programme, and to the party based on them: ideology, programme and party certainly act as tools of legitimation – but also, to a certain extent, of limitation – of power. Moreover, the propaganda bombardment conducted by the powerful US neighbour creates a situation of dual power on the ideological level, which can only be confronted by again resorting to the activity of the party. The seductive images of opulence broadcast by US television can only be countered by a deep-seated politicisation which appeals to the 'metaphysical questions' that have always been odious to Bonapartism in all its forms.

The moment in which a communist-led society seems to have come closest to the Bonapartist model is perhaps represented by the years of the Cultural Revolution in China, with the leader who, bypassing the party and leveraging his own personal charisma, addressed himself directly to the masses. Yet the latter were not called upon to express plebiscitary acclamation and then return to private life: on the contrary, they were insistently prodded into permanent political activity, albeit one guided and controlled from above. And this control was itself problematic and brought many strains. The extreme difficulty which Mao encountered in delimiting the forms of struggle and the objectives of the Cultural Revolution, and in concluding it at any given moment, provides further confirmation of the autonomous role that continued to be played, also on this occasion, by ideology and programme, as well as by political groups which, although sometimes clashing with the Communist Party or its leadership, also organised on the basis of this same ideology and programme. On the other hand, it is precisely for these reasons that liberal or conservative theorists reduce the Jacobin, Bolshevik, or communist revolutionary of whatever form to a very singular and decidedly dangerous anthropological type – the *homo ideologicus*, a species totally unacceptable to Bonapartism, with its furious loathing for 'indoctrinated' and ideologised masses or individuals.

Arendt's assimilation of communism to Fascism and Nazism on the basis of '[l]ack of or ignoring of a party program' is completely untenable, and can only be explained by her own preconceived stance.[102] It was, rather, a leader like Mussolini who repeatedly boasted of not being hampered by programmatic scruples, and instead of proceeding exclusively according to his creativity or his mood. It is Fascism and Nazism that insist on formal allegiance, irrespective of any determinate content, to an individual leader or Duce or Führer. This is the meaning of such formulae as 'Believe, obey, fight!' or 'Our honour is called loyalty!' Within the communist tradition, we encounter quite different watchwords: think of the one coined by Wilhelm Liebknecht and also dear to Lenin: 'Learn, propagandize, organize!'[103] – or that which Gramsci put in the masthead of *L'Ordine Nuovo*: 'Educate yourselves, because we shall need all our intelligence. Agitate yourselves, because we shall need all our enthusiasm. Organise yourselves, because we shall need all your strength.'[104] As we can see, in the first place appears the appeal to study – that is, to theoretical appropriation of the ideology and of the programme summoned to guide the movement transforming reality. If there is a trait that both Nazi-Fascism and communism share, it is simply their common inability – albeit for different reasons – to pass from the state of exception to normality, as instead happens in the

102 Arendt, *Origins of Totalitarianism*, p. 325.

103 Sergius Yakobson and Harold D. Lasswell, 'Trend: May Day Slogans in Soviet Russia 1918–1943', in Harold D. Lasswell and Nathan Leites, *Language of Politics: Studies in Quantitative Semantics* (Cambridge, MA: MIT Press, 1965), pp. 233ff.

104 *L'Ordine Nuovo*, 1 May 1919 et passim.

sphere of soft Bonapartism, to which we will soon devote greater attention.

As for the rest, we would need to look to other categories in order to understand the political developments that took place after the October Revolution. The theory of the revolutionary vanguard, formulated by Lenin and already present *in nuce* in Marx, had emerged with the aim of giving political subjectivity to what the liberal tradition considered the eternally 'childlike' multitude constitutionally incapable of expressing an autonomous will. In the history of 'actually existing socialism', this theory objectively ended in the prevalence of a new version of the theory and practice which it had been meant to overcome. For Gramsci, so long as the subaltern classes were an 'amorphous mass perennially swaying back and forth outside of any spiritual organisation', the 'working people' were doomed to remain 'easy prey for all' and simple 'human material' in the hands of the elites – 'raw material for the history of the privileged classes'.[105] This was the case, in particular, during World War I, when the 'childlike' multitude was thrown into the furnace of war, against its own will, by an elite that explicitly claimed its right to impart this energetic pedagogy of pain and sacrifice to a reluctant mass which clung to the banality of everyday existence and material interests. But it so happened that the vanguard called upon to direct the process abolishing this state of affairs turned itself into a new elite, investing itself with a superior knowledge absolutely inaccessible to a multitude that remained or returned to a childlike condition. For this reason, the political regimes that recently collapsed in Eastern Europe were rightly denounced in the common understanding as dominated by a nomenklatura – by a now-closed and sclerotic leadership group, a veritable oligarchy that developed on the basis of the central and privileged position of the Communist Party, although the latter itself constituted an obstacle to the development of Bonapartism proper.

Bonapartism did, however, begin to emerge in Russia, starting from the collapse of 'actually existing socialism'. Some time later, the press described Boris Yeltsin's role in the following terms: 'Elected president by the people, self-appointed prime minister of his government, now

105 Antonio Gramsci, *Cronache Torinesi 1913–1917* (Turin: Einaudi, 1980), p. 175; Antonio Gramsci, *L'Ordine Nuovo 1919–1920*, ed. Valentino Gerratana and Antonio A. Santucci (Turin: Einaudi, 1987), p. 520.

Boris "the Terrible" will also be Minister of Defence. The post is temporary . . . But in fact the leader of Russia now finds himself with enormous power, such as not even Gorbachev ever had in the Soviet Union.' What is more, Yeltsin would find himself directing an army that was not conscripted, and therefore scarcely reliable, but one that was at least intended to become 'completely professional, made up only of volunteers, who are soldiers "for their job" as in the US'.[106] Typical of Bonapartism were the declarations recently made by Yeltsin as he engaged in a tug-of-war with the congress: 'I gave my oath to the Russian people, not to a Constitution that is now outdated.'[107] The president's newly founded party proposed 'the calling of a referendum to dissolve parliament'.[108] As things stand today – at the beginning of December 1992 – one can only wonder whether, if the situation stabilises, the Russian leader will succeed in imposing a real Bonapartist regime, capable of passing easily from normality to a state of exception and back again, or whether we will instead see the state of exception growing autonomous, with the emergence of an openly authoritarian regime or a dictatorship of a more or less fascist type.

Caesarism, Dictatorship and Bonapartism

In the debate on the new political regime (based on a highly personalised executive endowed with very broad powers) that began its triumphal march in the major countries after World War I, we have seen how different categories were brought in upon different occasions. These categories were not always free of ambiguities, and merit further reflection. If Cobban referred above all to the institution of the Roman dictatorship, Weber spoke primarily of Caesarism. But, in this debate, the category of Bonapartism also clearly emerged: already present in Pareto and Mosca, it was discussed in greater depth by Sorel. A few weeks after the outbreak of the war, he stressed, in a letter to the Italian Missiroli,

106 Enrico Franceschini, 'I comunisti sfidano Eltsin e lo "zar" forma un esercito', *La Repubblica*, 17 March 1992.

107 Giovanni Bensi, 'Yeltsin: "Il Congresso è superfluo". Rabbia sul Baltico per la sospensione del ritiro delle truppe di Mosca', *Avvenire*, 31 October 1992.

108 Andrea Bonanni, 'Si apre la sfida al Congresso. Eltsin è pronto a ricorrere alle urne per contrastare l'opposizione', *Il Corriere della sera*, 1 December 1992.

the tendency in France to 'grant the president wide powers': 'a Bonapartist restoration' could not be ruled out, but the most probable result was perhaps a coup d'état to 'reform the Constitution, inspired by the example of the United States'.[109] And it was a tendency that did not end with the end of the war. More than ever, Bonapartism seemed to have gained renewed vigour and to be making a forward march:

> It must be observed that throughout Europe parliamentarism is moving towards a regime of personal power exercised by a great politician. The fact is especially remarkable in England. Lloyd George is truly a king without a crown, and a much more powerful king than the last Bourbons were in France . . . I believe that everywhere political customs are increasingly modelled on the fundamental principle of the [Bonapartist] Constitution of 1852: all the agents of the government must be responsible to a single head, who, in turn, is responsible only to the people.[110]

As we know, already on the eve of Louis Napoleon's coup d'état and the imposition of the 'Constitution of 1852', Bonapartist propaganda made reference to the American model. Now, as war was raging, it was Sorel who noted the elements of Bonapartism present in the political and constitutional order of the United States and the influence they had on the political evolution of many European countries:

> When Prince Louis-Napoleon was elected president on December 10, 1848, he considered himself invested with a national delegation that placed him far above the Chamber; a man appointed by more than half the voters was, to the Bonapartists' eyes, much more 'national' than the deputies, elected by virtue of local influence. The President therefore believed he could impose on the legislative Assembly an action conforming to the will of the people, as expressed on 10 December . . . In the United States, the president is elected directly by the people . . . Their presidents almost invoke the supreme law of common salvation when they speak in the name of the nation; the principle of dictatorship is implicit in the American constitution. The

109 Sorel, '*Da Proudhon a Lenin*', p. 510.
110 Ibid., pp. 244ff.

> way in which the history of the United States has unfolded during the last century has contributed to persuading presidents that, when the occasion arises, they must act as leaders responsible only to the whole country.[111]

In the French author's view, the political regime that was now spreading from the United States across Europe was not without its worrying aspects. Yet it seemed to be permanent, if not outright irresistible, in character: 'The more or less dictatorial acts of American presidents have not always been very felicitous . . . Despite the numerous demonstrations of what is dangerous in the semi-dictatorship of the American presidents, it would be difficult for things to change.'

Perhaps Sorel went further than anyone else in defining the characteristics of the new political regime that was now emerging, namely that (1) it was based on 'personal power exercised by a great politician', a sort of 'king without a crown' invested and legitimated by the 'will of the people'; (2) it was not a military dictatorship, but a regime within which 'the principle of dictatorship is implicit'; (3) this regime, characterised by the personalisation of power and the agility with which it manages to pass from normality to a state of exception and back again, found its main point of reference in the 'American Constitution' and in the political tradition of the United States.

Compared to Sorel, Weber is less precise, for he also uses other categories in addition to 'Caesarism'. He speaks positively of the 'Caesarist dictator' and the 'plebiscitary city dictators . . . in the great American municipalities' who had 'tamed' corruption.[112] In other cases, the German sociologist appears to consider the Caesarist leader to be 'like the military dictator, Napoleon I'. At times, he seems almost to express regret for the defeat of the last Bonapartist initiative in France, mounted by General Boulanger: 'France paid a price for this, in that the supreme powers lack authority with the masses, something that is typical of the country'.[113] Nonetheless, in spite of some oscillations in his language, also evident from the contempt with which he speaks of Napoleon III's 'shadow parliament' (which, despite everything, failed to tame the

111 Ibid., p. 243.

112 Weber, 'Parliament and Government in Germany', p. 221.

113 Ibid.

'domination of the street' and was swept away by the Paris Commune), Weber above all took as his model what I have called a regime of soft Bonapartism.[114] The German sociologist sheds light on another essential aspect of this latter regime, which remained in the shadows in Sorel's analysis: the Caesarist leader raised to power not through 'the usual "casting of votes" or "election" ' but rather through 'a confession of "belief" in the vocation for leadership of the person who has laid claim to this acclamation'.[115]

Weber primarily turned his gaze towards the United States, where parties were 'essentially organisations for the patronage of office ... lacking any specific convictions'.[116] They are thus unable to put obstacles in the way of a simple fiduciary relationship between followers and leader – a relationship from which the former can expect material rewards, even substantial ones, but certainly not the respect of programmatic commitments which have never actually been made. The power that this leader exercises is not a dictatorship, but is liable to turn into one, as the objective situation requires: 'Unless it wants to risk the kind of consequences affecting Russia at the moment, every government, even the most democratic and socialist, would be bound to institute summary jurisdiction against putsches, sabotage and other politically sterile outbursts of this kind, which occur in every country, although less frequently here than elsewhere.'[117]

After describing Kerensky's Russia in gloomy tones (noting how it was committed to continuing at all costs a war odious to the mass of the population), Weber invoked martial law to prevent in other countries the October Revolution that had overthrown this odious regime.

But our concern here is not so much to dwell on the great sociologist's own immediate political choices. More interesting is his theorisation of a Caesarist or Bonapartist regime, liable to transform into an open dictatorship in moments of acute crisis and able to return from a state of exception to normality, as happens among 'politically mature nations'.[118] From this point of view, Bismarck's main fault consisted in the fact that, although he was a great Caesarist leader, unlike those of the English-speaking

114 Weber, *Zur Politik im Weltkrieg*, p. 186.
115 Weber, 'Parliament and Government in Germany', p. 221.
116 Ibid., p. 152.
117 Ibid., p. 232.
118 Ibid.

countries he was not able to bring about a real Caesarist or Bonapartist regime. For Weber, the important function of the British parliament was not to exercise real power but to solve 'the problem of *succession*', i.e. the 'peaceful way of *eliminating* the Caesarist dictator when he has *lost* the trust of the masses' and the '*controlled nature* of his position of power'.[119] Yet this assertion was itself based on the understanding that this orderly and painless succession should give rise to the installation of another 'Caesarist dictator', or rather of a leader who is 'the (de facto) Caesarist representative of the masses', ready to turn into an open dictator at any moment.

119 Ibid., pp. 227, 222, emphasis in the original.

6

Universal Suffrage, Proportional Representation and the Reaction Against It

The Single-Member Constituency and New Forms of Property Discrimination

Even after the reintroduction of universal suffrage, French liberalism certainly did not recognise it unreservedly, not even in the liberal phase of the Second Empire. It continued to find a model in Britain, with its explicit discrimination based on property qualifications. Even the Reform Act of 1832, which had extended political rights to the bourgeoisie, was not always the object of enthusiastic evaluations: it favoured 'the triumph of mediocrity', while the previous system, even with all its feudal distortions, had sent 'the most capable men in England' to the Commons.[1] This judgement was made by an author whom we have already seen poking fun at the peculiar French idea that the vote is 'a natural, absolute right', and who emphasised the dangers of universal suffrage. This institution could be considered a good thing, but only 'on one condition', indeed a rather problematic one whose fulfilment depended on an uncertain future – namely, the condition 'that the great majority of the citizens are wise, moderate, friends of justice and truth'.[2]

1 Édouard Laboulaye, *Histoire des États-Unis* (Paris: Charpentier, 1866), vol. 3, p. 340.

2 Édouard Laboulaye, *L'état et ses limites suivi d'essais politiques* (Paris: Charpentier, 1863), p. 203.

It was necessary to beware easy and uncritical enthusiasms: 'I know that universal suffrage is a dogma: one does not discuss it, one adores it. I'm always wary of blind faith. In religion as in politics, it produces nothing but fanatics.'[3] The French liberal seemed to be searching for possible remedies to the massive extension of suffrage: without any preliminary work of instruction and education, political rights were granted to the mass stirring below the 'surface' of the 'old civilization', a mass in the grip of 'ignorance, credulity, weakness' and among whom 'revolutions find their soldiers'.[4] There was no sense in trying to remedy this situation by filtering the popular vote through a two-tier electoral system, Laboulaye observed – here following in line with Constant, of whose *Principles of Politics* he had been the editor. In a country where 'the passion for equality' was so strong, it was unthinkable to turn to the pluralist vote so dear to John Stuart Mill – a figure credited with advancing 'very bold' ideas which, if they might appear 'strange', had nonetheless imposed themselves on the debate and 'reflection' in Britain.[5] So, what was the solution?

Despite his many reservations about universal suffrage, the French liberal was conscious that in his country a return to open property qualifications was now unthinkable. However, it was possible to do something about the electoral system. Laboulaye again took up the polemic against the 'list vote', which had already been denounced by Bonapartist propaganda as an instrument for the falsification of the popular will by organised political groups and parties. This was set in contrast with the American example, in order to assert that '[i]t is the constant thought of free peoples' that 'it is necessary that elections be done directly, that the voters choose only one person and know well the person whom they choose'.[6] Laboulaye made the case not only for the single-member system, but also for small constituencies:

> In our old Houses, there was a considerable nucleus of deputies who had a relationship with their electors not based on political ties alone. Big proprietors, great industrialists, generals, magistrates, lawyers,

3 Laboulaye, *Histoire des États-Unis*, vol. 3, p. 341.

4 Laboulaye, *L'état et ses limites*, p. 211.

5 Édouard Laboulaye, *Le Parti libéral. Son programme et son avenir* (Paris: Charpentier, 1863), p. 150; *Histoire des États-Unis*, vol. 3, pp. 344ff.

6 Laboulaye, *Histoire des États-Unis*, vol. 3, p. 365.

> publicists, even poets had been in some way adopted as perpetual representatives of their place of birth or residence. Vitry knew only Mr Royer-Collard, Sedan was honoured to elect Mr Cunin-Gradin, Clamecy was proud of Mr Dupin, as Mâcon was of Mr de Lamartine. Deputies of this sort, attached to their constituency by the community of interests or of memories, by the authority of talent or of glory, exercised a moderating action in the House and in the country. They were forgiven for not being wedded to the passions of the moment; their advice was listened to and their opinion discussed. This was a great factor for calm and reason. Today, the extent of the constituency is so great, and its delimitation sometimes so arbitrary, that all these old relations of patronage and clientele have broken down. The new system has destroyed these personal influences, which had transient inconveniences and lasting advantages; the result is that today political sympathy almost exclusively decides the election. Between the voter and the deputy there is no longer anything in common outside of the opinion of the moment. The storm comes, there comes one of those terrible days when the country throws itself to the opposition: there will be a general election which will overthrow the House and tear apart the whole country.[7]

The advantages of this electoral system were thus identified in its ability to hold back too deep a process of politicisation, and to ensure an influence of local notables, sanctioned by custom and the traditional attitude of reverence towards them, observed especially by a rural or provincial population unmarred by the pernicious influence of political parties. Ensuring that the countryside prevail over the city was also the concern of Napoleon III, committed to leveraging the peasants to neutralise the restless and turbulent cities. But Laboulaye develops his argument further. After emphasising the importance of wealth in electoral results, he asked whether it was right to try to control or limit it by legislative means:

> Buying and paying for a voter's vote is real corruption; it is a crime punishable by law: but giving money to churches and hospices in the district, founding schools, opening kindergartens, building fountains

7 Laboulaye, *Le Parti libéral*, pp. 162–4.

> – could all this be forbidden to a citizen just because this citizen is a candidate? If these expenditures are declared suspicious or guilty, then also stopped is the generosity in which the ancients identified the virtue of republics, that attachment to the community which is the honour of free countries; if, on the contrary, these expenditures are declared innocent, whatever the intention of the donor – and I would incline to that solution, out of respect for liberty and love of the public good – wealth is given an electoral privilege which it will be able to take advantage of. It will be an indirect re-establishment of an electoral threshold.
>
> If these observations are correct, we see that universal suffrage is a less easy instrument to handle than may have been believed at first.[8]

In the French case at least, it would be problematic and dangerous to pull back from universal suffrage. Yet it was possible to undermine it by reintroducing, under the new conditions, the property-based discrimination which it was officially supposed to have abolished once and for all.

We can find similar concerns and conclusions in the British political thought of the time. We have seen Bagehot anxiously raise the possibility of 'a political combination of the lower classes, as such and for their own objects'. The choice of electoral system is also of great importance in heading off such an unfortunate possibility. The liberal author draws an interesting social-political picture of the Britain of his time:

> There are whole classes who have not a conception of what the higher orders call comfort; who have not the prerequisites of moral existence; who cannot lead the life that becomes a man. But the most miserable of these classes do not impute their misery to politics. If a political agitator were to lecture to the peasants of Dorsetshire, and try to excite political dissatisfaction, it is much more likely that he would be pelted than that he would succeed.[9]

Such a situation may well survive the extension of suffrage, but on the condition that it is not disturbed by an electoral system such as the

8 Ibid., pp. 167ff.

9 Walter Bagehot, *The English Constitution: Introduction to Second Edition*, in *Collected Works*, ed. N. S. John-Stevas (London: Economist, 1974), vol. 5, p. 380.

proportional system, whereby industrial towns would be able to send to parliament 'persons representing the beliefs or the unbeliefs of the lowest classes in their towns', craftsmen or workmen or other elements mixed in with them. This could be the beginning of an autonomous organisation of the lower classes, especially since proportionality favours the development and consolidation of parties, strengthens their influence, and puts 'isms' at the centre of the debate – that is, precisely the great questions that are likely to 'excite the lower orders'.[10] All this would end up giving political value to existing miseries, and it would undermine the satisfaction or dull resignation that the mass of 'miserable creatures' have hitherto felt with regard to their living conditions, despite everything.

If, incapable of comprehending general political questions, the 'childlike' multitude must confine itself to choosing a leader from among competing personalities drawn from among the ruling class, clearly the electoral system conforming to this objective must be the single-member constituency. Such an election may well be polarised between two candidates, both – even if in lively competition – committed to stirring up the 'vague dream of glory' which can divert the masses' attention from their tough living conditions and prevent them from connecting their misery with the existing sociopolitical system. But Bagehot goes further. For he makes no mystery of the fact that the electoral system he champions is intended as a dam against democracy: the basic defect of proportional representation is that it somehow follows in train with the 'ultrademocratic theory' which would confer an 'equal right to vote' on adult males (and even to women!), abolishing also the plural vote, so that 'the rich and wise are not to have, by explicit law, more votes than the poor and stupid'.[11] If it is not possible to block or drive back the tendency that seeks to level out the exercise of political rights, at least it should be restrained with the single-member constituency. For the English liberal, as for his French counterpart, this had the merit of allowing the basic 'advantages' of property-based discrimination to survive the expansion of the franchise.

10 Ibid., pp. 299, 304ff.
11 Ibid., pp. 380, 298.

Proportionality as the Completion of Universal Suffrage

On the opposite side to Laboulaye's and Bagehot's, the democratic movement also clearly identified the political and social significance of the debate on electoral systems that developed from the second half of the nineteenth century. We can look to an intervention in France from the end of the century: 'Proportional representation, our opponents claim, will allow for the representation of unconstitutional or revolutionary parties', will open the doors of parliament to 'umbrella traders', 'ragpickers' and 'drunks', 'to "dangerous" elements and parties.'[12] The single-member constituency is meant to keep the classes traditionally considered 'dangerous' at bay, outside of representative bodies. It can be understood, then, that in France not only the democratic movement but also a wider public opinion demanded the proportional system as the concrete realisation of 'universal and equal suffrage', which was otherwise condemned 'to exist only on paper'.[13] Indeed, it was necessary not only to abolish property qualifications, but also to reject proposals such as plural voting – so dear to Mill, and at this moment also implemented in practice outside England, in a country like Belgium. But was plural voting the only way to make suffrage unequal? Let us look at the effects of the single-member constituency: 'At the very most, 45 out of 100 voters are represented: thus parliament does not even represent half of the country: who, then, does the majority in parliament represent? . . . Today, of the approximately 10 million Frenchmen who have the right to vote, only four and a half million are represented: Is this your understanding of universal suffrage?' Instead, it was 'necessary that all votes should have equal value'; and if democracy was 'the government of all', then it is clear that its concrete realisation, its future, was 'intimately linked to the question of proportional representation'.[14]

Certainly, the definition of democracy presupposed here implies 'the participation of all in public affairs', 'the effective and proportional participation of all citizens in the designation of the state organs'.[15]

12 Nicolas Saripolos, *La démocratie et l'élection proportionnelle. Étude historique, juridique et politique* (Paris: Rousseau, 1899), vol. 2, pp. 169, 172, 177.

13 Ibid., p. 166.

14 Jean-Paul Laffitte, *Le paradoxe de l'égalité et la représentation proportionnelle*, 2nd edn (Paris: Hachette, 1910), pp. 254ff, 159, 263.

15 Saripolos, *La démocratie et l'élection proportionnelle*, vol. 2, p. 144.

Political freedom is also the exercise of political power, not simply its delegation: 'Universal Suffrage was not established to decide whether this or that parliamentary group will have the totality of representation in an electoral college; it was established to enable all citizens to exercise their share of sovereignty.'[16] And hence, 'minorities have the same right as majorities to be represented in proportion to their electoral strengths: in a regime of political equality, every vote must have the same representative value.' The attainment of this objective is rendered impossible by the 'uninominal ballot', the supporters of which – it was polemically pointed out – did no more than follow the policy of the 'Bonapartist regime' which, in this way, managed to 'obtain enormous majorities in the legislature'.[17]

From the foundation of the Third Republic, the 'revolution' to be completed through the introduction of proportional representation was seen as the realisation of the watchwords of freedom and equality which had emanated from 1789, and as the development of the 1848 revolution which had first affirmed the principle of universal suffrage.[18] Already in 1864, from the exile to which Louis-Napoleon had forced him, one of the protagonists of that revolution had raised the demand for proportional representation in the name of the 'equality' that constitutes the 'essence of democracy'. Louis Blanc raised this demand in polemic against any electoral system which, in condemning minorities and especially the lower classes to silence, sanctioned 'the rule of privilege'.[19] The collapse of the Bonapartist dictatorship, to which the single-member constituency was so dear, seemed to give impetus to this demand. Now, together with universal suffrage, proportional representation, called upon to make the principle of 'one man, one vote' a concrete reality, was demanded, invoking the 'Declaration of the Rights of Man which confers on every citizen the right to participate, "personally or through his representative", in the elaboration of the law':[20]

16 Georges Lachapelle, *La représentation proportionnelle en France et en Belgique* (Paris: Alcan, 1911), p. 49.

17 Ibid., p. 35, 1ff.

18 Saripolos, *La démocratie et l'élection proportionnelle*, vol. 2, p. 470.

19 Louis Blanc, 'De la représentation proportionnelle des minorités', in *Questions d'aujourd'hui et de demain* (Paris: Dentu, 1873), vol. 1, p. 252.

20 Raymond Huard, *Le suffrage universel en France 1848–1946* (Paris: Aubier, 1991), p. 167.

> Proportional representation is the logical complement of universal suffrage, of which Lamartine gave the following definition: 'The right is equal for all citizens and is absolute. No citizen can say to another: I am more sovereign than you!' For this principle to be applied, it is necessary that the representative value of each vote should be the same, that the vote of a Radical voter should have the same value as that of a Socialist or a Moderate voter, and vice versa. Now it is clear that this result can be achieved only by attributing to each important fraction of the electoral body a representation proportional to the number of votes it has, and not by deciding that only the majority of the electors in each constituency will be represented.[21]

But would not proportional representation end up producing 'a strong organisation of rigorously disciplined parties', resulting in a serious limitation or erasure of voter freedom? This was the accusation raised by the opponents of the new electoral system. Yet its supporters retorted that the 'organisation of political parties on the basis of clear and precise principles' had a positive meaning; indeed, it was thanks to this that 'political freedom will become a reality'.[22] If the critics of universal suffrage and partisans of the thesis of the 'childlike' multitude believed that the latter was able to pronounce only on persons and not on programmes, the advocates of proportional voting condemned a system in which 'the personal element takes first place' and 'the elector votes for one man rather than another'. For the supporters of this system, the 'omnipotence of local groups', boards of company directors, or the 'irresponsible committees of the constituencies' main towns' had to be replaced by 'the initiative of broad party associations' and 'real political associations'.[23]

Proportional representation then became an integral part of the programme of France's Socialist Party, which approved this demand at its Limoges Congress in 1906, and then at the Marseilles Congress in 1908. Even if the replacement of the single-member constituency were not to bring any immediate electoral advantage, and even in the hypothetical case that the party should suffer some loss, the new electoral

21 Lachapelle, *La représentation proportionnelle*, pp. 36ff.
22 Saripolos, *La démocratie et l'élection proportionnelle*, vol. 2, pp. 182, 188.
23 Lachapelle, *La représentation proportionnelle*, pp. 51, 46.

system – Jaurès, among others, pointed out – would nevertheless contribute to adding a moral dimension to the elections and to pushing the deputies – the Socialist ones, in any case – to overcome any corporatist vision and exclusive defence of the interests of their own voters or of some limited local or social group.[24]

Proportional representation was also sometimes credited with an effect of social stabilisation or reabsorption of radically subversive impulses, precisely because it allows for the representation of minorities who could otherwise only express themselves through frontal opposition to the existing social and political order. In this sense, the single-member constituency, guaranteeing the monopoly of representation to the majority, is 'anti-social', insofar as it is founded on 'exclusion', and thus a harbinger 'of battles, struggles and passions'. Conversely, the proportional system was presented as the realisation not only of 'freedom' and 'equality', but also of the 'brotherhood' proclaimed by the French Revolution.[25] Backed up by such arguments, it found support even outside the socialist and radical-democratic movements. But whatever the perspective from which proportional representation was advocated, the single-member system was identified and denounced as the heir of discrimination based on property qualifications. Indeed, apart from the different and opposing value judgements attached to them, this was not so dissimilar from the analyses set out by Laboulaye and Bagehot.

In Italy, the Left fought for proportional representation even before universal suffrage had been achieved: in 1900 the Socialist Party included it in its 'minimum programme'.[26] But the significance of this demand, put forward in the name of the 'great principle of the equivalence of suffrage', was best clarified by an MP for the Italian Republican Party, who polemicised against the single-member system in the following terms: 'while we fight those who advocate the plural vote, because it is detrimental to the principle of equality, we witness every day, undismayed, the constant rejoicing at this injustice that is intimately bound up with Italian electoral legislation.'[27]

24 Huard, *Le suffrage universel en France*, p. 169.

25 Saripolos, *La démocratie et l'élection proportionnelle*, vol. 2, p. 470ff.

26 Filippo Turati, *Socialismo e riformismo nella storia d'Italia. Scritti politici 1878–1932*, ed. Franco Livorsi (Milan: Feltrinelli, 1979), p. 107.

27 Roberto Mirabelli, *La rappresentanza proporzionale* (Naples: Ruggiano, 1900), p. 17.

Between Emancipation and Disemancipation: Women's Suffrage

With the outbreak of World War I and the October Revolution, the exclusion of vast popular strata from political rights became highly problematic. It was riskier than ever to cling to restrictions based explicitly on property qualifications, such as had been swept away by the upheavals that had taken place in Russia and now threatened to infect the West as well. Moreover, how was it possible to continue enforcing such restrictions even after the call for a general and total mobilisation? Could the right to vote really be denied to citizen-soldiers who had been called upon to resist, suffer and die in the trenches in the name of the nation? Could the nation deny that the proletarians from whom it demanded even the greatest sacrifice had the full capacity to understand and to choose – the same proletarians who in Russia had been the protagonists of a revolution that stoked constant distress among the ruling classes of all the belligerent states?

The total mobilisation effort also involved women: those in the workplace who took over from men sent to the front, and those whose skins bore the marks of the grief and sacrifice that the war entailed. Should they, too, be admitted to political citizenship? In his time, Spencer had stated that granting women political rights would entail a violation of the principle of equality: since they were exempt from military service, if they enjoyed political rights without being exposed to the serious and mortal risks to which males were subjected, their position would be 'not one of equality but one of supremacy'.[28] But did the liberal philosopher's reasoning still make sense in the new situation? In his 30 September 1918 address in favour of women's suffrage, the American president Wilson underlined the important contribution that women had made to the national cause of total mobilisation. They could not be admitted to the 'partnership of sacrifice and suffering and toil' only to be excluded from the 'partnership of privilege and of right'.[29]

28 Herbert Spencer, *The Principles of Ethics*, ed. T. R. Madian (Indianapolis, IN: Liberty Classics, 1978), vol. 2, p. 183.

29 Woodrow Wilson, *War and Peace: Presidential Messages, Addresses and Public Papers (1917–1924)* (New York: Harper, 1927), vol. 1, p. 265.

The war had such a powerful impact that even a leading exponent of French conservatism proposed granting the right to vote to the widows or mothers of fallen soldiers. This was not a matter of women's suffrage, and not only because, in such a scenario, women would continue to be largely excluded from voting rights. Maurice Barrès – the conservative we are talking about – declared that his project aimed to provide for the 'suffrage of the dead', that is, of the males fallen in battle, who, unable to express themselves directly, would instead do so through female relatives, meaning either their spouses or their mothers.[30] However grotesque and even macabre this proposal may seem, it was, in any case, a sign of the cracks now beginning to emerge in the edifice of sexual discrimination, which was in danger of collapsing, and in some countries did collapse, partly because of the blows received from the upheavals taking place in Russia. One year after the October Revolution, other revolutions would sweep away the Hohenzollern and Habsburg dynasties, marking the victory of women's suffrage in Germany, Austria and Czechoslovakia, before it then also established itself in Britain and the United States.

But Barrès's stance is also indicative of the ambiguities that would continue to plague the question of women's suffrage. On the one hand, well before the outbreak of the war, the demand for women's suffrage was a decisive element of the platform of the movement for emancipation and the struggle against the various forms of discrimination in the exercise of political rights. Not to turn too far back, in 1892 the German Social Democratic Party started its campaign for a truly universal suffrage – one not limited to men alone.[31] Writing in the course of World War I and immediately after the fall of Tsarism, Lenin denounced not only the persistence of property qualifications, more or less camouflaged by means of residence requirements or other '"petty" – supposedly petty – details of the suffrage', but also 'the exclusion of women'.[32] The situation in Russia had in the meantime been altered by the February revolution, already hailed by Gramsci as a 'proletarian revolution'

30 Huard, *Le suffrage universel en France*, pp. 221ff.

31 Mariette Sineau, 'Le donne nella sfera della politica: diritti delle donne e democrazia', in *Storia delle donne in Occidente, Il Novecento*, ed. Georges Duby and Michelle Perrot (Bari: Laterza, 1992), p. 535.

32 V. I. Lenin, *State and Revolution* (Moscow: Foreign Languages Press, 2020), p. 87.

because of the sway of the councils and of the popular masses therein; he enthusiastically underlined the fact that it had 'destroyed authoritarianism and substituted it with universal suffrage, extending it to women as well'.[33] Indeed, the Provisional Government had announced the creation of a Constituent Assembly on this basis, and the Central Committee of the Bolshevik Party had already pronounced in this sense on 13 March (28 February) 1917.[34]

On the other hand, women's suffrage has long been viewed from an entirely different, and even opposed, political and social perspective. A few years before the outbreak of World War I, in lamenting the 'improvised' way in which universal (male) suffrage had been introduced in France after the revolution of 1848 – a measure at fault for granting political rights even to so many people incapable of exercising them properly – a scholar of electoral law listed some possible remedies: 'the distribution of voters by categories, as in Austria; plural suffrage, as in Belgium, with a double and even triple vote according to property, ability or the quality of father of the family'; and, finally, 'two-grade voting, which would in some way filter and regularise' suffrage, especially that of the popular classes. Unfortunately, these measures were unpopular and felt to be in contradiction with the principle of equal political rights. But by now, the French author concluded,

> universal suffrage has acquired the right of citizenship in our public law and can now celebrate its fiftieth anniversary. To seek to undermine it in order to reduce and transform it would be the most reckless of undertakings and the most illusory of theories. If, some day or other, it should need defending against itself, that will instead be done through its wider extension. Who can say whether, in the twentieth century, women's suffrage will not be France's greatest reserve of conservatism?[35]

At the end of the nineteenth century, American nativists began to turn to the conservative use of women's suffrage, hoping in this way to

33 Antonio Gramsci, *La città futura 1917–1918* (Turin: Einaudi, 1982), pp. 138ff.

34 Gérard Walter, *La Rivoluzione russa* (Novara: De Agostini, 1972), p. 412.

35 Antonin Lefèvre-Pontalis, *Les Élections en Europe à la fin du XIXe siècle* (Paris: Plon, 1902), p. 37.

counter 'the corrupting tendencies of the polyglot metropolis' polluted by immigrants.[36] This was a time when access to political citizenship for women of the upper classes in the United States was intertwined with the exclusion of blacks, immigrants and even poor whites. The temptation to use women's suffrage for conservative ends was also felt during World War I, and this is perhaps the context in which Barrès's proposal should be placed. On the other side of the scales, in addition to the weight of difficult-to-eradicate prejudices, there was concern over the social upheaval that could result from granting political rights to women, and the consequent break with a centuries- or millennia-old tradition of subordination. After the end of the conflict, demobilisation aggravated the problem of unemployment: Was it possible to re-confine women in the role of angel of the hearth, after they had participated in the total mobilisation effort and also become full citizens? The remedy of votes for women risked being worse than the disease it was intended to cure. This is why, in countries such as Italy and France, women's suffrage could only triumph after a fresh wave of immense upheavals which saw women actively participate in the Resistance, including with guns in hand.

Democracy, Parties and Proportional Representation in Kelsen

It is telling that a moment that saw a powerful process of political emancipation – and a now-serious crisis of the explicit discrimination based on property, race or sex that still regulated the exercise of political rights – also corresponded to the triumph of the principle of proportional representation in countries such as Italy, Germany and Austria. In this moment, it seemed as if this electoral system was now inseparable from universal suffrage, as per the claim of the democratic movement which had grown especially under the French Third Republic. In Germany, after the November revolution, the Council of People's Commissars proclaimed that 'all elections to representative assemblies must be carried out on the basis of an equal, secret, direct, universal vote, granted to everyone over twenty years of age, of both sexes, and according to

36 Walter Dean Burnham, *Critical Election and the Mainspring of American Politics* (New York: Norton, 1970), pp. 76–7.

proportional electoral principles'.[37] Kelsen is perhaps the most important theorist of this development of democracy, which occurred in certain major Western countries. Publishing an essay in a review in the immediate postwar years, which was later revised and issued as a standalone book, Kelsen polemicised against not only the communist movement, but also those who viewed with unease or hostility the democratisation process which was changing the face of Austria after the revolution and the end of the Habsburg dynasty.

Also to be set within this landscape is Kelsen's clear stance in favour of democracy, understood also in its classical and etymological sense: democracy meant universal suffrage and participation in political choices, and, in this sense, Rousseau was to be considered an 'apostle of freedom' and 'possibly the most important theorist of democracy'. Kelsen had no doubts about the fact that 'the hostility of the old monarchies toward parties [is] nothing more than thinly disguised attacks on democracy'; this attitude survived in Austria after the collapse of the old dynasty, yet 'Only self-deception or hypocrisy could lead one to suppose that democracy is possible without political parties.'[38] The enemies of the party system and of multi-partyism opposed proportional representation, which 'more than any other electoral system . . . presupposes the organization of those who possess political rights into political parties. Where this organization has not yet sufficiently occurred, proportional representation has the explicit tendency to speed up and strengthen this process.'[39] But this is yet further reason to take a stand in favour of such an electoral system, which is the logical consequence of universal suffrage and democracy: 'The aforementioned fundamental principle is that of freedom, i.e., of radical democracy. Just as I only want to obey a law that I have helped create, so I only want to recognize someone – if anyone at all – as my representative in government, if he was chosen for this position by, and not against, my will.'[40]

But a further observation by the great jurist deserves particular attention. Unlike the single-member constituency, which is based on the 'antinatural principle of territoriality' (which he assimilated to the

37 Sergio Ortino, *Riforme elettorali in Germania* (Florence: Vallecchi, 1970), p. 48.

38 Hans Kelsen, *The Essence and Value of Democracy*, ed. Nadia Urbinati and Carlo Invernizzi Accetti (London: Rowman & Littlefield, 2013), pp. 29, 30, 39.

39 Ibid., p. 73.

40 Ibid., p. 72.

majoritarian system, given that, on the scale of the nation or the individual electoral district, both discriminate against and strongly penalise the minority), proportional representation relies on the 'principle of personal status'.[41] Kelsen hints here at a question of extraordinary importance. In Britain, the electoral system based on the single-member constituency was heir to a long pre-modern tradition that sees as the bearer of representation not the individual, but rather communities and guilds. In this sense, equal universal suffrage, based on the representation of the individual and the principle of 'one person, one vote', requires proportional representation. Only this gives real form to democracy, which 'implies that all individuals are of equal political value'.[42]

It can thus be understood why America could not represent a model, either: and not only because that country had borrowed from Britain an electoral system rooted in a pre-modern conception of representation. For there is also another factor. Contrary to Weber and many of his contemporaries, the great jurist had no sympathy for Caesarism, however democratic or otherwise. He criticised 'plebiscitary' practices, which even a 'thoroughly liberal' thinker like Pareto had suggested to the Fascists, and saw that 'in a so-called presidential republic', with executive power entrusted to a president not elected by parliament but directly by the people, 'the principle of popular sovereignty is . . . weakened . . . Where there is only one elected individual for millions of voters, the idea of popular representation must lose every last pretense of legitimacy.' This is also true, on a reduced scale, of the single-member constituency, which creates a local leader, marginalising the parties that Kelsen sees as the backbone of democracy. The national leader not controlled by parliament is even more dangerous: 'the chances of an . . . autocracy' may in some cases be greater in a presidentialist regime than under a hereditary monarchy; and direct popular election, far from banishing or lessening this risk, further aggravates it.[43]

Weber also agrees that the single-member constituency is congenial to a Bonapartist regime – or, in any case, one founded on a radical personalisation of power. Yet he does so on the basis of a different and

41 Ibid., pp. 70–1.

42 Hans Kelsen, 'Foundations of Democracy', *Ethics* 66: 1, Part 2 (October 1955), p. 25.

43 Kelsen, *Essence and Value of Democracy*, pp. 56, 89–90.

opposed value judgement, for which 'Caesarist democracy' (*Führerdemokratie*) is incompatible with the proportional system, which is capable of producing only a 'leaderless democracy' (*führerlose Demokratie*). Such a democracy may be fine for 'Swiss cantons' and in 'normal times', but not for a great power that must be prepared for an emergency situation at home and abroad. The proportional system is 'the exact opposite of any dictatorship'. If we want to put an end to the 'miserable impotence of the French president' by resorting to 'a "dictator" . . . a man trusted by the masses and elected by them', we must instead look to countries like America and Britain and their political and electoral system.[44] A theorist of democracy as political participation, Kelsen opposed any form of Bonapartism. This is why, while he was suspicious of the political regime developing in countries such as the United States, he did identify with the democratic regimes in Austria and Germany that followed the fall of the Habsburgs and the Hohenzollerns.

Corporatist Parliament and Plural Voting

It is impossible to understand twentieth-century history adequately in abstraction from the struggle between emancipation and disemancipation that has characterised this century, as well as the contemporary world as a whole. Even as far as universal male suffrage is concerned, there has been strong resistance. We can thus see, in the effort to restrain it, the re-emergence of various suggestions and proposals which had already been put forward by the above-cited French scholar at the beginning of the century, but which he considered impractical. If it was necessary to grant suffrage to all, without exception, could one not, at least, try to 'organise' and control it within the framework of a corporatist constitution? Ideas and suggestions of this kind circulated in Germany during World War I, and we can say that they circulated widely, judging by Max Weber's efforts to refute the many proposals for 'professional and class representation' (*berufsständische Vertretung*), which he rightly considered nostalgic for a social order now passed, which was

44 Weber, *Gesämmelte politische Schriften* (Tübingen: Mohr, 1958), pp. 543ff, 474, 499.

incompatible with the mobility of modern industrial society.[45] It should not be forgotten, however, that a tendency towards corporatist representation can also be found within the liberal tradition: the plural vote dear to Mill – as one of his opponents observed at the end of the nineteenth century – applied the model of the joint-stock company also to the political community: but, if the lower classes needed twice as many votes as the upper classes to elect a deputy, or, if in parliament the fifty deputies of the agrarian party had the same hundred votes as a hundred socialist and worker deputies, effectively this would mean reintroducing the vote by estates or orders.[46] On the other hand, corporatist representation characterised the parliament of national-liberal Prussia until the end of World War I – and the political-electoral system in force there was considered 'truly reasonable' by many intellectuals and academics in America at the beginning of the century.[47] We can thus understand the fascination that corporatist representation still exercised in certain liberal circles in Italy after World War I, before it became an unambiguously fascist agenda. In 1919, Benito Mussolini, who still posed as a 'revolutionary', in pronouncing himself in favour of 'universal suffrage, for men and women', and even for 'proportional representation', made this significant addition:

> The current political representation cannot be enough for us; we want a direct representation of the individual interests, so that just as I, as a citizen, can vote according to my ideas, as a professional I can vote according to my professional qualities. It could be said, against this programme, that we are going back to the guilds. No matter. The important thing is to create Councils for categories, which integrate a sincerely political representation.[48]

Immediately after the March on Rome, the man who had by then become the leader of Fascism reiterated: 'While maintaining absolute centralisation in Rome, I want to create a kind of corporatist parliament, elected by farmers, seafarers, and the professionals of every major

45 Max Weber, *Zur Politik im Weltkrieg. Schriften und Reden 1914–1918*, ed. W. J. Mommsen with G. Hübinger (Tübingen: Mohr, 1988), pp. 160ff.

46 Saripolos, *La démocratie et l'élection proportionnelle*, vol. 2, pp. 149ff.

47 Weber, *Gesämmelte politische Schriften*, p. 495.

48 Benito Mussolini, *Opera Omnia* (Florence: La Fenice, 1951), vol. 12, p. 326.

industry.'[49] The proposal for 'professional forms of representation' was supported by the Catholic Murri, as well as by a liberal right-wing leader like Antonio Salandra.[50] The latter cultivated a project of 'decisive reforms, to integrate the [existing] system of representative institutions' through the use of forms of corporatist representation.[51]

Sometimes, the plural vote was proposed as an antidote to universal suffrage. In 1917 Weber noted in critical tones that such a proposal enjoyed 'great popularity' in Germany.[52] It is easy to understand the reasons for this: it would make it possible to continue to marginalise the working classes, while formally recognising their political rights, through an electoral mechanism that was still in force in Britain and was thus backed up by the prestige of a country which insisted that it had entered the war in a crusade for democracy! Immediately after the March on Rome, Mussolini – who had in the meantime also changed his mind about granting political rights to women – spoke out in favour of the plural vote:

> I am a partisan of universal suffrage, but not of women's suffrage . . . our reform will be particularly concerned with the inequality of electoral rights; it is absurd to grant the same privileges to an uneducated man and to a university rector. It is not by lowering the upper classes that a common equality is created . . . I am ascribed the idea of restricting universal suffrage. No! Every citizen will keep his right to vote for the Parliament of Rome. But a university professor or a great technician must have one more word to say than a porter or an illiterate.[53]

In this position favouring the plural vote, using arguments that seem drawn from John Stuart Mill, Mussolini was hardly alone. Taking a similar stance, in April 1924, the liberal-nationalist Maffeo Pantaleoni proposed a combination of the plural vote and corporate representation,

49 Ibid., vol. 19, p. 12.

50 Piero Gobetti, *La Rivoluzione liberale. Saggio sulla lotta politica in italia*, ed. E. Alessandrone Perona (Turin: Einaudi, 1983 [1924]), p. 142.

51 Renzo de Felice, *Mussolini* (Turin: Einaudi, 1966), vol. 2: i, p. 478 notes.

52 Weber, *Zur Politik im Weltkrieg*, p. 156.

53 Mussolini, *Opera Omnia*, vol. 19, pp. 9ff, 12.

in order to 'strike at the source of demagogy'.[54] At the end of 1924, the head of government received a letter from a Fascist MP, Agostino Lanzillo, who advocated 'double voting for voters over fifty years of age' and 'a multiple vote for commanders of men, captains of industry, presidents of organisations, etc.'[55] It is interesting to note that, until 1925, Mussolini remained faithful to the idea of the plural vote; it was explicitly stipulated in the original electoral-law bill confirming the destruction of democracy and the establishment of the dictatorship. However, Edmondo Rossoni intervened in the debate in the Chamber of Deputies, representing the corporations, claiming for them 'the pride of having reconciled a large part of the working masses with the Fatherland', and expressing the fear that the plural vote, by discriminating against the working masses or putting them at a disadvantage, might again alienate them from the regime.[56]

Nationalists, Fascists and the Single-Member Constituency

While the debate on universal suffrage developed at a European and even global scale, it became particularly important in Italy in the period surrounding the Fascist coup. The reasons are easy to understand: this was a country shaken by profound social and political upheavals, in which the Red peril seemed to be on the rise. This was a danger that Weimar Germany itself seemed to have averted, achieving a certain degree of stability – albeit later swept away by the crisis of 1929 – precisely thanks to the electoral and popular legitimacy on which the new rulers confronting the persistent communist agitation could draw. Thus, at the beginning of 1919, the organ of the Italian nationalists could rejoice:

> The German people has spoken. Summoned by the meetings [to vote] for the Constituent Assembly, with the most universal suffrage, with an extraordinary percentage of voters, reaching the hyperbolic proportion of 98 per cent of those registered – and the registered

54 De Felice, *Mussolini*, vol. 2: i, p. 593.
55 Ibid., p. 700 notes.
56 Ibid., p. 51.

> voters represented the entire adult population – the German people gave the overwhelming majority of its votes to the bourgeois parties. This is no longer a question of an oligarchy – whether of a court or of the public square – which, usurping the sovereignty legitimately expressed by the people summoned in their free assemblies, establishes its caste or class privilege through the violent seizure of the state. The rule of the Hohenzollerns, like the Spartakus dictatorship, is over. Today it is the whole German people, with all its layers and classes, which, against every regime of privilege, establishes in the most liberal and legitimate forms, by means of universal, direct and secret suffrage, its sovereignty in the Constituent Assembly, which is to found the new regime in Germany.[57]

But the elections that took place in Italy shortly thereafter, with universal suffrage and a proportional system, far from legitimising the existing social order, seemed to put it radically into question. Hence, the extension of political rights and the changes in the electoral system that had taken place between 1913 (the advent of 'quasi'-universal suffrage among the male population) and 1919 (the introduction of the proportional system) became the target of a relentless press campaign by the same circles that had also celebrated the outcome of the elections in Germany. Yet even the violence of these polemics did not cancel out the awareness that it was no longer possible to restore open property-based discrimination. This same nationalist organ was forced to recognise as much, in gloomy tones, at the end of 1922: 'We have lowered the moral and intellectual level of the political voter too far by granting the vote also to illiterates; raising it again by restricting this right is perhaps impossible without serious disturbance.'[58]

In order to avoid such a popular reaction, it was thus necessary to resort to other methods that would be able to hollow out universal suffrage from within. But which methods were there? In the *Politica* of 31 January 1920, Alfredo Rocco continued to thunder against a reform that had invested the masses with 'a function that they do not understand, do not appreciate, and are unable to exercise' and that, as far as Italy was concerned, it seemed ought to be blamed on Giolitti's 'senile

57 Franco Gaeta, *La Stampa nazionalista* (Bologna: Cappelli, 1965), pp. 158ff.

58 Ibid., p. 400.

decadence'.[59] But this leading nationalist and future jurist of the Fascist regime concentrated his fire less on universal suffrage than on the proportional system – namely, 'the new electoral system' imposed by 'a brief but lively press campaign staged by the socialists and the Catholics'. This system had the serious fault of favouring organised mass parties: 'The list vote with large constituencies and with proportional representation could not but succeed in favouring those like the Socialist and the Catholic parties, which are the only ones to possess a vast organisation extending across the entire national territory, and have more or less numerous groups in even the smallest centres.'

Conversely, traditional notables were heavily penalised: 'As could easily be foreseen, and as experience has shown, in an electoral struggle no longer limited to the narrow sphere of the single-member constituency, but extended to an entire province, in some cases to several provinces, the personal action and influence of the candidate is no longer sufficient.' This was especially true given that 'the list vote, having multiplied the expenses for organisation and propaganda, has left little margin for individual corruption'.

However influential, rich and prestigious he might be, the provincial notable would face difficulties in competing with a party present throughout the national territory, sometimes even with an extensive and deep-rooted organisation. 'Such an organisation cannot be improvised'; and if the Popular Party could 'draw on the millennia-old organisation of the Catholic Church', in turn the Socialists 'in thirty years of work have now gathered around them most of the industrial workers, and in some parts of Italy also a good number of peasants, so that in northern and central Italy the Socialist section, the league, the cooperative, reach the remotest centres and bring the word and the will of the party there'.[60]

But particularly telling is the article published a little more than a year later by another fervent nationalist, Armando Zanetti. He devoted this text to unmasking a commonplace central to what he termed the 'many lies or illusions of the democratic-reformist mentality' – a commonplace having to do with 'so-called proportional representation'.

59 Alfredo Rocco, 'Ritorni del Medievo', in Angelo D'Orsi, ed., *I nazionalisti* (Milan: Feltrinelli, 1981 [1920]), pp. 302, 295.

60 Ibid., pp. 299ff, 303.

This electoral system was guilty, first of all, of attacking the sleepy life of the agricultural areas in the shadow of the bell tower, which had hitherto come under the – quietly accepted or passively suffered – sway of local notables. Now, there came in its place

> The disturbance of entire regions due to rallies, demonstrations, conflicts for which it is not always easy to identify those responsible, a confusion of ideas among the good old provincials and especially among the peasants, among whom the poison of politicking is carried in a form little accessible to their simple mentality and under the criminal and ruinous form of incitement to class hatred . . . Let the provinces and the countryside go back to sending us their landlords and their lawyers, their little bosses and their provincial councillors, practitioners of local needs and local administrations; their rose-water socialists elected even with bourgeois votes and themselves bourgeois in spirit and in manners . . . A little healthy traditionalism, a little true spirit of conservation will do Italy much more good than all the programmes and all the reforms and all the subtleties of proportionality in calculating the relative weight of the various elements of a political conscience that does not always and does not everywhere exist. And perhaps it is not even desirable that it should develop beyond measure.

Together with proportional representation, 'two legends, two democratic prejudices are to be destroyed . . . the first is that fortune, birth, and large agricultural estates, which in many cases constitute a candidate's electoral base in the single-member constituency, are a residue of feudalism to be fought against. This is a very serious error: these human realities, I would say historical realities, are also undeniable, useful, and practically indestructible with a democratic electoral law'.[61] The grave fault of the proportional system was that it substituted for local notables' somehow natural leadership over a population content with its lot and distant from political agitation, replacing this with the artificial and demagogic leadership of the mass party – and, for that matter, the 'party understood in a purely classist sense'.[62]

61 Gaeta, *La Stampa nazionalista*, pp. 395–7.

62 Ibid., p. 401.

So, as soon as the new electoral system was introduced – or rather, as soon as it was won on the wave of upheavals caused by the world war and the October Revolution – it began to be violently challenged. It was questioned not only and not mainly by recourse to the argument that it would hamper the formation of solid parliamentary majorities (though this argument surely was raised). More important was the consideration that this system marked the passage from the government of notables – or of the enlightened classes, according to the generous definition or self-definition offered by nostalgists for the good old days – to the government of the mass parties and of the masses organised in parties.

Initially, substantial sectors of the Fascist movement and party declared themselves in favour of a return to single-member constituencies. Particularly interesting, not least given its 'authoritative' status, was the stance taken by Roberto Farinacci, expressed in an open letter to Mussolini in February 1923: 'I am wholly certain that only with this return to the single-member constituency will it be possible to form that government majority that is necessary, so that Fascism in power can worthily, completely fulfil its lofty mission, in the supreme interest, not of a party, but of the Nation.'

The aim was not only to consolidate the executive and the power of the new government, but also to strengthen the personal ties between candidates and the electorate, beyond the mediation of parties:

> First of all – with a return to the previous electoral system – the selection of candidates, besides being the work of the party, would also be the work of the electoral body, whose trust in the elected member would be nourished by the personal knowledge it would have of him, as well as by that of the party, and by the direct evaluation of his qualities: this would be a double guarantee, to have objective certainty that he really is the expression of the popular will and of our political faith.[63]

For all these reasons, the 'ultra-Fascist' leader declared himself in favour of a system of single-member elections without a run-off contest, thus adopting the British model.

63 De Felice, *Mussolini*, vol. 2: i, pp. 521ff.

The Single-Member System and the Political and Social Control of the Electorate

There was a moment, between the murder of Giacomo Matteotti and the open establishment of the Fascist dictatorship, when Mussolini himself advocated a return to the single-member electoral system.[64] He was conscious that, even with this electoral system, he would have been able to 'decimate Socialist, Popular and Communist opposition', and to gather around the Fascist candidates an overwhelming bloc that would have allowed him practically to silence all opposition. This was especially the case given that the single-member constituency presented further advantages for those who already held power. After all, the government, 'unless it shies from interference and high-handedness, does not find in the single-member constituency organised political masses to resist it, except perhaps in the major cities'. This was explained by Antonio Salandra, who was well aware of the room for manoeuvre that that electoral system gave to Giolitti and his 'hatchet-men', but continued to be an inflexible opponent of the proportional system.[65]

Ever since the creation of the French Third Republic, opponents of the single-member constituency pointed out that it powerfully favoured 'official candidacies' imposed from above, as was already the case under the Bonapartist regime. This need not necessarily mean violence or forms of illegal pressure coming from 'prefects' and other authorities sometimes responsible for the 'most arbitrary rulings' – though these were hardly lacking. In reality, as one of the protagonists of the French parliamentary debate of the time explained, within the framework of such an electoral system, a deputy who had received 'a sort of private mandate, particular to local interests', was easily led to try to solve the problems entrusted to him and to secure his own re-election by entering into a relationship with the existing powers-that-be:

64 TN: Matteotti was a reformist-socialist MP murdered by Fascist Blackshirts on 10 June 1924, at a time when Mussolini's government still presided over a multi-party system. While the killing prompted a political crisis, leading the other parties to leave parliament in protest, the episode was ultimately a milestone in the consolidation of an open Fascist dictatorship which banned all opposition parties.

65 De Felice, *Mussolini*, vol. 2: i, pp. 698–700.

> It may be feared that a representative may have too many things to settle with the executive power, on which the affairs which he deals with depend, to be an inconvenient restraint and to counteract the policy of a government on which he relies. If he has an acquiescent attitude (justified in his eyes by his duties to his clients), the powerful cannot but desire the return to parliament of such a governmental or ministerial deputy, according to the language of the time; and there is always a slippery slope from this desire to active help. Thus between the electors, the elected member and the government's ministers, an exchange of favours takes place in which the country and its general interests, its policy and its future are less considered than they ought to be. If this regime endures for some time, power will be without restraint, deputation without authority, and the representative system will become a fiction again.[66]

But from the single-member system there also flow other advantages to the incumbent authorities. After all, this system also affords it the possibility of carefully redrawing electoral constituencies, so that, again in the Third Republic, in one instance, 1,478 votes were enough to win election, but at the other end of the scale it took 20,286![67] By no means was this a phenomenon limited to France. In Bismarck's Germany, and even afterwards, up to World War I, 'the inequality of the constituencies has only increased, without their proportionally representing the number of voters. Thus, in the city of Berlin, a constituency which has only 30,000 inhabitants is represented by one deputy, as is one which has 142,000, and this irregularity, without which the Socialists could double their number of deputies, is not about to disappear.'[68]

On the other side of the Atlantic, the practice of gerrymandering, that is, the instrumental and manipulative redrawing of constituencies – which has, moreover, a long-established tradition behind it – acquired a new magnitude at the end of the nineteenth century. Indeed, it became one of the instruments of the process of disemancipation that developed in these years: workers and immigrants, already penalised by registration laws and by the fresh obstacles set up against naturalisation, were

66 Lachapelle, *La représentation proportionnelle en France*, pp. 1–6.

67 Ibid., p. 14.

68 Lefèvre-Pontalis, *Les Élections en Europe*, p. 127.

further discriminated against by a redefinition of electoral constituencies that disadvantaged the cities and urban agglomerations to the advantage of rural communities (considered more malleable) and of 'true Americans'.[69] Only in 1981 did the US Supreme Court declare such practices unconstitutional.[70]

Gobetti, the Proportional System and Britain

The reactionary meaning of the return to the single-member constituency, invoked by a large and varied group of people in post–World War I Italy, was clearly understood by the various mass parties that expressed their support for the proportional system. Luigi Sturzo's new-born Popular Party also expressed this view. Significantly, together with its rejection of the single-member system, its programme made the demand for 'legal recognition and freedom of class organisation in the unity of the trade union'.[71] The growing weight of the trade unions and political organisations of the popular masses marked the decline of the liberal Italy of the notables, also dear to the nationalists who were in the front line of denouncing the ruinous and subversive effects of the abandonment of the single-member constituency. Later, in the *Prison Notebooks*, Gramsci would observe:

> To a much greater and more organic extent than in 1913 (when the single-member constituency restricted possibilities and falsified the political positions of the masses through the artificial delimitation of constituencies), in 1919, throughout the whole territory, on the same day, the whole of the most active part of the Italian people asked itself the same questions and tried to resolve them in its historic-political consciousness.[72]

69 Burnham, *Critical Election and the Mainspring of American Politics*, p. 81; Marie-France Toinet, 'La Participation politique des ouvriers américains à la fin du dix-neuvième siècle', in *À l'ombre de la statue de la liberté. Immigrants et ouvriers dans la République américaine 1880–1920*, ed. Marianna Debouzy (Vincennes: Presses Universitaires de Vincennes, 1988), p. 297.

70 Liliane Kerjan, *L'égalité aux États-Unis: mythes et réalité* (Nancy: Presses universitaires de Nancy, 1991), p. 125.

71 Luigi Sturzo, *Opere scelte*, ed. G. De Rosa (Bari: Laterza, 1992), vol. 1, pp. 42ff.

72 Antonio Gramsci, *Quaderni del Carcere*, ed. Valentino Gerratana (Turin: Einaudi, 1975), p. 2005, Q 19 (X) §19.

This was not, therefore, simply a matter of a different electoral system from the previous one. Rather, the important development was that, with the proportional system, the masses were called upon for the first time to express themselves not in order to choose, on a fragmentary local basis, between this or that candidate, or between this or that notable, but between different and opposed political parties and alternatives, of national importance. Naturally, all this was sure to contribute to the deep politicisation of the country, even in its most remote corners. Hitherto, the latter had remained sheltered from the anxieties of politics and modernity, to the great joy of the nationalists and the national-liberals.

But the most articulate intervention in the debate on the electoral system was owed to Piero Gobetti – this singular liberal revolutionary who proved in many respects to be closer to *L'Ordine Nuovo* than to the official Liberal Party. Some elements of his analysis take up themes and arguments we have seen already: the single-member constituency 'succeeded in being the ideal most accessible to the peasants, alien to participating in the life of the state, satisfied to elect the deputy, incapable of controlling him'. Gobetti defended and championed proportional representation not as an 'instrument of conservation' – that is, for integrating minorities otherwise condemned to exclusion from representative bodies – but, rather, as the electoral system best suited to 'democracy', given that it 'obliges individuals to fight for an idea, and wants interests to be organised, and for the economy to be elaborated by politics'. Already, a certain novel element emerges here, especially if we bear in mind Gobetti's condemnation of any form of 'professional representation': and the single-member college was itself denounced as an instrument of 'corporatism', for breaking up the 'classes' into 'categories'. So, we can understand the reasons for the 'struggle against the proportional system' waged by the Fascists – who, not by chance, explicitly favoured corporatism, and who needed the corporatist dissolution of the working class in order to complete their conquest of power. Gobetti posed a drastic alternative: Italy would either 'live in a regime of modern democracy' under the banner of proportionality, or else regress towards 'Mussolini's Middle Ages', notwithstanding his efforts to disguise his 'stratagems of vulgar restoration as futurist discoveries'.[73]

73 Gobetti, *La Rivoluzione liberale*, pp. 141–3.

Yet one objection imposed itself. After all, the Fascists stood for an electoral system with a long tradition behind it in the most classic country of the liberal tradition. Gobetti had no hesitation in writing:

> The single-member constituency was the ideal system in a country (England) that had renounced feudalism to guarantee itself against a statolatrous sovereign; it is still economically and politically a feudal form, it presupposes a limited vote and the existence of an aristocratic class, it is adequate to a traditional and sedentary type of life, free from the spirit of adventure.[74]

This judgement may at first sight seem paradoxical, but it is one that we have seen implicitly formulated even by a great jurist like Kelsen. We should not forget the picture that Britain presented in these years in terms of its politics and electoral law. It had already become clear that, thanks to the prevalent single-member system (immediately handing the constituency to the candidate who has obtained the highest number of votes, even if with a minimal advantage, thus in fact representing a minority of the overall electorate), a majority in parliament might well correspond to a minority in the country. But the 1924 elections displayed a particularly glaring disproportion. The table below compares the actual allocation of seats in the House of Commons with the distribution that would have occurred under the proportional system, which would thus have conformed to the real balance of forces in the country.

	Seats, as calculated according to the proportional system	Seats actually allocated, based on the single-member system
Conservatives	288	413
Labour	206	151
Liberals	110	40

Also telling was the Proportional Representation Society's calculation of the number of votes that each of the three parties needed to win one seat, shown in the second table:

Conservatives	20,000
Labour	39,000
Liberals	90,000

74 Ibid., p. 141.

In the period of the Weimar Republic, these figures and calculations were reported by an authoritative German scholar who rightly observed that, given the strident 'contradiction between the will of the people and its representative expression' under such an electoral system, the 'theory of the mandate' becomes completely meaningless. On the contrary, 'the popular will manifested in elections is falsified on the level of representation, to an extent which makes a mockery of all the maxims of democracy'.[75] The Labour Party seems to have understood this: at its June 1918 conference, in demanding the full realisation of universal suffrage (which, at that moment, still had its limits even with regard to the male population), it also called for 'the best practical arrangements' to ensure that 'every minority has its proportionate and no more than its proportionate representation'.[76] Subsequently, it was the Liberals who published a manifesto for electoral reform aimed at 'ensuring a real correspondence between parliamentary representation and electoral strength'. But, in the meantime, the Labour Party, which had itself become a beneficiary of bipartisanship, seemed to forget the link it had established between universal suffrage and proportional representation, allowing the Liberal bill for the reform of the electoral system to fall in the House of Commons.[77]

It is worth probing the underlying reasons why Britain remained immune to the wave that led to the triumph of proportional representation in various countries, including Italy, Germany and Austria. At this point, we are forced to return to Gobetti's evaluation. Traditionally, in Britain, the bearer of the right of representation is not the individual but a community or a guild: and this feudal inheritance was preserved, to some extent, through the successive laws which extended the franchise. This may explain the fact that, even up to the mid twentieth century, there persisted not insignificant traces of plural voting, whose links with professional and corporatist representation we have seen already. The single-member constituency was seamlessly grafted onto this tradition:

75 Karl Loewenstein, 'Minderheitsregferung in Großbritannien. Verfassungsrechtliche Unte suchung zur neuesten Entwicklung des britischen Parlamentarismus', in *Annalen des deutschen Reichs für Gesetzgebung, Verwaltung und Volkswirtschaft*, 1925), pp. 62, 55, 47ff.

76 Ralph Miliband, *Parliamentary Socialism: A Study in the Politics of Labour* (New York: Monthly Review, 1964), p. 63.

77 Karl Loewenstein, 'Minderheitsregferung in Großbritannien', pp. 49, 65.

quietly distorting the will of the people in parliament and the distribution of seats, it certainly runs counter to democracy, but is in perfect harmony with a political vision that continues to see not individuals but communities or electoral constituencies as the bearers of the right to representation.

Universal Suffrage, the 'Present Tragedy of the Bourgeoisie' and Its Possible Remedies

We can thus understand why the campaign against proportional representation in Italy harked back to a British example. The latter country was sometimes cited as an example by Italian nationalists, who claimed to be pursuing their cause in the name of the 'proper functioning of parliamentary institutions', and to be drawing on the example of 'serious, even if exquisitely parliamentary, countries', where there was no place for 'democratic abstractionism' or for the proportional system.[78] Not by chance, this was a political movement which, a few years earlier, had declared in its press organ that it wanted to be 'the initiator of alliances among the constitutional parties, especially Catholics and liberals, against socialism', towards which it instead felt 'implacable hatred'.[79] But, in these years, prominent liberals also took an active part in the battle against proportional representation. For Giolitti, this primarily meant putting an end to 'the cursed electoral law', the 'real disaster' of the proportional system, by reintroducing first-past-the-post, on the British model. As we can see, this was the same proposal as Farinacci's.[80]

But this is not the essential consideration. More important is the fact that, in both Fascist and Liberal circles, the preference for such an electoral system was motivated, sometimes even explicitly, by the intention of neutralising universal suffrage. Let us turn back to the letter addressed to Mussolini by Agostino Lanzillo. In expounding his plans for electoral reform, he began from an important premise: 'I do not think we can touch the concept of universal suffrage.' This aside is telling, as an

78 Gaeta, *La Stampa nazionalista*, pp. 401ff.

79 Ibid., pp. 7ff.

80 De Felice, *Mussolini*, vol. 2: i, p. 392; Gabriele De Rosa, *Giolitti e il fascismo* (Rome: Edizioni di storia e letteratura, 1957), p. 19.

expression of both regret for the loss of the previous situation and dismay that it now seemed to be an unchangeable fact. The Fascist MP did not conceal his 'ardent anti-democratic spirit'; yet, if it was not possible to reintroduce property qualifications explicitly, some remedy could and should be devised: the plural vote was one, but others could be imagined. It might be possible to

> modify and restrict eligibility. Today, almost everyone who is an elector is eligible, and this makes no sense because being a legislator is as difficult as few other functions in life. Eligibility to be a candidate for political deputation should require a series of qualifications, especially moral ones . . . for example professional practice, life abroad, one's working experience, publications, recommendation by class organisations, etc., all with the aim of showing that the candidate possesses a minimum of qualities to be eligible.[81]

So, here was a new proposal: to dissociate active citizenship from passive citizenship, and to link the latter to requirements of property and education, or to a two-tier electoral system based on professional or corporatist criteria (the 'recommendation by class organisations'). The various suggestions arising from the Italian debate all referred to the history of the liberal tradition, and emerged on a particular terrain: namely, concern over the popular masses' tumultuous entry onto the political scene and the related desire to dampen the fuse of universal suffrage. To this end, it was necessary to proceed in a cautious and indirect manner, given that a frontal attack on universal suffrage would risk igniting the situation and making the explosion yet more ruinous.

But none too different was the attitude taken in that same period by a liberal or liberal-conservative like Gaetano Mosca. Taking up the image dear to Constant, he stressed that there were those 'minds who are and will forever be minors'.[82] From this perspective, the granting of universal suffrage could only be judged a 'colossal mistake'. The ideal would be to return to the situation in which non-property-owners, and in any case proletarians, were excluded from political rights. But

81 Felice, *Mussolini*, vol. 2: i, p. 700 notes.

82 Gaetano Mosca, *Elementi di scienza politica*, ed. Benedetto Croce, 5th edn (Bari: Laterza, 1953), vol. 2, p. 239.

unfortunately it would not be easy to mount 'a restriction of political suffrage': 'the granting of universal suffrage was one of those mistakes which are made lightly and in obedience to the suggestions of logic, which it is then difficult and dangerous to correct'.[83] This explained 'the present tragedy of the bourgeoisie . . . prisoner of the lie it accepted when it wanted to enact universal suffrage, believing that it would always be possible to render it harmless with the well-known ploys, and now that it finds itself drowning it can no longer renege on the principle it accepted'.[84]

Universal suffrage, the result of a long process, the 'almost certain product of the democratic logic', in the long run makes it impossible for the representative regime to function. For it ends up putting into doubt the very economic and social foundations on which this regime relies:

> From the time of Aristotle . . . the difficulty of reconciling political equality, which gave preponderance to the poor over the rich, with economic inequality was noted. It is thus no wonder that after the granting of universal suffrage, the European and American ruling classes found themselves faced with the same difficulty; if before the Great War they were able to confront it with relative ease and up to a certain point overcome it, this partly owed to the political unpreparedness of the popular classes, who in many countries at first allowed themselves to be easily regimented within the framework of the bourgeois parties.[85]

Prey to a deep-rooted pessimism, which sometimes led him to draw parallels between the decline of the ancient world and the upheavals of his own time, the elitist theorist did not delve into analysis of the various electoral systems.[86] Yet one basic indicator does emerge from his identification of the causes of the crisis of the 'parliamentary regime': 'Unfortunately, in the years between 1919 and 1922 Italy suffered a degeneration of this system . . . two most great errors were committed, the first immediately

83 Ibid., p. 240 notes.

84 Gaetano Mosca and Guglielmo Ferrero, *Carteggio (1896–1934)*, ed. C. Mongardini (Milan: Giuffrè, 1980), p. 308.

85 Mosca, *Elementi di scienza politica*, vol. 2, p. 242 notes, pp. 207ff.

86 Mosca and Ferrero, *Carteggio*, pp. 307ff.

before the war and the other immediately after: here I mean to allude to universal suffrage and proportional representation.'[87]

The 'two most great errors' denounced here seem to be closely connected. Insofar as it was possible to indicate a remedy for the enormous harm caused by granting political rights to individuals who are 'eternally minors', this could only consist in the suppression of proportional representation. We have seen the Italian nationalists ascribe to the single-member constituency the merit of stemming any widespread mass politicisation, especially in the countryside. For Mosca, the efficacy of this electoral system ought to be strengthened by legislative measures which – while refraining from attacks on the 'representative regime' itself, and leaving 'intact the freedom of scientific inquiry and the exercise of honest criticism of rulers' acts' – would prevent or make as difficult as possible 'that corruption of minds, which are and will be eternally [those of] minors, which has hitherto been freely exercised in some European nations'. The politicisation along socialist lines of the 'childish' multitude previously excluded from political rights was to be prevented by restricting the freedom of the press as well as of association. The return to the single-member constituency, assisted by these legislative measures, thus served as a proxy for the abolition of universal suffrage, which the spirit of the times had, unfortunately, rendered impossible or at least inadvisable.[88]

The meaning of the attitude taken a few years earlier by liberal-conservatives, nationalists and Fascists in Italy was explained, with customary lucidity, by Max Weber. Considering inevitable the universal suffrage demanded even by the humblest citizen, also in his guise as a soldier, the sociologist observes: 'While other questions of electoral law (e.g. the proportional system), despite all their political importance, are nevertheless felt to be "technical" matters, the question of equality in electoral law is, even subjectively, such a purely political question that it must be put to rest if sterile struggles are to be avoided.'[89]

From this statement there transpires an implicit recognition of the nexus that exists between universal suffrage and the proportional

87 Gaetano Mosca, *Partiti e sindacati nella crisi del regime parlamentare* (Bari: Laterza, 1949), p. 283.

88 Mosca, *Elementi di scienza politica*, vol. 2, pp. 230–40.

89 Weber, *Zur Politik im Weltkrieg*, p. 156.

system. But awareness of this link was not widespread, and it could therefore be broken without provoking violent mass reactions – on condition, of course, of continued formal respect for the principle of the equal electoral capacity of all citizens.

Liberalism, Fascism and Disemancipation

An extremely broad and variegated line-up thus ended up identifying proportional representation as its primary target, violently challenging a system deemed the main obstacle to the disemancipation project that was now being cultivated. The debate that preceded the establishment of the Fascist dictatorship in Italy was not, therefore, especially different from the one that had developed, for example, in France after the revolution of 1848: in both cases, it was a question of finding a remedy to the exercise of political rights by the popular masses, which was considered politically and socially intolerable and a factor for subversion. The crisis in France led first to a redefinition of universal suffrage (albeit without attacking it head-on), by significantly reducing the electorate, to the detriment of the poorer classes. The second stage was constituted by Bonapartism; it abandoned property qualifications (which had been reintroduced in a camouflaged way by the liberal bourgeoisie), but, at the same time, replaced list voting with the single-member constituency, within a regime characterised by the iron power of the executive. In the Italian case, after making a mockery of 'universal suffrage and like genres' (as its leader put it in 1923), Fascism entertained the idea of neutralising it, before it proceeded to establish its dictatorship and a war-Bonapartism of its own.[90] It contemplated neutralising suffrage by reducing the political weight of the working class in particular, through reforms or counter-reforms ranging from plural voting to single-member constituencies, or the split between active and passive citizenship (with the consequent increase in eligibility requirements), not to mention the professional and corporatist representation to which it would remain faithful to the last. Seen in this perspective, Fascism, at least in its initial phase, is one of those moments of disemancipation that have accompanied the tormented and tortuous history of suffrage.

90 Mussolini, *Opera Omnia*, vol. 19, p. 195.

Also in this case, projects for political disemancipation directly concerned the socioeconomic sphere: their aim was to reaffirm the inviolability of private property and head off the danger of income redistribution, which the liberal tradition constantly tied to the 'excessive' extension of political rights. We see this connection also in Mussolini's inaugural address as head of government. Having already the previous year called for a 'strengthening of the state' as a police and repressive apparatus, but simultaneously for the 'gradual demobilisation of the economic state' and its return to the 'Manchesterian state', Mussolini now set out a programme for dismantling state intervention in the economy, abolishing the Ministry of Labour, reducing direct taxation and increasing indirect taxation. 'All this' – a gratified Luigi Einaudi commented in the *Corriere della Sera* – was 'classical liberalism'.[91]

At that moment, Italy seemed to be back in the 'paradise of the classical economy'; the finance minister in the new government was De Stefani, 'a rigid laissez-faire individualist' who, not by chance, recycled himself in the post-1945 news media as a free-market economist.[92] It was this that had provided the basis for the initial encounter between Fascism and the liberals, themselves often highly critical (to varying degrees and in varying intensity) of universal suffrage, and especially of the proportional system. Maffeo Pantaleoni, who favoured the combination of plural and corporatist voting, praised the aforementioned laissez-faire address by the Fascist leader and head of government: 'I do not recall in the Italian Chamber, over the last twenty years, a more radically anti-socialist and anti-demagogic speech, more Manchesterian, than the one that Mussolini gave on 21 June.'[93] As we have seen, the liberal statesman Salandra was a partisan of combining individual and professional representation. In subscribing, even in 1927, to Mussolini's condemnation of any 'demo-liberal regime', Salandra defined himself as an 'old right-wing liberal (without the demo-)'; and the following year, in a letter to Benedetto Croce, he wrote that 'in Italy liberalism was

91 Luigi Salvatorelli and Giovanni Mira, *Storia d'Italia nel periodo fascista*, 3rd edn (Milan: Mondadori, 1972), vol. 1, p. 249; De Felice, *Mussolini*, vol. 1: i, pp. 62, 127.

92 Alfred Cobban, *Dictatorship: Its History and Theory* (New York: Haskell, 1971), p. 129; Silvio Lanaro, *Storia dell'Italia repubblicana. Dalla fine della guerra agli anni novanta* (Venice: Marsilio, 1992), p. 32.

93 De Felice, *Mussolini*, vol. 2: i, p. 127 notes.

extinguished by democracy'.[94] In each case, he was expressing nostalgia for a world not yet contaminated by democracy and universal suffrage.

'The believers in "Universal Suffrage"', 'the believers in St Democracy' and the followers of 'beneficial proportional representation' were also the object of Vilfredo Pareto's mockery.[95] Like Giolitti, he was a fervent laissez-faire liberal, though he suggested the use of Bonapartist measures as a first solution to the crisis. This, in the end, would be the path taken by Mussolini, albeit showing a radicalism that the sociologist had not wished for. After various ups and downs, Fascism preferred to entrust its fortunes to a law designed to ensure an overwhelming majority for the national-Fascist bloc. Giolitti voted in favour, based on the recognition that this was still a measure 'mitigat[ing] the defects of the proportional system', indeed of the 'real disaster' that was this electoral system – though its failures could be better and more definitively overcome, the liberal statesman maintained, by a return to the single-member constituency, which he considered to be sooner or later inevitable.[96] It is significant that even in 1925, with the dictatorship already in place, Mussolini himself considered introducing plural voting, as we have seen already. This served as a demonstration of Mussolini's dogged attachment to dis-emancipation projects built on the critique of equal universal suffrage and of the proportional system – a critique that fired the enthusiasms of a multiform array of liberals, liberal-nationalists and Fascists, each committed to fighting this system.

The long crisis that had begun in Italy with the Great War finally led to the establishment of a sort of war-Bonapartism, based on a permanent state of exception. This outcome certainly had its own particular traits. But it also fitted well into a general landscape characterised by the acceleration or triumph of Bonapartist tendencies.

94 Ibid., vol. 2: ii, pp. 429, 430 notes; Benedetto Croce, *Nuove pagine sparse*, 2nd edn (Bari: Laterza, Bari, 1966 [1949]), vol. 1, pp. 390ff.

95 Vilfredo Pareto, *Trattato di sociologia generale*, ed. G. Busino (Turin: UTET, 1988 [1916]), § 2,183; *Scritti politici*, ed. G. Busino (Turin: UTET, 1974), vol. 2, pp. 907, 797.

96 De Rosa, *Giolitti e il fascismo*, pp. 19ff.

7

The Twentieth Century: Between Emancipation and Disemancipation

The 'Childlike' Multitude, Democracy and the Market

If, as we have seen, the emancipation movement triggered by the upheavals of the war and the revolution in Russia spurred a reaction in Italy, this was no isolated phenomenon. In Austria, Mises took a polemical stand against Kelsen. Unlike the great jurist, he felt rather ill at ease with the society of his time, and mounted a ruthless indictment of the multiparty system. His polemic was especially targeted against the class parties, the 'destructiveness' of the trade unions, and even the 'legal protection of labour' and the legal regulation of working hours. While the latter measures were advocated by 'statist writers', they too ought to be counted as 'destructive policy', considering that they reduced 'the quantity of labour performed and the profit of the economic production process'.[1] The concern that the new political situation caused to the existing social order was such that, even in 1927, when the spectacle of the open and permanent terrorist dictatorship established by Mussolini was clear for all to see, Mises paid tribute to fascism for having saved 'European civilisation', thus acquiring a 'merit' that 'will live forever in history'. Despite granting fascism such acknowledgement, this was still

1 Ludwig von Mises, *Liberalismus* (Jena: Fischer, 1927), p. 149; Ludwig von Mises, *Die Gemeinwirtschaft. Untersuchungen über den Sozialismus* (Jena: Fischer, 1922), pp. 469, 460ff.

a liberal author who saw it only as a 'momentary remedy dictated by the emergency situation'; he called for the foundations to be laid for a return to the golden age of the liberal regime and the market economy.[2]

The fact remains that Mises's critique concerned the entire democracy that had sprung from the collapse of a liberal world that, throughout Europe, still bore notable traces of the *ancien régime*.[3] The Austrian author took up the classical liberal tradition's denunciation of the ever-'childlike' multitude: 'The great mass does not possess the ability to think logically . . . Most men do not have the capacity of the mind that is necessary to understand the rather complicated problems of social life.' Even if, by adventure or miracle, they were able to rise to such a height, they would lack the firmness and strength of will necessary to place general and permanent interests above their own particular and momentary ones. The masses demonstrate their perennial political immaturity through their inclination towards socialism or political 'interventionism' in the economic field, or even simply through their demand for a progressive income tax.[4] In these same years, a protagonist of the conservative revolution in Germany, which preceded the advent of Nazism, thundered against 'fiscal Bolshevism' (*Steuerbolchevismus*).[5] With some variations, this is a theme we also find in Mises, though he, above all, followed the classical liberal tradition, which justifies discrimination based on property as an indispensable instrument to defend it from the 'deadly taxes' to which the destitute would inevitably have recourse once they had obtained or wrested access to political rights and representative bodies.[6] Indeed, the Austrian author, citing Thiers and his polemic against progressive taxation, mounts a severe critique of democracy:

> He who stands up against the rich, he who in any way tries to arouse the resentment of the most disadvantaged, can count on a large following. Democracy merely creates the conditions for the unfurling of this spirit which is always and everywhere present in latent form.

2 Mises, *Liberalismus*, p. 45.

3 Arno J. Mayer, *The Persistence of the Old Regime: Europe to the Great War* (New York: Pantheon, 1981).

4 Mises, *Liberalismus*, p. 138; Mises, *Die Gemeinwirtschaft*, p. 481.

5 Oswald Spengler, *Politische Schriften* (Munich: Beck, 1933), p. 263.

6 Mises, *Die Gemeinwirtschaft*, p. 481.

> This is the reef against which all democratic states thus far have been shipwrecked. The democracy of our time is on the right path to follow their fate.[7]

Mises's mistrust or hostility towards universal suffrage is transparent; this was confirmed decades later, when he denounced what he saw as the basic contradiction of the welfare state. For Mises, the latter could be justified solely on the grounds that 'the wage earners lack the insight and the moral strength to provide spontaneously for their future' – but it would not, then, be legitimate to make such ill-equipped people the country's arbiters. The state system of social security assumes the need to 'impose upon the wage earners a restriction concerning the spending of their total income' – yet it is the wage-earners themselves who ultimately decide on the structure of the state and on the formation of the government called upon to remedy their childish imprudence. But is it not 'absurd to make those people supreme in the conduct of government who are manifestly in need of guardians?'[8] It hardly needs saying that this reasoning can be easily reversed: on the one hand, the classical liberal tradition, so dear to Mises, excludes the propertyless from political rights with the argument that they are ultimately minors; on the other hand, those who claim to be their self-appointed guardians deny these eternal children any assistance. But, despite appearances, there is complete coherence in the positions of both supporters and opponents of popular suffrage: if, in Robespierre, the theorisation of the 'natural right' to vote goes hand in hand with the affirmation of the 'right to life', among his antagonists, the overcoming of property-based discrimination is suspected of favouring the legislative affirmation of the right to life through a redistribution of income.

From distrust or hostility towards universal suffrage immediately springs the rejection of proportional representation: it is absurd to expect parliament to be 'a reflection of the social stratification of the country in miniature'. If democracy is not to be reduced to an 'ochlocracy', it must be ensured that it is primarily members of the 'upper social strata', who provide 'the nation's best political heads', that sit in the

7 Ibid., p. 60.

8 Ludwig von Mises, *Human Action: A Treatise on Economics*, 4th edn (San Francisco: Fox & Wilkes, 1996).

representative bodies, rather than the 'elements of lesser value' and 'the trade union and peasant leaders, who have stamped the mark of spiritual desert on the German and Slavic parliaments'. Admittedly, the 'upper social strata' constitute a minority, but their 'influence on men's minds is far greater than their numbers'. If these classes were not present in the representative bodies in sufficient force, a contradiction would open up 'between the public opinion of the country and the opinion of the parliamentary bodies', fatal to the functioning of the latter. Thus, Mises calls for these bodies to reflect the hegemony that the upper social strata already exercise at the level of civil society and the distribution of wealth. Once again, the continuity with the classical liberal tradition is evident, and Mises in fact seems to look at the 'gentleman without profession, who plays a great role in the English parliament' as the figure worthiest of performing a political function.[9] He explicitly holds up the 'Anglo-Saxon' countries as a model, with particular reference to nineteenth-century Britain: the parliamentary regime can only function when there are only two parties, and neither of these must express class interests, i.e. have its point of reference in the organised movement of the lower classes.[10]

Starting from his distrust and hostility towards universal suffrage, Mises criticised not only proportional representation, but also the very idea of representation: the deputy 'represents me no more than the doctor who treats me, or the cobbler who makes my shoes'. But what about democracy itself? While, at times, the Austrian author does not hesitate to take explicit aim at democracy, he generally prefers to proceed in a more cautious way, limiting himself to a radical reinterpretation of it: the market is the authentic and peaceful democracy, in which 'every penny represents a vote' and every mandate can be revoked at any moment by the consumer, who is therefore the true 'master of production'.[11] There is no other democracy to be claimed, beyond the market that exists already; if anything, it is the latter that needs protecting, from a democracy that – based on universal suffrage, and even on proportional representation – inevitably ends up under the sway of the multitude's puerile and

9 Mises, *Die Gemeinwirtschaft*, pp. 57ff.
10 Mises, *Liberalismus*, p. 149.
11 Mises, *Die Gemeinwirtschaft*, pp. 57 notes, 435ff.

selfish tendency to interfere or intervene in the world of the economy, property and the market.

The Critique and Redefinition of Democracy in Schumpeter

The theory of democracy-as-market leads us to another author of Austrian origin. It may first be interesting to note that Joseph Schumpeter similarly takes as his starting point the critique of suffrage as an inalienable subjective right. In reality, so-called universal suffrage applies only to persons 'above the age limit' established by law. But then, why should other kinds of restriction not be lawful or justifiable?

> If persons below the age limit are not allowed to vote, we cannot call a nation undemocratic that for the same or analogous reasons excludes other people as well. Observe: it is not relevant whether we, the observers, admit the validity of those reasons or of the practical rules by which they are made to exclude portions of the population; all that matters is that the society in question admits it. Nor should it be objected that, while this may apply to exclusions on grounds of personal unfitness (e.g., 'age of discretion'), it does not apply to wholesale exclusion on grounds that have nothing to do with the ability to make an intelligent use of the right to vote. For fitness is a matter of opinion and of degree. Its presence must be established by some set of rules. *Without absurdity or insincerity* it is possible to hold that fitness is measured by one's ability to support oneself.[12]

As we can see, here re-emerge all the themes of the polemic against universal suffrage developed by the liberal tradition since Constant: if an age limit can be set for the exercise of political rights, then the law can decide on other limitations and restrictions, too. It follows that suffrage is a social function and not a subjective right: the Austrian-American sociologist insists that 'we do not define democracy by the extent of the franchise'.[13] Moreover, 'discrimination can never be entirely

12 Joseph Schumpeter, *Capitalism, Socialism and Democracy* (London: Routledge, 1994), p. 244. Emphasis in original.

13 Ibid., p. 276 notes.

absent': for instance, the United States (and Schumpeter was writing in the 1940s) 'excludes Orientals . . . from citizenship; in the southern part of the United States Negroes are also often deprived of the vote'.[14] To equate the exclusion of minors, on the one hand, with that of blacks or Orientals, on the other, is in fact to take up the category of the eternal child which Constant had used for wage-earners and to apply it, in the wake of Mill, to a 'minor race', with racist implications that hardly need underlining. In the years in which Schumpeter was writing, blacks were not only excluded from the franchise, but subjected to lynching for attempting to register on the electoral roll or for union activities. Similar observations apply to Orientals, subjected to a discrimination not limited to the strictly political sphere: in the second half of the nineteenth century, the Chinese, having already being deprived of the possibility of testifying in trials involving whites, were also exposed to the threat of being lynched; and that is not to mention that this hatred against Orientals culminated, in the course of World War II, in a mass deportation of Japanese-origin Americans, not motivated by reasons of military security alone.[15] Obviously, the *permanent* denial of political rights to a social class or ethnic group considered incapable of rising to the level of maturity and full capacity to understand and decide cannot plausibly be collapsed into the *momentary* exclusion of those who have not come of age but are destined ultimately to obtain these same rights.

To demonstrate that suffrage is a social function and not a subjective right, Schumpeter offers a further example: the exclusion of Jews from political rights in Hitler's Germany.[16] This last example is doubly unfortunate. Firstly, because it does not draw on the category of the eternal child, lacking – to use Schumpeter's language – the 'ability to make an intelligent use of the right to vote' – but quite another one, though the latter, too, refers in some way to the liberal tradition. This was the category of the foreigner who cannot be assimilated to the nation in which he lives and thus, in times of war or acute conflicts, can be equated to an accomplice or agent of a foreign power, or to a pathogen that attacks and infects a healthy organism from the outside. The latter category is

14 Ibid., p. 244 and notes.

15 Thomas F. Gosset, *Race: The History of an Idea in America* (New York: Schocken, 1963), pp. 270, 290.

16 Schumpeter, *Capitalism, Socialism and Democracy*, p. 244 notes.

certainly not alien to the treatment reserved for blacks and Orientals in the United States – but it would above all become central and decisive in the history of antisemitism. However, this added example adduced by Schumpeter is disconcerting mainly for another reason, namely that it refers to the terrible condition of an ethnic group that was already under the sinister shadow of the 'final solution'. Of course, our object of discussion here is not the great economist's own immediate political choices; himself Jewish, he made his way to the United States already in 1932. The fact remains that, starting from his theoretical presuppositions, which are those of the classical liberal tradition, just as it is not possible to claim suffrage as an inalienable subjective right, so it is not possible to condemn disemancipation. That is, it provides no grounds to condemn either the process to the detriment of blacks and immigrants, as well as poor whites, which developed in the United States at the end of the nineteenth century, nor that which took place, in the Third Reich, to the detriment of the Jews. Indeed, in initiating their disemancipation with the Nuremberg Laws, which deprived them of political rights and subjected them to a sort of apartheid, Hitler's Germany at times referred, through the mouths of its more 'moderate' exponents (such as Hjalmar Schacht, president of the Reichsbank), precisely to the discriminatory practices against blacks and Jews that were already in force in the United States![17]

But let us see, in broad terms at least, how Schumpeter further makes the case for his reinterpretation of democracy. Given that it is impossible unequivocally to define either the people called upon to decide (children, blacks, immigrants, Jews, etc. can be excluded) or the 'common good' that should be the object of a supposed 'popular will' (not only are interests different and conflicting, but the satisfaction of needs can also be defined in a different and conflicting way), it follows that democracy needs to be formulated in a new way. Renouncing the old idea and claim of government by the people, this reformulation should instead understand democracy as a peaceful competition between different leaders or leaderships. In this sense, democracy is the political analogue of the market, with the competition and plurality of choices that the latter entails. And yet, in particularly difficult moments, such competition

17 Raul Hilberg, *The Destruction of the European Jews* (New York: Holmes & Meier, 1985), p. 36.

and plurality can be suspended without the country thereby ceasing to be democratic:

> In fact, democracies of all types recognize with practical unanimity that there are situations in which it is *reasonable* to abandon competitive and to adopt monopolistic leadership. In ancient Rome a non-elective office conferring such a monopoly of leadership in emergencies was provided for by the constitution. The incumbent was called *magister populi* or *dictator*. Similar provisions are known to practically all constitutions, our own included: the President of the United States acquires in certain conditions a power that makes him to all intents and purposes a dictator in the Roman sense, however great the differences are both in legal construction and in practical details.[18]

I have italicised the word 'reasonable' to underline the fact that, after all the talk about the impossibility of defining in unequivocal terms 'a Common Good . . . which every normal person can be made to see by means of rational argument', here the category that was previously banished and mocked is effectively presupposed.[19] Locke had justified the 'power to act according to discretion'[20] emanating from the state of exception in the name of the 'public good' and the 'benefit of the community', just as the United States justified the suspension of constitutional liberties, for instance during World War I, in the name of 'public safety'. This is also the substantial meaning of the adjective used by Schumpeter, who also ends up using the category of 'public good', so much so that the Austrian-American economist credits Ramsay MacDonald, who declared his government 'proud and jealous of, and prepared to maintain, the Empire', with having made 'a sacrifice in the national interest'.[21]

Recourse to a category by stealth invariably entails its uncritical use. In order to deal with the state of exception constituted by the war, President Wilson established a sort of dictatorship; yet this could be

18 Schumpeter, *Capitalism, Socialism and Democracy*, p. 296.

19 Ibid., p. 250.

20 Locke, *Two Treatises of Government*, p. 375, §160–1.

21 Ralph Miliband, *Parliamentary Socialism: A Study in the Politics of Labour* (New York: Monthly Review, 1964), p. 112; Schumpeter, *Capitalism, Socialism and Democracy*, p. 369.

considered 'reasonable' only on condition that intervention in the gigantic bloodbath that was already underway is itself considered 'reasonable' – that is, in accordance with the interests of the country as a whole. So here, instead of solving the problems bound up with the theory of democracy, elitism further aggravates them. By reducing the role of the people to the choice of a leader or a group of leaders, it confers on the latter the power to invoke a state of exception which not only entails very grave sacrifices for the citizens forced to fight and die, but, at the domestic level, implies the recourse to dictatorship and the suspension of that 'competitive leadership', which is meant to console the people, having renounced the sovereignty attributed to it by classical democratic theory.[22] Here, I have given the example of an international war; but perhaps even more significant is the case of a civil war or a situation of serious social-political crisis that seems liable to provoke the state of exception: again, in this case, the establishment of a dictatorship can appear 'reasonable' only on condition that we presuppose the need to defend some 'common good'. Schumpeter thus calls upon this category only at the very moment when its fraudulence is most blatant, given that society is now divided into antagonistic fractions. Moreover, if the existing authorities are able to invoke a state of exception in order to suspend the rules of the game, it is unclear why it cannot be invoked also by social classes or political organisations that are in opposition, having become unable to bear a bloody war or a crisis situation that involves the destitution or even starvation of a considerable mass of people. This highlights the basic limit of any definition of democracy based exclusively on respect for formal criteria and the rules of the game. Rather, the validity of these rules requires a minimum common denominator in a society, such that it can face possible external states of exception in a united way and avoid the emergence of states of internal exception, that is, socio-political antagonisms so acute as to cause an emergency situation. After all – as the authors who commit to a merely formal definition of democracy themselves recognise – such a situation ends up undermining or annulling the very rules of the game that are supposed to define the inalienable essence of the political regime in question.

But the difficulties inherent in Schumpeter's theory are also apparent even if we focus exclusively on periods of normality. Within the

22 Schumpeter, *Capitalism, Socialism and Democracy*, p. 284.

democratic political market, Schumpeter tells us, 'on principle at least, everyone is free to compete for political leadership'.[23] If this is an absolutely necessary condition for us to be able to speak of a democracy, it would be alien to the United States where, at the time the great economist was writing, blacks and Orientals were excluded from political citizenship, and therefore evidently did not have the possibility of competing for 'political leadership'. Yet, if this condition can simply be circumvented, it is not clear in what sense a political market that excludes substantial social and ethnic groups a priori can be defined as free. But then, what exactly does it mean to say that, within the framework of the market-democracy, 'on principle at least, everyone is free to compete for political leadership'? The same objections that Schumpeter levelled with regard to the subject of an inalienable right to vote – that is, as envisaged by the classic demand for universal suffrage – can also be made to apply to this 'everyone'. In both cases, children and other categories must be excluded, and the definition of the free political market encounters the same difficulties and uncertainties that the great Austrian-American economist underlines with respect to the definition of 'the people'.

From the Joint-Stock Company to the Market

As well as reducing democracy to the market, Mises also criticised parties (especially socialist and communist ones). By taking as their point of reference one class in opposition to the others, they rejected 'the liberal doctrine of the solidarity of all interests' and forget the fact that, 'above the different opinions, there must remain the firm conviction that there is, in the last analysis, an identity of intentions and desires, while the divergence concerns only the means of achieving the desired end'.[24] This is a bit like the theory of the 'common good' that Schumpeter later attributed to the classical conception of democracy, thus demonstrating his rather precarious assumptions. In the years after World War I, this theory was instead upheld by fervent liberals or neoliberals in polemic against radical democratism. Interesting here is the fact that the

23 Ibid., p. 272.
24 Mises, *Liberalismus*, pp. 142, 149.

reduction of democracy to the market could be arrived at by starting from different and even opposing assumptions.

In reality, the theory dear to Schumpeter (and Mises) was a redefinition of democracy in the classical terms of the liberal tradition. One central thread of continuity is now clear: the denial that suffrage is an inalienable subjective right. Others can also be identified. According to Schumpeter, rather than referring to the will of the people, as in the classical conception of democracy, parliament is instead to be understood as an organ of the state. As we have seen, in the British political tradition representation is never based on individuals, but on communities and collective subjects to which is delegated the function of contributing, through their representatives, to a better balance of powers. In this sense, the upper and lower chambers are indeed organs of the state, and nothing more. For Schumpeter, as for Mises, parliament does not so much express the will of the people as respond to the need, proper to any complex society, for a division of labour. It is interesting to note that, in addition to the representative regime, Sieyès also speaks of 'representative work': just as in the political world the deputies, who come only from the circle of active citizens, represent in some way the whole nation, so in the economic world, with the roles reversed, the mass of active workers carries out work in representation of the whole nation, and each individual worker carries out his work in representation of the others.[25] In this sense, 'In the social state, everything is representation. It takes place everywhere, in the private as well as in the public sphere; it is the mother of productive and commercial industry, as well as of liberal and political progress. I go even further: it merges with the very essence of social life.'

In Sieyès's usage, the noun *représentation* retains its link to the idea of fiction and theatrical performance. The editor of the French liberal's speeches rightly points out that, in Sieyès, the idea of representation blends into the idea of the 'division of labour. Men represent each other to the extent that they exercise different activities from which a mutual utility arises.'[26]

25 Emmanuel-Joseph Sieyès, *Écrits politiques* (Paris: Éditions des archives contemporaines, 1985), p. 62.

26 Paul Bastid, ed., *Les discours de Sieyès dans les débats constitutionnels de l'an III* (Paris: Hachette, 1939), pp. 16, 57.

The reading of the political community on the model of the market was not lacking in historical precedents. Alongside the division of labour, another category also taken from the world of economics has followed the history of the liberal tradition like a shadow, namely the assimilation of society to the model of the joint-stock company. According to Burke, certainly, 'all men have equal rights', but even so, the 'dividend' is shared 'in proportion' to the capital put in by each. In turn, Sieyès points out that the 'real shareholders of the great social enterprise' are 'the real active citizens, the real members of the "association"', while the rest, the non-proprietors, having paid in no capital, have no right to participate in the management of the joint-stock company, and must therefore be only passive citizens.[27] The sociopolitical significance of this metaphor is clear by now: it makes it possible to pay homage to the call for equality that emanated from the French Revolution while simultaneously justifying the exclusion of the majority of the population from the circle of political rights. According to another devotee of the theory of the joint-stock company, Justus Möser – in a sense, the German Burke – the 'philosophical theories' of the radical Enlightenment and the French revolutionaries, in substituting the concept of 'man' for that of 'shareholder', had arbitrarily flattened and levelled the different contractual positions of the different members of society.[28] Likewise, the category 'political market' again reduces the idea of equality to equality between producers or consumers of goods. In addition to producing a tendency to delegitimise property-based discrimination in the field of political rights, the call for equality that emanated from the French Revolution introduces an element of mismatch and tension between the political world and that realm of inequality that is the economic world – a delegitimation, mismatch and tension that, thanks to the metaphor of the joint-stock company or the market, can be eliminated or reabsorbed by reducing the citizen or man to the shareholder or consumer. The latter figure is much more expansive than that of the shareholder, and it is natural that it should take its place in a historical period characterised by universal suffrage, or the generalised demand for it. And, given the contemporary tendency

27 Sieyès, *Écrits politiques*, p. 199.

28 Domenico Losurdo, *Hegel and the Freedom of Moderns* (Durham, NC: Duke University Press, 2004), pp. 193–4.

towards the extreme personalisation of power (soft Bonapartism), we can also understand that, while Sieyès indicated a more or less narrow elite as the real subject of power, Schumpeter instead pointed to the more or less charismatic leader, exercising 'a formative leadership of public opinion beyond the lines of party, toward national leadership', located 'outside both party and Parliament'.[29]

Yet, despite these differences, the central thread of continuity is fully apparent. An understanding of the political community exclusively in terms of the division of labour, on the model of a joint-stock company or market, is what I have called repressive individualism. On this basis, in Sieyès's era the French bourgeoisie banned trade unions, which were deemed disruptive of the market and the division of labour; similar accusations are echoed in our own time by a theorist of the democracy-as-market such as Mises. If Schumpeter reduces democracy to the simple choice between competing leaderships, Sieyès asserts that the representative regime consists simply in the delegation of full powers to a 'representative elite' that cannot be disturbed by petitions or pressure of any kind. This is also the opinion of the Austrian-American economist, according to whom there is no place for 'back-seat driving' a democratic society (as he characterises it); on the contrary, such a society requires that 'people stand by patiently' even 'while somebody is attacking their most vital interests or offending their most cherished ideals'.[30] Like the doctor, the cobbler or the engineer, parliamentarians and rulers must be able to do their work without being subjected to the pressures of the public square. To Schumpeter's eyes, the organised parties, if not trade unions, must be seen as a disturbing element in the quiet and orderly progress of the division of labour and the political market. But, of course, as even Adam Smith recognises, to stifle workers' associations is to give clear favour to coalitions of employers – just as, we might add, to limit as much as possible or remove the space for organised parties is largely to silence the voice of the subaltern classes, to the advantage of the most powerful industrial and financial lobbies and groups.

By flattening the political community into the joint-stock company and entirely reducing it to a division of labour, Sieyès fully legitimises the

29 Schumpeter, *Capitalism, Socialism and Democracy*, p. 277.
30 Ibid., p. 295.

distinction between active and passive citizens, while declaring unfounded the claim to a subjective right to suffrage. Similarly, Schumpeter, starting from the reduction of democracy to the market, justified the exclusion from political rights of blacks, Orientals, Jews, and this or that ethnic or social group. But today, at a time when it no longer seems possible openly to question the principle of universal suffrage, the redefinition and restriction of democracy are important above all from another point of view. Through the assimilation of the political community to a joint-stock company or a market, the subaltern classes that aspire to see guarantees of the right to life and the dignity of a human existence are pushed back into the same world of commodity distribution that they had hoped to transcend.

It should be added that the theory that condemns the classical conception of democracy as archaic and incompatible with the complexity of today's industrial society itself displays pre-modern propensities. We see this in a 1945 speech of Schumpeter's, consumed with anguish at 'social decomposition', the 'current disorganisation', and the 'moral disorganisation' resulting from the 'utilitarian philosophy of the last century', based on 'individual egoism'. He suggests as a remedy not only the 'corporatist principle' and 'corporatist organisation', but also a theory of leadership extending beyond the political sphere proper: according to Schumpeter, the cause of this tragic situation lay in the lack of conscious, recognised leaders 'in families, in factories, in societies'. In particular, the 'business leader' – far from rightly being considered an adversary or an enemy, as in Marx's theory of the 'class struggle' – is 'essentially a worker who is the leader of other workers', and thus more properly compared to a 'military commander'.[31] Here, we can note obvious pre-modern echoes, and nostalgia for a world without unions and class parties; a world, moreover, based on a fiduciary relationship between leaders and followers, in society as in the workplace. This speech is all the more remarkable considering that, although it was delivered in Montreal, it was given by an exile from Austria, which had now been swallowed up by the Third Reich. This country was thus now subject to a regime under which, with the 'elimination' of the class struggle, the factories, too, were subject to the

31 Joseph Schumpeter, 'L'avenir de l'entreprise privée devant les tendances socialistes modernes', in *Comment sauvegarder l'entreprise privée?*, ed. Association Professionnelle des Industriels (Montreal: API, 1945), pp. 105–7.

Führerprinzip – that is, the principle according to which the industrial manager was to be considered akin to a military leader, able to count on the trust and loyalty of his entourage.

The Emancipation Process and the Theorisation of 'Social and Economic Rights'

World War II ended with a fresh expansion of democracy, and not only because of the collapse of fascist dictatorships. Women's suffrage triumphed in countries such as Italy and France; with the disappearance of the remaining traces of plural voting, equal universal suffrage and the principle of 'one person, one vote' also forcefully asserted themselves in Britain; in the United States, the discrimination against blacks and poor whites introduced by the disemancipation movement at the end of the nineteenth century began to be put into doubt; and the return to proportional representation in Italy further democratised the electoral and political system, blocking attempts to return to the regime of notables that had preceded World War I and the October Revolution. Not only did this period see the universalisation of political rights, but they were also given material substance: the Constitution of the Italian Republic established a relationship between freedom and the removal of the 'obstacles of an economic or social nature' that thwarted it or threatened to thwart it: in many countries, governments declared their intention to pursue a policy of full employment and social security for all. Even in the United States, where the laissez-faire tradition is more deeply rooted, Franklin Delano Roosevelt spoke in 1940 of 'freedom from want' as one of the essential, and indeed inalienable, democratic freedoms.[32] The theorisation of 'social and economic rights' was enshrined in the Universal Declaration of Human Rights adopted by the United Nations in 1948. Commenting on the approval of this text, Eleanor Roosevelt, who had herself promoted it, declared that it should be accepted 'as the international Magna Carta for all mankind'.[33] To all this must be added

32 Henry S. Commager, *Documents of American History* (New York: Appleton-Century-Crofts, 1963), vol. 2, p. 449.

33 Noberto Bobbio, *Il terzo assente. Saggi e discorsi sulla pace e la guerra* (Turin: Sonda, 1989), p. 71.

the decolonisation process, which had begun with World War I and the October Revolution, and was now gaining new momentum. This was the moment when the emancipation movement of the twentieth century reached its highest point, having overcome the hurdle of fascism, and likewise surmounted the other resistance and countertendencies we have seen already.

This is the context in which we should set the reflection of an author like Harold Laski. If Schumpeter had found nothing to complain about in the exclusion of blacks from political rights in the Southern states of the United States, the English liberal-socialist denounced the fact that the Fifteenth Amendment of the American Constitution (meant to prohibit racial discrimination in the exercise of political rights) continued to remain a dead letter, since neither the executive nor the Supreme Court were really willing to enforce it. But Laski went further. Taking seriously the Rooseveltian watchword of 'freedom from want', he considered it intolerable that, in the United States, 'richer today than any country has ever been in history', a considerable proportion of citizens lived in poverty or on its margins. With reference to the Third World, he then pointed out that, in countries like Egypt and Saudi Arabia, so closely linked to the liberal West, one could speak of freedom only for a narrow circle, while the mass of the population endured conditions of life and work not very different from those of the 'slaves of ancient Greece or Rome'. In any case, in examining the problem of freedom, one could not continue to separate 'economics and politics'.[34]

In this same context should be placed the reflection that Norberto Bobbio developed in the 1950s and 1960s. It is interesting to observe how he engaged in his polemic with Palmiro Togliatti: while insisting, rightly and far-sightedly (as is today clear) on the inalienability of 'formal' freedom and its juridical-institutional guarantees, the Turin philosopher also credited the socialist states with having 'initiated a new phase of civil progress in politically backward countries, introducing traditionally democratic institutions of formal democracy, such as universal suffrage and the electivity of offices, and of substantial democracy, such as the collectivisation of the instruments of production'. At this point in time, Bobbio's judgement on the political and social

34 Harold Laski, *Liberty in the Modern State* (London: Allen & Unwin, 1948), pp. 77, 16ff, 22.

transformations that had taken place was so clearly positive and flattering that the new 'socialist state' was called upon merely to transplant liberal guarantee mechanisms into its own bosom, pouring 'a drop of oil into the machinery of the already accomplished revolution'.[35] My concern here is not with his subsequent radical change of evaluation of the historical event that began with the October Revolution; what is more important is the fact that, at this point, a 'substantial democracy' was also being theorised alongside 'formal democracy'.

In these years, the demand for a democracy with socioeconomic substance was so widespread that its effects were notable even in authors who sought to position themselves in line with the classical liberal tradition, and later even became points of reference for neoliberal literature. In 1948, such a figure as Karl Popper declared himself in favour of the aim of 'securing full employment at high wages for the whole labouring population'.[36] In *The Open Society and Its Enemies*, we find a general consideration of the link between the formal and material dimensions of freedom:

> Even if the state protects its citizens from being bullied by physical violence (as it does, in principle, under the system of unrestrained capitalism), it may defeat our ends by its failure to protect them from the misuse of economic power. In such a state, the economically strong is still free to bully one who is economically weak, and to rob him of his freedom. Under these circumstances, unlimited economic freedom can be just as self-defeating as unlimited physical freedom, and economic power may be nearly as dangerous as physical violence; for those who possess a surplus of food can force those who are starving into a 'freely' accepted servitude, without using violence.[37]

The theorist of the open society has a nice way of classifying Marx among the 'false prophets'. Whether he is aware of it or not, directly or indirectly, Popper ends up deducing from the German philosopher the criticism of liberalism formulated in this text: there is not only physical

35 Norberto Bobbio, *Politica e cultura* (Turn: Einaudi, 1977 [1955]), pp. 164, 280.

36 Karl Popper, *Conjectures and Refutations: The Growth of Scientific Knowledge* (London: Routledge, 2002), p. 345.

37 Karl Popper, *The Open Society and Its Enemies: New One-Volume Edition* (Princeton, NJ: Princeton University Press, 2013), p. 333.

coercion, there is also economic coercion that can reduce even legally free individuals to conditions of substantial 'servitude'.

In the first years following 1945, the demand for 'social and economic rights', proclaimed and enshrined even by the UN, seemed so irresistible that it was not so much openly opposed as stripped of its critical potential by means of a reassuring and sometimes even rose-tinted reading of the existing realities. Popper acknowledged the debt that the 'modern democracies' owed to Marx (having been forced to take into account the relationship between politics and economics, and the fact that freedom also has a material dimension). But he did so only then to add that these democracies had made the *Communist Manifesto* obsolete, simply by putting 'most' of its programmatic points 'into practice'.[38] In these years we see a paradoxical phenomenon at work. The utopia denounced in Marx is contrasted with a sort of realised utopia: the political and social reality of the time is, in fact, seen and celebrated as a society that has not only fully realised, together with the other freedoms, also 'freedom from want', but is even characterised by the progressive disappearance of class privilege and – according to certain particularly apologetic descriptions – by the disappearance of social classes as such.

This is how Dahrendorf, writing in the 1950s, summarised the goals now achieved by the capitalist system: 'Today, the allocation of social positions is increasingly the task of the educational system.' Property had lost all importance, being replaced instead by merit: 'the school has become the "first and thereby decisive point of social placement"'. And this is not enough; there is 'increasing equalization of the social status of incumbents of different social positions' and 'as a tendency the process of leveling social differences cannot be denied'.[39] The author of this rose-tinted picture is, moreover, forced to polemicise against other sociologists, according to whom there is now a spontaneous movement towards a situation 'in which there are no classes and no class conflicts, because there is simply nothing to quarrel about'.[40]

There is no need to underline the radically erroneous character of such predictions, which sometimes even claimed to be a simple

38 Ibid., p. 350.

39 Ralf Dahrendorf, *Class and Class Conflict in Industrial Society* (Stanford, CA: Stanford University Press, 1959), pp. 59, 63.

40 Ibid., p. 64.

recognition of fact. But we should not lose sight of the fact that such a reassuring picture of reality also expressed – albeit in a distorted and mystifying way – an awareness that, after the political upheavals of the twentieth century, in a society characterised by a great development of the productive forces and of social wealth, it was no longer legitimate to restrict the meaning of freedom to its essential formal dimension. Even from this honeyed description of the existing reality, there emerges an objective recognition of the 'social and economic rights' that seem to have become part of the common consciousness in these years.

Hayek and the Nostalgia for a World Uncontaminated by Universal Suffrage

Like all the preceding moments in the expansion of democracy, the postwar period also saw manifestations of resistance and the emergence of efforts towards disemancipation, especially overtly expressed in an author like Hayek. It may be interesting to examine this neoliberal patriarch's rereading of contemporary history. According to Hayek, from 1848 onwards, '"social" or totalitarian democracy' began its baleful struggle against 'liberal democracy'; in 1870, there were already clear signs of the decline of the 'tradition of liberty', which he instead intended to restore in its pure, authentic form.[41] Especially interesting is this periodisation, which connects the first manifestation of the crisis of liberalism to the first appearance of modern democracy. If 1848 marked the affirmation of universal male suffrage in France, the second date takes us to the years after the collapse of the Bonapartist dictatorship and the brief flare-up of the Paris Commune, and, after the failure of attempts at both Bourbon restoration and disemancipation, through the return to open property-based discrimination or the introduction of plural voting. It was in these years that the Third Republic began to function as a parliamentary democracy based on universal (male) suffrage.

These facts do not cause the least disturbance to Hayek, who does nothing to conceal his sovereign attitude of indifference or haughty

41 Friedrich A. Hayek, *The Constitution of Liberty* (Chicago: University of Chicago Press, 1979), p. 55.

disdain towards what is commonly called 'political freedom' (the quotation marks are the neoliberal patriarch's own). By this he means, 'the participation of men in the choice of their government, in the process of legislation, and in the control of administration . . . a free people in this sense is not necessarily a people of free men; nor need one share in this collective freedom to be free as an individual'.[42] That is, freedom taken in its most authentic meaning – indeed, in the only one acceptable to the patriarch of neoliberalism (the autonomy and inviolability of the individual sphere) – does not necessarily need democracy and the recognition of political rights for all. This is why Hayek has no problem in mounting a periodisation that has the beginning of the crisis of the 'tradition of liberty' coincide with the advent of mass suffrage. The extension of political rights has nothing to do with liberty: 'It can scarcely be contended that . . . resident aliens in the United States, or persons too young to be entitled to vote do not enjoy full personal liberty because they do not share in political liberty'.[43]

Significantly, the examples given here (foreigners and minors) are the same ones Constant resorts to in order to justify the exclusion of non-proprietors from political rights: 'No nation has regarded all the individuals living in its territory, in whatever way this might be, as members of the political association'; even the 'most full democracy' excludes from political rights 'foreigners and those below the age decreed by the law'.[44] As Laboulaye emphasises in a note, 'women must be added to children, that is, half of the nation. Universal suffrage is thus exercised only by a minority of citizens. This proves clearly that it is a political function and not a natural right.' If women (not to mention children) can be excluded from political rights, why could not the propertyless be excluded, too? Similarly, Hayek argues:

> It is useful to remember that in the oldest and most successful of European democracies, Switzerland, women are still excluded from the vote and apparently with the approval of the majority of them. It

42 Ibid., p. 13.

43 Ibid., pp. 13–14.

44 Benjamin Constant, *Principles of Politics Applicable to All Governments*, transl. Dennis O'Keeffe (Indianapolis, IN: Liberty Fund, 2003), p. 165. The Laboulaye comment appears in the edition cited in Domenico Losurdo, *Princìpi di politica* (Rome: Editori Riuniti, 1970), pp. 99 notes.

> also seems possible that in primitive conditions only a suffrage confined, say, to landowners would produce a legislature sufficiently independent of the government to exercise effective control over it.[45]

We have seen Laboulaye make the case that suffrage is only a 'political function', and certainly not a 'natural right'. This is, once again, the opinion of the patriarch of neoliberalism. Hayek insists that the denial of political citizenship to certain social groups – and, as we shall see, also ethnic groups – not only does not harm the freedom of those thus excluded, but also does not violate the principle of 'equality before the law'. Thus:

> If in the Western world universal adult suffrage seems the best arrangement, this does not prove that it is required by some basic principle . . . However strong the general case for democracy [understood as the recognition of political rights for all adults], it is not an ultimate or absolute value and must be judged by what it will achieve. It is probably the best method of achieving certain ends, but not an end in itself.[46]

By now, it is clear: Hayek takes up the arguments with which the liberal tradition of the nineteenth century had justified property qualifications, as it resisted each step forward made by the suffrage movement while also leaving the door open to further restriction through disemancipation measures. In the years of the July Monarchy, in the country where memories still survived of the political rights enjoyed by almost the whole adult male population during the Jacobin phase of the Revolution, Thiers had stated: 'we do not believe that one is an elector by right. One is an elector for the utility of the country. The only electors are those whom the country has believed to be useful and declares as such by a law.'[47] After Louis-Napoleon reintroduced universal suffrage, in the more or less liberal phase of the Second Empire, Laboulaye insisted that 'neither in England, nor in America, nor in any other country in the

45 Hayek, *Constitution of Liberty*, p. 443.

46 Ibid., pp. 105–6.

47 Raymond Huard, *Le suffrage universel en France 1848–1946* (Paris: Aubier, 1991), p. 23.

world, has the electoral right been supposed to be a natural right': this last peculiar idea had exclusively emerged in a country that was devastated by a ruinous revolutionary process.[48] Hayek, in turn, after contrasting the Anglo-Saxon political tradition with the French one – at fault for favouring, from 1848 onwards, the inauspicious rise of '"social" or totalitarian democracy' – denounced the political regime dominant in the France of that time as a 'dictatorship of the *ouvriers*' – indeed, 'an uncompromising aristocracy of the *ouvriers*'.[49]

This judgement, which Hayek himself fully embraced, was taken from an American author who had written these words in 1848. That was the year of the introduction of universal male suffrage, with the extension of political rights also to the workers – whom the author denounced as a new privileged and tyrannical caste.[50] He articulated this judgement in a paper republished in the 1960s in the *New Individualist Review*, the publication in which Milton Friedman – another illustrious name of the neoliberal current – also collaborated alongside Hayek. The nostalgia which transpires from these pages for a world not yet contaminated by egalitarian mass suffrage is no merely individual weakness. Hayek steers well clear of questioning the restrictions based on property, 'culture' or race that had been in force in the United States when this 1848 text was written. Still, in 1975 there were those in that country who envisaged a fresh disemancipation, to be achieved through the introduction of plural voting. As we can see, distrust or hostility towards equal universal suffrage died hard.

The Nineteenth- and Twentieth-Century Critique of Democracy and Its End Point

Not only does Hayek take up the arguments developed by the classical liberal tradition in support of property-based discrimination regarding political rights; more precisely, he refers directly and explicitly to those late Victorian British authors who looked with

48 Édouard Laboulaye, *Histoire des États-Unis* (Paris: Charpentier, 1866), vol. 3, pp. 319–22.

49 Hayek, *Constitution of Liberty*, p. 55.

50 Francis Lieber, 'Anglican and Gallican Liberty' (1848), *New Individualist Review* 4: 2 (Winter 1966), p. 35.

horror at the expansion of suffrage that was then ongoing. This is the context in which we should see Hayek's positive statements regarding Lecky – an author who considered essential to 'British liberty' the exclusion of non-taxpayers from political rights – and above all the 'eminent thinker', or rather one of the 'greatest political thinkers of the nineteenth century', Lord Acton, who is repeatedly cited, and passages of whose are often used as an inscription for this or that text.[51] And here we are dealing with an author who never tired of underlining the 'abominable' results of universal suffrage, which everywhere proved 'absolutist and retrograde'.[52] Given the associations of this tradition, it is easy to understand why Hayek would like to erase the term 'democracy' and replace it with the less compromising 'isonomy'.[53]

After emphasising the full legitimacy of the property-based forms of discrimination dear to the liberal tradition, Hayek concludes: 'It is also by no means obvious that proportional representation is better because it seems more democratic.'[54] A similar approach is taken by Schumpeter; while considering legitimate the exclusion of this or that ethnic or social group from political rights, he does not explicitly reject the principle of universal suffrage. Rather, he mounts an indictment of proportional representation, which he accuses of promoting instability by 'offer[ing] opportunities for all sorts of idiosyncrasies to assert themselves'.[55] Several have noted the debt that Schumpeter owed to Italian elitism, and to authors such as Mosca and Pareto; as we have seen, the latter were critics of equal universal suffrage and proportional representation, moreover denouncing the latter as the electoral system that, by realising equal universal suffrage in its most complete form, lays bare its subversive and catastrophic effects.[56] The condemnation of proportional representation was the end point of the expressions of unease and criticism of

51 Hayek, *Constitution of Liberty*, p. 401; Friedrich Hayek, *The Road to Serfdom* (London: Routledge, 2001), p. 13; Hayek, *Constitution of Liberty*, pp. 176, 234; Hayek, *Road to Serfdom*, pp. 1, 105, 138, 225; Friedrich Hayek, *The Fatal Conceit: The Errors of Socialism* (London: Routledge, 1990), p. 52.

52 John E. E. D. Acton, *Selected Writings* (Indianapolis, IN: Liberty Classics, 1985).

53 Hayek, *Constitution of Liberty*, pp. 164–5.

54 Ibid., p. 105.

55 Schumpeter, *Capitalism, Socialism and Democracy*, p. 272.

56 Ettore Albertoni, *Storia delle dottrine politiche in Italia* (Milan: Comunità, 1990), p. 719.

democracy, in Italy as in Austria, after the enormous revolutionary upheavals that followed World War I.

The Italian elitists, in turn, harked back to the lessons of authors such as Bryce and Ostrogorski. Looking at the United States, they had engaged in inflamed denunciations of the deep damage caused by organised parties, which suffocated enlightened elites and vigorous personalities with a 'machine' all the more ruinous the more it dragged behind it the muddy mass of blacks, immigrants and illiterates, unwisely admitted to the exercise of political rights and inclined to cause social and workplace unrest. In a certain sense – taking its cue from reflection on America, where universal male suffrage was introduced first, albeit limited to the white community – elitist theory returned, with Schumpeter, to its starting point, after having passed through Italy and Europe.

Each stage in this bumpy journey was marked either by a disemancipation process or a project that pointed in that direction. In America at the end of the nineteenth century, the critique of democracy resulted in the explicit exclusion of blacks, immigrants and poor whites from political rights, through the enactment of registration laws that hindered the lower classes' access to the ballot box. In Italy after World War I, after a debate that contemplated the most diverse measures, on the eve of the establishment of the Fascist dictatorship (which, with its brutality, would strip the previous debate between emancipation and disemancipation of all meaning), criticism of democracy flowed into denunciation of the proportional system, seeing as it was impossible directly to attack universal suffrage, by now too deeply rooted in people's conscience. On the wave of the conquest of universal suffrage, especially in the France of the Third Republic, the democratic and socialist movement had demanded the introduction of proportional representation. The condemnation of this electoral system would likewise lead to a more or less explicit critique of universal suffrage itself, after World War I and until the period following World War II.

It is in this perspective that we should set the various reinterpretations of democracy and the representative regime as a political market, and as a procedural mechanism for the production of leaders – or as a simple 'isonomy'. Not by chance, as in Mises, these took their cue from the debate that developed as a challenge to the emancipation process that had followed World War I and the October Revolution. Such reinterpretations (which, by erasing the very idea of representation, constitute the most radical critique of the demand for proportional representation) not only expunge 'social and economic' rights from the catalogue of rights, but also make democracy compatible with the exclusion of certain social and ethnic categories from political citizenship.

In issuing their condemnation of proportional representation, both Schumpeter and Hayek cited the German-American scholar of electoral systems, Ferdinand Hermens. In his work, too, we can find a somewhat lukewarm, or reserved, attitude towards universal equal suffrage. The book in question is preceded by an introduction that credits the British and their 'incomparable practical sense' for their maintenance of 'special seats in parliament for the great universities'. While this is not explicitly mentioned, it was an institution connected with plural voting (for the benefit of both 'the universities' and 'business centres') that would endure until 1948. Moreover, the author of this introduction acknowledges that these seats are 'actually survivals of the corporate representation of medieval times', but insists that they 'serve a modern purpose'.[57]

Universal Suffrage and '"Social" or Totalitarian Democracy'

According to the patriarch of neoliberalism, the theorisation of 'freedom from want' and of 'social and economic rights' was to be blamed on the ruinous contagion that had developed since the 'Marxist Russian revolution'.[58] In fact, the claim to suffrage rights for the propertyless and those without financial means had gone hand in hand with the theorisation of the 'right to life' already in Robespierre; subsequently, the revolution of 1848, which sanctioned universal male suffrage, also saw the rise of the demand for the right to work. But it is correct that the development of this movement cannot be understood without the lesson of Marx. It is worth reflecting for a moment on the latter's fundamental critique of the bourgeois society that resulted from the French Revolution. It 'completed the transformation of the political into social

57 Carl J. Friedrich, 'Introduction', in Ferdinand Hermens, *Democracy or Anarchy? A Study of Proportional Representation* (New York: Johnson Reprint, 1972 [1941]), p. xxvii notes.

58 Friedrich Hayek, *Law, Legislation and Liberty* (London: Routledge, 1982), p. 103.

estates, or changed the differences of estate of civil society into mere social differences, into differences of civil life which are without significance in political life.'[59] Even in its most developed form, even where it removes property-based restrictions from the electoral law, the bourgeois state in fact merely 'closes its eyes and declares real contradictions to be non-political contradictions which do not disturb it'.[60] In this sense, to the extent that the rights of man regard the poverty, even desperate poverty, of broad masses of people to be a merely private matter, they are only formal in character. The theorisation of 'freedom from want' and of 'social and economic rights' cannot be understood without Marx's lesson. This theorisation would develop even in political circles very distant from Marx, in response to the challenge posed by the real movement largely inspired by the authors of the *Communist Manifesto* and resulting in the October Revolution, as well as the hopes or illusions this revolution aroused among vast popular strata all over the world.

In this sense, Hayek is right to connect the theorisation of 'social and economic rights' with a cultural and political tradition he considered odious. But insofar as he proceeds to deny these rights, the patriarch of neoliberalism is a theorist of disemancipation also in one further sense: namely, that, even though he does not openly question universal suffrage (also for reasons of political opportunism), he does somehow deny its legitimacy. For Hayek denounces universal suffrage as providing the foundation and the premise for despotic and liberticidal pretensions to realising supposed 'social and economic rights' and so-called 'freedom from want'. The path to the new serfdom and despotism is marked by increasing state interventionism and by the demand for a coercive redistribution of income – a pretension which itself results from the indiscriminate granting of political rights:

> at the time when the dependent and propertyless were growing most rapidly in numbers, they were also given the franchise, from which most of them had been excluded. The result was that in probably all countries of the West the outlook of the great majority of the

59 *Marx-Engels Collected Works* (*MECW*) (London: Lawrence & Wishart, 1975–2004), vol. 3, p. 80.

60 *MECW*, vol. 4, p. 96.

> electorate came to be determined by the fact that they were in employed positions. Since it is now their opinion that largely governs policy, this produces measures that make the employed positions relatively more attractive and the independent ones ever less so. That the employed should thus use their political power is natural. The problem is whether it is in their long-term interest if society is thereby progressively turned into one great hierarchy of employment.[61]

Had not many liberal authors of the eighteenth and nineteenth centuries claimed that putting the right to vote in the hands of the unpropertied posed a grave danger to property? Did not Constant already denounce progressive taxation as a measure that was not only despotic but turned the poor into a new 'privileged caste'? Pursuing an even more vigorous offensive, Hayek insistently condemns progressive taxation as an attack not only on liberty but also on equality before the law, since it discriminates against and penalises the highest incomes.[62] And, much like Constant, this latter-day neoliberal portrays this odious discrimination as the ruinous consequence of universal suffrage: 'Taxation comes to be based on a conception of income which is essentially that of the employee. The paternalistic provisions of the social services are tailored almost exclusively to his requirements.'[63] According to Hayek, now that the worker enjoys political rights, it is he who controls the legislature.

The liberticidal pretension to impose 'social justice' and the pursuit of 'the mirage of social justice' can also be traced back, directly or indirectly, to universal suffrage: and the inevitable outcome of this ruinous course is '"social" or totalitarian democracy'.[64] After reporting and embracing Mises's denunciation of the welfare state as guilty of granting political rights to minors in need of assistance, Hayek asserts that it is 'also possible for reasonable people to argue' that it would be better if 'all recipients of public charity were excluded from the vote'.[65] Indeed, one can go much further. Even in the most democratic countries, the universal suffrage proclaimed in theory is denied in practice through the

61 Hayek, *Constitution of Liberty*, p. 119.

62 Friedrich Hayek, *New Studies in Philosophy, Politics, Economics and the History of Ideas* (London: Routledge, 1990), p. 142.

63 Hayek, *Constitution of Liberty*, p. 123.

64 Ibid., p. 93; Hayek, *New Studies*, vol. 2.

65 Hayek, *Constitution of Liberty*, p. 105.

denial of voting rights to minors, criminals, foreigners, and so on: 'If only persons over forty, or only income-earners, or only heads of households, or only literate persons were given the vote, this would scarcely be more of an infringement of the principle than the restrictions which are generally accepted.'[66] Even if this maximal objective was unachievable, what could be done was to redefine democracy, expunging any idea of an inalienable subjective right to suffrage and, even more so, of economic and social emancipation.

Disemancipation and 'Minimising' Democracy: The Case of Popper

But it is not only the authors I have just mentioned who worked to redefine and reduce the scope of democracy. Here, I will limit myself to two examples that can give a sense of what today seems to be the main tendency. Popper's evolution is significant. *The Open Society and Its Enemies* is characterised by a basic contradiction. On the one hand, it establishes a link, as we have seen, between freedom and material rights (which have either been realised in practice or compel attention also thanks to the contribution of Marx and the movement that takes its cues from him). On the other hand, the definition of democracy is very formal. In the philosopher's subsequent evolution, the first consideration has been completely overshadowed and even erased by the second. It is the latter that we should now deal with. The theorist of the open society presents as a fundamental discovery, in the field of political science, the 'new approach' which compels us to recognise that 'the old question "Who shall be the rulers?" must be superseded by the more real one "How can we tame them?"'.[67] At the time the author published this book –and even more so at the moment of its conception – universal suffrage was far from well established worldwide, and not only because in many countries women continued to be excluded from political rights: in America, the laws that had sanctioned the disemancipation of blacks, immigrants and poor whites had not yet been struck down; in Britain, the plural vote endured; not to mention a country like

66 Ibid.
67 Popper, *Open Society and Its Enemies*, p. 341.

South Africa, where racial discrimination appeared in all its monstrosity, including with regard to the exercise of political rights. But the approach taken by the theorist of the open society effectively delegitimises the fight for suffrage.

Nevertheless, this alleged discovery would become the central or even only theme of the late Popper, who defines democracy as 'the type of government which can be removed without violence', or in which 'the government can be got rid of without bloodshed'.[68] In reality, these two definitions are not at all equivalent, and the thesis according to which the sociopolitical system dominant today in the West would allow a peaceful transition to a genuinely different one remains wholly unproven. But, leaving aside the variations and imprecision of language, the theorist of the open society means to say that a regime in which the change of parliamentary majority, of government and of governmental formulae takes place painlessly and in compliance with the rules of the game is to be considered democratic. This is, in substance, also the definition we shall see in Bobbio's more recent works. But it has one further aggravating factor: for, while the Turin philosopher sometimes seems to include, among the conditions for a 'minimum definition of democracy', respect for the individual rights of all citizens, Popper's formulation is characterised by an even more radical formalism. In this reading, even a slave-owning country like the pre-1865 United States could come under the rubric of democracy: this was, after all, still a society in which one president succeeded another and one party alternated with the other in an orderly and peaceful fashion – and this is the only condition that the theorist of the open society establishes for distinguishing 'democracy' from 'tyranny'.

Pushed to the extreme, the formalism of a definition based exclusively on the proper functioning of the rules of the game ends up by considering irrelevant not only citizens' political rights (let alone their material rights), but even their civil rights. It is no coincidence that Popper mounts an impassioned celebration of the 'Athenian democracy' – its 'mistakes' and 'crimes', if there were any, lay in its foreign policy; but he forgets to mention that it was founded on the enslavement of the large majority of the population.[69] We see what a remarkable trajectory

68 Popper, *Conjectures and Refutations*, pp. 345, 350.

69 Karl Popper, *The Lesson of This Century*, interview by Giancarlo Bosetti (London: Routledge, 1997 [1992]), pp. 67–8.

the liberal tradition has followed: in challenging the claim of the unpropertied to voting rights and political participation, Constant polemically pointed out that the Athenian democracy to which the Jacobins harked back was in fact founded on slavery. In our own time, driven by its thirst for self-celebration and desire to reject excessive material claims, this same tradition proceeds, with Popper, to a definition of democracy so formalistic that it can even embrace a regime of slave owners!

However, even an author such as Hayek agrees with the formulation advanced by the theorist of the open society – though, as we have seen, he was also somewhat suspicious of the term 'democracy' itself. Insofar as this category evokes the right of all citizens to participate in political life, it is doubtless a disturbing one for a nostalgic of a society not yet contaminated by universal suffrage. Yet this term can easily be accepted, once it has been subjected to a redefinition that lends itself well to the re-legitimation of even the most oligarchic liberal regimes in a democratic key.

To grasp the full extent of Popper's evolution, however, let us turn back to *The Open Society and Its Enemies* – and, more particularly, to the pages which, in underscoring the link between freedom and the material conditions of life, deem the *Communist Manifesto* now obsolete because its demands have supposedly already been realised in the West. It is worth dwelling on one of these for a moment, namely what Popper describes as the call for a 'heavy progressive or graduated income tax'. Given that he is referring to the *Communist Manifesto*, we may presume that Popper actually means to refer to the 'starke Progressivsteuer', 'the strongly progressive taxation' which Marx and Engels called for.[70] Such a demand is now superfluous, observes Popper, since it has already been largely 'put into practice' in the 'modern democracies'.[71] But this progressive tax is itself condemned as a synonym of oppression and despotism – and indeed, set in close relation with the advent of universal suffrage – by Hayek. He does not, therefore, seem to consider irrelevant and misleading the 'old question' ('Who shall be the rulers?') that Popper attributes to the 'enemies of the open society'.

As we know, the patriarch of neoliberalism traced progressive taxation back to the nefarious influence of the 'Marxist Russian revolution'

70 *MECW*, vol. 6, p. 350. Translation edited.
71 Popper, *Open Society and Its Enemies*, p. 350.

– and, in the Reagan years, the United States wanted to erase this influence as much as possible. This offered an opportunity for Popper to revise his judgement on the obsolete character of certain programmatic demands, especially now that even the aim of 'securing full employment at high wages for the whole labouring population' – an objective which he had in 1948 attributed to 'British social policy' – had in the meantime been clearly set aside, first of all in the United States and Britain.[72] Already some time earlier, having abandoned the fantastical predictions of the 1950s, Dahrendorf had noted that the United States was seeing 'an increase in the percentage of the poor'.[73] In the brief period since then, the situation has worsened even further. But the theorist of the open society, rather than revise his judgement, prefers to rail against those intellectuals who still dare to adopt a critical attitude towards existing realities:

> But when the new well-being had only just been established and everything was going well in the West, a great racket started up and intellectuals issued their curses on our wicked age, our society, our civilization, our beautiful world . . . But irresponsible intellectuals have managed to see only evil in our Western world . . . They wanted to be original and to say things that fly in the face of the evidence. And they succeeded in overturning not only the evidence but the objective truth. But I do not mean to go on blaming intellectuals. I would like to ask them to accept their responsibility for mankind and for the truth. Our freedom allows them to say everything, even to insult the free world and to paint it as an evil world.[74]

Such language is symptomatic of the growing aggressiveness of the ongoing process of disemancipation, seemingly determined to break down the obstacles that stand in the way of its onward march.

72 Popper, *Conjectures and Refutations*, p. 345.
73 Ralf Dahrendorf, *Per un nuovo liberalismo* (Bari: Laterza, 1988), p. 122.
74 Popper, *Lesson of this Century*, pp. 88–9.

Disemancipation and 'Minimising' Democracy: The Case of Bobbio

It may seem strange to put the recent works of Bobbio in this same context. But the object of concern here is not the Turin philosopher's own immediate political choices; rather, I am interested in examining his recent evolution on a strictly theoretical level. According to the 'minimal definition' of democracy that he proposed some years ago, this political regime presupposes that 1) decision-making power is attributed 'to a very high number of members of the group' or of the collectivity, and 2) decisions within the group or collectivity, and choices between 'real alternatives', are freely made on the basis of the 'fundamental rule of democracy [which] is the rule of the majority'.[75] It is interesting to note that the first rule specified here does not in any way require that a majority of the members of a given group or collectivity (that is, of individuals who have reached the age of majority) be empowered to make decisions. According to Bobbio, the 'very high number' required by the first condition cannot be quantified: 'it can only be said that a society in which adult male citizens have the right to vote is more democratic than one in which only property-owners vote, and is less democratic than one in which women also have the right to vote'.[76] So, even the liberal societies of the nineteenth century in which only a minority, and even a small minority, decided (for the electorate excluded not only women, but also unpropertied men) are still to be considered democratic. Paradoxically, when Bobbio refers to the need for majority rule, this is applied *within* the group empowered to make decisions, not to the relationship between this group and the population as a whole: the field of application of what is defined as 'the fundamental rule of democracy' is thus seriously and arbitrarily restricted. On this basis, it is no longer possible to distinguish between democracy and an oligarchy capable of perpetuating itself, respecting the rules of the game within its own ranks. The holes in such a 'minimum definition of democracy' are clear to see: Why should those who are left excluded bow to the principle of majority rule which is explicitly trampled upon by the minority that

75 Norberto Bobbio, *Il futuro della democrazia. Una difesa delle regole del gioco* (Turin: Einaudi, 1984), pp. 4–7.

76 Ibid.

proclaims its lone right to decide? Is the possibility of participation not the preliminary, foundational condition of the validity of the rules of the game? Why should the classes who are not admitted to political citizenship – the 'foreigners', according to Constant's definition – and who are subjected to a legislation that comes to them from outside, feel bound by the rules of a game that not only does not concern them, but is based on their exclusion?

Defending the full legitimacy and reasonableness of a regime in which '32 million men are governed by the vote of 240,000', Thiers rejected the accusation levelled by those who claimed that, given the restriction of suffrage, with the July Monarchy 'the aristocracy of the nobility had been replaced by the aristocracy of the bourgeoisie'.[77] At the level of the philosophy of history, if not of his immediate political choices, Bobbio agreed with the French premier rather than with his opponents. For, starting out from Bobbio's current positions, no objection of principle can be raised against the disemancipation that took place in the France of 1850 or the United States of the end of the nineteenth century. Without doubt, they each thereby became less 'democratic' – but why should this backward step not be taken, as compelled by the conditions of the time, when the ground of 'democracy' is not itself abandoned? Meanwhile, this reading delegitimises the great milestones that mark the advent of modern democracy – starting with the revolution of 1848. Based on Bobbio's approach, this revolution appears as a completely unjustified *coup de force* against a society that was itself democratic. This, even if this society was itself the product of an earlier *coup de force*, though surely one he would find it hard to justify, given that the Restoration France against which the July revolution rose up was also 'democratic' (albeit even less so) insofar as it had a far from homogeneous representative body operating on the basis of the majority principle. It could be objected that the revolutions of 1830 and 1848 were prompted by the decision to restrict constitutional freedoms that the dominant power had in each instance taken just beforehand; but, as we have seen, similar decisions characterise the history of all representative regimes in crisis situations.

On the level of the reading of history, Bobbio does not succeed in effectively countering Hayek: and both seem far from the positions of

77 Adolphe Thiers, *Discours parlementaires* (Paris: Calman Lévy, 1879), p. 484.

the protagonists of the February revolution who, in introducing universal suffrage, declared their intention to call all 'the people to the exercise of the supreme right of man, that of his sovereignty'.[78] In his insistence that suffrage is not a right but a simple function regulated by society, Hayek is merely reiterating a central theme of the liberal tradition. For all its talk of individualism and the overcoming of all forms of holism, this tradition still today often refuses to recognise suffrage as a subjective right. It instead presents it as a gracious concession to be bestowed according to circumstances, but always, in the words of an author dear to Hayek, 'on grounds of expediency or, in other words, for the benefit of the State'.[79] It is this approach, energetically affirmed by the patriarch of neoliberalism, which the Bobbio of recent vintage proves unable to question or overcome, having clearly regressed with respect to the positions he had earlier expressed. On the one hand, the Turin philosopher articulates the thesis that democracy presupposes the overcoming of 'holistic conceptions of society and history' and the recognition of the individualist principle of 'one person, one vote'. On the other hand, by subsuming under the category of 'minimal democracy' even regimes in which the right of suffrage belongs to a small minority of the population, and in which the figure of the modern individual sometimes does not even exist (and, as we have seen, for a long time in England only communities and guilds were entitled to the right of representation), Bobbio ends up theorising a sort of holistic democracy. That is, a 'democracy' that grants political rights exclusively on the basis of the holistic calculation of the 'benefit of the state', as interpreted by the restricted circles of the ruling class.

Here we get a measure of Bobbio's involution as compared with the positions he expressed in the 1950s. Then, he considered 'universal suffrage' an integral part of 'formal democracy' – though it did not exhaust the scope of democracy as such, given that he also theorised a 'substantial democracy'. Certainly, even in recent times, Bobbio's immediate political positions have been clearly different from Hayek's. But the fact remains that, on the philosophical level, the renunciation of the category of 'substantial democracy' is the analogue of the neoliberal

78 Huard, *Le Suffrage universel en France*, p. 34.

79 William E. H. Lecky, *Democracy and Liberty* (Indianapolis, IN: Liberty Classics, 1981 [1896]), vol. 1, p. 1.

liquidation of 'social and economic' rights. Equally, the expulsion of universal suffrage from 'formal democracy' (in its 'minimal definition') is the analogue of a vision that considers democracy compatible with the exclusion of vast social and ethnic groups from political citizenship. Indeed, based on this 'minimum' definition of democracy, it would be easy for this category to embrace even a regime which, after depriving a large part of its citizens of political rights, then ventures into economic and foreign policies which condemn them to death by starvation or to mass sacrifice in war (however unjustified this might be).

The Weakness of the Resistance to the Disemancipation Process

While the tendency towards disemancipation is clearly prevalent, it would be schematic and wrong to paint a picture of today's political theory that takes into account *only* this tendency. To give just one example, the evolution of Popper and Bobbio can be contrasted with that of Dahrendorf. Putting aside the reassuring picture of reality that he painted in the 1950s, Dahrendorf went on to denounce the poverty and unemployment extending even into the capitalist metropole as a threat, and even a nullification of 'civil rights':

> Equality before the law has little meaning if there is no universal suffrage and other opportunities for political participation. Opportunities for participation remain an empty promise if people do not have the social and economic position to benefit from that which laws and constitutions promise them. Little by little, the idea of citizenship has been given substance. From being a formal quantity of rights, citizenship has become a status, which includes, in addition to the right to vote, a decent income and the right to lead a civilised life, even when one is ill or old or unemployed.[80]

Here, not only universal suffrage but also social and economic rights make up part of the definition of democracy. Abandoned by Bobbio, the category of substantial democracy ends up re-emerging in this passage of Dahrendorf's, even with regard to the terminology he uses. And yet,

80 Dahrendorf, *Per un nuovo liberalismo*, pp. 122, 124.

even in this case, the resistance to the disemancipation movement is weak and contradictory. Moreover, these comments show no awareness of this movement, and remain subordinate to the reading of history developed by its leading theorists. For Dahrendorf, the category of citizenship also includes material rights, the theorisation of which, according to Hayek, is to be blamed on the political tradition that resulted in the October Revolution and paved the way for totalitarianism. Yet Dahrendorf formulates only weak reservations concerning the patriarch of neoliberalism.[81] The Anglo-German sociologist does not even seem to be fully aware of the debt that his most recent theoretical elaboration owes to Marx; nor does he seem willing to revise – as would be necessary – the commonly traced history of democracy. If, in its fullest meaning, democracy implies universal suffrage and social and economic rights, then, in the first place, it refers to the tradition that leads from the Jacobin French Revolution to the October Revolution, rather than to the 'blessed if not altogether perfect island' – that is to say, to Britain.[82] As we have seen, the latter in fact arrived only with considerable historical delay at the idea of modern representation and the principle of 'one person, one vote'. Alongside the classic homeland of the liberal tradition, he refers with great warmth to Edmund Burke, the implacable enemy of the rights of man and of the 'swinish multitude', who subsumes the wage worker under the category of *instrumentum vocale* dear to the ancient theorists of slavery. Dahrendorf nonetheless celebrates him as the first theorist of the 'open society', in opposition to the 'totalitarian tendencies' already emerging from France in 1789! The reference to the author of the first great indictment against the French Revolution delegitimises that political tradition from which sprang the 'idea of citizenship . . . given substance' that Dahrendorf wants to affirm and defend today, but which Hayek considered ruinous. The latter, after paying homage to the 'great seer' Burke, contrasts the Anglo-Saxon political tradition with the French one, which he indicts for its 'totalitarian' tendency to theorise a social democracy that Dahrendorf, too, would today seem to have taken to heart.[83]

81 Ralf Dahrendorf, *Reflections on the Revolution in Europe* (London: Routledge, 2017 [1990]), pp. 32–7.

82 Ibid., p. 123.

83 Hayek, *Law, Legislation and Liberty*, p. 22.

Dahrendorf also expresses his admiration for the more recent works of the theorist of the open society.[84] But, when he realistically and critically analyses the worsening social question in the West, he objectively ends up being one of those intellectuals of whom the late Popper loves to stand in condemnation.

We are thus in the presence of a variegated and contradictory scenario. Yet the main tendency, in a process which is still underway, is the theoretical downsizing of democracy. Since democracy is not fulfilling its promises, in terms of either material rights or citizens' participation in political choices, a minimalist redefinition of democracy is being advanced in order to adapt it to the existing situation. In the last analysis, this is how the liberal or liberal-democratic theorists of our century have generally behaved; and this is how Bobbio and Popper are proceeding today – the former in pained fashion, the latter with the magniloquence of a judge delivering his verdict.

Disemancipation and the 'New World Order'

But the terrain on which the disemancipation process does not seem to encounter *any* resistance worthy of note is the level of international relations. Indeed, the process being discussed here cannot be examined in exclusively national terms or limited within the bounds of the West; such a picture would be not only incomplete but also distorted. After all, as we have seen, historically the emancipation process that developed in the context of a determinate state, national or ethnic community has often been intertwined with the disemancipation and even enslavement of ethnic groups and populations located outside that community. In the years of the colonial expansion of Europe and the West, the de-racialisation process that had developed in the capitalist metropole, to the benefit of those previously excluded from citizenship and considered 'foreigners' and members of a different and inferior people, became deeply intertwined with another process that heavily naturalised the cultural diversity of the peoples subjugated or destined to be subjugated – transforming them into minor and barbaric races, thus summoned to meekly bow to what John Stuart Mill explicitly called the pedagogical

84 Dahrendorf, *Reflections on the Revolution in Europe*, p. 161.

'despotism' of their tutors. From this point of view, the twentieth century represented a crucial turning point. For, starting from the appeal that the October Revolution launched to the slaves of the colonies, calling on them to break their chains, a powerful decolonisation process developed which pitched into crisis the previous interconnection between emancipation within a determinate (state, national or ethnic) community and disemancipation outside it. So, how should we fit together the pieces of today's situation?

After the Gulf War and the collapse in Eastern Europe, the system of international relations seems to oscillate between two different temptations. The first is what we might call a planetary Bonapartism. At present, the conditions for this seem to be in place. The extreme concentration of the means of information that guarantees, within the individual capitalist countries, a monopoly to the 'trumpets' of the bourgeoisie, is even more accentuated in the relationship between, on the one hand, the former colonial powers, and even more so the sole surviving superpower, and, on the other, the countries of the Third World: 'the news market is the quasi-monopoly of four agencies: Associated Press and United Press (United States), Reuters (Britain) and Agence France-Presse. All radio, all television chains, all newspapers in the world subscribe to these agencies. Sixty-five percent of the world's "news" originates in the United States.'[85]

The disappearance or extreme weakening of international organisations such as Comecon and the non-aligned countries is the equivalent of the phenomenon at the level of individual states that has led or is leading to the liquidation or marginalisation of organised mass parties based on political programmes. No longer hindered by these annoying filters, and availing himself of the monopoly of the means of information, Bush presented himself as what the compliant press called the 'president of the planet'.[86] Having obtained formal, plebiscitary investiture from the United States, Bush was able to proceed without any kind of hindrance in defining the timing, modes and objectives of the war he so determinedly sought. In this context, we can well understand the United States' annoyance at the International Court of Justice. This

85 Serge Latouche, *L'Occidentalisation du monde: Essai sur la signification, la portée et les limites de l'uniformisation planétaire* (Paris: La Découverte, 2007), p. 45.

86 TN: The 1989–1993 US president, George H. W. Bush.

country had already dismissed the court's legitimacy when it condemned it for having mined the ports of Sandinista-ruled Nicaragua, and it also bypassed it during the recent crisis with Gaddafi, in which Bush was determined not to wait for, and indeed 'to ignore the sentence of the International Court in the Hague and escalate the confrontation with Libya'.[87] Even if the court ultimately ruled in the United States' favour, the fact remains that this is a body that reduces the speed and fullness of powers of the 'global' executive. Most importantly, it puts up obstacles to the United States' direct and immediate relationship with the mass of Third World countries, which are atomised and in a condition of clear inferiority and subalternity, both at the level of their economies and in terms of information.

It is true that military expeditions in the former colonies are today carried out in the name of the 'New World Order'; but it is worth remembering that the establishment of peace and the passage from the 'state of nature' to the 'social state' – with the legal regulation, if not of international relations as such, at least of those relating to Europe and to truly civilised countries – is another old theme of Bonapartist propaganda.[88] In its time, it managed to deceive a vast public opinion, and even – for example, in 1811, on the occasion of the invasion of Russia – great intellectuals such as Johannes von Müll and Goethe, who saw in that event the beginning of the realisation of the beautiful dream of 'perpetual peace'.[89]

Partly an alternative to the tendency towards 'planetary Bonapartism', but also partly bound up with it, is the drive to definitively transform the United Nations into an explicit instrument of the hegemony of the rich countries. In the years in which the influence of the Third World (accounting for the overwhelming majority of the world's population) was making itself felt in this organisation, there was no lack of voices in the United States calling for a reform that would in some way guarantee power of control to the states that made the largest financial contributions. These calls and aspirations sometimes expressed a project of disemancipation which would even be formalised through the

87 Ennio Caretto, 'L'Onu vuole punire la Libia', *La Repubblica*, 29–30 March 1992.

88 Napoléon III, *Œuvres* (Paris: Plon-Amyot, 1861), vol. 1, p. 155.

89 Domenico Losurdo, *Hegel und das deutsche Erbe. Philosophie und nationale Frage zwischen Revolution und Restauration* (Cologne: Istituto italiano per gli Studi filosofici, Pahl-Rugenstein, 1989), Chapter 6.4.

enshrining in the sphere of international relations of the principle dear to the liberal tradition whereby representation is primarily or exclusively the prerogative of those who pay the highest taxes. In his day, Churchill stated that 'the government of the world must be entrusted to satisfied nations, who wished nothing more for themselves than what they had. If the world-government were in the hands of hungry nations, there would always be danger.'[90] So, we can understand the current tendency to turn the Security Council into a club of rich countries – one to which Germany, Japan or a body like the European Economic Community would indeed like to be admitted.

Discrimination based on property is, moreover, already being felt today, at different levels and in different areas. When it comes to voting in the Security Council or the UN General Assembly, the poorest (and most populous) countries are exposed to the sometimes explicit blackmail of the richest. Not long ago, we could read in the press that 'China has opposed sanctions against Libya and the three Western powers have threatened commercial reprisals.'[91] And, of course, the countries weaker and poorer than China are even more disarmed to resist the pressures of the rich and powerful.

But this property-based discrimination also plays a significant role in other areas. Take the issue of armaments: not only nuclear weapons, but also chemical weapons, long- and medium-range missiles, super cannons, and so on. All of these must be kept out of the hands of small and poor countries, and remain the monopoly of the great powers (apart from some possible exceptions decided or allowed by them). This, even though the latter do not even feel obliged to commit to never making first use of weapons of mass extermination, which must be banned even at the planning stage when it comes to the small and poor countries. All this is somehow reminiscent of the exclusion of passive citizens from the national guard. The monopoly of armed force that the bourgeoisie sought to establish at the national level after the French Revolution is today the objective of the club of rich countries at the international level. It barely needs adding that this monopoly is also the rule when it comes to deciding the direction of the so-called international police corps. If some obstacles do still stand in the way of the full development of this

90 Noam Chomsky, *Deterring Democracy* (London: Verso, 1991), p. ix.
91 Ennio Caretto, 'L'Onu vuole punire la Libia', *La Repubblica*, 29–30 March 1992.

discrimination based on the various states' wealth, they would appear to be nothing more than the residue of a very particular historical constellation (the considerable weight and prestige of the USSR at the end of World War II and the unforeseen victory of the revolution in China), and by now consigned to the past.

Founded at the moment when the process of decolonisation and emancipation at the international level began to develop following the defeat of fascism, the United Nations charter stipulates 'the sovereign equality of all its Members' (art. 2, § i). This declaration of principle has never reflected the reality. Yet it has played an important positive role in promoting the overcoming or questioning of the international relations handed down as the legacy of colonialism, including relations of political inequality. Today, there are many signs that the trend has reversed: the delegitimation of the International Court of Justice; the US assertion of its right to capture and 'try' a head of state (Manuel Noriega) who was first pampered and financed and then disgraced; and the reaffirmation of the Monroe Doctrine in its most brutal form. Upon Bush's trip to Moscow in the summer of 1991, one newspaper reported: 'On Castro, the president was very explicit: "We have discussed it repeatedly. His presence eighty miles off our coast is intolerable".'[92] All this seems aimed at formalising the inequality between great powers and small countries. This is also the context in which we should place the ongoing rehabilitation of colonialism. After the triumphant war against Iraq, in France a professor, Georges Boudarel, was exposed to public shame for having opposed the French war in Indochina: his persecutors, among them a former minister of Giscard d'Estaing's, were all the more emboldened by the fact that – they declared – 'public opinion today is rediscovering the civilising role' of the French army.[93] It is easy to understand, then, that the revelations about the central role that oil played, as we shall see, in the crusade against Iraq, or about the American determination to 'exterminate the already unarmed and fleeing Iraqis' do not stir particular emotions.[94]

In this context, we witness the disconcerting fact that a philosopher like Bobbio (who kept his silence over the invasions of Grenada and

92 Enrico Carretto, '"A Mosca chiederò la testa di Castro". Bush annuncia le sue richieste per aiutare le riforme in Urss', *La Repubblica*, 19 July 1991.

93 Gianni Marsili, 'Crimini contro l'umanità per Boudarel', *L'Unità*, 23 March 1991.

94 Giorgio Bocca, 'Dimenticare Hitler . . .', *La Repubblica*, 6 February 1992.

Panama, the mining of Nicaraguan ports, and even the crimes that the West's then-proxy Saddam Hussein committed during the war of aggression against Iran) wanted to give his backing to the expedition against Iraq, only to continue to remain silent, for example, on the US administration's repeatedly claimed right to 'liberate' Cuba – in the meantime imposing, outside the UN, a deadly blockade that indiscriminately strikes at that country's civilian population. The inequality of treatment in international relations between rich and powerful and poor and weak countries does not seem to distress today's theorists of democracy – not even the most tormented consciences.

Colonial Ideology, Old and New

However, this inequality is explicitly theorised by Popper. In two revealing interviews, the theorist of the open society declared: 'We must not be afraid to wage wars for peace. In the present circumstances it is inevitable. And sad, but we must do it if we want to save the world.'[95] But who is this 'we' to whom Popper refers? The Crusade is to be declared in the name of 'civilised states' – that is, 'states of the civilised world'. And which states are these? He clearly means the 'West', whose geographic and political boundaries are not specified, but which makes the sovereign decision as to who is 'civilised' and who is not.

Is this not the ideology that has traditionally accompanied colonial and imperial expansionism – one founded on the assumption of the primacy of the great 'civilised' powers and the mission incumbent upon them? The theorist of the open society does not shy away from this ideology; he is just as fearless in rereading history as he is in demanding the deployment of armed force. To Popper's eyes, colonialism clearly and unequivocally represented progress. But what about the devastation and massacres that the colonial conquest brought? What about the 'extermination of the lower races' which was denounced at the beginning of the twentieth century by a liberal (albeit a left-wing one) like

95 Karl Popper, 'Kriege führen für den Frieden', interview by Olaf Ihlau, *Der Spiegel*, 23 March 1992, pp. 202–11; Karl Popper, 'Io, il Papa e Gorbaciov', interview by Barbara Spinelli, *La Stampa*, 9 April 1992.

Hobson?[96] For Popper, all this is nonexistent or irrelevant; indeed, he does not hesitate to increase the dose: he insists that 'we liberated these states [the ex-colonies] too hurriedly and too simplistically', and that this was like 'abandoning a kindergarten to itself'. Here, we are confronted with an explicit disemancipation at the level of international relations: Popper would like to make the ex-colonial peoples regress to a condition of subalternity, rolling back the emancipation process which, starting from World War I and the October Revolution, led them to shake off the yoke imposed by the great powers. Here, we get back to the language of the golden age of colonialism, when whole 'races' – to quote Mill – were considered 'minors' or – as Kipling had it – half-children and half-devils. We find a similar reasoning in the theorist of the open society. For Popper, insofar as the countries and peoples of the Third World prove to be rebels and devils, civilised countries have the right and the duty to launch a crusade against them in the name of civilisation and peace, or what he calls the *pax civilitatis*.

Here, again, we come across a classic theme of colonial ideology. It was Theodore Roosevelt – this 'herald of modern American militarism and imperialism', and even, to some degree, of 'racism' – who claimed an 'international police power' for the United States and the great powers of 'civilized society'.[97] The leader of a great power, Roosevelt explicitly arrogated to himself the right, in his role as guardian of order in the Western Hemisphere, to use a 'big stick' against the recalcitrant peoples and countries of Latin America.[98] Those who believe that the watchword of 'international police power' is something new would do well to read the entire chapter devoted to this theme as part of a brilliant overall analysis of the ideology of 'nationalist expansionism in American history'.[99] And if we turn from the United States to Britain, we see talk of world government coming from such a passionate champion of the British Empire as Winston Churchill, who, as we know, claimed such a

96 John A. Hobson, *Imperialism: A Study* (London: Allen & Unwin, 1905), p. 251.

97 Richard Hofstadter, *The American Political Tradition and the Men Who Made It* (New York: Knopf, 1973), p. 314; Commager, *Documents of American History*, vol. 2, p. 33.

98 Theodore Roosevelt, *The Strenuous Life: Essays and Addresses* (New York: Century, 1901), p. 288.

99 Albert K. Weinberg, *Manifest Destiny: A Study of Nationalist Expansionism in American History* (Chicago: Quadrangle, 1963), pp. 413–50.

government for the 'satisfied nations': the great powers who had been the protagonists of colonial expansion.

Lastly, it should be remembered that a brutal, massacre-strewn colonial enterprise like the great powers' joint expedition to suppress the Boxer Rebellion in China was, in its time, celebrated, as Lenin noted and denounced, as the realisation of 'the dream of idealist politicians – a United States of the civilised world'.[100] Colonial expansion constantly brandished not only the watchword of 'international police power', but also the slogan of peace. We find this in a champion of imperialism like Cecil Rhodes, and so too in Mill.[101] The latter celebrated the British Empire as 'a step, as far as it goes, toward universal peace and general friendly co-operation among nations'. However, despite the good intentions it cites as its inspiration, this ideology immediately reveals itself to be an instrument of war: since 'a vigorous despotism' is the only method capable of raising backward peoples (or, rather, 'barbarians') to a higher level, it turns out that colonial conquests (and wars) are in the interest of peace and civilisation, and must therefore be extended to embrace the entire globe: it is already a 'common condition' for the 'more backward populations to be . . . held in direct subjection by the more advanced', and this is to become the 'universal' condition.[102]

The correspondence of today's realities with the colonial ideology of the pacifying *mission civilisatrice* – or, rather, the celebration, so dear to Kipling, of the white man's (or Westerner's) burden – clearly transpires from the day-to-day news coverage on the conduct of the great powers. We read that 'in the new design of the zones of influence in the world, the USA wants, at least from the commercial point of view, Latin America to belong to it', and that 'Somalia . . . should be able to remain largely within Italy's sphere of influence'.[103]

No doubt. But what methods are being used to achieve an objective that is not the altruistic and disinterested one of which colonial ideology, both old and new, likes to boast?

100 V. I. Lenin, *Lenin Collected Works* (Moscow: Progress, 1974), vol. 39, p. 684.

101 Basil Williams, *Cecil Rhodes* (London: Constable, 1921), pp. 51ff.

102 John Stuart Mill, *Considerations on Representative Government* (New York: Henry Holt, 1873), pp. 342, 345–7.

103 Carlos Elordi, 'Castro tenta l'ultima battaglia', *La Repubblica*, 19 July 1991; Renzo Cianfanelli, 'Somalia: italiani tra le polemiche', *Il Corriere della Sera*, 14 December 1992.

> The only two great powers [the United States and France] that today exercise a direct influence on that continent, are now competing for that market, even at the cost of increasing the conflicts between the warring factions in various countries. Supporting one or the other of these factions, depending on whether they are considered better suited to looking after their respective interests. This is the case in Liberia, where war rages between the factions allied to the incumbent president Charles Taylor and his opponents.[104]

So, before they invest themselves with the role and mission of firemen at the service of the New World Order, the great powers behave like unscrupulous arsonists. Let us continue to leaf through news organs that can hardly be suspected of Third Worldist leanings:

> *The New Yorker* magazine reports on a 1986 mission by George Bush, who allegedly asked King Hussein of Jordan and Egyptian President Hosni Mubarak to 'put pressure on Saddam to intensify the bombing of Iran'. The plan's objective was to force Tehran to turn to the United States for missiles and anti-aircraft defence weapons. In exchange, Washington supposedly requested the liberation of the American hostages in Lebanon.[105]

Barely touched on here is an argument that would deserve probing much more deeply. Presenting themselves as guarantors of world peace are the great powers that make enormous profits from the arms market, just as those who organise humanitarian missions by sending food and medicine are those who claim the right to impose, sometimes with an avowedly hegemonic intent, a total embargo on this or that rebel country in the Third World. Meanwhile, the official journal of the US Army War College is already predicting 'the Second Gulf War'.[106]

---

104 Franco Fabiani, 'Bérégovoy: resistere all'America', *La Repubblica*, 20 November 1992.

105 'Nuovi scandali, sempre più pericolose le relazioni con Saddam', *Il Corriere della Sera*, 26 October 1992.

106 Gianni Riotta, 'E nell'anno 2012 i soldati di pace faranno un golpe', *Il Corriere della Sera*, 14 December 1992.

The Return of 'Foreigners' and the Future of Democracy

For this reason, too, it is impossible to agree with the assessment of those who see in the collapse of the Eastern Bloc simply the fall of the old regime or the triumph of the 'demands for traditional civil and political liberties', and thus celebrate these outcomes.[107] This view undoubtedly captures an essential aspect of the reality. Certainly, there was no possibility of survival for regimes which, by eternalising the state of exception, were unable to achieve normality and ended up reproducing the figure of the 'childlike' multitude guided by an elite claiming to be enlightened. But we should not overlook certain other factors that are also essential. Firstly, the collapse in the East seems to be fuelling the disemancipation process to the detriment of the former colonial peoples. When Fidel Castro declared that 'the disappearance of the USSR is a tragedy for the Third World', he seems to have expressed an opinion and a feeling widespread in the countries forced to suffer the arrogance of the great powers.[108] Even leaving aside questions of international relations, we cannot overlook the fact that in Eastern Europe we are witnessing the explicit removal from the catalogue of rights of those 'social and economic rights' that Hayek – today the prophet of the regimes that have taken the place of 'actually existing socialism' – blames, not by chance, on the October Revolution. Thus, emancipation and disemancipation are closely intertwined. This becomes even clearer when we reflect on the fact that those stripped of the 'right to life' or 'freedom from want' in Eastern Europe – in today's Russia, 'more than half the population is below the poverty line' – and thus forced to emigrate, upon reaching their destination countries lose their political rights, and sometimes face threats even to their civil rights.[109]

The figure of the 'foreigner' – in Constant, a metaphor to define the juridical situation of non-property-owners deprived of political rights – is beginning to become a substantial reality also in Western Europe, as it has always been in America. Fleeing from a Third World now lacking

107 Dahrendorf, *Reflections on the Revolution in Europe*; Noberto Bobbio, *L'utopia capovolta* (Turin: La Stampa, 1990), p. xv.

108 Aldo Garzia, 'Fidel: la sinistra ricomincia', interview with Fidel Castro, *Il Manifesto*, 5 December 1992.

109 Andrea Bonanni, 'Si apre la sfida al Congresso. Eltsin è pronto a ricorrere alle urne per contrastare l'opposizione', *Il Corriere della Sera*, 1 December 1992.

even the hope of development, or from former socialist countries that, instead of reaching the level of the more advanced Western countries, as hoped, risk regressing to underdevelopment, masses of immigrants are pressing the borders of the European Economic Community, often succeeding by adventurous means to cross them, and thus constitute the class of foreigners. Here, too, the American model has won, or is winning. And, once again, a racialisation process is underway that confines newcomers to the lowest-ranking segments of the labour market and tends to externalise social conflict, identifying in immigrants an external pathogenic agent, and perhaps a scapegoat for unresolved or worsening problems.

The people excluded from democracy and the guarantees of the 'rules of the game' at the level of international relations suffer a similar violation of rights when they arrive in the capitalist metropole. There is evidently a relationship between the casting of formerly colonial countries as 'kindergartens', or, worse, as a jumble of barbarians outside the 'civilised world' – deserving, if necessary, to be hit by the punitive expeditions of the great powers – and the racist agitation developing in the capitalist metropoles. This agitation, too, considers non-Europeans unworthy of the rights due to other men, and sometimes hits them with beatings and punitive expeditions – reproducing in miniature the ones organised by the countries that claim 'international police power' for themselves. No one willing to look reality in the face can fail to notice that skinheads basically radicalise the discourse dear to Popper and all those others who, regretting the overly 'hurried' end of colonial domination, justify and welcome the ongoing recolonisation of the Third World. Even in the second half of the nineteenth century, the ideology of the 'white man's burden' or 'mission' accompanied both the great powers' gunboat diplomacy and the lynchings of blacks or Orientals by the Ku Klux Klan and other racist groups.[110]

But the 'foreigners' of the developed capitalist world are not only the immigrants living within its borders, but all those who help produce its material wealth without being able to influence its choices. At the beginning of the twentieth century, British liberal critics of imperialism provided some elements of a history of the figure of the foreigner, on

110 Oscar and Lilian Handlin, *Liberty in Peril 1850–1920* (New York: Harper Collins, 1986), p. 131.

which it is still worth reflecting. For centuries, the West had engaged in raiding backward countries for servile or semi-servile labour-power (first black slaves, then Chinese or Indian coolies):

> In ancient times the employer would not, if he could, go away from his own country to employ Libyans or Scythians in their native places. If he left home, it was not so easy to come back. He was practically in exile. In the second place, he was not sufficiently master of his slaves in their own country. If they were all of one nation and all at home, they might rebel or break loose.[111]

But then, as a result of the development of both industry and the means of communication, it was no longer necessary to deport the indigenous labour force to the heart of the capitalist metropole, since it could instead be employed in the exploitation of local raw materials. The figure of the foreigner living in the capitalist world did not disappear, but it took a back seat to that of the foreigner living outside it. Certainly, since the time when this analysis was elaborated, colossal upheavals have taken place, changing the face of the earth. Especially starting with World War I and the October Revolution, these largely swept away – together with colonialism, at least in its classical form – also those forms of servile labour which, Hobson noted, still endured at the beginning of the twentieth century.

Yet there are also elements of continuity. The English liberal published the first edition of his book in 1902; little over ten years later, through an agreement with the crisis-ridden Ottoman Empire, the British Empire created the state or protectorate of Kuwait. It absolutely needed this latter's oil for its vast programme of naval rearmament, in the context of its growing rivalry with Wilhelm II's German empire, which would soon give rise to World War I.[112] Let us now take a leap forward to the present. During the Republican Convention in Houston, immediately preceding the 1992 presidential election campaign, Bush did nothing to hide the fact that Operation 'Desert Storm' was necessary to prevent 'our energy

111 Hobson, *Imperialism*, p. 248.

112 Enzo Santarelli, *Imperialismo, socialismo. Terzo mondo. Saggi di storia del presente* (Urbino: QuattroVenti, 1992).

sources being taken hostage'.[113] On the other hand, even newspapers who had been in the forefront of the crusade against Iraq let slip the real objectives of the Gulf War: the decision to 'severely punish Saddam Hussein' had been taken by 'all the industrial powers' firmly determined to keep the price of oil low, 'destroying any possibility of another oil crisis that would have slowed down the expansive momentum of Western capitalism'.[114] At this point, we may recall an observation of Hobson's: 'the most profitable use of the hired labour of inferior races is to employ them in developing the resources of their own lands under white control for white men's profit'.[115] The oil needed by the capitalist West is extracted by workers who are foreigners twice over. For not only can they not influence the political destiny of the countries that are the prime beneficiaries of this essential raw material; they are also foreigners in the sheikhs' Kuwait, which continues to exclude them from political rights.

Moreover, the link between internal 'foreigners' and the others external to the capitalist metropole arises also from a classic of neoliberalism. In proceeding with his work of demythologising universal suffrage, and in any case questioning whether the vote is an inalienable subjective right, Hayek observes that everyone considers 'reasonable' the exclusion from political rights of 'resident foreigners' and 'inhabitants of special regions or territories'.[116] This last expression seems to allude to the situation of Puerto Rico, whose inhabitants are American citizens but do not have the right to vote in US elections. Of the utmost interest here is the juxtaposition between foreigners proper and the population of a Caribbean island that was subjugated by the United States after the war with Spain, and is still today kept in a semi-colonial condition. The exclusion of the Puerto Rican population from political rights is no problem for the patriarch of neoliberalism, who instead uses this example to demonstrate that there should be no cause for scandal if those whom the classical liberal tradition assimilated to foreigners – the destitute, the illiterate, and 'recipients of public charity' – were deprived of political citizenship. In 1926, after the gigantic process of emancipation

113 Cited in 'Votate Bush o vi derubberanno', *L'Unità*, 22 August 1992.

114 Eugenio Scalfari, 'Al pettine i nodi di Reagan e Thatcher', *La Repubblica*, 26–27 January 1992.

115 Hobson, *Imperialism*, p. 248.

116 Hayek, *Constitution of Liberty*, p. 105.

and extension of suffrage that followed the war and the October Revolution, a great reactionary political scientist, Carl Schmitt, wryly observed that, in the British Empire, so-called universal suffrage concerned only 100 million of the total 400 million inhabitants:

> When one speaks of British democracy, of 'universal' rights of suffrage and 'universal' equality, one coolly overlooks these hundreds of millions, just as coolly as slaves were overlooked in Athenian democracy. Modern imperialism has put into practice new forms of domination, corresponding to economic and technical development which extend to the same degree as democracy develops in the motherland. Protectorates, mandates, treaties of intervention and similar forms of dependence now make it possible for a democracy to dominate a population that is heterogeneous to it, without making citizens of it; to make it dependent on the democratic state, while keeping it distant from this state.

In this sense, the figure of the 'foreigner' is here considered essential to democracy and inseparable from it. But had not the October Revolution promoted and ordained the revolt of the colonial slaves and sanctioned the conquest of human dignity by the barbarians alien to the West? Had it not thus proclaimed the end of the figure of the racialised 'foreigner'? But let us see Schmitt's reply: 'In general, a democracy always includes slaves, that is to say, men who are deprived of rights in whole or in part and excluded from the exercise of political power, whether they are called barbarians, uncivilised, atheists, aristocrats, or counter-revolutionaries.'[117]

Clearly, the category of those excluded from democracy is too broad here, since it coolly amalgamates figures as diverse as, for example, slaves in the colonies and aristocrats during the French Revolution who were momentarily deprived of political rights. It should be added that the great political scientist then greeted Nazism's rise to power: so, having started by unmasking the slavery or semi-slavery camouflaged within the democracies, he then adhered to a regime that explicitly set out to subject to slavery the lower races and sub-humans of Eastern Europe. In this sense, in the words of the young Marx, with the

117 Carl Schmitt, *Positionen und Begriffe im Kampf mit Weimar-Genf-Versailles* (Berlin: Duncker & Humblot, 1988 [1940]), pp. 60ff.

reactionary critique of ideology 'the false flowers have been plucked from the chains in order to wear real chains without any flowers'.[118]

But this is not a reason to ignore the theoretical challenge that comes from Schmitt. Notwithstanding the enormous changes that have taken place, we may well wonder whether Western democracy's self-exaltation does not somehow continue to bear an illusion similar to that of Tocqueville, who believed that property qualifications had disappeared in the United States simply because they instead took the form of racial and ethnic discrimination. Of course, contrary to what Schmitt seems to suggest, it is not true that there is nothing new under the sun. After all, the Third Reich was an attempt to impose a gigantic disemancipation, as Schmitt himself ended up suggesting when, in 1936 (immediately after the issuing of the legislation that deprived Jews of political rights, because they were of a different race to the German-Aryan one), he credited Nazism with 'substituting the concept of "man" with the concepts of "citizen" and "foreigner"'.[119] In an Eastern Europe now assimilated to the traditional colonies, the disemancipation pursued by Hitler aimed at imposing, as in the golden age of colonialism, servile or semi-servile labour conditions which could also be introduced into the heart of the Empire. This burden was, of course, to be placed on the shoulders of the 'lower races', who were to be deprived of political rights and coercively confined to the lower segments of the labour market, as in America before the War of Secession or in the decades that saw the disemancipation of the blacks and their re-subjection to a condition 'comparable to serfdom'. But the Nazi attempt ultimately failed, notwithstanding the gigantic material means at its disposal and the extreme brutality with which this effort was conducted (with heavy effects even on the '*Herrenvolk* race', itself forced to undergo a terrorist dictatorship imposed by the permanent and total state of war necessary to achieving the objectives pursued). On the other hand, the very history I am here reconstructing shows how it has become practically impossible, in our day and age, to question the principle of universal and equal suffrage openly. Hence movements and attempts at disemancipation – which are

---

118 *MECW*, vol. 1, p. 205; Domenico Losurdo, 'Le catene e i fiori. La critica dell'ideologia tra Marx e Nietzsche', *Hermeneutica* 6 (1986), pp. 87ff.

119 Domenico Losurdo, *La comunità, la morte, l'Occidente. Heidegger e l'"ideologia di guerra"* (Turin: Bollati Boringhieri, 1991), § 3.1.

far from lacking – are forced to move with caution, making concessions to the principle they set out to neutralise.

On closer inspection, the history of the fight for suffrage is only one particular aspect of a wider story. It was no accident that the unpropertied, who won political rights with the revolution of 1848, finally felt themselves elevated to the 'rank of men'. And Marx identifies the meaning of the *égalité* which sprang from the French Revolution not in the assertion of the simple equality of buyers and consumers in the market, but in the 'unity of human essence', as humans develop a consciousness and behaviour as members of the same species.[120] Thus, the broader history in which the struggles for suffrage, for political and social rights, and against the racialisation of difference must be included is that of the construction of the universal concept of man and humanity as a species. This is the common thread running through the revolutions of the contemporary world – a history that is far from over.

120 *MECW*, vol. 4, p. 39; Domenico Losurdo, 'L'égalité e i suoi problemi', in Alberto Burgio, Domenico Losurdo and Jacques Texier, eds, *Égalité/Inégalité* (Urbino: Istituto italiano per gli Studi filosofici, QuattroVenti, 1989).

8

The Triumph of Soft Bonapartism

Democracy, Market, Total Manipulation

The twentieth century began and ended with two victories for soft Bonapartism. The first has already been discussed. Before dealing with the second, it is worth dwelling on some of the characteristics of the political regime in question, returning for a moment to Le Bon. After stressing the emotionality and irrationality of crowds, he proposed, as an antidote to universal suffrage, a Caesarist regime that could make skilful use of propaganda devoid of rational arguments, but instead built around the model of commercial advertising. For Schumpeter, it was necessary to acknowledge the 'serious blow' that the French sociologist had dealt to the assumptions underlying 'the classical doctrine of democracy' by demonstrating the irrationality of crowds that was supposed to be the subject of popular sovereignty.[1]

In fact, this demonstration itself needs revisiting. In support of his thesis Le Bon cites, among other things, the chauvinistic excitement of the masses which, in 1870, dragged France into 'a terrible war' with Prussia and into the defeat at Sédan; on the occasion of World War I we saw Guido Dorso, an exponent of democratic elitism, chide the masses for their reluctance to accept intervention in the immense

1 Joseph Schumpeter, *Capitalism, Socialism and Democracy* (London: Routledge, 1994), p. 257.

bloodbath.[2] 'An indirect tax' – continues Le Bon in his indictment – 'however exorbitant it be, will always be accepted by the crowd'; while it would raise a hue and cry over any immediately visible tax 'on wages or income', it pays no attention to the modest and barely perceptible variations in the prices of consumer goods, once again confirming its irrationality.[3] Conversely, Mises demonstrates this same irrationality precisely by citing the mass support for the demand for a progressive income tax. Again according to Le Bon, 'The crowds that go on strike do so far more in obedience to an order than to obtain an increase of the slender salary with which they make shift'; yet this same French sociologist points out, in critical tones, that 'by association' and organising themselves in unions, 'crowds have come to procure ideas with respect to their interests which are very clearly defined if not particularly just, and have arrived at a consciousness of their strength'.[4]

But what, then, is the alternative to the irrationality of crowds? It is certainly not provided by the intellectuals; for Le Bon, as for Constant, they are devoid of practical sense, full of *ressentiment* towards the upper classes and inclined to chase chimeras and utopias, and thus constitute a further factor clouding political life with passions. Once the monopoly of political rights held by the proprietors (the only ones, according to the classical liberal tradition, able to provide guarantees of rationality and political maturity) has collapsed, there is nothing left but to rely on the leaders of whom Bagehot speaks. This means relying on the 'Caesars' also invoked by the French sociologist – that is, the men explicitly called upon in each case not only to exploit irrationality but to fuel it, stirring up some 'vague dream of glory' through an intensive campaign in the country using 'thousands of speakers', or, even better, using obsessive 'repetition', modelled on all-pervasive commercial advertising.

Schumpeter's attitude also presents unique aspects of its own. The irrationality of crowds, demonstrated once and for all by Le Bon, demands a new definition of democracy, which is now to be understood only as a political marketplace in which different leaders compete. But to what extent is this market also rational and democratic in character?

2 Gustave Le Bon, *The Crowd: A Study of the Popular Mind* (New York: Macmillan, 1896), p. 21; Mario Stoppino, 'Élites, democrazia e partecipazione', in Peter Bachrach, *La teoria dell'elitismo democratico* (Naples: Guida, 1974), p. vii.

3 Le Bon, *The Crowd*, p. xxii.

4 Ibid. p. 44, xi.

Already in the strictly economic sphere, we see that consumers 'are so amenable to the influence of advertising and other methods of persuasion that producers often seem to dictate to them instead of being directed by them'. The situation of the consumer-voters in the political market is even worse, as here verifying the quality of the product purchased or voted for is even more problematic: 'The picture of the prettiest girl that ever lived will in the long run prove powerless to maintain the sales of a bad cigarette. There is no equally effective safeguard in the case of political decisions.'[5] But this observation does not lead to the logical conclusion that such a regime has little about it that is rational or democratic; nor does it suggest the practical necessity of enlarging such a political market as much as possible, so that the multiplicity of competing political products and advertising campaigns reduces as much as possible the effect of the spell over the consumer-voters. Much less does there follow from this a need to block or mitigate in some way the bombardment of advertising by encouraging the development of political parties and organisations which, by promoting their own internal political education and discussion, break or crack the monopoly of communication in the hands of highly centralised mass media.

We have seen Mises consider bipartisanship as an indispensable requirement of the market-democracy he theorised. And Schumpeter moves in the same direction when he condemns the proportional system. The process of oligopolistic concentration is already clearly more advanced and less controllable at the political level than at the economic level. Rather than being hindered, as antitrust laws theoretically propose to do in the economic sphere proper, in the political sphere this oligopolistic concentration is clearly favoured by a whole series of measures, also related to the electoral system itself, that tend to introduce or produce bipartisanship. This is, moreover, a bipartisanship that sees as competitors not two clearly characterised programmes but rather two aspirant leaders. At this point, we can consider definitively complete the reduction of the political community to a market deciding between two political products that, even though they compete with each other, resemble each other as a tube of toothpaste or a bar of soap resembles another of a different brand:

5 Schumpeter, *Capitalism, Socialism and Democracy*, pp. 257, 263.

> The ways in which issues and the popular will on any issue are being manufactured is exactly analogous to the ways of commercial advertising. We find the same attempts to contact the subconscious. We find the same technique of creating favorable and unfavorable associations which are the more effective the less rational they are. We find the same evasions and reticences and the same trick of producing opinion by reiterated assertion that is successful precisely to the extent to which it avoids rational argument and the danger of awakening the critical faculties of the people. And so on. Only, all these arts have infinitely more scope in the sphere of public affairs than they have in the sphere of private and professional life.[6]

Le Bon had already emphasised the systematic 'repetition' of an assertion, in the absence of any rational argument, as the fundamental propaganda tool of the 'Caesar' or 'hero' called upon to tame the universal suffrage which also elevates him to power. Schumpeter analyses market-democracy in analogous terms. It might seem that this is a critical observation. But, to the extent that this reality is considered insurmountable and without alternatives, the critical element dissolves completely. The Austrian-American economist's new theory is thus reduced to the empirical description of the de facto reality in a country like the United States, passed off as the very essence of democracy.

It would seem, then, that this political regime should be reduced to a 'subtle manipulation of the market which has become completely capitalist. Advertising has become the model of political "enlightenment" with the aid of an outrageously persuasive mass media.' The observation is Lukács's, but he goes further when he adds: 'Hitler already clearly understood this when he looked upon a good soap advertisement as a shining example for all political propaganda.' Yet, a 'direct connection between Hitler and capitalist advertising is out of the question, in fact, a strict contrast exists. Hitler's political propaganda was overtly ideological.'[7]

Obviously, radically different political regimes cannot be hastily juxtaposed – or, worse, assimilated under the banner of manipulation,

6 Ibid., p. 263.

7 Georg Lukács, *The Process of Democratization* (New York: State University of New York, 1991), p. 85.

as the Frankfurt School sometimes tends to do.[8] But there is a real problem that cannot be neglected: Le Bon, a writer in many ways linked to the liberal tradition, also became an authority in circles very different to Schumpeter's own. As Gramsci noted, the French sociologist became the model for Mussolini, who boasted of having read all of his work and of having meditated at length on *The Crowd* in particular.[9] Goebbels also got to grips with this text; he, too, was fully convinced of the effectiveness of propaganda based on the model of commercial advertising and systematic repetition without recourse to rational arguments.[10] Yet, developing as it did in between two world wars and in preparation for a total war, Nazi (and Fascist) propaganda could not but become immediately and explicitly ideological. Conversely, it is in the context of soft Bonapartism and periods of normality that political propaganda tends not only to model itself on commercial advertising, but to identify with it.

The Twentieth Century and the New Victory of Soft Bonapartism

The Cold War, which ended with the collapse of the Eastern European regimes, featured two propaganda apparatuses with quite different characteristics. It has been observed that 'the mass media's persuasive effect operates at a much deeper level in countries with a pluralistic democracy (and a market economy) than in totalitarian countries'. Indeed, conscious attention represents more of an obstacle to than a vehicle for the transmission of persuasive messages. And this is why, paradoxically, the media maximise their power of influence precisely in democratic countries, where the explicit ideological content of messages is relatively low and their potential for indirect persuasion is very high.

Particularly instructive is the comparison between the two countries separated by an artificial wall that attempted to divide a nation with a

8 Max Horkheimer and Theodor W. Adorno, *Dialectic of Enlightenment* (Stanford, CA: Stanford University Press, 2002), pp. 94ff.

9 Antonio Gramsci, *Quaderni del Carcere*, ed. Valentino Gerratana (Turin: Einaudi, 1975), Q9, §78, pp. 1145–6; Renzo de Felice, *Mussolini* (Turin: Einaudi, 1966), vol. 2: ii, p. 298.

10 Ralf G. Reuth, *Goebbels*, 2nd edn (Munich: Piper, 1991), p. 112.

long national tradition behind it: 'the old methods of Marxist-Leninist despotism were defeated by the West German media, which for years silently exerted their persuasive influence on the citizens of "democratic Germany" [i.e. the East].'[11] The United States' victory in the Cold War – as Bush himself described it – was also the triumph of the mass media over the party school, of subliminal messaging and of covert persuasion over conscious and overt indoctrination.

Just as the twentieth century began with the demonstration of the superiority of the American model, at the moment of its intervention in World War I and then in the course of its development, the century ended with a brilliant new victory for soft Bonapartism. At its centre is a leader able to base himself on plebiscitary-type popular investiture; on the very broad powers he exercises, which he can expand beyond all measure through the state of exception; on the holy aura that comes from being the interpreter of a sacred mission of freedom; and on the possibility of drawing on a gigantic apparatus of propaganda and covert persuasion. To identify this victory immediately with the onward march of democracy is to subscribe uncritically to the ideology of war and the empire of freedom. This ideology has constantly accompanied the history of the United States, beating the rhythm of its worldwide rise, and enshrining the triumph of soft Bonapartism in our own time.

The theorists of today's triumphant political regime have proceeded to redefine and drastically scale down democracy, which is now purged of any idea of emancipation and even of citizen participation in political decisions. But does soft Bonapartism at least manage properly to safeguard what the liberal school defines and celebrates as negative liberty? To answer this question, we should turn to an author usually considered a classic of liberal-democratic thought:

> What is an *absolute* monarch? He is one at whose command, if he says, 'war is necessary', a state of war immediately exists. What is a *limited* monarch, on the other hand? He who must first consult the people as to whether war is or is not to be; and the people say, 'there is to be no war', so there is no war. For war is a situation in which *all* political power must be at the disposal of the sovereign. Now the

11 Danilo Zolo, *Il principato democratico. Per una teoria realistica della democrazia* (Milan: Feltrinelli, 1992), pp. 201, 199ff, p. 199 note 78.

> British monarch has conducted wars aplenty without seeking the consent for them. Therefore, this king is an absolute monarch who ought not to be one, of course, according to the constitution; but he is always able to bypass it because precisely through those political powers, namely, that he has it in his power to dispense all appointments and posts, he can consider assured the assent of the representatives of the people.[12]

A regime such as the one in force in the United States would therefore have to be considered despotic. According to its admirers, who would like to propose this as a model for countries like Italy as well, this regime grants the president 'such a wide autonomy from the legislature in making decisions' that he can 'send the army to war even without a prior congressional decision'.[13] 'On the other hand', Kant continues in his denunciation, 'only children can allow themselves to be dazzled by the constitutional dictate which requires that war spending be approved by parliament. In the meantime, the latter is called upon to intervene too late when hostilities have already begun at the initiative of the executive, which then has ample room for manoeuvre to ratify the fait accompli. A people living under such a regime, and sent to war without the consent of itself or its representatives, is not "free" but "oppressed"'.[14]

Are we to consider such analysis and argumentation obsolete and now unserviceable? In reality, historical developments have given further validity and freshness to a denunciation formulated in an era when compulsory conscription was still unknown, or rather limited. According to a nineteenth-century English liberal philosopher, compulsory conscription reduced the soldier to a condition of slavery, as he was subjected to rigid discipline and even forced to run towards his own death.[15] But under today's regime of soft Bonapartism, an executive that has taken the

12 Immanuel Kant, *The Conflict of the Faculties*, transl. Mary J. Gregor (New York: Abaris, 1979), p. 163 notes.

13 Sebastian Messino, *La grande Riforma. Uomini e progetti per una nuova repubblica* (Bari: Laterza, 1992), p. 59.

14 Immanuel Kant, *Gesammelte Schriften* (Berlin: Königlich-Preussischen Akademie der Wissenschaften, 1900), vol. 19, pp. 606ff.

15 Herbert Spencer, *The Man versus the State: With Six Essays on Government, Society, and Freedom* (Indianapolis, IN: Liberty Classics, 1981 [1843–44]), p. 72.

initiative in involving its country in an international conflict also has the possibility of imposing conscription on large strata of the population, and even the entire population. Kant further observes – as he denounces the despotic character of a regime that entrusts the executive with the de facto imposition of a state of war, if not its formal declaration – that in an armed conflict '*all* political power must be at the disposal of the sovereign'.[16] And today's sovereign has a far vaster concentration of power at his disposal than was true at the end of the eighteenth century, with the possibility of making more or less onerous interventions into citizens' essential rights, up to total regimentation in the case of large-scale conflicts.

After the experience of Vietnam, even a limited war (limited, that is, from the viewpoint of the great power or superpower involved) entails the substantial suppression of freedom of information. Upon the invasion of Grenada in 1983, 'the White House prevented journalists from covering military operations, entrusting disclosure of what had happened to news bulletins published by the Department of Defense . . . One journalist would later comment, "The administration seemed to want a monopoly on news, as long as it was able to shape public opinion".'[17]

The same technique was pursued in subsequent conflicts, reaching the peak of perfection in the Gulf War: 'The management of information during the first conflict to be broadcast on live TV began a new era of wartime communication, consolidating the administration's control over the media.' Here I limit myself to citing the accounts of journalists who can hardly be accused of anti-Americanism.

> With a pointed strategy, which does not hesitate to resort to censorship, disinformation and rigid control of journalists, the White House and the Pentagon manage to ensure and maintain the consensus of a large share of American public opinion, notwithstanding any isolationist or pacifist inclinations . . . If in the last century the Prussian general Karl von Clausewitz asserted that the condition for victory was the cohesion of all the combatants, the electronic media had demonstrated that in a modern democracy the first condition for victory was the cohesion of public opinion.[18]

16 Kant, *Conflict of the Faculties*, p. 163 notes.

17 Enrico Brivio, *Come comunica la Casa Bianca* (Milan: Bridge, 1992), p. 91.

18 Ibid., pp. 105, 202ff.

The subordination of information to the needs of mobilisation and the regimentation of the war is so complete as to suggest the image of a 'second front' no less important than the battlefield proper.[19]

But even more significant is the fact that the experience accumulated in war does not vanish even in times of peace. Hence recourse to a colossal and intensive propaganda apparatus becomes the normal condition for the exercise of power:

> Not to see this gigantic mechanism for building political consensus, executive power, international politics, and public relations, is simply to fail to understand the heart of American democracy. The American president is more than just a political leader. He is a symbol of national unity, he represents the government, but also the country, he is the heir to an unbroken tradition leading back to the country's founding father George Washington.[20]

Two Competing Plebiscitary Investitures

Soft Bonapartism constitutes a regime not only by virtue of the orderly and painless succession from one leader to the next, but also because competition develops on the basis of an essentially unified platform common to the various candidates competing for the office of the nation's supreme leader and interpreter. This is particularly the case in the United States. Here, I will focus mainly on the 1988 presidential election, not only because a considerable amount of research is already available on the subject, but also because it comes closest to the ideal-typical model under investigation here. Let us begin by examining the conventions of the two major parties, following in the footsteps of a scholar whose analysis closely traced how each of them unfolded. The Democratic convention took place in Atlanta and ended with Michael Dukakis's acceptance speech, greeted by a 'prolonged ovation':

19 John R. Macarthur, *Second Front: Censorship and Propaganda in the Gulf War* (New York: Hill & Wang, 1992).

20 Gianni Riotta, 'Prefazione', in Brivio, *Come comunica la Casa Bianca*, p. 14.

> As the delegates sang *God Bless America*, Dukakis, Bentsen [the vice-presidential candidate], the other primary candidates, and all the Democratic leaders, filed into the gallery together, surrounded by their families. The gathering of the entire party behind its candidate is acclaimed with the liveliest enthusiasm. The Orthodox Bishop of Atlanta recites a prayer of thanksgiving, before the delegates part in a great spirit of unity.[21]

Let us move on to the Republican Convention in New Orleans. In his acceptance speech, Bush, who had already been 'unanimously nominated by the delegates', insisted on the need to maintain 'the obligation for teachers to have their students give the pledge of allegiance to the national flag' in America's classrooms. His words were met with collective enthusiasm: 'after a long ovation, the Convention ends with a prayer recited by the Orthodox Archbishop of New York; down to the smallest detail, the Republicans make their reply to the [Democrats'] Atlanta Convention.'[22]

It is not enough to say that 'Presidential conventions, once forums of decision, become in the electronic-age ceremonies of ratification.'[23] We must go further: in each case, we are witnessing two plebiscitary investitures, consecrated also on the religious level. The beneficiaries of this sort of Caesarist acclamation were two leaders who were indeed competitors, but whose competition, even if very bitter on a personal level, did not exclude a common profession of faith. It is interesting to note the main arguments with which they confronted each other. This time, let us start with Bush, who attacked his Democratic competitor as follows:

> [Dukakis] sees America as another pleasant country on the UN roll call, somewhere between Albania and Zimbabwe. And I see America as the leader – a unique nation with a special role in the world. And this has been called the American Century, because in it we were the dominant force for good in the world. We saved Europe, cured polio, we went to the moon, and lit the world with our culture. And now we

21 Patrick Gérard, *George Bush président: histoire d'une élection* (Nancy: Presses Universitaires de Nancy, 1989), p. 97.

22 Ibid., p. 123.

23 Arthur M. Schlesinger, Jr, *The Cycles of American History* (Boston, MA: Houghton Mifflin, 1999), p. 272.

> are on the verge of a new century, and what country's name will it bear? I say it will be another American century. Our work is not done – our force is not spent.

There is a 'mission' that belongs to the United States, the 'nation under God's protection'. Is Bush here justified in accusing the Democratic nominee of disregarding the mission and the unique role belonging, by the grace of God, to the United States? In fact, in Atlanta, Dukakis had declared that what was at stake was not 'ideology' and 'meaningless labels', but rather 'American values': 'And just as we Democrats believe that there are no limits to what each citizen can do, so we believe that there are no limits to what America can do.'[24] Even more significant is the official party platform issued by the Democratic Convention in Atlanta, with this profession of faith at its core:

> WE BELIEVE in a stronger America ready to make the tough choices of leadership in an ever-dangerous world; militarily stronger in our overall defense and anti-terrorist capabilities and in the cohesion of our military alliances; economically stronger at home and in the global marketplace; intellectually stronger in the advances of our schools, science and technology; and spiritually stronger in the principles we exemplify to the world.[25]

The two candidates, each enjoying plebiscitary investiture by their respective parties, then faced each other in a duel that had to demonstrate who was the privileged interpreter of the American mission in the world. This mission was not itself subject to question. Of course, there was no lack of differences and contrasts between the candidates. But not only did these develop on the basis of a common ground, but they are expressed by a language and an ideology common to both parties, which tend to externalise social conflict. According to the Democratic platform passed in Atlanta, the Republicans are at fault for having 'converted this proud country into the world's largest debtor nation', now forced to

24 Gérard, *George Bush président*, pp. 125, 134, 98ff. [TN: the candidates' acceptance speeches from the 1988 and 1992 elections and the Democratic Party platform cited below are all available at presidency.ucsb.edu.]

25 Ibid., p. 91.

suffer 'an unhealthy dependence on foreign energy and foreign capital, and the increasing foreign ownership of our land and natural resources'.[26] The serious social problems of the United States are somehow ascribed to a kind of foreign invasion that the Republicans have proved unable adequately to confront.

As for the duel that developed in 1992, this time between Bush and Clinton (though complicated by Ross Perot's presence), it had similar characteristics. The former gave an address to the Republican Convention in Houston which was shot through with pride at both the military superiority of the United States and its unique and exceptional role as bearer of the right to 'liberate' Cuba and to intervene in every corner of the world. Bush even issued a slogan ('America is the land where the sun is always peeking over the horizon') that seemed to echo Charles V's famous boast that the sun never set on his vast empire. In turn, Clinton concluded his speech accepting the Democratic nomination by painting the picture of 'An America with the world's strongest defense, ready and willing to use force when necessary . . . An America that will not coddle tyrants, from Baghdad to Beijing . . . God bless America.'[27] Again, the 1992 electoral contest took place on the basis of a common belief in American leadership which, even before being political-military in character, is enshrined in moral and religious terms.

Hence, the 1992 campaign had Clinton challenging the incumbent president to intervene also in the former Yugoslavia, and blaming him for having squandered US economic supremacy; and Bush, in reply, accused the Democratic Party of besmirching America, attributing to it an imaginary weakness, and forgetting that it was 'still the strongest economy in the world'.[28] In his contest with Dukakis in 1988, Bush had proudly stressed that he had learned the meaning of America's 'mission' in the world from his own military involvement in World War II; and similarly, four years later, he accused his challenger Clinton of shirking his duty to fight for his country in Vietnam.[29] It is not even asked what the concrete meaning of any particular war may have been: whatever it

26 Ibid., p. 89.

27 Bill Clinton, 'Cara America, ti restituirò un sogno. L'arringa di Clinton: guerra alla povertà e all'ingiustizia', *La Stampa*, 18 July 1992. English text from presidency.ucsb.edu.

28 Ibid.; 'Votate Bush o vi deruberanno', *l'Unità*, 22 August 1992.

29 Gérard, *George Bush président*, p. 124.

is, if it involved American soldiers, it is cast as a mission that no citizen can shirk. And most importantly, a politician aspiring to lead the nation on which this mission is incumbent must himself be worthy of it. This explains Bush's confession that he felt fully the president only after his baptism of fire in the invasion of Panama.[30]

In his victory speech on election night 1988, referring also to the congratulations he had received from Dukakis, in the 'great tradition of American politics', Bush had said: 'And I – I thank God for the faith he's given me, and as I grow older, as I grow older, I'm more aware of the spiritual element in life and I ask for God's help . . . and now we will move again, for an America that is strong, and resolute in the world, strong and big-hearted at home.'[31]

The 1988 contest that had started with two competing plebiscitary investitures ended as it began, with the reaffirmation of the American mission in the world, which was once again religiously consecrated. But, this time, this mission was reaffirmed by a leader who had received the investiture of the entire nation, and who could therefore make use of the extraordinary breadth of powers granted to a president who is the sole interpreter of the people (congressmen, who are elected according to the single-member system, instead represent an individual district and the particular interests prevailing in it). More than that, the US president is the interpreter of a people with a global role so peculiar and unique that it can be considered, to quote one twentieth-century American senator (Albert J. Beveridge), to be the one that God marked as 'His chosen nation to finally lead in the regeneration of the world.'[32]

The 1992 contest ended in a similar fashion: not surprisingly, one of the winner's first acts was to reaffirm the continuation of his predecessor's foreign policy, and the ideology that inspired it, built on America's global mission.

---

30 Jonathan Alter, 'The Limits of Schmooze', *Newsweek*, 10 August 1992, p. 39.

31 Gérard, *George Bush président*, p. 210.

32 Albert K. Weinberg, *Manifest Destiny: A Study of Nationalist Expansionism in American History* (Chicago: Quadrangle, 1963), p. 308.

Soft Bonapartism, Competitive Monopartisanship and the Power of Lobbies

Because of the ideology – rather, because of the common national religion – they express, the two major and, as we shall see, somewhat official electoral competitors seem to refer more to different factions within one party than to two different parties. The statement may seem excessive. But even in Tocqueville we can read: 'One would say that here there are factions, but not parties properly so called. Men are everything, principles are little.' This is an opinion expressed in the course of a conversation with the president of the Bank of the United States, who, in turn, observes that, at least since the Jackson presidency, 'there have been no parties proper, opposed to one another and professing conflicting political faiths. The fact is that there are now no two practicable ways of governing this people and that political passions can be exercised in matters of administrative detail and not over principles.'[33]

Doubtless, the image of America that emerges from this interview is rather rose-tinted. When Tocqueville claims that, in the country of 'universal suffrage', 'the people are everything and no one still dares to struggle against them', and that 'opinions differ only by nuances', it is clear that he has in mind exclusively the white community.[34] And the situation which the two authoritative interlocutors describe is explained by the fact that blacks had no opportunity to express themselves politically, paired with the camouflaging and softening of conflicts within the white community by means of expansion into the Far West at the expense of the Native Americans. So, far from being an expression of a conciliated and peaceful society, the absence of real parties rests on the violent externalisation of conflicts and tensions within the dominant 'race', to the detriment of the populations condemned to silence. The substantial agreement on the basic choice to externalise conflicts explains why the two political groups in the white community are configured, in Tocqueville's language, more like two 'factions' than two real political parties, limiting their opposition, according to the

33 Alexis de Tocqueville, *Œuvres complètes*, ed. J. P. Mayer (Paris: Gallimard, 1951), vol. 5.1, pp. 122ff.

34 Alexis de Tocqueville, *Democracy in America*, ed. Eduardo Nolla, transl. James T. Schleifer (Indianapolis, IN: Liberty Fund, 2012), pp. 285, 310.

American banker's description, to 'administrative details'. When, for a series of reasons, the agreement on the externalisation of conflicts broke down, this produced not only a sharp political clash but a bloody civil war. Yet the two parties rebuilt their unity, and again became effectively two factions of the same party thanks to a compromise which, while not formally reintroducing slavery, nevertheless effected a ruthless disemancipation of the blacks.

This political system seemed to plunge into crisis again in 1896, when, in unusual circumstances, William Jennings Bryan – a populist figure, or in any case one strongly influenced by the populist movement of the poor peasants and other popular strata – became the Democratic Party's presidential candidate. Not by chance, upon this same election, the votes of substantial sectors of the Democratic Party rallied behind the Republican candidate. Party loyalty was defeated by class solidarity among the privileged strata of US society. This confirmed the fact that, having overcome the previous crisis, the Democrats and Republicans increasingly started to behave not as two parties, but as two factions of a single party, now tending to become an official, state party. In 1968, the Supreme Court had to intervene to declare unconstitutional the legislative measures in some states aimed at limiting the possibility of running in presidential elections to the candidates of the two major parties alone. Yet, in April 1975, an authoritative American journal observed that all states restricted ballot access to third parties and independent candidates. The list of obstacles is endless: in some states, acceptance of a candidacy was conditional on the payment of a tax, sponsorship by a certain number of voters or a commitment to respect the Constitution – intended to discourage 'radical' parties.[35]

Finally, no one can meaningfully take part in the electoral contest without being able to draw on enormous sums of money. As far as presidential elections are concerned, there are provisions for federal contributions, and yet only candidates who achieve 10 per cent of the votes in one of the two parties' primaries can draw on these funds.[36] This is a further measure to support and protect bipartisanship – or, rather,

35 'Developments in the Law-Elections', *Harvard Law Review* LXXXVIII: 6 (April 1975), pp. 1111ff.

36 Gérard, *George Bush président*, p. 173; Marie-France Toinet, *Le Système politique des États-Unis* (Paris: Presses universitaires de France, 1987), pp. 423ff.

competitive monopartisanship. When an outsider to the dominant political system manages to overcome the various legislative obstacles and secure a place on the ballot in every state – well, here is where media censorship intervenes. Let us take the 1988 elections: Who, even in the United States itself, knew that, in addition to Bush and Dukakis, a certain Leonora B. Fulani was running for president? Fulani? She was a black woman, a psychologist from New York, supported by the black community disappointed by the Democratic Party, who expressed a pacifist agenda, friendship with Cuba and solidarity with the Palestinian people. The television stations that organised the electoral debates were very careful not to invite her on, or even mention her name. This resulted in an appeal to the commission that is supposed to guarantee 'equal opportunities' for the various candidates. The television companies had 'deprived the American electorate of the knowledge that there is a third national candidate': this was the basis of the appeal, which was rejected on the grounds that the television companies had – as was their right – considered Ms Fulani's candidacy 'not newsworthy enough'. Yet, in those same days, a public opinion poll (conducted by the *Wall Street Journal* and NBC News) showed that 63 per cent of voters did not feel represented by either the Republican or Democratic candidate.[37] In fact, in a country where the electoral contest mainly plays out as a televised duel, the participants are largely decided by the large monopolistic corporations who control the TV channels and the major media outlets – condemning Fulani to silence and excluding other 'minor candidates', but not Perot. The soft-Bonapartist political regime does not develop in a vacuum; nor does it hover above existing social relations, which it instead ratifies and tends to eternalise.

In the countries where the hollowing out of political parties has gone furthest, we are in fact witnessing the return of discrimination based on wealth:

> The party has lost control of the lines of information and communication. It has also lost control of the selection of top candidates . . . The party, in addition, is losing control of campaigns. Television and the computer have produced a new class of electronic political specialists . . . Campaigns abandon the traditional paraphernalia of mass

37 Gérard, *George Bush président*, pp. 173–6, 166.

> democracy: volunteers, rallies, torchlight processions, leaflets, posters, billboards, bumper stickers. Political action, once labor-intensive, becomes capital-intensive.[38]

Again with regard to the United States, observers agree in noting 'the appallingly high costs of recent election campaigns', whose rise far outstrips inflation: 'Between 1976 and 1988, legislative election expenditures nearly quintupled (they multiplied by 4.3 times over), while the price index over the same period more than doubled, from 57 to 119.' 'The result is increasingly to limit politics to candidates who have money of their own or who take money from political action committees', primarily meaning lobbies.[39] The functioning of the American model, often cited as an example, is clear: 'it costs a hundred billion to win the White House', and the highest office in the land is in fact 'bought' with a river of 'money'.[40]

An Instrumental Reading of History, and the Advent of 'the Chancellor's Democracy'

While the American model had already been a source of fascination in Europe, especially after World War I, in recent decades it has borne even greater concrete influence on our continent. The political regime established in Germany after World War II is often called a *Kanzlerdemokratie* (a term modelled on the *Führerdemokratie* dear to Weber) – that is, a democracy hinging on the figure of the chancellor, who strikes the pose of being both responsible to the nation and its privileged interpreter.[41] In this case, the undermining of the proportional system is only partial. Yet we must not forget the threshold clause – an obstacle to parties that achieve under 5 per cent of the votes from entering parliament – and the harassment or persecution of communists, who were first officially

38 Schlesinger, *Cycles of American History*, pp. 271–2.

39 Toinet, *Le Système politique des États-Unis*, p. 429; Schlesinger, *Cycles of American History*, p. 270.

40 Vittorio Zucconi, 'Costa cento miliardi vincere la Casa Bianca', *La Repubblica*, 27 February 1992.

41 Franz Alt, *Es begann mit Adenauer. Der Weg zur Kanzlerdemokratie* (Freiburg: Herder, 1975).

outlawed and then, through the *Berufsverbot* (which has still not been revoked), kept on the margins of legality and banned from the state apparatus and public employment. On the whole, these measures were motivated not so much by the concern to ensure governmental stability – which certainly does not seem to run any great risks in Germany – as by the desire to ensure the political and social homogeneity of parliament by barring access to the Communist Party. Its presence would have been troubling not only because of its political ideas and the Cold War, but also because, as an organised political party, despite its small strength, it objectively countered the tendency, already seen in Bonapartism, not to tolerate filters between leader and nation and to deprive the subaltern classes of any independent political representation.

In the early years of the federal republic, the residual social-democratic resistance to the dismantling or downsizing of the proportional system was overcome with the help of a historical analysis that blamed the previous electoral system for the rise of Nazism and Fascism.[42] This thesis, formulated in 1941 by a German-American sociologist, then became a sort of official state doctrine in the Federal Republic of Germany.[43] Of course, the claim that Hitler would have been blocked by a system of single-member constituencies – that is, the electoral system invoked by authoritative Fascist circles in Italy on the eve of Mussolini's dictatorship – has yet to be proved. In any case, a historical balance sheet that, in seeking to explain the irresistible rise of Nazism, starts from the Weimar Republic and not from the catastrophe of World War I – the beginning of a crisis from which the country was unable to recover – is surely rather instrumental. Such a reading objectively ends up indicting the very political and social forces which, after 1918, drawing on the terrible lesson of the war, intended to build a peaceful and democratic Germany based on the proportional system – that is, the forces characterised by their stance in favour of a rupture of the imperial and Bonapartist tendencies manifested, already starting with Bismarck, in the Second Reich (with its single-member system), responsible for

42 Sergio Ortino, *Riforme elettorali in Germania* (Florence: Vallecchi, 1970), p. 102.

43 Ferdinand Hermens, *Democracy or Anarchy? A Study of Proportional Representation* (New York: Johnson Reprint, 1972 [1941]).

dragging the country into an unprecedented bloodbath. We have seen, on the other hand, Weber – a fervent chauvinist to the last – calling for the fullest development of the Bonapartist and Caesarist tendencies and, to this end, coming out clearly in favour of a system based on presidentialism and the single-member constituency.[44] For Weber, this would have allowed Germany more effectively to fulfil a great-power role, responding to the challenge of the powers that had defeated it and preceded it in consistently following the path of Caesarism. Paradoxically, in his condemnation of proportional representation, German-American sociologist Ferdinand Hermens refers to this same Weber – who also aroused the interest of General Ludendorff – as he makes his attempt to indict the forces who fought for democracy and proportionality in the Weimar Republic for their supposed role in Hitler's triumph.[45]

In reality, in the very first months following the defeat of the Third Reich, the occupying Western powers, including Britain and the United States, appear to have favoured the continuation of the electoral system that had been in force in the years preceding Hitler's coming to power.[46] A simple distraction? Another explanation seems more probable: initially, the dominant concern was the possibility of a revanchist Germany rising from the ashes. Against such a danger, this electoral system – not by chance, already adopted in the Weimar Republic by the democratic forces who had been won to the cause of peace – might well prove useful. But once the Cold War began to rage, and it was deemed necessary to expel the Communists from representative bodies, the proportional system immediately became a great impediment.

The capital sin of this electoral system – Hermens, the sociologist dear to Schumpeter and Hayek had already noted in 1941 – was that it made it possible, even in a country like Britain, for Communists to be elected to parliament from the 'industrial centers of the country'.[47] This observation takes us back to a theme that was common currency in the nineteenth-century debate. It was above all Bagehot, to whom Hermen repeatedly refers, who pointed out that proportional representation had the great drawback of allowing industrial centres to send to parliament

44 Domenico Losurdo, *La comunità, la morte, l'Occidente. Heidegger e l'"ideologia di guerra"* (Turin: Bollati Boringhieri, 1991).

45 Hermens, *Democracy or Anarchy?*, p. 77 notes.

46 Ortino, *Riforme elettorali in Germania*, p. 101.

47 Hermens, *Democracy or Anarchy?*, p. 112.

'persons representing the beliefs or the unbeliefs of the lowest classes in their towns'. The 'isms' – the great political and ideological issues – would make their way into representative bodies together with workers and craftsmen. Hermens in turn observes that, even if the Communist group formed in the British parliament thanks to proportional representation might be very small, it would still seriously hinder the Labour Party's move towards the centre. This would itself undermine the character that elections in Great Britain had, and everywhere should have, as the plebiscitary investiture of the leader of one of the two great parties.[48] Thus re-emerges the preference for a regime with more or less Bonapartist characteristics – a preference that Hermens shares with Weber, but also with Spengler and other implacable enemies of the Weimar Republic, who violently indicted it for its weakness on the international stage.

Gaullism and the Presidential Republic in France

When we examine the onward march of soft Bonapartism after World War II, events in France are particularly significant. The events leading up to the replacement of the French constitution began with a military *pronunciamento* in Algiers on 13 May 1958. Declared to the cry of 'The army to power', it developed with the landing of paratroopers in Corsica ten days later, who rapidly occupied the island. The coup ended with the rise to power of a general still surrounded by the aura of glory he had taken on during World War II. This was a classic Bonapartist scenario; and similarly classic was the recourse to a referendum to legitimise the results of the coup and the new Constitution, based on a radical personalisation of power. Official propaganda hammered home the message that saying yes to De Gaulle meant saying 'Yes to France'. Again, we see the habitual technique of externalising conflict, tending to pass off opponents of the coup as substantially foreign to the national soul. It was no accident that the general-president immediately set himself up as the privileged interpreter of eternal France and its national grandeur. Yet this was how the referendum that marked the birth of the Fifth Republic unfolded:

48 Ibid.

> the campaign was brief, but fervent, equal to the importance of what was at stake. The Yes vote overwhelmed the No vote, both in terms of the number of movements that supported it . . . and in terms of the superiority of the means placed at their disposal by the public authorities. Posters, leaflets, millions of copies of a newspaper written for the occasion pushed the Yes vote with an obsessive insistence that opponents denounced as abusive. In fact, the official envelope sent to every citizen contained, in addition to the ballot paper and the text of the Constitution subject to referendum, the speech delivered on 4 September by General De Gaulle recommending its adoption.[49]

As Weber made clear, the Caesarist leader does not come to power through any 'normal "vote" or "election"', but by means of a plebiscite. And when the hegemony held at the level of civil society, deriving primarily from the monopoly of the means of material and mental production, is not enough to guarantee control of the media, state power also intervenes. The Caesarist leader, Weber further underlines, is raised to power not on the basis of a programme with determinate political contents, but by virtue of a 'profession of "faith"'; and immediately after the referendum, the most authoritative French press outlets spoke of the 'blank cheque' that had been handed to De Gaulle.[50] As at the time of Louis-Napoleon, political parties were now in the firing line, as was any electoral system that favoured them. For the latter introduced a troublesome filter in the direct and immediate relationship between the atomised masses and the leader, hindering the 'profession of faith' that must bind them to him.

The new Constitution, whose drafting drew, among other things, on a study of the Bonapartist Constitution of 1852, immediately introduced the single-member constituency.[51] In this regard, there was a significant change in De Gaulle's attitude. In 1945, damning the instability of the Third Republic based on single-member constituencies, he had introduced proportional representation, albeit altered and modified so as to favour the major parties.[52] Thirteen years later, the general had radically

49 René Rémond, *Le retour de De Gaulle* (Brussels: Complexe, 1987), p. 134.

50 Jacques Chapsal, *La Vie politique sous la Ve République: I. 1958–1974* (Paris: Presses Universitaires de France).

51 Rémond, *Le retour de De Gaulle*, p. 120.

52 Chapsal, *La Vie politique sous la Ve République*, p. 58.

changed his mind, now having fully understood the functionality of the single-member system in relation to the Bonapartist regime he was preparing to implement. Unlike Louis-Napoleon, the general-president did not set up a personal Bonapartist dictatorship, which would have been incapable of lasting over time and of ensuring an orderly succession. Rather, he established a regime – one that functioned so well that it then saw the rise and extended rule, across two seven-year terms, of the same François Mitterrand who had earlier combatively denounced the Bonapartist inspiration of what he rightly defined as the 'coup d'état' of 1958.[53] Here, again, we can see the agility with which, within the framework of soft Bonapartism, it is possible to move from normality to the state of exception. This was again apparent at the most acute moment of crisis in 1968, when De Gaulle mysteriously disappeared, only to resurface after he had a reassuring conversation in Baden-Baden, across the West German border, with General Massu, the head of the most tried and tested military units. The president was ready to turn into a dictator upon the enactment of a state of exception, of whose advent he was the sole judge.

The Single-Member System, Bonapartism and the Political Decapitation of the Subaltern Classes

Thus far, Italy has been an exception. The drives towards Bonapartism owing to foreign-policy factors have been absent or weaker in this country. Moreover, the convergence of two political traditions (Communists and Christian-Democrats), though so different from each other, has so far played a role in defending the proportional system and a democracy founded on parliament and the parties. Already in the early postwar period, they opposed the variegated bloc (liberals, nationalists, and even fascists) that called for a return to the single-member constituency. Indeed, while this call again raised its head in 1945, it had little chance of success in the political and spiritual climate of the time: the spirit of the Resistance still prevailed, fed and directed by organised mass parties fighting against a regime that had enjoyed the support, complicity or benevolent detachment of economic and political circles who after 1919

53 Rémond, *Le retour de De Gaulle*, p. 19.

still dreamed of the return to Italy of the single-member constituency and of the rule of notables.

In the Constituent Assembly elected in 1946, Palmiro Togliatti declared that the organised mass parties (which these other forces sought to liquidate by scuttling the proportional system) were 'the new classes that are rising and organising themselves to control their own representation, to participate in the political direction of the country'. A few years ago, a Catholic historian, Roberto Ruffilli – later the victim of a barbaric and mysterious terrorist crime – observed that the single-member system tends 'to dismantle the positions of organised mass parties in favour of parties of opinion, and perhaps of those most able to assert themselves through the mass media and political spectacle'.[54] At least until recently, Communists and Catholics were well aware of the not only political but also social significance of proportional representation: the attack against it was seen as an integral part of the conservative attempt to drive the popular classes back into a condition of political subalternity and to guarantee the big monopolies and financial groups control even of representative bodies.

But today the situation is completely different. For there are three projects, both competing and intersecting, for the liquidation of the First Republic. The first is that which is expressed by the Lega Nord, whose most radical and extremist sectors seem to envisage a Northern Republic founded on some form of disemancipation of Southern immigrants. This is the only way to understand the Lega's threatening intimations against Southerners, and the indignant denunciations of their supposed effect in 'taking Northerners' jobs', and taking up too much space in the public sector and in the apparatus of administration and government. Leafing through the Lega's propaganda, or at least its more extreme variants, you get the impression of rereading the texts of late-nineteenth-century US nativists, who demanded the disemancipation of immigrants, or at least the drastic lengthening of the terms for their naturalisation. The latter, too, were portrayed as dirty, incapable of serious and honest work or serious and honest participation in political life, and above all denounced as a germ of criminal contamination. The American nativists' campaigns redoubled in intensity in periods of crisis; and in the context of today's Italy it is easy to understand the

54 Messina, *La grande Riforma*, pp. 30, 39.

racialisation process to the detriment of Southerners, who were welcomed quite differently at the time of the postwar 'economic miracle', with its soaring demand for labour power. As we have seen, even when it did not formally deprive them of political rights, the process of disemancipation that developed in America at the end of the nineteenth century confined immigrants to the lower segments of the labour market. It cannot be ruled out that – albeit in different conditions, presenting objectively greater hurdles to the *leghisti* – something similar could happen in Italy, too.

The other two projects for institutional reform or counter-reform refer to the American model, in these cases consciously. In the first case, rather than altering the mechanism of election, important social and political forces are pursuing the creation of a 'presidential republic' based, as has been observed, on 'a way of forming government leadership that breaks the monopoly of the large mass parties through an accentuation of the personal and charismatic quality inherent in leadership'.[55] Then there is the project fronted by Mario Segni, summarised as follows in the authoritative *Il Sole-24 Ore*:[56] through the single-member constituency, possibly in the British style (i.e. without run-off elections) or, secondarily, in the French style (i.e. including such run-offs), it would seek 'a dualistic alignment of the party landscape'; these parties, moreover, should be 'firmly and sincerely, even in their diversity, "bourgeois"'.[57] Here, we have the basic premises of competitive monopartisanship, whose structure can be completed with appropriate 'integrative reforms', to be introduced at a later date.[58]

As we can see, while these three projects are competitors in tactical terms – given their different dimensions and the rival interests and calculations of the parties and political forces behind them – on a more properly strategic level they are intertwined and convergent. We have seen that the single-member system has always been a favoured tool of Bonapartism – as also suggested by its systematic recourse to the 'abrogative referendum' which, as Weber authoritatively clarified, constitutes 'the specific instrument of purely plebiscitary democracy'.[59] In rejecting

55 Federico Stame, 'La prima riforma è la sinistra unita', *Micromega* 4, 1990, p. 40.
56 [TN: A business daily broadsheet].
57 Giovanni Bognetti, 'Tanti programmi per nulla', *Il Sole-24 Ore*, 26 March 1992.
58 Ibid.
59 Max Weber, 'Parliament and Government in Germany under a New Political

proportional representation, Bonapartist propaganda has also constantly denounced the scourge of parties that stand between the authentic will of the people and the leader, whether that means the leader of the individual local constituency or the supreme leader of the nation. This immediate relationship is distorted, again according to Bonapartist propaganda, by the presence of organised parties. Indeed, the target under fire from all the current rival reform projects in Italy is the so-called 'partyocracy'. It is proposed that this 'system of domination by the parties' should be literally thrown away, through secession from the part of the country considered incurably infected, or else drastically counterbalanced by means of a strong executive or the suppression of the proportional system, thus leaving room only for 'decentralised and "weak" party structures, somehow of the American style'.[60] As we have seen, in this 'model' country, the monopoly of political representation by the propertied has practically been reintroduced. This is most evident in the case of elections to congress, where there is no form of the public financing that some now seek to abolish in Italy.[61] Also pushing in this same direction are the proposals that seek to penalise minor parties by denying parliamentary representation to lists that do not reach some threshold of votes. Leaving aside the petty concerns of immediate electoral calculations, these measures are the contemporary analogue of the nineteenth-century imposition upon the press of various taxes and deposit payments, which the ruling classes used to hinder the newspapers that gave voice to the subaltern classes, thus ensuring their own media control through supplementary political means. Now that the mass media, especially those with the greatest impact, are the unchallenged monopoly of the big bourgeoisie, all that remains is to force the disappearance or downsizing of those parties that still purport to function as autonomous centres of intellectual production.

It is interesting to examine the ideology on which the campaign against organised parties is based: they are accused of constraining a 'frank and healthy individualism'; given the 'irrepressible existential difference of each individual', their claim or aspiration to represent

Order', in *Political Writings* (Cambridge: Cambridge University Press, 1994), p. 226.

60 Giovanni Bognetti, 'Tanti programmi per nulla'.

61 Schlesinger, *Cycles of American History*, p. 270.

classes or interests is absurd.[62] As we have seen, these are the same arguments that the ruling classes has long used in order to ban workers from forming associations. The indiscriminate campaign against parties claims to be targeting corruption. This was the same watchword that presided over the movement in the late-nineteenth-century United States, which resulted in the disemancipation of blacks, immigrants and poor whites. In his day, Tocqueville – certainly not a champion of ideological and internally structured parties – remarked that, from the absence of parties, America had gained 'a great deal in happiness, but not in morality'.[63] In the late-nineteenth-century United States, the weakening of the parties – touted as the answer to the phenomenon of political corruption – ended up sanctioning the rapid growth of the intertwining of, and exchanging of favours between, the political and business worlds, and the excessive power of the lobbies, leading even a conservative critic of parties to underline 'the cynical audacity with which they have often used their wealth to seduce officials and legislators from the path of virtue'.[64]

To those who think that returning to single-member elections, with the related hollowing out of the parties, would in itself offer a remedy to corruption, we may suggest that they read good old Gaetano Salvemini. In Giolitti's Italy, the single-member constituencies, besides being infested with corruption, were under the joint domination of organised crime (the Camorra) and the police: 'What use would they be, if the government did not have to use them in case of necessity?'[65] But how could the work of the 'minister of the underworld' and his hatchet men continue undisturbed? A journalist of the time explained: in the small constituencies of the single-member electoral system, with its weak or nonexistent parties, the 'political struggle' saw only the opposition between 'personal factions competing to thieve the most from public affairs':

62 Giovanni Bognetti, 'Tanti programmi per nulla'; Paolo Flores D'Arcais, 'Partito a misura di cittadino', *L'Unità*, 6 April 1990.

63 Tocqueville, *Democracy in America*, p. 281.

64 James Bryce, *The American Commonwealth* (London: Macmillan, 1888), vol. 3, p. 668.

65 Gaetano Salvemini, *Il ministro della mala vita, con scritti di Ugo Ojetti e Luigi Lucatelli*, 2nd edn (Rome: La Voce, 1919), p. 8.

> Political life was as if confiscated by local factions that usurped public property and civil rights. They supported any government, so long as it allowed the systematic robbery of their followers to flourish and reciprocated their mercenary obedience with illicit favours. Puglia was charged with providing a large contingent to that murky parliamentary mass that ministers summon by telegraph in moments of battle; it is known in the corridors of the Chamber as the 'cattle cart' on account of the bovine docility with which it serves any master.[66]

Moreover, in 1920, regretting the results of the first elections held under the proportional system, it was the ardent nationalist proponents of the single-member constituency who lamented the fact that 'the list vote . . . left little margin for individual corruption', with the effect that the latter had 'become relatively minimal'.[67] We see what is really at stake today when a supporter of the single-member system and bipartisanship (or competitive monopartisanship) declares that this is 'a question of opening up public and social services (health, school, pensions), at least partially, to the logic of the market', and of dismantling once and for all what he defines as the 'welfare state in partyocratic sauce'.[68] As in the past, the attack on universal suffrage or on the proportional system goes hand-in-hand with the assertion of a free-market economic policy. This is the same context in which we should also set the rise of the Leagues which, radicalising their fight against the much-denounced redistribution of income in favour of the South, have ended up calling for Northern secession.[69]

Yet, in Italy, Bonapartism and the single-member system are still having a hard time achieving victory. There is no lack of signs of impatience: 'All [constitutional] revisions respond to that sort of unwritten law that experts call the rule of the external event. This principle says that modern constitutions are altered or even totally replaced because of

66 Luigi Lucatelli, 'La Federazione degli Insegnanti Medi e le candidature Salvemini', in Salvemini, *Il ministro della mala vita*, pp. 125ff.

67 Alfredo Rocco, 'Ritorni del Medievo', in *I nazionalisti*, ed. Angelo D'Orsi (Milan: Feltrinelli, 1981 [1920]), p. 303.

68 Bognetti, 'Tanti programmi per nulla'.

69 TN: The Lega Nord's formation as a single party was preceded by the 1980s development of 'Leagues' for individual regions of northern Italy, such as Lombardy and Veneto.

external and traumatic events.'[70] This observation can also provide a key to interpreting the murky happenings that have marked Italian political life for some time now.

The Trajectory of Today's Liberalism

We have seen that, even according to its admirers, the West's leading country is characterised by a political system in which the leader holds such sweeping executive powers that he can independently decide to go to war, and invoke and introduce the state of exception. We have seen that even in periods of normality, this leader can draw on an apparatus of propaganda and covert persuasion that would have been the envy of Joseph Goebbels. Such a situation confronts liberal thought with a new situation which – judging by the watchwords it has constantly raised throughout its history – ought to have sounded its alarm bells. But this has not been the case. On the contrary, we can well speak of an involution, of which Popper perhaps represents the most extreme example. In declaring misleading and dangerous the question of 'who should rule', the theorist of the open society pointed to the control and limitation of power as the central problem of philosophy and political life. In a 1955 essay, he had even raised a disturbing question: 'How far do publishers' monopolies establish a kind of censorship?'[71] The gigantic concentration of political and multimedia power – which showed its enormous potential for censorship, disinformation and manipulation during an episode like the crusade against Iraq – is plain for all to see. But anyone who expected the theorist of the open society to pay attention to such problems would be gravely disappointed. On the contrary, Popper not only seeks to silence or blame the few voices of dissent, but also promotes new punitive expeditions on the model of the Gulf War, which would inevitably lead to a new and gigantic concentration of power in the belligerent countries.

Quite different, and much more balanced, is of course the position of Norberto Bobbio. He recognises the 'inversion of the relationship

70 Alberto Sensini, *Presidente o Cancelliere? Viaggio ragionato nel labirinto delle riforme istituzionali* (Milan: Sperling & Kupfer, 1992), p. 3.

71 Karl Popper, *Conjectures and Refutations: The Growth of Scientific Knowledge* (London: Routledge, 2002), p. 353.

between controllers and controlled', given that, 'through the unscrupulous use of the mass media, elected representatives now control the voters'.[72] But, instead of drawing the conclusion that the now-dominant political regime does not even meet the requirements he himself defines as the 'minimum' to fall under the category of democracy, the Turin philosopher seems to encourage resignation. This resignation sometimes goes as far as endorsing projects for electoral and institutional (counter-)reform, which aim, in the last analysis, at achieving a competitive monopartisanship that would itself entrench the 'inversion of the relationship between controllers and controlled'.[73] Such projects would themselves eliminate, or further drastically reduce, the possibility of choosing between 'real' alternatives, which the Turin philosopher identified as one of the minimum requirements of democracy.

But, beyond the attitude taken by this or that single author, there is a general trend to be noted. Today, we are witnessing a paradox. The liberal tradition has long stressed the need for intermediate bodies as a counterweight to despotism. It is a theme that Tocqueville long emphasised, looking not so much at the danger constituted by monarchical power as at that constituted by the 'omnipotence of the majority', or at least by a power consecrated by popular vote: without 'associations', including, in the first place, political ones, there is no longer 'any dike against any sort of tyranny'.[74] Even the French liberal was not entirely consistent in the approach to which he laid claim: he does not seem to have fought for the legalisation of workers' associations, which in France were persecuted even by the governments of the Second Republic to which Tocqueville himself belonged. But today one cannot even speak of inconsistency: the stages in the rise of soft Bonapartism are regularly patterned by a campaign that pursues, and ultimately succeeds in, the cutting back and marginalising of organised political parties – that is, the only intermediate bodies today capable of hindering a power that has assumed much more disturbing proportions than those foreseen or feared by the author of *Democracy in America*.

72 Noberto Bobbio, *L'utopia capovolta* (Turin: La Stampa, 1990), p. xv.

73 'Il giudizio di Norberto Bobbio: "Segni e compagni sono l'unica novità" ', *La Repubblica*, 20 October 1992.

74 Tocqueville, *Democracy in America*, pp. 402, 307.

Despite their formal homage to the liberal tradition, its followers today seem to be concerned not with the limitation of power, but exclusively with its efficiency and capacity for rapid action. This phenomenon manifests itself at various levels. Not only Kant, but also the Anglo-Saxon political tradition, long expressed great distrust for the standing army. Yet the standing army of the time was less worrying than the powerful professional armies today's liberals praise.

A similar fact can also be noted regarding the debate on electoral systems. As is well known, John Stuart Mill insisted on the absolute necessity of proportional representation, to avoid the 'collective despotism' of the 'numerical majority', which was already at least raising its head in the United States.[75] Yet the electoral system recommended by the author of *Considerations on Representative Government* as an effective antidote to power is today resolutely condemned and abandoned just when, from the standpoint of liberal theory, such an antidote would appear most necessary, given the enormous expansion of this power in the intervening period. But if this is a remarkable reversal of positions, it does have a certain logic. Mill feared that, with the extension of suffrage, the 'working classes', in Britain and Europe – much more widespread and numerous than their counterparts in the United States – could gain a majority, using it to 'substitut[e] the class ascendency of the poor for that of the rich'. The 'rule of the numerical majority' would end up becoming 'a class government', in the sense that it would sanction the undisputed power of the 'majority of poor' over 'a minority who, in contradistinction, may be called rich', who, in the absence of the proportional system, would be denied any representation.[76] This is why the English liberal both recommended plural voting, tilted to the advantage of the rich and intelligent, in order to readjust the balance of power; and, bearing in mind the difficulties of introducing unequal suffrage, he also insisted on the abandonment of the (first-past-the-post) electoral system then in force, which heavily penalises or even silences the minority.

But Mill was wrong: he was still thinking about a situation in which the trumpets of the bourgeoisie could be countered by the bells of the working classes. The substantial monopoly of the press and mass media

75 John Stuart Mill, *Considerations on Representative Government* (New York: Henry Holt, 1873), p. 166.

76 Ibid., pp. 166, 133.

makes his concerns obsolete: the 'class government' that actually exists today is certainly not the 'working-class' one he feared, and it is liberal politicians and thinkers who condemn proportional representation. Such is the case of Giolitti, Pareto, Mosca, Hayek and Schumpeter – and, it seems, also of Bobbio. In Italy, a vast array of forces claims to want to change the political and electoral system in order to impose not only bipartisanship, but a bipartisanship that, having as protagonists two 'bourgeois' parties, is in fact structured as competitive monopartisanship. To put this in Mill's language, it means a class government that ensures itself the monopoly of parliamentary representation.

Soft Bonapartism and Marx's Analysis of 'Bourgeois' Democracy

I have defined the regime that is heading towards triumph in our century as a soft Bonapartism. As we conclude, it is worth dwelling for a moment on this category, comparing it with other competing ones. Some have spoken of 'democratic elitism'. But such a definition helps very little in understanding the political reality of our times. First, let us focus on the adjective. Does it make sense to define as democratic a reality and a political conception that not only considers irrelevant the problem of citizens' participation in the choices meant to determine the fate of the community in which they live, but that explicitly theorises mass electoral abstentionism as a positive and indeed essential factor for the stability and proper functioning of the system? Abstentionism has taken the place of the explicit denial of political citizenship of large social strata once seen by the theorists of census discrimination as the ineliminable presupposition of the representative regime. It has been rightly observed that 'all elite theories are founded on two basic assumptions: first, that the masses are inherently incompetent; and second, that they are, at best, pliable, inert stuff or, at worst, aroused, unruly creatures possessing an insatiable proclivity to undermine both culture and liberty'.[77]

But is this not exactly the assumption that provided the classical liberal tradition with its basis for denying suffrage to the 'childlike'

77 Peter Bachrach, *The Theory of Democratic Elitism: A Critique* (Boston, MA: Little Brown, 1967), p. 2

multitude? There is likewise little that is democratic about the elitism which, in Schumpeter's formulation, considers the exclusion of this or that ethnic, and possibly social, community from political rights as normal and uncontroversial. And it is doubtful even that such an elitism can be defined as liberal, given its sympathy for a regime of personal power so broad that it can decide autonomously on war and the state of exception – that is, it can make use of prerogatives that, according to good old Kant, are proper to despotism alone. In a certain sense, even the noun is to be considered misleading: it does not take sufficient account of the personalisation of power, a characteristic that clearly distinguishes the current political and institutional order from the regime directed by the 'representative elite' so dear to Sieyès.

The category of 'democratic Caesarism' is more appropriate. But even this is not fully satisfactory. The noun has the disadvantage of referring to an event in the distant past, rather than to a chapter of contemporary history that begins with mass or universal suffrage. Moreover, the adjective risks acting as a pretext for legitimation.

The category I propose exposes itself to the objection already raised against political categories and analyses suspected of excessively comparing the political and constitutional structure in today's West to dictatorial regimes and those resulting from coups d'état.[78] In reality, the French Fifth Republic was itself the product of a coup; and, as we have seen, even when it comes to the genesis of the US Constitution, there has been no lack of historians who have spoken of a more or less camouflaged coup d'état. Above all, this objection fails to take into account the distinction between a Bonapartist dictatorship of a single personality and a Bonapartist regime based on an ordered and regulated succession, capable of ensuring its continuation over time.

The most recent developments in reality, and even in political theory, in the West have fully validated Marx's analysis, which is today, paradoxically, even more fitting and illuminating than at the time it was formulated. Let us quickly revisit the key passages:

1) 'The ideas of the ruling class are in every epoch the ruling ideas . . . The class which has the means of material production at its disposal,

78 Luciano Cavalli, *Governo del leader e regime di partiti* (Bologna: il Mulino, 1992), p. 15.

consequently also controls the means of mental production.'[79] This is a text I have reflected upon already, and whose extraordinary relevance is confirmed every day by the more precise analyses of what has aptly been defined as the 'multimedia principality'.[80] However, it must be added that this latter term refers to the realm of the social class that controls the mass media, exercising a power that in some ways runs even deeper than Marx had envisaged. For today, the control of the means of material production entails the control of means of mental production so powerful as to allow a 'manipulative pressure' that is exercised upon individuals' 'acts of volition' even before it shapes their 'external behaviour'.[81]

2) According to *Capital*, the 'freedom' and 'equality' of which the bourgeois theory of democracy speaks refers only to the sphere of circulation, and constitutes its ideological expression.[82] Reduced by Schumpeter to the market, democracy no longer even implies political equality – which Bobbio, too, expels from the 'minimal definition' of democracy. At the end of the nineteenth century, the national-liberal Treitschke expressed his admiration for American democracy, which was able to control the plebs much more effectively than imperial Germany:

> Let us examine the most delightful plebs in the world, in New York. It is the collection of the refuse that has flowed in from all over the earth, and yet, left to themselves, these corrupt elements are forced to control themselves. Do you think there is a Prussian police force capable of restraining them as they are restrained by the strict law of necessity? Everyone knows this much very well: that no one will pay any attention if I starve.[83]

It would seem that such a model is coming back into vogue.

3) Democracy conceived in this way was limited, according to Marx, to giving the electorate the possibility of 'deciding once in three or six

79 *Marx-Engels Collected Works* (*MECW*) (London: Lawrence & Wishart, 1975–2004), vol. 5, 59.

80 Zolo, *Il principato democratico*, pp. 172ff.

81 Ibid., pp. 172ff, 133.

82 *MECW*, vol. 35, p. 186.

83 Heinrich von Treitschke, *Politik. Vorlesungen gehalten an der Universität zu Berlin* (Leipzig: Hirzel, 1897–98), vol. 2, p. 272.

years which member of the ruling class was to misrepresent [*ver- und zertreten*] the people in Parliament'.[84] The most recent political theory conceives democracy precisely as the competitive investiture of a leader granted such sweeping powers that he can involve the entire country in military adventures of his own independent volition. Soft Bonapartism has developed with the state of exception in mind – a situation in which the leader can transform himself into a dictator, at least in the Roman sense of the term, without difficulty. And, precisely by examining this transformation, Marx sees the moment of dictatorship which is already latent and implicit in 'bourgeois' democracy.

The New Disemancipation and the Long-Term Future of Democracy

Without doubt, this extraordinarily insightful phenomenology of power ends up with a utopian and utopic 'solution' – the withering away of the state, a 'solution' that has played a catastrophic role in all attempts to build a post-capitalist or non-capitalist society. It is not possible to dwell here on a theme that I have already analysed elsewhere.[85] The fact is that, already in Marx, and even more so in the tradition that took its cue from him, one senses the negative influence of the anarchist tradition, with its irreducible hostility towards the idea of representation, suggesting to Bakunin the idea of Saturn who 'represented his children to the extent that he devoured them'.[86] This is the case even of Lenin's *State and Revolution*. It was published at a time when the denunciation of the liberal or liberal-democratic representative regimes was at its bitterest, as it could not fail to be, given that in World War I these regimes really did function in the way described by the anarchist leader, calmly immolating millions of men – the 'represented' – in a gigantic sacrificial rite. In *State and Revolution*, we read that even the most developed democracy cannot do without 'representative institutions'.[87] Yet the myth of the

84 *MECW*, vol. 22, p. 333.

85 Domenico Losurdo, 'Gramsci, il marxismo e lo Stato', *Marx centouno* 8 (1992), pp. 42–58.

86 Mikhail Bakunin, 'Circolare ai miei amici d'Italia', in *Stato e anarchia e altri scritti* (Milan: Feltrinelli, 1968 [1871]), p. 397.

87 V. I. Lenin, *State and Revolution* (Moscow: Foreign Languages Press, 2020), p. 46.

withering away of the state continued to fuel mistrust of the idea of representation. This, even the very moment when – as Kelsen aptly observes – the leaders of Soviet Russia were increasing the number of representative bodies (which the soviets undoubtedly were), and did not shy away even from second-degree representation.[88]

Marx, like the tradition inspired by him, sometimes contrasts direct democracy to parliamentary democracy. This opposition stems from the rejection of a representation that is reduced to a simple theatre without real effect in the factories and workplaces. There, the workers are 'organised like soldiers. As privates of the industrial army, they are placed under the command of a perfect hierarchy of officers and sergeants' and continue to be subjected to a 'despotism' which in practice deprives them of that same negative freedom that even the liberal tradition claims to cherish.[89] Yet, this counterposition seems to spring from the illusion that, with the disappearance of the mediation of representation, the people is thus able to express its own authentic charge of emancipation, without obstacles or distortions. This illusion is well understood from the epistemological assumptions of anarchism, which sometimes takes on irrationalist tones, with Bakunin's constant devotion to celebrating 'instinct' and 'life', as opposed to 'thought' and its pretence to 'prescribe rules to life'.[90] But such an illusion can hardly be reconciled with Marx's thesis that the dominant ideas are the ideas of the ruling class – that is, the same class that monopolises the material and mental means of production.

In our day, we face a paradox: the proponents of 'direct democracy' – not the kind that takes place in factories and workplaces, but the kind that dispenses with the mediation of parties – are the real proponents of 'soft Bonapartism'. Here, the leader of the nation (under the presidential regime) or the leader of a given electoral constituency (under the single-member system) must be designated directly by the atomised people,

88 Hans Kelsen, *The Essence and Value of Democracy*, ed. Nadia Urbinati and Carlo Invernizzi Accetti (London: Rowman & Littlefield, 2013), pp. 54–6, note 7.

89 *MECW*, vol. 6, p. 491.

90 Mikhail Bakunin, 'Programm und Reglement der Geheimorganisation der intemationalen Bruderschaft und der intemationalen Allianz der sozialistischen Demokratie' (1868), in *Staatlichkeit und Anarchie und andere Schriften* (Frankfurt: Ullstein, 1981), p. 73; Bakunin, 'Circolare ai miei amici d'Italia', pp. 143ff; Bakunin, 'Programm und Reglement', pp. 560ff.

deprived of their modest means of autonomous mental and political production, and helplessly delivered up to the totalitarian power of the mass media monopolised by the big bourgeoisie.

Despite its fundamental limitations, Marx's analysis still has a lot to say with regard to the construction of democracy in countries with high industrial development and a ramified and complex civil society. It has been rightly observed that democracy increasingly becomes an empty slogan unless measures are taken 'to promote democratic political communication. In spite of the extreme difficulty of the task, it would be necessary to free multimedia communication from its subordination to both the political system and the system of production, and to liberate it from the advertising paradigm that increasingly unites these two subsystems.'[91]

This is a courageous conclusion that seems to run against the dominant trend: the formal volatilisation of democracy develops just as it has become clear that, without interventions capable of affecting or in some way controlling the monopoly of intellectual production, not even 'minimal' democracy can be saved or achieved. And nor can the de facto reintroduction of property-based discrimination be prevented. This is particularly evident in the United States, the country in the vanguard of the reduction of democracy to a market. Here, with organised parties having been de-powered and marginalised, and the mass media alone deciding the outcome of electoral competition, the most important elected offices tend to become the prerogative of great wealth or of lobbies with the interest and ability to pay the enormous sums of money now required.

The analysis proposed here seems to deny the 'self-evident' existence of democracy in the West. But we might reflect on the fact that, historically, even authors who were far from revolutionary have sometimes expressed the awareness that property-based discrimination can manifest itself in ways other than formal and explicit exclusion from the enjoyment of political rights. In 1866, a moderate French liberal underlined how the lack of remuneration for British MPs in fact benefited only the aristocracy, which thereby controlled the representative bodies and, moreover, made itself look good by flaunting its alleged

91 Zolo, *Il principato democratico*, p. 207 notes.

disinterest.[92] Non-payment for parliamentary offices was a different way of excluding certain social classes from elective offices – offices which in fact continued to be the monopoly of the richer classes. Has this monopoly disappeared, or is it disappearing, today? Or are we witnessing the implementation of new instruments to perpetuate it, and even to restore it in its entirety where it had been partially broken?

On the eve of the generalised collapse of property-based restrictions that followed World War I and the October Revolution, Lenin analysed how, despite the great extension of suffrage achieved through long struggle, political institutions continued to exclude or marginalise the subaltern classes. On the one hand, there is the 'purely capitalist organization of the daily press'; on the other, certain minute aspects of electoral legislation which discourage the poor 'from active participation in democracy'.[93] Enormous changes have taken place since then: albeit through a long and laborious process, the legislative norms that considerably denied political rights to blacks and poor whites in America even past the midpoint in the twentieth century have collapsed. Equal universal suffrage has become an unshakeable bottom line: hence the failure of the attempts, continuing almost up to the present, to introduce or maintain plural voting. Yet the 'restrictions, exceptions, exclusions, obstacles for the poor' of which Lenin speaks have not completely gone away: we need only think, in the US case, of the registration laws to which eminent American sociologists attribute an at least objective discriminatory effect – a discrimination in the last analysis based on wealth. Indeed, still in 1975, one American senator saw in these laws a 'disenfranchisement on a massive scale' of the poorer classes.[94]

This is the same context in which we should place the turn towards the single-member constituency. To quote Weber, himself a supporter of this system, this is only apparently a merely technical instrument. In fact, it has long been considered by a whole series of liberal and conservative politicians, as well as authors, as the only viable alternative to the abolition of universal suffrage, which is itself now unfeasible. All this may seem astonishing and even unheard-of. However, we have seen that

92 Édouard Laboulaye, *Histoire des États-Unis* (Paris: Charpentier, 1866), vol. 3, p. 365.

93 Lenin, *State and Revolution*, p. 87.

94 Steven J. Rosenstone and Raymond E. Wolfinger, 'The Effect of Registration Laws on Voter Turnout', *American Political Science Review* 72: 1 (March 1978), p. 22.

the single-member constituency pre-dated the advent of universal suffrage, related as it is to a pre-modern concept of representation held by communities and guilds, rather than by individuals. Moreover, it has been thought of and theorised in opposition to universal suffrage, as an instrument to continue substantially to exclude the 'childish' multitude from political life. The latter is henceforth called upon not even really to choose between this or that plenipotentiary leader, on the basis of alternative programmes and rational arguments, but merely to let itself be charmed and influenced by one or the other.

From Britain, where the idea of individual representation emerged much later than elsewhere, the electoral system based on single-member constituencies then moved on to America. There, it continues to prove vitally important, and not only because of the weight of tradition behind it. First of all, it is a system that in both these countries has proved perfectly congenial to a political regime characterised by the personalisation of power and uninterrupted imperial expansion – whether in colonies across the oceans, or in the Far West and other territories contiguous to the metropolitan core. A further consideration should be made in reference to the US case. This is a country where work is largely handed off on foreigners, whether that means blacks – who were first slaves and then long endured semi-servile conditions, and in any case were excluded from political rights – or immigrants, also often not admitted to political citizenship. It is also a country that, for very many decades, had at its disposal the pressure valve represented by the territories taken from the Native Americans or Mexicans. In such a context, the white community has appeared fairly homogeneous and devoid of the bitter social contradictions typical of Europe. The single-member constituency responds to this situation. It is no accident that, in the 1960s and 1970s, American political figures concerned about the spread and worsening of racial tensions proposed the introduction, at least at the level of local government, of the proportional system as an instrument to allow blacks, too, to express themselves politically. But these proposals were rejected with the argument that the abandonment of the single-member constituency would have allowed for the election of militant or extremist elements – that is, also of blacks not fully integrated into the existing system.[95]

95 Hermens, *Democracy or Anarchy?*, pp. 477ff.

The Los Angeles revolt in 1992 is the other face of the rejection of the principle of proportional representation and the political decapitation of the subaltern classes. With the reduction of democracy to its most minimal, market variant, no longer considered bearers of socio-economic rights, deprived of any party organisation on which they could rely, with no access to media, and even kept from voting by way of registration laws, blacks – still affected by not inconsiderable racial discrimination – are ultimately unable to make their voices heard on a more properly political level. They can protest only through recourse to a kind of urban jacquerie, an angry and destructive revolt which, however, does nothing to change the existing state of affairs.

As the example, in particular, of the French Fifth Republic shows, even in the twentieth century, the march of Bonapartism has been marked by the triumph of the single-member constituency. Electoral legislation further multiplies the effects of the monopoly which the wealthy hold over a mass-media apparatus of unprecedented power, thus accelerating and reinforcing the political decapitation of the subordinate classes. As the American model triumphs, the phenomenon of urban jacqueries – fed by immigrants, underclasses and subaltern and marginalised social classes – is destined to repeat itself in Europe, too. Indeed, this is already happening, in Britain in particular.

In the last two centuries, the emancipation process wrested universal equal suffrage (one person, one vote); demanded proportional representation in the name of the 'equal representative value' of each vote; challenged the monopoly, however configured and disguised, of representative bodies by wealth; connected political rights with social and economic ones; and saw and celebrated democracy as the emancipation of classes, 'races' and peoples held in a subaltern condition. Today, this process seems to have suffered a serious setback. In this sense, we are witnessing a phase of disemancipation. Similar such phases have marked democracy's long and tortuous path throughout its history. But as far as the current one is concerned, the end is not yet in sight.

Index